P9-ECS-795

HISTORY OF
PHILOSOPHY

*the text of this book is printed
on 100% recycled paper*

About the Author

William S. Sahakian completed graduate studies in philosophy at Harvard University and at Boston University, receiving the Ph. D. degree from the latter university in 1951. He is Professor of Philosophy and Psychology and Chairman of the Department of Philosophy at Suffolk University. He has lectured at Northeastern University and in Massachusetts Department of Education courses at Harvard University and has also served as consultant to research organizations and educational publishers. Among his outstanding recent works are the following: *Ideas of the Great Philosophers* (in the Barnes and Noble Everyday Handbook Series); *Systems of Ethics and Value Theory; Psychology of Personality; Realms of Philosophy; History of Psychology; Psychotherapy and Counseling;* and *Philosophies of Religion.* He has been a member of national associations, including the New York Academy of Science; the American Philosophical Association; the American Association for the Advancement of Science; the American Ontoanalytic Association; the American Association for Humanistic Psychology; and the Association for Realistic Philosophy.

HISTORY OF PHILOSOPHY

WILLIAM S. SAHAKIAN

Professor of Philosophy
Suffolk University

BARNES & NOBLE BOOKS

A DIVISION OF HARPER & ROW, PUBLISHERS

New York, Hagerstown, San Francisco, London

© Copyright 1968

BY BARNES & NOBLE, INC.

All rights reserved. No part of this book may be reproduced or utilized in any form or by any means, electronic or mechanical, including photocopying, recording or by any information storage and retrieval system, without permission in writing from the Publisher.

L.C. catalogue card number: 68–26401

80   12 11 10 9

PRINTED IN THE UNITED STATES OF AMERICA

Dedicated to my brother
Van Sahakian
in appreciation of the fond memories
of my roommate of boyhood years

Preface

The history of philosophy provides an ideal introduction to the entire field of philosophical thought. Its chronological approach helps to illuminate complex modern and contemporary philosophies by tracing them back to their historical origins and stages of development. It brings into bold relief the differences and similarities among the ideas of the great philosophers. For each philosopher, it explores the backgrounds of his thinking and shows how his point of view fits into the stream of philosophical ideas progressively unfolding from the dawn of history to the present. Furthermore, the history of philosophy explores the entire system of each philosopher, not merely his conclusions in specialized areas, such as logic, ethics, or the philosophy of religion.

The term *philosophy* is from the Greek *philosophia*, meaning literally "the love of wisdom." It is used today to signify the *critical evaluation of the facts of experience*. The key word in this definition is *evaluation* (rather than *critical*), for philosophy differs from the sciences essentially in that it does not simply analyze, describe, or criticize, but especially assigns values to human experiences. Scientists, though they must be concerned about the truth and accuracy of their work, nevertheless do not as scientists make value judgments. For example, the psychologist describes but does not praise or censure behavior of a given kind, and, similarly, the political scientist analyzes but does not morally evaluate the actions of the government. In these instances, however, the philosopher would not hesitate to make value judgments, for he would appraise and either approve or condemn the individual's behavior and the government's policies.

The earliest philosophers in ancient times sought rational solutions to certain fundamental problems of mankind, asking questions about the nature of the universe and the meaning of human experience. They were concerned with specific problems: What is the world made of? Is it one or many substances? What are the differences, if any, between matter and organic life? Is there a soul or a God? How can things change and yet remain the same things? What is the highest good for man to pursue? It was not until the appearance of Plato and Aristotle that all such problems were brought together and integrated into unified systems of philosophy. Each great philosopher thereafter attempted to solve these specific problems from his individual point of view and as part of his complete system of thought. The history of philosophy throughout ancient, medieval, and modern times has generally followed the precedent of system-building initiated by Plato and Aristotle. Recently some philosophers have advocated the exclusion of some problems which they regard as unreasonable, futile, or of dubious worth. But their approach, too, seems to result in a complete system of thought based upon their particular point of view, while many of their conclusions owe much to the philosophical systems of the past.

It is hoped that this Outline will help the reader to understand the difficult concepts of contemporary philosophers and to appreciate their debt to predecessors. It is also hoped that for this purpose the reader will be motivated to explore the original writings of the philosophers discussed.

The author is indebted to many students and colleagues for comments and suggestions; to the Editorial Department of Barnes and Noble, Inc. for invaluable assistance in the preparation of the final manuscript; and especially to his wife, Dr. Mabel Lewis Sahakian, of Northeastern University, who responded untiringly with professional counsel and helpful reactions despite the author's numerous unreasonable requests.

Beacon Hill,
Boston, Massachusetts

WILLIAM S. SAHAKIAN

Table of Contents

CHAPTER   **PAGE**

1. The Problem of Matter—The Milesians   1
Thales   1
Anaximander   2
Anaximenes   3

2. The Problem of Identity and Change   5

Xenophanes, the Theological Eleatic   5
Heraclitus of Ephesus   6
Parmenides, the Metaphysical Eleatic   9
Zeno, the Dialectical Eleatic   10
Melissus of Samos   12
The Metaphysical Pluralists   13
Empedocles of Agrigentum   13
Anaxagoras of Clazomene   15
Leucippus of Abdera   16
Democritus of Abdera   17
The Pythagoreans—Mathematical Philosophy   20
Philolaus and the Pythagorean Philosophy   21

3. The Problem of Man—from the Sophists to Plato   24

The Sophists   24
Protagoras of Abdera   25
Gorgias of Leontini   27
Socrates   30
The Lesser Socratics: Four Socratic Schools   33
Stoicism: Indifference to Pain and Passion   37
Hedonism—Pleasure as the Highest Good   41
Epicureanism: A Life Devoted to Pleasure   44
Skepticism: The Suspension of Judgment   47
Eclecticism: Amalgamation of the Best Doctrines Available   50

4. Systematic Philosophy—Plato and Aristotle   52

Plato   52
Platonic Idealism   52
Plato's Philosophy of Religion   54
Plato's Ethical Theory   55
Plato's Political Philosophy   57

CHAPTER	PAGE
Aristotle	62
Aristotelian Logic	62
Aristotelian Metaphysics	65
Aristotelian Philosophy of Religion	69
Aristotelian Ethics	72
Aristotle's Social and Political Philosophy	76
Aristotle's Aesthetics	78

5. The Religious Problem — 80

Origins of Neo-Platonism	81
Plotinus	82
Schools of Patristic Philosophy	85
Origen	86
St. Augustine	88

6. Scholasticism — 93

Problems of Medieval Philosophy	93
Neo-Platonism, the First Period of Medieval Philosophy	94
John Scotus Erigena	94
St. Anselm of Canterbury	96
Roscellinus—the Philosophy of Nominalism	99
Peter Abelard—the Primacy of Reason	100
Aristotelianism, The Second Period of Medieval Philosophy	103
St. Thomas Aquinas—The Philosophy of Intellectualism	104
John Duns Scotus—the Primacy of Will	112
William of Occam	115
Nicolas of Cusa	117

7. Renaissance Philosophy — 119

Social and Political Philosophy of the Renaissance	121
Niccolo Machiavelli	121
Sir Thomas More	123
Francis Bacon—Social and Political Philosophy	124
Thomas Campanella	125
Thomas Hobbes	126
Natural Law and the Philosophy of Science	128
Francis Bacon—Philosophy of Science	128
Scientific Method of Galileo, Kepler, and Newton	129

8. The Continental Rationalists — 132

René Descartes	133
Cartesian Solutions	139
Benedict Spinoza	140
Gottfried Wilhelm Leibniz	145
Leibnizianism	151

9. The British Empiricists — 153

John Locke's Metaphysical Agnosticism	153
George Berkeley's Metaphysical Idealism	158

CHAPTER   PAGE

David Hume's Metaphysical Skepticism   161
Thomas Reid and the Common Sense School   164
Philosophers of the French Enlightenment   165

10. The German Idealists   169

Kant's Transcendental Idealism   169
Fichte's Subjective Idealism   180
Schelling, Schiller, and Schleiermacher   184
Hegel's Absolute Idealism   187
Neo-Hegelianism   201
Arthur Schopenhauer   204
Eduard Hartmann   211
Neo-Kantianism and the Marburg and Baden Schools   212

11. British Utilitarianism   215

Jeremy Bentham   215
James Mill   217
John Stuart Mill   217
Henry Sidgwick   221
Hastings Rashdall and George Edward Moore   222

12. Evolutionary Naturalism   224

Lamarck   224
Darwin   225
Herbert Spencer   227
Friedrich Nietzsche   229
Thomas Henry Huxley   231
Henri Bergson   233
Samuel Alexander   235

13. Classical Positivism   241

Comte's Positivism   241
Classical Positivism after Comte   244

14. Dialectical Materialism: Marxian Communism   246

Marx and the Marxists   246
Nikolai Lenin   251
Mao Tse-tung   253

15. Pragmatism   255

Charles Sanders Peirce   255
William James   258
John Dewey   263
F. C. S. Schiller   268

16. Idealism and Personalism   269

Types of Idealism   269
Personalism (Bowne, Knudson, Brightman, Rashdall, Sorley, McTaggart)   270

CHAPTER   PAGE

Absolute Idealism (Green, Bradley, Royce)   279
Italian Neo-Idealists (Croce, Gentile)   285

17. Neorealism and Critical Realism   288

American Neorealists (Perry *et al.*)   288
American Critical Realists (Santayana *et al.*)   291
British Neorealists (Moore, Russell, Whitehead)   292

18. Logical Positivism   299

The Influence of Ludwig Wittgenstein   299
Alfred Jules Ayer   301
Moritz Schlick   302
Otto Neurath   303
Rudolf Carnap   304
Alfred Tarski   306

19. Analytic Philosophy   307

Cambridge Philosophy (Moore, Russell, Wittgenstein, Wisdom)   308
Oxford Philosophy (Ryle, Austin)   313

20. Neo-Scholasticism and Neo-Thomism   316

The Twenty-four Theses of Thomism   317
Jacques Maritain   319
Etienne Gilson   323

21. Phenomenology   327

Franz Brentano   328
Edmund Husserl   329
Max Scheler   334
Nicolai Hartmann   338
Maurice Merleau-Ponty   339

22. Existentialism   342

Søren Kierkegaard   343
Martin Heidegger   349
Jean-Paul Sartre   353

INDEX   359

Chapter 1

The Problem of Matter— The Milesians

Philosophy in the Western world is traditionally traced back to ancient Greece, particularly to the region of Ionia, which includes Attica (especially Athens), Samos, Miletus, Ephesus, and the islands strung along the Aegean Sea from southeastern Greece to the western coast of Asia Minor. The three men regarded as the first philosophers were Thales (c. 624–546 B.C.), Anaximander (c. 610–545 B.C.), and Anaximenes (fl. 585–528 B.C.). Since they lived in Miletus (which was probably the capital of Ionia during the sixth century B.C.), these philosophers and their followers became known as the Milesian school.

The Milesian philosophers are also referred to as Ionian Physicists because of their almost exclusive interest in physics or, more properly, cosmology, as this term is used in philosophy. Cosmology is that branch of metaphysics which deals with the nature or essence of the orderly universe—the cosmos. The Ionian philosophers set for themselves the task of ascertaining the nature of substance, of cosmic matter, of the very stuff out of which the entire universe is composed.

THALES

History attributes remarkable intellectual accomplishments to Thales, the first of the Milesians, who predicted the eclipse of the sun (for May 28, 585 B.C.), determined the height of the pyramids (by measuring their shadows), and invented a device for calculating the distance of ships at sea.

Our information about the ideas of the ancient philosophers of Miletus is so fragmentary that we must often supplement it with a certain amount of conjecture in order to explain the basis for their theories. Thales made his principal contribution to philosophy by postulating a single substance, water, as the cosmic stuff comprising the universe. It is not difficult to understand why he selected water as the basic component, for water exists in all three forms of

1

matter: liquid, solid, and gas. Furthermore, with keen insight he decided that all matter must consist of a single substance which remains the same despite such different states of aggregation. Using these theories to explain the position of the earth among the planets, he concluded that the earth is floating in space, just as a ball floats in water.

Thales and other Ionian philosophers believed in the doctrine of *hylozoism* (or *hylopsychism*), the theory that matter possesses life or sensation—that life and matter are inseparable. The Milesians ascribed life or soul to substance, and, according to Thales, God is in everything, in all three forms and manifestations of matter. Thus he even attributed a soul to the magnet because it has the power to attract metallic objects.

ANAXIMANDER

None of the writings of Thales have been preserved, and only a fragment is extant from the works of Anaximander, this being a slight portion of his book, *Peri Phuses* (*Concerning Nature*). Nevertheless, from the writings of later philosophers the principal thesis expounded by Anaximander became widely known.

Ultimate cosmic matter, said Anaximander, consists of *Apeiron*, that is, *the Boundless, or the Infinite.* The fundamental elements of matter are of necessity infinite; otherwise they could not account for the ceaseless, multifarious creations and changes which take place in nature. If natural processes were finite, they would eventually exhaust their creative potentialities and cease; consequently, the Boundless, God, must be infinite, unlike the finite forms of matter which proceed from it. The Boundless, which is an eternal reality beyond the limits of our experience, is distinct from that matter which we do experience; it is the reality to which the facts of human experience relate. Matter is perceptible, but that fundamental reality from which it originates, the Infinite or God, is imperceptible.

Within the *Apeiron* are contained all the elements of the world, and the Infinite makes use of heat and cold to produce qualitatively distinct characteristics in the realm of our experience. The basic substance, *fluid*, is formed by the action of these two influences (heat and cold), and from it are derived the three primary elements: earth, air, and fire. Building on the foundation of Thales' cosmology, Anaximander thus rounded out the philosophical system of the Ionian Physicists.

Anaximander also contributed a theory of evolution strikingly close to the Darwinian hypothesis, for he attributed organic life to the action of fluid in drying up sufficiently to form fish-like creatures which developed into animals through a process of adapting themselves to life on land. The human species was the end result of this process of adaptation.

Finally, Anaximander formulated a theory on the transmigration of souls. According to his theory (which appears to have been quite similar to the Hindu point of view) cosmic matter creates itself, disintegrates, and then recreates itself—in a perpetual life process of never ending transformations.

ANAXIMENES

The third great philosopher of the Milesian school, Anaximenes, differed both from Thales and from Anaximander concerning the nature of cosmic matter. Instead of water, as postulated by Thales, he selected air as the fundamental substance; also rejecting the Boundless of Anaximander, he attributed the origins of the entire universe to air. Since air is the most mobile of all elements, is omnipresent, and, furthermore, is essential to the growth of all natural objects and thus to life itself, it constitutes the only satisfactory basis for the explanation of reality.

According to Anaximenes, the *Originator* (as he called the basic substance air) takes on the characteristics of all kinds of matter by means of condensation and rarefaction. When air condenses, it assumes the forms of earth and the structured rocks; when it becomes rarefied, it appears as fire. Condensation is identified with cold, rarefaction with heat. There is a constant rhythm in this everlasting cycle whereby all the elements of the universe are continuously being created and destroyed in ceaseless succession.

From these meager beginnings among the Milesian thinkers, philosophy was introduced into the Western world. The way philosophy started proved to be most favorable to the development of science, for these earliest philosophers were interested primarily in scientific knowledge, that is to say, in knowledge about the physical world, an interest which has been the center of attention among modern scientists to the present. It was in a much later period than the Milesian, especially during the time of Socrates, that man's thoughts turned to a philosophy of practical life, a pragmatic philosophy which a person could practice and live by. Meanwhile, the Milesian philosophers had initiated the search for ultimate answers to questions about the true nature of the universe. A number of great philosophers followed the Milesians during the pre-Socratic period, beginning with Xenophanes of Colophon and Heraclitus of Ephesus. All of them concentrated on the problems of *metaphysics*, the attempt to unveil the mysteries of ultimate reality, to account for the origin of the physical universe, and to demonstrate how the phenomenal facts manifested in human experience stem from ultimate reality.

Chapter 2

The Problem of Identity and Change—Antithetical Philosophies Of Heraclitus and the Eleatics

---

The Ionian philosophers created the metaphysical problem which they left as a legacy to future philosophers, that is, the problem of identifying the ultimate reality which philosophers refer to as the *ontologically real*. The problem actually turned out to be twofold: that of ascertaining the nature of the basic substance of which the world is composed; and that of deciding whether the universe is one or many—whether the ultimate cosmic stuff is only one basic substance (*Metaphysical Monism*, as it is technically referred to) or a multiplicity of substances (*Metaphysical Pluralism*).

XENOPHANES, THE THEOLOGICAL ELEATIC

Inquiry into the nature of ultimate reality soon involved additional problems, such as those raised by Xenophanes of Colophon. Xenophanes settled in Elea in southeastern Italy and is generally regarded as founder of the Eleatic school of philosophy. He introduced two fundamental problems: the problem of *being* and *becoming*, and that of *rest* and *motion*. The problem of being and becoming hinges on the question whether anything in the universe has been fully or permanently developed (and thus is now in a state of being) or, on the contrary, everything is still in a transitory state of being perfected (and is thus maturing or becoming), on its way toward actualization or realization. The problem of rest and motion is inextricably woven into the first problem; its solution may explain how natural forces can be effective—how, for example, a flower develops from a seed to full blossom, or how any or all given events can be traced back to their causes.

Xenophanes formulated answers to these metaphysical questions on the basis of his belief in God. As the "theological Eleatic," he condemned the anthropomorphism of his day, the idea that the gods (or God) possess human characteristics. He noted that the Ethiopians made their gods both black and snubnosed like themselves, and he conjectured that if the oxen or lions had hands with which

5

to paint, they, too, would fashion the likenesses of their gods in their own images. According to Xenophanes, there is only one God, differing completely from mortal men in both form and mind; but, although he defended monotheism, the belief in one God, he was technically a Pantheist because he identified God with all that exists —the sum total of reality is God.

For Xenophanes, therefore, God and the universe are one and the same reality, a single, unchanging, universal Being who contains within himself the *Arche* (beginning, first principle, or primitive element) of all things. The cosmic principle is the cosmic deity, a cosmic mind, a World-God; he is a unity possessing homogeneity. This divine originator of all things is himself unbegun, eternal, and unchangeable; moreover, because he himself is immobile, it follows necessarily that the ultimate substance of which the world is composed is also immutable and consequently lacks the hylozoistic qualities posited by the Milesians. Hylozoism, as set forth in Milesian philosophy, states that "inanimate" objects actually possess life; it is an attempt to explain causal forces, development, growth. Xenophanes' assumption of a pantheistic God supplants the hylozoistic principle, for his theory explains how an immutable, immobile substance (God) can release forces which account fully for the phenomena and development of the entire universe. Although God, the *Arche* (originator), remains unchanged, he is the cosmic principle which creates the natural processes that both come into being and undergo change.

Thus Xenophanes attempted (through his doctrine of Pantheism) to reconcile the antithetical interpretations of nature, first, as an array of ever changing things and, second, as an infinite, never changing substance. Later philosophers debated the problem intensively, for they realized it would be necessary for them, too, to make the choice between two conflicting points of view. Thus Heraclitus of Ephesus (c. 544–484 B.C.) argued that the entire substance of the world is in a ceaseless process of change, while the Eleatic philosopher Parmenides (c. 540–470 B.C.) held to the opposing theory that the ultimate substance (Being) is unchanging and unchangeable, permanent. These two great thinkers set the stage for the metaphysical problems which commanded the attention of all philosophers during that period 2,500 years ago.

HERACLITUS OF EPHESUS

The chief doctrine of Heraclitus states that everything is in a state of *flux,* undergoing constant change. Permanent, immutable substance does not exist, for ultimate reality is essentially a mutable substance, always developing, hence constantly in a state of flux. The process of *strife*, which changes all things into their opposites, is the real Lord of the universe. Heraclitus regarded the world as a ceaselessly changing system (never complete or final in the sense of reaching its goal or coming to a stop in a state of perfection). This idea he expressed in the concise statement: "All things flow, nothing abides." He pointed out that it is impossible for a person to step into the same river twice inasmuch as new water is constantly entering the river while at the same time some water which was once part of the river is continuously flowing into the sea, thus no longer constituting part of the river. His conclusion was that the river is not the same in any two given moments; no matter how brief the time interval, change has already occurred. Hence, like everything else in the universe, the river lacks permanency.

In this way, Heraclitus deduced that things do not really exist as ready-made units (if *exist* means they are identical from moment to moment); in fact, they lack identity, for they possess only *Becoming* and they do not possess the permanency of *Being*. They are only in a transitory stage, always about to become something. Everything is in a continuous state of alteration, transmutation, from one condition to another, just as, for example, a human being must pass from childhood to manhood, unable to stop aging or to prevent changes in his relationship to time. Not only does time move constantly onward, but the whole perceptual world is in transition.

According to Heraclitus, the Originator (or *Arche*, this being the term applied by early Greek philosophers to the force responsible for the genesis of the world) was *motion*, which produces perceptual matter in all its multifarious characteristics. In this respect, he was in agreement with the Milesians, who believed motion to be self-contained in matter. This view was reflected in their hylozoistic doctrine that a vital element self-contained in all forms of matter activates every process in the ever changing universe, ranging from the sprouting of a tree from its seed to the movements of a river as it carves out its course to the sea.

Not the object of sense, but cosmic motion, is the eternal reality. This cosmic motion takes the form of *fire*, incessantly changing yet retaining its identity. For Heraclitus, therefore, fire is the genesis of all things, the substance responsible for motion, and the world stuff which changes everything, including itself. Despite its unceasing motion, fire remains uniform; consequently, the universe, although it changes and in this sense lacks permanency, must be an uncreated eternal mutability. In Heraclitanism we have a pantheistic hylozoism, inasmuch as Heraclitus identified the world principle, fire, with motion (which accounts for the genesis of the world), with ultimate reality, and with God. Fire, then, or God, is the cosmic process, the world principle, responsible for all of nature and its ongoing phenomena.

Although "nothing is permanent except change" itself, nevertheless the process of change takes place in accordance with reason, the one permanent aspect of the universe. Reason controls all the changing and recurrent forms in the world, it guides the rhythmic movement of ever changing phenomena, and it does these things according to law. To Heraclitus, therefore, we must grant the distinction of having been the first to discover natural law, the laws of science. This natural principle, reason (or the law of nature), which he termed *Logos,* is the rational principle which dominates nature; it governs the cosmic process in accord with universal and immutable law. The *Logos* of the world makes possible the orderly behavior of cosmic processes of action and reaction. These processes combine to make things grow and then to disintegrate in a ceaseless cycle from life to death, from composition to decomposition, from creation to destruction, from chaos to cosmos and vice versa, all in a sequence of rhythmical change. Everything in the universe undergoes this procedure of change and counter-change in a cyclical order, and only the *law* of change abides—that is, the *Logos.*

The *Logos,* as the universal reason in nature, is also the soul's inner source of nourishment, vitality, and perfection on all those occasions when the soul obeys its dictates. The soul, which Heraclitus described as fiery (fire being the ultimate reality of the world), is the spirit of the universe. During life it is imprisoned within the body, from which it transmigrates at the time of death, then must expect just retribution for its lifetime record of moral or immoral conduct. A dry soul, said Heraclitus, is superior to a moist one (fire and dryness go together); consequently, one should keep sober, bearing in mind the fact that, owing to its wet state, a drunken soul behaves incoherently instead of according to reason.

Heraclitus counseled men to make all their actions conform to reason (*Logos*). Even as nature obeys universal laws, so must man also, both in his personal (or ethical) and in his social (or political) life, for he must live according to rational rules, that is, ethical principles. Only through such conduct are serenity and happiness to be found; only by obeying reason are these desired results feasible and humanly attainable. Unfortunately, said Heraclitus, the masses are misled by their senses and mere appearances. The wise man will follow reason as the correct path to happiness and contentment.

PARMENIDES, THE METAPHYSICAL ELEATIC

Parmenides, who became the second great leader of the Eleatic school, developed a view in direct antithesis to Heraclitanism. Whereas Heraclitus interpreted all reality as change, Parmenides pictured the universe as a single, permanent substance (the theory of Metaphysical Monism). This had been the view of Xenophanes, the theological Eleatic. Now Parmenides developed it further on the basis of rational thought, building the thesis on a scientific foundation.

Parmenides stated that all thinking depends upon the things being thought about, that every idea has its corresponding object in the external world, and that, accordingly, thought has *Being* for its objective content. If a thought did not have a referent, it would be devoid of content and hence would refer to nothing whatever—such a thought would have no definite object. Conversely, no object that is inconceivable could exist, for it would be non-Being (nonexistent). In other words, all our concepts must have corresponding real objects in the external world, for otherwise they could not be thought. It is absurd to talk about nonexistent Beings, which would be identical with nothingness. Thought and the thing thought about are one and the same entity (Epistemological Monism).

For Parmenides, therefore, the object of abstract thought is the only thing which exists, and it exists as a single abstract Being—consisting not of basically different elements, but of one and the same substance. The nature of all things throughout the world is fundamentally the same essence. Consequently, the ultimately real world is one object, or Being, which is an uncreated, eternal, indestructible, unchangeable, unique, indivisible, homogeneous cosmic substance.

Moreover, according to Parmenides, all the numerous things we seem to perceive are actually one thing only, namely, Being. To say that a thing is, implies that it occupies space, but empty space does not and cannot exist, for the same reason that non-Being cannot exist. (Note the dual meaning of *Being*, as employed here by Parmenides: in the first instance it refers to ultimate reality, in the second to whatever occupies space.)

Consequently, in direct antithesis to Heraclitus, Parmenides denied the reality of change or motion, because motion implies empty space, an unoccupied area into which an object may enter, but empty space is nothingness, an unreality. In order for a thing to move, it must move into occupied space, and it cannot do that inasmuch as every space is already occupied. Therefore, nothing can move, and, since motion does not exist, Being is changeless. Motion and change are mere illusions, comparable to the phenomena created when still movies are shown in rapid succession on a moving-picture screen. These empirical facts of motion and change do not exist in reality; only the facts prescribed by rational thought exist. Hence the empirical world is nonexistent.

ZENO, THE DIALECTICAL ELEATIC

Zeno of Elea (*c.* 490–430 B.C.), was the most famous of Parmenides' disciples. Aristotle referred to Zeno as the originator of *dialectic*, who used dialectical ingenuity to defend his teacher's philosophical doctrine concerning the unity ("oneness") and permanency of ultimate reality—the doctrine of Being. Zeno's arguments were based on the premises of formal logic, on pure logical relations, not on the data of empirical experience; in debate he used logical reasoning to ensnare his opponent in contradiction and paradox.

Zeno realized that to deny the oneness (unity) of things (Metaphysical Monism) and the permanency of substance—or, alternatively, to assume multiplicity (Metaphysical Pluralism) and motion —would mean that time and space are infinite. But if time and space were infinite, then existing objects would be both infinitely large and infinitely small, and the infinitely large objects could be divided into infinitely small particles. In order to prove the absurdity of the conclusions advanced by the Atomists (who believed that the universe consists of many infinitely small units), Zeno pointed out that if the atoms had even the smallest dimensions, or any size whatever, it would be possible to split and divide them. On the other hand, these same atoms would be infinitely large as well, because if an object were composed of parts, then each part would be connected to another part, and that one to still another, and thus each object in the world would become infinitely large.

The problem of unity versus plurality is complicated indeed by the arguments of the Atomists and other Metaphysical Pluralists whose premises lead to the conclusion that the universe is both finite and infinite. A world of multiple objects would have to be finite, claimed Zeno, because there would be nothing else to add to the objects already in existence. But the same world of multiple objects would have to be infinite, for there would be something—a separating object—between any pair of things, and then there would have to be something between that separating object and the other two, and so on *ad infinitum*.

The Pluralists assumed that an object is in space; however, since space itself must be something, then space must either be in something else or in nothing. It would be absurd to think of space as being in nothing. Therefore it must be in something, and that something must be more space. Thus, one becomes involved in assuming an infinite number of spaces within space, an absurdity justifying the conclusion that empty space does not even exist. The absurdity is clear if we visualize space as finite, ending at a given point, and ask the questions, "What is on the other side? Still more space?"

Zeno confronted the Atomists and other Metaphysical Pluralists with the foregoing paradoxes. He also debated against advocates of the Heraclitan concept that the universe consists only of motion, change, that there is no permanency in things. He attacked the Atomists, too, in the same way, for they believed that individual atoms contain *kinesis* (motion capable of effecting changes such as take place in cause-and-effect relationships). He set forth a number of contradictory propositions (paradoxes) to prove his criticism.

One of Zeno's paradoxes stated that it is impossible to traverse an infinite number of points within finite time, because to go from any point A to any point B we would have to traverse the intermediate points. But since the distance between points A and B could be divided into an infinite number of points, then how would it be possible to travel an infinite number of spaces within the limited time in which we would have to do so?

Another of Zeno's paradoxes is one about a handicap race between Achilles and the tortoise. Giving the tortoise the lead will never allow Achilles to catch up to the tortoise because (since the tortoise is moving constantly at the same time that Achilles is striving to catch up to him) the moment Achilles tries to place his foot where the tortoise is, the tortoise will have moved ahead. So Achilles could never win the race. The same paradox is involved in our attempt to pinpoint the precise moment that separates past time from future time. We may say "Now" to indicate the present moment, only to discover that time had already moved onward even while we are referring to the present. Consequently, we can never catch up to time in the sense of holding fast to the present moment.

A third paradox uses the example of an arrow in flight to refute the belief in motion. At any given moment, an arrow flying through space (composed of points) must be at rest. A high-speed candid camera will catch the arrow in flight at any moment and show it at rest—that is, at a precise spot. But motion could not consist of a series of fixed positions; it must be an illusion, just as a rapidly appearing sequence of still pictures seem to move when shown on a moving-picture screen.

According to Zeno, motion is not real, but is merely a relative judgment. The apparent rate of movement depends on a comparison between two or more objects. A modern example may be cited: an automobile travelling at fifty miles per hour will seem to be moving swiftly when passing a stationary object such as a parked automobile, but it will seem to be moving much more slowly when passing another which is travelling at forty miles per hour. If motion were real, it would seem to be as swift in the first instance as in the second. Must we agree with Zeno that all motion is but a matter of judgment, an illusion?

Zeno's ingenious arguments against the existence of multiplicity and motion raised problems about the nature of space, time, and motion. They implied the non-empirical nature of time and motion —the assumption that time and space are capable of being statically divided infinitely. Unless we postulate the real existence of empirical time and motion on the ground, for example, that Achilles actually races past the tortoise, the paradoxes of Zeno still remain a mystery.

MELISSUS OF SAMOS

We have considered the problems raised by three of the Eleatics: Xenophanes, Parmenides, and Zeno. Another Eleatic philosopher, Melissus of Samos, wrote a treatise, *On Being*, to defend Parmenides' doctrine of Being. Melissus contributed the proposition that Being is not only permanent and imperishable, but also infinite, without a beginning or ending in space; in other words, Being is the *Apeiron* (boundless), to which Anaximander the Milesian had attributed the origin of all things.

THE METAPHYSICAL PLURALISTS

We shall now see how a subsequent school of Hellenistic philosophy—the Metaphysical Pluralists from Empedocles of Agrigentum to Democritus of Abdera—attempted to find a common meeting ground or synthesis to close the gap between the antithetical views of Heraclitus and the Eleatics. These Pluralists tried to solve basic metaphysical problems in a rational way that would yet be consistent with the facts of human experience. The Heraclitan doctrine of ultimate reality as *Becoming* lacked any element of fixed, stable reality, while the antithetical doctrine of Parmenides and the Eleatics lacked any element of changing, progressive reality. The mediating philosophical systems which sought to reconcile these two antithetical positions were developed by Empedocles of Agrigentum, Sicily (495–435 B.C.); Anaxagoras of Clazomene (499–428 B.C.); and two Atomists, namely, Leucippus of Abdera (fifth century B.C.), and Democritus of Abdera (460–370 B.C.). All four of these mediating systems were in agreement on two major assumptions: (1) that reality consists of a *multiplicity* of substances or elements (Metaphysical Pluralism); and (2) that there is a mechanism which explains their mode of behavior. In other words, they agreed that ultimate elements are in themselves permanent but do undergo change, variations in form, destruction, and creation as a result of a mechanical arrangement or rearrangement of these ultimate elements of which every object is composed.

EMPEDOCLES OF AGRIGENTUM

Empedocles, the first of these Metaphysical Pluralists attempting to reconcile Heraclitanism with the Eleatic point of view, met with considerable success but also raised additional problems. According to Empedocles, although the basic substances in the universe differ qualitatively, they are eternal and unchangeable, as the Eleatics had claimed; the unchanging substances are quantitatively divisible by mechanical processes, thus allowing for the introduction of change and rearrangement. The four basic elements (which he identified as fire, air, water, and earth) combine in various proportions to form everything that exists. Thus, by postulating a definite number of ultimate elements and noting their combinations in fixed mathematical proportions, he may be said to have founded the science of chemistry. In fact, his theory was considered valid even as late as the early eighteenth century.

In other words, Empedocles combined the idea of the indestructibility of matter (which, in Parmenides' doctrine, is both eternal and unchangeable Being) with the Heraclitan idea of Becoming—change, motion, and transition. The rearrangement of the four elements of Being account for construction and destruction, creation and annihilation, change and decay. But how does the rearrangement occur? Since the four elements (as changeless Being) cannot of themselves move into the various arrangements which make up the existing facts of the world, a *moving force* which causes their motion is a necessary postulate. Force and matter are distinct cosmic realities which must be related to each other. Empedocles assumed force to be dual in nature, inasmuch as it constructs, or creates, and also destroys. He termed these forces *love* and *hate*, respectively. Love, the universal law, is responsible for unity, for orderliness in the world, for its inherent goodness, while hate (destructive in nature) is the cause of disorder, disarray, separation, and decay or destruction of objects. Empedocles designated supreme, all-powerful love as God, who establishes a perfect harmony of the elements to create an orderly cosmos; if the forces of hate were to become supreme, they would produce a total separation and destruction of the elements.

Everywhere there is conflict between the two forces of love and hate; as a consequence, whenever either emerges as victor, there is a mixture of creation and decomposition, of order and destruction, with order or chaos dominant. But man is unlike other objects. When a man's body is destroyed, his soul transmigrates from body to body, remaining as the prisoner of one until hate destroys that particular body. Empedocles' belief in the doctrine of the transmigration of the soul is coupled with his belief that the human spirit is eternal. Prior to man's appearance on earth, his soul dwells in a blissful state in the divine community. He is expelled for committing sin, for which his punishment is physical imprisonment in the body during life on earth. Divine existence, a life elevated above the material world, is the true life.

The imprisonment of the soul within the body also limits human cognitive ability; sense perception does not yield true knowledge. Genuine knowledge is derived from the power of reason and reflection. Thus, we find a dualism in the philosophy of Empedocles: the natural world contrasted with the spiritual world. The philosopher uses the power of reason to discover the elements and relationships in both worlds.

ANAXAGORAS OF CLAZOMENE

Like Empedocles, Anaxagoras argued from the Eleatic premise that matter is indestructible, but, unlike the Eleatics who asserted that matter consists of a single kind of substance, and unlike Empedocles who posited only four basic elements of matter, Anaxagoras postulated innumerable elements of matter, each possessing its own distinctive form and sensory qualities (as in taste and color vision).

Inasmuch as matter is indestructible, it is misleading to refer to material objects as being really created and destroyed, since all the objects are fundamentally the same; rather Anaxagoras, like Empedocles before him, preferred to speak of the origin of an object as its state or stage of composition, and he referred to its separation as its state or stage of perishing or decomposition. Matter itself, whether in a state of composition or that of separation, is nevertheless at bottom the same unchangeable, eternal, uncreated substance as Parmenides posited it to be. On the basis of this reasoning, when objects change, their change is simply a mechanical process, not strictly a qualitative one in which the chemical properties change; the chemical composition is merely altered.

How then do qualitative changes occur? Original matter came into existence qualitatively different, each element differing qualitatively from the rest, and there existed a countless number of them dispersed throughout the world in an exceedingly fine condition. An individual object comes into existence when these elements compound in a given relationship; their disassociation, a state of separation, causes the object to pass out of existence.

At this point, however, the persistent problem as to how the *force* which produces change (i.e., the power of motion which is lacking in the original elements themselves) arose to plague Anaxagoras as it had plagued his predecessors. Empedocles had attributed the motive forces to *love* and *hate*, and the Milesian physicists had hypothesized that matter contained its own motion (expressed in their doctrine of *hylozoism*, stating that matter contains its own means of animation). Anaxagoras could not accept the explanation that elements themselves possess activity, nor did he believe in atoms, for he repudiated the atomic theory of his time. He concluded that the forces of nature must be pure forces, immaterial forces which impart force to objects of the universe. Thus, the forces of nature move themselves and are the cause of motion for everything else within the world.

The nature of these forces as such must be psychical, spiritual, or ideal in their natural constitution, a sort of soulness, soul substance, or animate materiality—an immaterial substance. This cosmic immaterial substance, which is akin to the nature of mind, he termed *Nous* (reason). This thought-stuff, this force type of substance called *Nous*, is essentially teleological, which is to say that its every act is purposeful, with a specific goal as its objective. The beauty of the world, its orderliness, its response to scientific understanding, its response to purpose, its intelligible functioning, and the harmonious cosmic systems are all due to *Nous*, the purposeful rational mind responsible for ordering them according to the goals for which they were intended and also according to the respective worth that each possesses. The world has a purpose, and the forces of nature which direct nature to its goal are determined by the purpose ascribed to them by *Nous*. The causal laws of nature which move objects to their respective individual and composite ends (which dominate nature teleologically, thereby establishing orderly movement in the universe) are attributable to the rational and purposeful *Nous*, a unique imperishable substance differing from all else. The worth of the world, together with its beauty and perfection, its ascent from chaos to cosmos, is credited to this mind substance, *Nous*. With the introduction of Anaxagoras' *Nous*, philosophy had its first unmistakable intimation of that enduring philosophy which eventually became known as *Idealism*.

LEUCIPPUS OF ABDERA

Leucippus, regarded as the founder of the school of Atomism at Abdera, disagreed in regard to basic principles with his predecessors among the Metaphysical Pluralists. Empedocles had posited only four basic elements that are qualitatively different, and Anaxagoras had assumed a countless number of *qualitatively distinct* elements. Leucippus reverted to the position of Parmenides, who had denied any qualitative distinctions among ultimate elements and had insisted that ultimate reality (Being) is composed of a single substance of homogeneous quality throughout (Metaphysical Monism). Although Leucippus held to these concepts that ultimate reality lacks qualitative distinctions and that its sole property consists in occupying space, he differed from Parmenides in that he assumed that this corporeality (called Being) is not a single substance, but is instead a multiplicity of *qualitatively identical* elements (Metaphysical Pluralism) which he termed *atoms* (indivisible inert dense bodies).

Leucippus also disagreed with Parmenides on the question of empty space (the Eleatic's non-Being), and he argued that non-Being is as real and necessary as Being, for within empty space (non-Being) the elements of atoms (each quantitatively distinct from the others) move about. This non-Being (something other than the object, Being) is a kind or mode of Being which is metaphysically real in its own right; it is an incorporeal substance, an empty space, an unlimited empty space which he called the *Apeiron*, the Boundless of Anaximander. Thus, absolute Being consists of two distinct entities: atoms and space.

The atoms, filling empty space, are characteristic of Being as Parmenides viewed it, alike in substance, indestructible. The term *atom* etymologically means uncuttable, hence indivisible. Although each atom exists in itself and in this way is distinct from the others, the atoms are all identical in their universal quality of occupying space. The illusion of qualitative differences among them is due to their quantitative differences in size, form, and arrangement. This premise of atomic structure can be used to explain the Heraclitan thesis of Becoming or change as due to the rearrangement (self-movement) of the atoms in space. Accordingly, the Atomism of Leucippus provides a synthesis of Heraclitan flux with Parmenidean permanency.

DEMOCRITUS OF ABDERA

The school at Abdera had as its most distinguished representative Democritus, the father of Materialism. After Democritus, the school rapidly passed into near oblivion as its followers diverted it into Sophism. From there it deteriorated further under the influence of Pyrrho who converted it into a philosophy of Skepticism.

The philosophy of Democritus reduced all phenomena to Materialism, to atomic substances mechanistically governed, a concept which he acquired from Leucippus. Mechanical relationships or arrangements of the atoms account for various characteristics of nature, the intimation here being that the natural order of the world resulted from chance. Qualitative distinctions, that is, differences in value or in the worth of one object as compared with another, are explained on the basis of mechanical arrangements. Mechanistic causes (atomic force or weight) account for all phenomena; teleological explanations, such as those based on Anaxagoras' *Nous*, are rejected. Even morality, the soul, and all mental life are reducible to mechanistic terms with physical imperceptible atoms as their basic structure. Spiritual reality does not exist; what appears to be spiritual is attributed simply to subperceptible atomic structure or else to mere superstition. Hence, the Democritan philosophy of mechanistic Materialism is complete, self-sufficient, and self-contained.

Atoms alone exist, possessing motion and filling empty space. These numberless, self-propelling, qualitatively identical atoms are imperceptible to human senses, but they are apprehended by the intellect, the mind, of man. Owing to their non-sensory nature and small size, they can only be thought, not directly observed. Nevertheless, the imperceptible atoms account for all observable phenomena of nature, those things which are manifest to the senses. Because sense observation is limited to phenomenal manifestation of the atoms only, sense knowledge is unreliable. Sense experience produces a multiplicity of opinions because people receive and interpret sensory phenomena from different perspectives. Knowledge derived from the senses is therefore *relative* to the person from whose experience it originates. Such knowledge is mere opinion, lacking validity and resulting in subjectivism. Actually, since sense knowledge never does reach reality—the atomic world of reality—one can never use the senses to attain truth, i.e., knowledge of the metaphysically real. This inability of the senses to disclose genuine knowledge or truth prompted the followers of Democritus, such as his disciple Pyrrho, to lapse into Skepticism—the doctrine that knowledge is unattainable, that nothing is known or can be known. Yet, Democritus not only repudiated Skepticism and the Relativism of Protagoras, Relativism's most influential representative, but he championed the cause of absolute truth and reality—the reality of the atoms discerned by reason. The primary qualities of the atoms, that is, their characteristics of solidity, weight, and form constitute the real material object itself and are known only to reason, whereas their secondary qualities, namely, the sensory characteristics, such as color, touch, and taste are derived from sense impressions. But the secondary characteristics are phenomenal manifestations only, lacking ultimate reality in contrast to the ontologically real, Being itself, which is an object of the understanding. Thus, in Democritus we find not only the synthesizor of the ideas of Parmenides and Heraclitus, but the intellectual predecessor of the great modern philosophers Locke and Descartes as well.

Democritus had an affinity for Pythagorean mathematical philosophy as reflected in his theory that geometrical *forms* are inherent in atomic matter. (These *forms* posited by Democritus will reappear in a later era as the Platonic Ideals.) His dependence upon the philosophy of Heraclitus is also clearly seen in his explanation of the soul and mental activity as due to the motion of fire atoms. Just as the *Nous* contributed a basic concept to the philosophy of Anaxagoras, the idea of fire atoms undergirded the philosophy and Behavioristic psychology (which he based upon Metaphysical Materialism) of Democritus. The activity of the human mind, of thinking, he attributed to the functioning (or motion) of the fire atoms. These fire atoms thus served as the basis of spiritual reality, while their movements were also held responsible for the cause and effect relationships in inert matter. The fire atoms, besides accounting for all functions of the human soul and reason, even form the basis for divine activity.

According to Democritus, the objective of metaphysical inquiry is to gain knowledge; and the ethical goal is to achieve happiness, that is, a state of well-being, of peace of mind—contentment. Democritus repudiated Hedonism as a doctrine derived from false sensory information. The true joys are those of the spirit, attained through knowledge of truth, not through sense experience. There are two kinds of atomic motion, the coarse and the refined. Coarse atomic activity provides sensual pleasure which terminates in emotional tension, disturbing the soul's equilibrium with its violent passions; but the refined fire atoms of the mind, holding to a rational course of behavior, lead not to stormy motions, but to gentle ones resulting in tranquility, pleasures of the spirit, a beautiful feeling of the mind, which constitutes happiness. True pleasures emanate from objective reality, nature, and atomic Being, hence have true worth, whereas sensual pleasures possess only psychological or phenomenal value and vary with different individuals owing to the subjective character of these pleasures. The wise man seeks to cultivate intellectual refinement as the path to temperance, self-control, and happiness, but the sensual man, lacking cultivation and knowledge, follows where his appetite leads him, remains ignorant and mentally inferior, and consequently contributes little to society.

The dualistic thought which runs throughout the philosophy of Democritus, beginning with his distinction between two basic types of knowledge (between sense experience and rational intellect) culminates in two interpretations of ethics (Hedonism and Eudaemonism) and two views of reality: as phenomenal reality and as metaphysical (or ontological) reality. Phenomenal reality refers to our knowledge of appearances, while metaphysical reality refers to our knowledge of real objects, the true essences of objects. The term *phenomenal reality*, apparently first used by Democritus, became a permanent part of the vocabulary of philosophers. In modern philosophy it has come to mean our relative knowledge of sense objects—the world which the senses depict for us—in contrast to genuine reality. By metaphysical reality Democritus meant the absolute, not relative, knowledge of Being or of the essences of objects. Plato, as we shall see, interpreted the objects themselves as Ideas constituting "ideal" reality. The great modern philosopher Immanuel Kant coined the term *noumena* to denote the real objects, the things-in-themselves. In fact it was Democritus who set the stage in metaphysics for the eventual development of two diametrically opposing points of view: Platonic Idealism, and Metaphysical Materialism coupled with Relativism.

THE PYTHAGOREANS—
MATHEMATICAL PHILOSOPHY

Pythagoras (c. 580–497 B.C.) formulated a practical, ethical, and religious philosophy which placed supreme value on intellectual activity but contained many ideas, such as the doctrine of transmigration of souls, that were quite foreign to Greek philosophy. We should distinguish between Pythagoras, who lived in the late sixth century B.C. and the Pythagorean philosophers (some of whom were closely associated with Plato's Academy) who later propounded a metaphysical view based on mathematics and science. Outstanding among these Pythagoreans was Philolaus, a contemporary of Socrates and Democritus.

Pythagoras himself founded a religion which taught the doctrine of the transmigration of souls. The members of his religious society, the Pythagorean Order, lived by a set of religious and ethical rules. His doctrine of transmigration, which made its first appearance among the Orphic cult, pictured ideal existence as a life of divine bliss attained after final escape from a cycle of intermediate births. This blissful final state of salvation could be reached through purification, the renunciation of worldly sensuality, and the observance of ascetic abstinence. But, since physical sensuality contaminates the soul, the noblest means of purification is intellectual activity, which liberates the soul from its bodily ties. The negation of sensuality prior to physical death enables the soul to achieve the ideal of spiritual purification, especially through music and science, and physical purification through the use of medicine and gymnastics.

Pythagoras' fundamental theory of the transmigration of souls became the basis for an ancillary doctrine asserting the brotherhood of all living things. All living things must be interrelated because their souls have each possessed a great number of different bodies during past transmigrations; therefore the practice of vegetarianism should become universal, all peoples should live in harmony and friendship, women should be granted equality with men, and slaves should be treated humanely.

The moral quality of one's present life determines the nature of the body which the soul will inhabit in the next life; a person is thus rewarded or punished accordingly. The preferred life is that of the physician, prince, or bard. As enlightened persons, the Pythagoreans assumed the responsibility of serving as spiritual guides and rulers; consequently, they prized and pursued careers in government.

PHILOLAUS AND THE PYTHAGOREAN PHILOSOPHY

The Metaphysical Pluralists sought to reconcile the Heraclitan idea of Becoming with Parmenides' concept of Permanence. Similarly Philolaus and other Pythagorean philosophers attempted (in the fifth century B.C.) to synthesize the two conflicting views of an ever changing universe and an eternal immutable world. They found the solution in mathematics.

Their interest in the practical applications of mathematics (the Pythagorean theorem, $A^2 + B^2 = C^2$, is a familiar example of their achievements) impelled them to formulate a mathematical explanation of all reality. They set out to prove that the phenomenal world of physical nature is grounded on mathematical principles. They demonstrated a mathematical relationship between musical sounds (such as octaves) and the lengths of vibrating musical strings. It seemed obvious to them that mathematical relationships must be taken into account in order to gain understanding and control of such natural phenomena.

The Pythagoreans believed that just as music obeys the laws of mathematics, all of nature—the phenomenal world of Becoming—must do the same, for, they said, ultimate reality (permanent Being) consists of numbers. Since in their view *all reality is number*, all physical phenomena stem from mathematical relationships. Numbers determine the permanent essence of physical things; numbers are the mathematical relationships or forms which natural objects take; and physical things are therefore ideal things, mere copies of these invisible mathematical relationships or forms. Physical objects are, as it were, poured into mathematical molds which constitute their essence. Physical things are mathematically limited; hence the controlling laws of nature must be regarded as mathematical principles, and for this reason physical nature can be understood only in mathematical terms. Furthermore, although physical nature is in transition, as correctly indicated by the concept of Becoming (or process) in the philosophy of Heraclitus, phenomena in nature possess a permanency and lasting order binding them together by means of their mathematical relationships. The permanent number relationships are invisible, yet they can be perceived and understood by the human intellect which senses them, not as things which create physical nature but as phenomena designed according to mathematical relationships. In this sense, physical things are in reality copies of numbers. These permanent mathematical forms of the Pythagoreans later were to become the Ideals of Plato who similarly interpreted them as belonging to a higher order than the phenomenal or physical reality (the Heraclitan Becoming), for the Ideals constitute absolute, ultimate, and permanent reality, whereas empirical phenomena are merely copies of the mathematical forms constituting original Being.

The Pythagoreans regarded everything in the world as a duality; they attributed to each object a corresponding opposite, to every thesis an antithesis. The opposing objects co-operate to produce a harmony; and just as in music harmony emerges from opposites, so the opposing forces in the universe are reconciled by a harmony of numbers. They formulated ten pairs of opposing ideas, each consisting of a thesis and its antithesis as follows: (1) limited and unlimited; (2) odd and even; (3) the one and the many; (4) left and right; (5) male and female; (6) rest and motion; (7) straight and crooked; (8) light and dark; (9) good and evil; and (10) equally square and unequal. The arbitrary selection of precisely ten pairs of concepts reflected their belief in the sacred character of the round number ten.

The Pythagorean philosophy was the last of the pre-Socratic systems of Greek philosophy to seek a compromise between conflicting views of the Heraclitans and the Eleatics. The next great development in the history of philosophy came during the period of the Greek Enlightenment, when the Sophists and Socrates turned away from metaphysical paradoxes to concentrate their attention on the ethical problems of man, his moral situation, and his philosophy of life.

Chapter 3

The Problem of Man—
From the Sophists to Plato

With few exceptions, philosophers prior to the Sophists (whose teachings became influential during the Greek Enlightenment in the fifth century B.C.), were primarily interested in cosmology, the systematic study of the universe as a whole, devoting little attention to problems of man as part of the universe. The Sophists turned the course of philosophy to the problem of man himself and formulated a philosophy of civilization and ethics. Among their predecessors, only Xenophanes, Heraclitus, and Pythagoras had seriously considered questions of ethics, of politics, or of religious philosophy; now, with the rise of the Sophists, these questions became fundamental philosophical issues. The new emphasis was reflected in the teachings of Socrates, who regarded the problem of man as the most important thing in the world.

THE SOPHISTS

The Sophists (a name derived from the Greek word meaning *wise*) sought to popularize scientific learning; they were the first professional teachers of philosophy, the first to require students to pay for instruction. Their foremost critic and adversary, Socrates, condemned this practice of accepting financial remuneration for teaching philosophy, stating that the search for scientific knowledge should never be debased in this way. Nevertheless, the Sophists defended the practice as justified by their mission of introducing the common man to a higher standard of culture—imparting to him the values and skills of sophisticated philosophical inquiry and communication and thus enabling him to live a more useful and better life. At first the Sophists' motives were noble ones, but we are told by Plato and Aristotle that the later practices degenerated into hairsplitting of words, frivolous argumentativeness, and eristic discussions designed to confuse the issue. Consequently, the name *Sophist* which had earlier been applied to all philosophers (including even Socrates and Plato) became an opprobrious term. Sophists such as

Euthydemus and Dionysodorus brought the method into disrepute
with quibbling and fallacious argumentation. Nevertheless, for over
a century the Sophists had contributed much to the advancement
of learning by their discussions of grammar, poetry, tragedy, lin-
guistics, and social reform. Protagoras founded the science of grammar, and Gorgias developed new artistic elements of Attic prose.

The Sophists based their philosophy on the doctrine of the relativity of truth; their emphasis on individualism eventually led to
complete Skepticism. At first they were influenced mainly by Heraclitus and his followers who rejected the idea of absolute truth and
interpreted reality as a process of constant change. The leading
Sophist philosopher, Protagoras, applied the idea of change to epistemology—the study of what knowledge is and how it is obtained.
He concluded that knowledge and truth are both dependent on judgments by the individual. The Pythagorean concept of unchanging
mathematical relationships as the essence of reality and the Eleatic
principle that nature obeys laws of permanent Being, that the laws
of physics are fixed and permanent (note that the Greek word for
physics means unchanging nature), were propositions analyzed crit-
ically by the Sophists. They inquired whether such unchanging laws
of nature could be accepted as the basis for laws governing man.
In other words, are there real ethical principles or is morality merely
a set of arbitrary conventions, the creation of man? Are the laws
of the State comparable to the laws of nature or mere arbitrary
rules? Are there genuine moral laws, norms for evaluating human
behavior, comparable to the laws which govern physical nature?
To assert that moral principles and legal codes are relative would
cast serious doubt upon their validity, yet this is what the Sophists
did, and thereby shook the foundations of society. Since knowledge
was at best relative, then truth was unattainable. Because of his
belief in the unavailability of absolute truth, the Sophist turned his
concern to the art of debate, to techniques for convincing or con-
verting one's opponents. Instead of trying to make truth prevail,
the Sophist was interested only in winning an argument. Thus the
Sophist's deep interest in grammar was motivated by the desire to
manipulate it to serve his personal ends, as illustrated particularly
in debate.

PROTAGORAS OF ABDERA

Protagoras of Abdera (*c.* 481–411 B.C.), not to be confused with
Pythagoras of Samos who founded the Pythagorean Order, was

the most influential leader of the Sophists. He based his entire philosophy on the concept of the relativity of truth, expressed in the statement, "Man is the measure of all things, of things that are, that they are, and of things that are not, that they are not." This point of view had an enduring impact on the history of philosophy down to contemporary times. Not only did Protagoras of Abdera thus proclaim the relativity of truth (that what is true for you is true only for you and what is true for me is true only for me) and the relativity of morals (that right and wrong are matters of personal opinion or choice), but also, as a most remarkable corollary, he derived from this principle the doctrine of equal rights for all mankind, including women and slaves. The doctrine that each individual must decide for himself as to the validity of any proposition became a principle of social reform, for it placed all persons on an equal footing as judges of the truth and thus served as an impetus toward cosmopolitanism, the unification of city-states into nations. No one group or city-state could be superior to the rest. The dictum of relativity implied equal rights for all, and Protagoras therefore demanded that sweeping social and political reforms be instituted by democratic means. Since laws and morals are social conventions arising from man's subjective nature, they should be binding only upon the group of individuals who have taken part in democratically enacting them. (Note that some philosophers have interpreted the Protagorean dictum as referring to man as an individual, while others have interpreted it as referring to man in the generic sense, hence as meaning that men in groups are the measure of all things, that ethical conduct and justice depend upon the moral codes of groups instead of the moral practices of individuals.) Without morality and justice, societies cannot be established; nevertheless, specific social codes are conventions, not absolute principles, and they ought to be obeyed only for selfish reasons—for the individual's own good.

The doctrine of the relativity of truth implied to the early Greek philosophers the assumption that human character can be improved by education, especially during childhood years, an objective which the Sophists sought to accomplish. Socrates derided their attempts, contending that no one can convert a bad soul into a good one or replace false feelings with sincere ones. Plato compared the Protagorean doctrine of the relativity of knowledge to the Heraclitan assertion that physical objects are in a state of constant flux—with both the objects of knowledge and knowledge itself ever changing; neither of them is permanent or absolute.

Although he held that absolutes do not exist in regard to morality, law, or religion, Protagoras did advance a moral philosophy of life based upon the natural law of self-preservation, the only law which to him was not reducible to mere social convention. Self-preservation, which he regarded as a force necessary for the survival of the species, implied a purpose which nature has devised for man and one which man is expected to fulfill. Nature has equipped man with intelligence, making him superior to physically stronger animals, and enabling him to create means of survival, such as suitable clothing, shelter, and other necessities. Yet even more remarkable is the fact that, using his divine reason, he has created language, morality, religion, society, and government. Man's innate nature predisposes him to live in society, but he must deliberately choose the specific rules of conduct for the group, develop its native language, and adopt a preferred religion or morality, all of which are equally conventions and become established as such through practice in everyday living.

For Protagoras and his followers, the doctrine of relativity holds good in all fields, even in geometry, whose propositions must be regarded as valid, not for application to individual cases, but for use as ideal principles only. The doctrine was reflected in the epistemological ideas of Democritus, who concluded that man is incapable of discerning the essences of things, their physical laws, by means of sense experience or perception.

GORGIAS OF LEONTINI

Another leading Sophist, Gorgias of Leontini (483–375 B.C.) had been a disciple of Empedocles, but later was impelled to accept Skepticism by Zeno's dialectical arguments. In his *On Nature, or the Nonexistent*, Gorgias propounded a nihilistic philosophy based upon three premises: (1) nothing exists; (2) if anything did exist we could never know it; and (3) if by chance we should come to know it, it would remain a secret because we could not communicate it to others.

Just as the Heraclitan concept of universal flux had paved the way for Protagoras' principle of the relativity of truth, so the Eleatic concept of changeless Being and the dialectical paradoxes of Zeno impelled Gorgias to formulate a philosophy of complete Skepticism.

According to Gorgias, it is difficult to prove that our ideas correspond with the object which they are intended to identify; the words used to denote real objects are merely linguistic expressions in no way related to those objects. Since absolute truth cannot be shown to exist, all that remains are ideas in the form of words. Consequently, Gorgias applied himself to the teaching of rhetoric instead of vain attempts to expound truth, science, or virtue. His pursuit of rhetoric led him to the founding of poetics, aesthetics, Attic prose, and the psychological science of suggestion. Abandoning the search for absolute proof, he settled for the concept of the mere probability of knowledge. Through drama and poetry, he said, the minds of men can be persuaded, though neither poetry nor drama can be accepted as true. He regarded them as justifiable deceptions which possess some practical value, for desirable moral results can be achieved through such intellectual activity.

The marked influence of Gorgias on his contemporaries was unquestionable, but since his adherence to Skepticism made it impossible for him to advocate positive conclusions on philosophical problems, his followers dealt with such problems in their own way and drew contradictory inferences from his premises. Thus, on moral questions they disagreed profoundly among themselves, developing two contradictory theories based upon ethical naturalism, that is, upon natural law: the first stated the doctrine that might makes right, the second the democratic concept that by virtue of natural law all men are born free and equal.

The doctrine that might makes right assumes that any person endowed by nature with superior power or strength has the moral right to impose his will on weaker individuals. The law of the jungle—the law of tooth and claw—therefore is accepted as the proper standard of human conduct. Each man has the right to follow his impulses and fulfill his desires if he is strong enough to defy antagonistic forces, including civil laws enacted by weaker persons to protect themselves. Civil or moral laws are mere conventions which must give way to nature's basic law, the law which justifies complete expression of his instincts as the natural right of a free man. In contrast to conventional morality which prohibits the strong from doing an injustice, natural morality—the edict of nature —deems it disgraceful for the strong to suffer injustice at the hands of the weak. Consequently, the strong never permit others to treat them unjustly. The Sophists adhering to this theory held that through institutions and laws the strong man becomes a victim of deception perpetrated by the weak to prevent him from exercising the power with which nature has endowed him. The shackles fashioned by the weak members of society must be broken so that the men of power can exercise their duty to attain mastery over them. The history of all living creatures testifies to the dominance of the strong over the weak, justifying the will to power and accepting it as the moral goal of the strong, their natural responsibility, to rule the weak. (In modern times the philosopher Nietzsche adopted this same theory of ethics.)

According to these disciples of Gorgias, moral laws as well as the civil laws of the State are techniques for harnessing the brutality in man, for taming the animal nature within him. Religion contributes to the use of such deceptive means of restraining the beast in man by instilling fear in those who would otherwise prefer to violate the moral or civil laws. The fact that our crimes may have escaped notice is of no consequence, inasmuch as divine invisible beings are at all times observing our behavior.

Two other disciples of Gorgias, namely, Lycophron and Alcidamas, taught the equality of man and the social contract doctrine of the State. They opposed divine or hereditary right, claiming that the concept of nobility is based on a false assumption perpetrated upon the people, that nature designed all men equal, that the State is created by means of a social contract (a mutual agreement subscribed to by its citizens), that men are born free, that nature makes no man a slave. Appealing to natural law, Lycophron and Alcidamas called for the emancipation of slaves together with equal rights for women.

Still another Sophist, Anonymus Iamblichi, added the argument that the laws of physics and those of the State are alike, and that moral and political laws emanate from human nature. Therefore the right of the stronger is an infeasible fiction, and any man who sets himself up as a superman or a master will find himself defeated by the combined strength and efforts of the multitude who have chosen to conduct themselves in accordance with law.

In time, *sophistry* became a term of reproach. Socrates, Plato, and Aristotle regarded Sophism as an infamous philosophy. Socrates left no writings, but the works of Plato and Aristotle condemned its tenets and methods; for example, Plato subjected the Sophists Euthydemus and Dionysodorus to searching criticism and ridicule. However, although Plato depicted Socrates as a staunch opponent of the Sophists, yet, in a sense, the Sophists were merely attempting to accomplish much of what Socrates himself had set out to do.

SOCRATES

It is true that the Sophists represented much that was antithetical to the philosophical views of Socrates (470–399 B.C.), who was a staunch defender of the objectivity of truth, and an outspoken critic of Sophism. Thus, in ethics, whereas the Sophists felt that there was more disgrace in suffering injustice than in committing it, Socrates taught that it was preferable to suffer wrong than to commit it. The Sophists believed in the subjectivity of conduct, advocating moral choices based upon the individual's feelings or desires, while Socrates sought objectivity, valid principles which could be used to guide the actions of all mankind. The Sophists' goal of human freedom was to be achieved through the independent and free expression of passions and impulses; Socrates had the same goal of freedom, but to him it meant freedom from enslavement by passion, a freedom to be attained through control of the self by insight, and a self-sufficiency (*autarkia*) characterized by freedom from needs.

Insight (*arete*) became the watchword for Socrates. The term *insight* had various connotations, including virtue, excellence, capacity, and prudence; it referred to the true good which man should seek. According to Socrates, transitory emotions and vague feelings are a questionable and unsafe guide to human conduct; only the person whose guide in life is accurate knowledge (not merely of the world without, but also of his own inner nature) will be capable of acting correctly. During the period of the Greek Enlightenment the Sophists were imparting to the masses scientific knowledge which had been the exclusive property of the learned elite, and Socrates was doing the same thing, but for Socrates scientific knowledge meant truths that provided an objective (not Sophism's subjective) basis for directing human activity so that man would become efficient and virtuous, understand correctly his true calling in life, and attain happiness.

Self-Knowledge. It is not the subjective feelings of the Sophist, but insight alone which should be regarded as a reliable criterion in making value judgments. But scientific knowledge about the external world is not enough since it provides us only with universals, principles which hold true for us all in common. What is needed in addition is self-knowledge, gained through self-examination; the principal value of scientific knowledge is simply to gain better understanding of oneself to enable one to live a better life. Know thyself (*gnothi seauton*) is the secret of self-control and thereby of happiness.

Know yourself, and you will be virtuous, inasmuch as virtue is identical with knowledge. If you know what is right, you will do it automatically, willingly, and effortlessly, with the spontaneity and motivation necessary for achieving what is good. Virtue is the same thing as knowledge of the good; consequently, whoever is virtuous must be knowledgeable. Similarly, whoever is enlightened must be virtuous.

Virtue and Knowledge.   Socrates taught that the good consists of a state of happiness which evolves from useful actions. For an act to be good it must first be useful, that is, useful in the sense that it is in agreement with one's real purpose in life and therefore is appropriate to the true goal of man. Socrates was concerned with determination of the proper goal of mankind and conceived this to be moral improvement. For Socrates, good deeds bring success and genuine happiness, whereas evil deeds bring failure and misfortune. The very act of doing good constitutes happiness, defined as a state of well-being accompanied by a sense of satisfaction.

The Socratic search for the good, that is, for what is genuinely valuable in life, rejects external goods, the paths of luxury or carnal pleasure; it directs mankind toward virtue in the attainment of knowledge of the good through deepest insight. Virtue is identical with knowledge, but evil deeds indicate a process of self-deception, not simply a lack of knowledge. Virtue consists of being truthful to oneself, maintaining one's integrity, enabling one to recognize truly useful acts and genuine happiness. The spiritual welfare of the soul takes priority over worldly gain. Strength does not rest with the physically superior but with the spiritually superior, for the good man is stronger than the evil one. No real harm can come to a good person, not even at the hands of an evil man, because real harm is spiritual, therefore beyond the reach of the evil person who would commit the harmful deed. Happiness can be assured only through the proper care of the soul, that is, right living.

Socrates' assumption of an intellect-directed will suggests a kind of intellectual determinism. The intellect, equipped with knowledge, directs the will into the right path. Knowledge possesses sufficient potency to motivate a person to do good deeds which result in concomitant happiness. Both happiness and knowledge are inherent elements of virtue, since knowledge is virtue and virtue is happiness —knowledge produces virtue and virtue produces happiness. A man who commits evil is an unenlightened person, because to do wrong knowingly or intentionally is madness. Just as a sane man would not knowingly or intentionally do himself physical harm, by the same token he would not purposely do moral harm; any other conclusion would be tantamount to saying that a man intentionally avoids doing good for himself and knowingly causes harm to himself. Since good is that which benefits a man, and evil is that which harms him, evil is identical with error.

Virtue, inasmuch as it is knowledge of what is good, can be taught to anyone; consequently, man, through instruction, can improve his moral lot and thereby his happiness. Men should therefore aim to practice self-examination and reciprocal examination of one another in order to achieve mutual moral perfection. It is precisely for this reason that friendship becomes an important value, for friends strive for one another's betterment, seeking the good of all as their common aim.

Notwithstanding the self-evident fact that Socrates was awakening the ethical conscience and promoting the moral welfare of the community, the hostile government, which accused him of corrupting Athenian youth by means of his teaching (he applied reasoning instead of tradition and religious doctrines to solve human problems), demanded that he surrender his lifelong philosophical principles under penalty of death. He preferred to suffer the extreme penalty, placing on the ruling establishment the onus of committing legalized murder, and thereby won his greatest victory. His action in rejecting opportunities to escape, and in drinking the poison hemlock as prescribed by law, dramatized the things he taught and the ideals for which he died.

The Socratic Method. Although Aristotle credited Socrates with being the founder of the inductive method as applied to ethical and scientific problems, Socrates did not write any books or found any school of philosophy. He was self-taught, and his teachings have come down to us chiefly in extensive works of his students Xenophon and Plato. (Some references are also contained in the writings of Aristotle.) Using the technique of *Socratic irony*, Socrates posed as an ignorant person, always asking questions, never offering answers, but seeking information from others. By means of this technique he was able to draw from the youth of his time truths which they had never before realized. Thus, on one occasion his questions elicited from one boy the rationale of the Pythagorean theorem which the boy in this way learned for the first time. Noting the results achieved through his *maieutic method*, as it is called, Socrates considered himself to be a sort of midwife, drawing truth from its repository in each man's soul, where truth is dormant and simply needs to be awakened. He concluded that all truths have been inherited by the individual before birth, that is, from an existence prior to his earthly existence. Moreover, Socrates felt that truth consists of definition, which discloses the basic meaning, the element or essence common to each particular thing in a class of things. Truth is laid bare through the *Socratic dialectic*, a method of conversation by which all possible points of view regarding a problem, issue, or subject are set forth and debated from every angle. Many persons took refuge in ambiguous and vague language, trying to prove an assertion by using words which lacked a precise meaning. Socrates employed his technique of irony which led such people into self-contradictions and compelled them to define their terms. He devoted his life to the search for definition, that is, conclusive definition of the good; yet the close of his life found him still engaged in that endless search.

THE LESSER SOCRATICS:
FOUR SOCRATIC SCHOOLS

Although Socrates did not found any philosophical school, and in fact had no intention of so doing, his teachings were indirectly responsible for the systems of thought sponsored by groups of his disciples. Four of these became known as the "Lesser Socratics" ("Minor Socratics"), namely, the Megarians, the Elean-Eretrians (which started as a branch of the Megarian school), the Cynics (who later become the Stoics), and the Cyrenaics (Hedonists). The latter two schools represented a development which lasted for many centuries. Eventually, however, the influence of all these schools declined and thereafter was recovered only during the intermittent leadership of noted individuals; consequently, for the sake of systematic analysis, we shall discuss them as types of philosophy instead of recording a strictly chronological review of their eminent exponents.

The Megarian and Elean-Eretrian Schools. Soon after the death of Socrates, Euclid of Megara (*c.* 450–380 B.C.) formed a group of Socratic disciples. The group developed into two branches, one of which lasted only for a short time before being amalgamated with the Cynic and Stoic schools. Among its chief adherents were Eubulides of Miletus, Alexinus of Elis, Diodorus Cronus of Caria, and Stilpo. Another branch of the Megarian school, known as the *Elean-Eretrian,* was founded by Socrates' favorite disciple Phaedo in his home in Elis; the philosopher Menedemus subsequently transferred its headquarters to Eretria. At first, all adherents in both groups agreed upon the essentials of Socratic doctrine. Phaedo accepted Euclid's interpretations of the fundamental Socratic principles.

These philosophers attempted to synthesize the Eleatic doctrine of *Being* with the Socratic idea of the *good,* formulating the concept of one permanent immutable Being identified with the good; this concept of Being as virtue was equated with the idea of *God, mind,* or *intelligence.* In other words, the Socratic view of the world as a moral reality was fused with the Eleatic view of the world as a metaphysical reality. The two ideas of goodness and of Being became the single idea of unified, ultimate essence in the universe.

The Megarians made no further contributions to the development of ethical theory, but they continued to debate metaphysical problems and issues, eventually lapsing into futile Sophistical eristics. Attempting to emulate Zeno, they set forth numerous paradoxes (of no real value), such as the classic paradox of *The Liar* by Miletus.

Cynicism: Independence and Self-Control; Virtue as the Only Good. It is especially desirable to understand the essentials of Cynicism because that school of thought developed into Stoicism, the major philosophy of the Stoics which lasted for centuries and left its mark upon the medieval and modern philosophies of the Western world.

ANTISTHENES OF ATHENS. The earliest representative of Cynicism was Antisthenes (445–365 B.C.) of Athens, who felt that he was following in the true spirit of Socrates. Theopompus, the historian, cited him as the most illustrious of the Socratics. Antisthenes studied both with Socrates and with Gorgias the Sophist.

As an adherent of Cynicism, Antisthenes advocated self-reliance, endurance, and diligence; he regarded virtue as the highest and sole good, that alone which is capable of producing happiness. For him happiness is not a mere concomitant of virtue, but is identical with virtue itself. "The chief good of man consists in living according to virtue." Virtue he understood to be intelligent living, a life devoted to the practice of morality. "Virtue is a weapon." Whoever lives such a life finds contentment rooted in a feeling of having become independent, of having been liberated from whatever course the world may take either for good or for ill. Virtue, then, is practiced for virtue's sake, because virtue makes for happiness regardless of life's vicissitudes. Only virtue is capable of liberating man, of making him independent of life's erratic course, so that his happiness will not be contingent upon fortune, nor dependent upon the fulfillment of his desires. Since we are powerless to control the world around us, then we must control the world within, the inner world of desire. For it is desire which holds us in bondage, making slaves of us all, whereas in the inhibition of desire, through the reduction of our needs to barest necessity, lies our salvation. "One must prepare oneself a fortress in one's own impregnable thoughts." Virtue therefore may be regarded as a way of life marked by liberation from want, indifference to desire, the elimination of egotistical passion, and the practice of self-control. Antisthenes preferred to be victimized by madness rather than by desire: "I would rather go mad than feel pleasure." The opposite of virtue, sin, is an evil; whatever else remains is inconsequential.

The Cynics sought a return to a state of nature. Consequently they repudiated civilization and all it represented: wealth, refinement, art, learning, science, and mathematics (but the latter two disciplines might be approved if they contributed to better living). Antisthenes attacked both democracy and tyranny, promoting the individualism of Socrates and seeking to emulate him in numerous ways, especially in demanding precision in the definition of terms. But the assumptions and standards he set for determining the right definitions made factual or scientific conclusions impossible. Thus he insisted that a simple concept is indefinable,[1] ignoring the principle that defining a simple idea in terms of its characteristic qualities merely distinguishes among its constituent parts. Furthermore, like the Pythagoreans, he assumed that a person could not contradict himself anyway, inasmuch as any contradictory statements will actually refer to contradictory things. The upshot of his Socratic philosophy was a relapse into anti-Socratic Sophism.

The Cynic's extreme individualism (which caused him to withdraw from society and return to nature) had as its concomitants a lack of concern about the values of life itself, a rejection of family

---

[1] Contemporary philosophy has made much use of the indefinability of the simple.

relationships or loyalties, and contempt for civilization. The Cynic felt obligated to regenerate the contemporary social order (including the most respected classes and institutions) which he regarded as morally corrupt. Yet, he was a cosmopolitan philosopher, regarding all men as brothers; consequently he disapproved of war and slavery, sympathized with the suffering of the disadvantaged, and advocated reforms such as the establishment of special communities of mothers and children. Antisthenes himself believed in monotheism, in one invisible God, although he did not accept the idea of human immortality.

DIOGENES OF SINOPE. This most famous of the Cynics, Diogenes of Sinope (412–323 B.C.), who was a student of Antisthenes, took delight in referring to himself as the dog, for the term *Cynic* literally means *dog-like*. Some of the ancient Cynics boasted of living in a barrel (Diogenes lived for many years in his tub), thus proclaiming their yearning for independence, their disdain for civilization, and their contempt for the prevailing culture. Advocating a return to nature, Diogenes declared, "I recoin current values," a revolutionary assertion which the modern philosopher Nietzsche reiterated, along with some of the moral ideas of the Sophists, as the basis for his ethical theory.

Diogenes lived in two cultural centers of the ancient world (Athens and Corinth), but he rejected their ways of living as unnatural and artificial. The natural life meant for him the satisfaction of basic human desires in defiance of the accepted codes of society. With superb wit and irony, he denounced the superficial hypocritical values of contemporary civilization. He dared to meet Alexander the Great, world conqueror, face to face as an equal. His cynical realism is reflected in the legend that he went about in the full light of day with a lantern as if he were searching for an honest man. This "Socrates gone mad," when taken into slavery, told his captor that he, Diogenes, was a ruler of men, searching for a master worthy of being ruled by him. He held that pain and deprivation helped men to achieve virtue, that pleasure must be avoided, that the good life is one of simplicity and self-control.

CRATES OF THEBES. The third and last of the noteworthy Cynics was Crates of Thebes (one of Diogenes' students) who lived in the latter part of the fourth century B.C. and became a link between the Cynic and Stoic philosophies. Disposing of his great wealth, Crates lived as a mendicant ascetic. He and his wife, who was also a person of wealth when she joined him in austere living, adhered to the Cynic belief in the "happiness of poverty." He was considerably more moderate in his doctrines than Diogenes had been, and his winsome personality exuded kindness. Unlike his teacher's biting wit, his humor was characterized by kindly sentiments, as in his *The Wallet,* a poem extolling the blessedness of poverty.

He regarded polytheism as a subjective conclusion, a mere opinion, whereas the true God, he said, is a monotheistic deity embedded in the course of natural phenomena.

Cynicism eventually was linked with the early period of Stoicism; the Cynic traditions were perpetuated, but in a more moderate form, during the development of Stoic philosophy. Whereas the original Cynics emphasized the extinction of desire, liberation from want, and physical endurance, the later Cynics viewed life as if it were a drama in which God as the author has assigned to each man a specific part to play, a life role which he must accept and fulfill well, whether it be that of a man blessed with wealth, health, and freedom, or, on the other hand, that of a man afflicted by poverty, illness, and enslavement. This new point of view in Cynic philosophy made it easier for individual adherents to adjust to adversity by adopting an attitude of indifference to it and a passive, fatalistic acceptance of their lot. Moreover, this later form of Cynicism (also referred to as Hedonistic Cynicism) attracted eminent adherents, such as Bion of Borysthenes in Sammatia (third-century B.C. satirist) and Menippus of Gadara in Syria (satirist, *c.* 250 B.C.).

STOICISM: INDIFFERENCE TO PAIN AND PASSION

As indicated above, Cynicism blossomed into Stoicism; in fact, although the earliest Stoic philosophies modified Cynicism considerably, they acknowledged their debt to the Cynics, and they found in the doctrines of Socrates, Antisthenes, and Diogenes their ideal conception of the wise man. They traced their own philosophic systems back to Cynic interpretations of Socratic philosophy. Stoic philosophy passed through several stages, referred to as earlier, middle, and later Stoa. It has, in fact, exerted a permanent influence extending into early modern and contemporary periods, as reflected in Christian theology and in the works of Shakespeare, Spinoza, Butler, and other classical philosophers.

The Greek name for Stoicism, *Stoa Poikile* (Painted Porch), referred to the portico in Athens where the early adherents held their meetings. The movement was founded by Zeno of Citium (*c.* 340–265 B.C.), who was a disciple of the Cynic Crates, and taught the first Stoic groups in that center. Among his eminent contemporary Stoics were two heads of the Stoic school: Cleanthes of Assos in Troas (*c.* 303–232 B.C.), who had also been a student of Crates and was the purported author of a monotheistic hymn (*Hymn to the Most High*) to Zeus; and Chrysippus of Solsus (280–206 B.C.), who integrated many of the Stoic doctrines and classified their terminology. Two students of Chrysippus, namely, Zeno of Tarsus and Diogenes of Babylon, succeeded him as leaders of Stoic philosophy in the third century B.C.

The Stoics of the middle period (second and first centuries B.C.) modified the doctrines of early Stoa to take into account the doctrines of the Platonic philosophers of the Academy and the Aristotelian Peripatetics. The founder of this form of Stoicism was Panaetius of Rhodes (*c.* 180–110 B.C.) who was greatly influenced by some of the views of Plato even though he disagreed with the fundamental Platonic principles expounded by Carneades, head of the Academy. Subsequent leaders of the Stoics during this middle period were Antipater of Tarsus and Boethus of Sidon (*d.* 119 B.C.).

Later Stoa, which prevailed during the first two centuries of the Christian era, was dominated by two groups of Roman philosophers, one concerned chiefly with Stoic interpretations of reality, the other with applied morality, that is, a religious belief in God's relationship to and interest in mankind and the universe. To this period belonged Arius Didymus of Alexandria (63 B.C.–A.D. 10) author of commentaries on Greek philosophical works; L. Annaeus Seneca, tutor and for some years an advisor to Nero, who condemned him to death in A.D. 65; C. Musonius Rufus of Volsinii; Epictetus of Hierapolis (c. A.D. 50–138), the most articulate Stoic exponent of moral philosophy; and the Roman emperor Marcus Aurelius Antoninus (A.D. 121–180).

Stoic Ethical Philosophy. Beginning with acceptance of the Cynics' doctrine of self-control and their attitude of indifference to worldly affairs, the Stoics introduced their rational interpretations of evil as consisting only of vice, and of virtue (wisdom) as being the only good. To the Stoics evil meant the failure of man's reason to control his passions, thus allowing them to rule over his reason; virtue meant the act of living in accordance with nature, allowing reason to control one's passions. Thus Stoicism identified reason with nature and virtue with obedience to reason (moral action based on Socratic insight). According to Stoic philosophy, since passions are a disease of the soul, the individual must expel them completely from his personality; he must never allow his feelings to deteriorate into passions, which are both unnatural and irrational. Man conquers the world only by overcoming his own impulses. External things cannot control him unless he by an act of his own will permits them to do so; and he will gain self-control and self-sufficiency if he shows utter indifference both to pleasure and to pain. A person must maintain an unconquerable will, which surrenders to no man. The Stoics warned each individual: let no one break your will. Stoic philosophy interpreted values as consisting of three things: (1) actions in harmony with nature, which are norms or true values; (2) unnatural actions (actions contrary to nature), which are called disvalues; and (3) actions neither good nor bad (hence being matters of indifference), which constitute neutral values.

Thus virtue (which the Stoics regarded as identical with wisdom) is the only necessary prerequisite for happiness, and it is the only good. True happiness is a state of inner tranquility, of freedom from disturbance, a state of mental composure, or peace of soul. This state of happiness reflects the rational character of the soul which enables it to attain an inner peace. Thus the Stoics agreed with Socrates in identifying virtue with knowledge (rational insight). Knowledge of what is morally right strengthens the will and the powers of the individual so that his mind becomes impervious to worldly vicissitudes and disturbances.

Meditation strengthens the soul, improves its health, and serves as a means of identifying and attaining virtue. Although virtue is essentially the same as wisdom, it also becomes manifest as four main virtues: the primary virtue of *meditation* and the three resulting virtues of *courage, self-control*, and *justice*. (Note that Cleanthes, however, preferred *endurance* instead of meditation, as the primary virtue.) Unlike Aristotle, who interpreted virtue as a mean between two extremes, the Stoics believed that each virtue has one, and only one, opposing vice; for example, the vice opposite to virtue is depravity, while the opposite of wisdom is foolhardiness. Whoever has not yet attained genuine wisdom is intellectually deficient and, similarly, whoever has not yet attained true virtue is morally in a state of evil or vice. Moreover, the descent from virtue to vice may be abrupt and immediate. Only by gaining wisdom can one make certain that he will remain virtuous. Perfection, then, is what the Stoic seeks, and perfection is the *sine qua non* of happiness, while inevitably imperfection results in unhappiness. All human beings, as frail mortals, are lacking in wisdom, hence in happiness. Just as wisdom accompanies virtue, so foolhardiness is accompanied by vice; just as the healthy mind constitutes happiness, so the diseased or evil mind constitutes chaotic unhappiness. But as the individual gains virtue, the more holy or divine-like he becomes; he who excels in virtue will be comparable to Deity in the enjoyment of happiness.

Stoic Social Philosophy.   Stoics were indifferent to nationalistic loyalties or distinctions, for they displayed a high regard for self-sufficiency, individuality, and personal independence. Nevertheless, they valued friendship between individuals chiefly as a means of satisfying social impulses and needs. Friendship, they said, is natural, hence good. The cosmopolitan outlook of the Stoics may be attributed to this faith in the social value of friendship between individuals. Common brotherhood and common legal prescriptions should be prized as natural laws, two of which—justice and brotherly love—are innate in human nature. Marriage is an accepted institution insofar as it is infused with moral spirit. The Stoics viewed man as a citizen of the world and regarded the world state as the only natural and proper form of political control. Their cosmopolitan spirit was reflected also in their defense of the natural rights of slaves. The Stoic social philosophy harmonized with Christian ideals and its point of view was buttressed by the rise of Christianity.

Stoic Philosophy of Religion and Metaphysics.   The Stoic philosophy of religion was closely allied with ethical naturalism; piety was identified with knowledge, and religious obedience with universal laws of nature. Stoic religious naturalism acquired pantheistic characteristics, emphasizing the belief that God and nature are one, although it differentiated the essential nature of God from the world of nature. Their metaphysics, which was decidedly Heraclitan, posited fire as the fundamental principle in things. It was their view that man's fate is determined by the mechanistic laws governing all natural phenomena. They linked religion closely with philosophy. Although they permitted recourse to polytheistic spirits as media for the worship of God, they held steadfast to a monotheistic doctrine and made their belief in one supreme, universal Deity (as creator and sustainer of the universe) the foundation of their moral philosophy.

Three types of Stoic theology were common, each emanating from its respective source: (1) philosophers, (2) statesmen, and (3) poets. Consequently, the Stoics remained sympathetic to the central themes of their religion. Their point of view was optimistic about nature, but pessimistic about man's moral insight. Stoic pessimism was vividly reflected in their acceptance of suicide (*taedium vitae*) as a permissible solution to extreme exigencies of life. This practice seemed to them a symbol of moral strength, evidence that they could choose to be indifferent to life itself. Accordingly, they felt justified in ending life whenever the natural course of events made such a course appear to be an appropriate way of dealing with insufferable problems. Zeno committed suicide, as did Cleanthes, who deliberately starved himself to death. It may be noted that the Stoics were not always consistent in their ideology. Thus they adhered to the doctrine of self-preservation as the most fundamental law of nature, yet this doctrine was precisely contrary to their belief in suicide as a rational solution.

HEDONISM—PLEASURE AS THE HIGHEST GOOD

In direct antithesis to everything for which the Cynics stood was the philosophy of the Cyrenaic Hedonists. Both philosophical systems developed out of the teachings of Socrates; while the Cynics emphasized the Socratic concept of virtue, the Cyrenaics stressed the Socratic principle that happiness results from the practice of virtue. Whereas the former argued that virtue itself is happiness, the latter taught that the virtuous man is he who knows how to achieve happiness or has the talent necessary for achieving it. Although both philosophies agreed that happiness is a state of mind, for the Cynic the term means the serenity and mental security which a self-sufficient man experiences, whereas for the Cyrenaic it referred to that satisfaction which follows upon the fulfillment of physical appetite. Both schools derived their basic concepts from Socratic philosophy and their leaders have been included among the Lesser Socratics. Moreover, both schools developed into more sophisticated thought—the Cynics into Stoicism, and Cyrenaic Hedonism into Epicurean Hedonism. Just as basic concepts of Stoicism have been perpetuated in Christian doctrine, and in the philosophies of Kant, Spinoza, and other leading philosophers, so the fundamental views of Hedonism have been incorporated in the philosophies of the Utilitarians, Freudians, and some Darwinians.

Cyrenaic Hedonism: The Pursuit of Momentary Pleasures. The founder of Cyrenaic Hedonism, Aristippus of Cyrene (435–355 B.C.) was influenced by the teaching of the Sophist Protagoras and subsequently became a disciple of Socrates. His philosophy reflects both sources, particularly the Protagorean doctrine of relativism and the Socratic belief that virtue is a *sine qua non* of happiness.

Since the Cyrenaics equated pleasure with happiness, they concluded that pleasure is man's highest attainable good.

Moreover, according to the Cyrenaic Hedonists, since pleasures are of a single kind, namely, physical satisfactions, there should be no attempt to designate any of them as inferior or superior to the others, the only discernible difference among them being their intensity or duration. The Cyrenaics' theory that pleasures lack qualitative distinction, that they differ only quantitatively from one another, is known as quantitative Hedonism. A corollary of this doctrine is the conclusion that pleasure itself is never evil, that only the laws and customs of the community designate some as good, others as morally bad—the central thesis of ethical relativism.

How did the Cyrenaic Hedonists define this experience of pleasure, which they accepted as man's highest good? Aristippus described it as a sensation of gentle motion in contrast to the violent motion of painful experience—but it must be understood that the Cyrenaics did not use the term *motion* in the sense of merely physical movement. Their interpretation came much closer to the modern conception of *emotion*. They held that there are two basic emotions, the emotions of pleasure and of pain. The emotion of pleasure, or the sensation of gentle motion, resembles the pleasant feeling of the hungry person immediately after he has satisfied his appetite. The Cyrenaics ascribed no significance to the state of apathy, the absence of emotion, which the Cynics regarded as a worthy goal.

Since the Cyrenaic Hedonists believed pleasure to be the only good, they ignored all scientific, mathematical, and cultural pursuits except those with useful applications. In this sense they could be classified as Utilitarians, for they devoted themselves to the study of logic because of its practical utility. The Utilitarian view of epistemology (the study of how man obtains knowledge) colored their entire philosophy. Accepting the doctrine of Protagoras, they agreed that human knowledge is limited to sensations and does not extend to the real objects to which the sensations correspond—a basic thesis of Protagorean relativism. Consequently, man is aware of nothing but his own subjective states of feeling; for Aristippus, therefore, feeling is the only valid criterion of truth. The feelings which we experience are the essence of our existence. During our span of life, we should experience as much pleasure as possible; therefore, Aristippus insisted that we must pursue the pleasures of the moment, for tomorrow we shall die. We must enjoy immediate experience inasmuch as the future does not lie in our hands.

Virtue, then, is the means whereby we can achieve pleasure and increase our capacity for enjoyment. But the indiscriminate gratification of pleasure is to be eschewed; at this point in the philosophy of Aristippus, the influence of Socrates is discernible. The sage, or wise man, while enjoying pleasure, remains in control of it. Aristippus claimed that the Cynics erred in seeking independence by abstaining altogether from pleasure, for "not he who abstains, but he who enjoys without being carried away, is master of his pleasures." [1]

Diogenes Laertius, discussing the Cyrenaic philosophers, emphasized their view that man's proper goal is to control pleasure and never to be controlled by pleasure. In order to achieve the highest ends of life, man must retain mastery over his experience by means of adaptation to circumstances, self-control, wisdom, the curbing of momentary desires, and an optimistic outlook and temperament.

Other leading Cyrenaic Hedonists included Aristippus' son, Aristippus the Younger, and daughter, Arete; Theodorus, the atheist; Anniceris; Euhemerus; and Hegesias.

Theodorus contended that the specific momentary gratification of pleasure is an inconsequential matter and that, consequently, the primary objective should be to develop an optimistic, cheerful attitude toward life. In other words, the wise man knows that true happiness can be found only within the mind of the individual—as a result of an appropriate inner mental disposition. Anniceris raised Cyrenaic Hedonism to a higher level by designating friendship, gratitude, piety, and aid to others as the true sources of pleasure. Euhemerus contributed the theory that men who had achieved distinction in their lifetime became divine beings in the hereafter. Finally, Hegesias, "the death-counsellor," introduced the doctrine of eudaemonistic pessimism, the theory justifying suicide as a way out of the pain and suffering which dominate the lives of the vast majority of human beings. According to Hegesias, since the frustration of human desires is a universal experience, man should prefer death as a happy, pain-free alternative. Thus, ironically, the philosophy which set out to promote the pursuit of pleasure became a self-defeating philosophy as a consequence of critical deficiencies in its rationale.

---

[1] Friedrich Ueberweg, *History of Philosophy* (New York: Charles Scribner's Sons, 1891) I, 97.

EPICUREANISM: A LIFE DEVOTED TO PLEASURE

The philosophy of Epicureanism, named after its founder Epicurus (341–270 B.C.), can be traced back to discussions of the
Epicurean Society at Athens in 306 B.C. There had been a few
temporary meetings of these philosophers in Mitylene and Lampsacus. Thereafter the society met in the gardens of Epicurus, and
were therefore known as "Philosophers of the Garden."

Epicurus, who regarded philosophy as medicine for the soul, wrote
three hundred books to set forth his views. The basic principles of
his philosophy were derived chiefly from two sources: Cyrenaic
Hedonism, and the physics, metaphysics, and psychology of Democritus. From the Cyrenaics he accepted the theory that pleasure
is the sole good. He agreed with Aristippus that pleasure consists
of a gentle motion (the modern equivalent of pleasant emotion),
and with Theodorus that the goal of life is an optimistic disposition.
From Anniceris came the concept of the great value of friendship,
and from Hegesias the conclusion that life's principal objective is
to avoid or escape from suffering. Epicurus accepted the atomic
theory of Democritus as the foundation of his metaphysical system,
which was to serve as the substratum of his Hedonistic ethics.

Epicurean Ethics.   Epicurus defined life's sole good as happiness, which he equated with pleasure. Each individual is impelled
by the laws of his inner nature to seek to attain happiness and,
conversely, to avoid pain—a basic doctrine of Psychological Hedonism. The Epicureans asserted, moreover, that only one's own personal pleasures should motivate his behavior. The moral quality of
any action depends upon the amount of pleasure to be derived
therefrom, that action being morally right which produces the most
pleasure and that action being wrong which produces pain. Friendship has value insofar as it augments personal pleasure, and it must
be used to fulfill selfish, not altruistic, purposes—notwithstanding
Epicurus' statement that the sage loved friends as he did himself
and that it is more pleasant to do than to receive good.[1] In con-
formance with these ideas, the Epicureans cultivated friendship,
beneficence, gratitude, and co-operation as means of deriving pleasure from human relationships. But, although they agreed that
society contributes an essential function, in that its laws can protect
the individual from injustice and oppression, they advocated a large

---

[1] *Ibid.*, 211.

measure of privacy, even to the extent of "living hidden," that is, at considerable social distance from other people. They had a dim view of marriage and the entire gamut of family relationships, considering these to be a questionable involvement.

The Epicureans held that sensory experience is the only acceptable criterion of moral value, that the feeling of pleasure must be identified with the individual's sense of the good, and that the feeling of pain is identical with an awareness of evil. The most virtuous person is he who can most often ascertain and choose the most satisfying pleasures while, as far as possible, avoiding painful experience. The wisest men—the sages—have mastered the techniques of avoiding pain; if this goal is in some cases impossible because apparent pleasures turn out to be painful events, they know how to minimize the pain. Some pains should be endured for the sake of future pleasures, while, on the other hand, certain pleasures apt to result in future pain should be rejected. The safest and most desirable policy is to live a life of simple pleasures, a rational life controlled by prudence, the greatest of all goods. According to the Epicureans, even though some may fail to obey the dictates of reason and yet be lucky enough to achieve desired pleasures, nevertheless, it is far preferable for each individual to be guided by intelligent decisions based upon logical reasoning. Despite the fact that, as Democritus taught, events are determined by the mechanistic activity of atoms, man possesses a will which enables him to choose among alternative courses of action.

Epicurus' philosophy diverged from the physical principles expounded by Democritus in ascribing even to atoms a kind of self-direction and freedom from the compulsion of natural laws. As a Materialist, however, Epicurus accepted the idea that the soul consists of atomic material which disintegrates at death, at which time all sensation ceases. Consequently, he said, death need not be a matter of anxious concern, inasmuch as it is merely the state in which all sensation ceases. He borrowed nearly all the concepts of physics from Democritus but he insisted that physical laws must be subordinate to and serve the purposes of the moral law, i.e., the law conducive to effective, successful living.

As noted above, Cyrenaic Hedonism counseled the individual to seek pleasure and to avoid pain, a doctrine to which Epicurus fully subscribed. But to him the avoidance of pain was of even greater concern than the pursuit of pleasure. In this respect he differed from the Cyrenaic Hedonist Aristippus, who considered the absence of emotion to be merely an indifferent, inconsequential state, a sort of neutral no-man's land between the desirable state of pleasure (a gentle emotional experience) and the undesirable state of pain (a violent emotional experience). Epicurus valued highly the pleasure of rest—that freedom from pain which he referred to as negative pleasure. He regarded the experience of living as pleasurable insofar as it is not disturbed by intermittent disappointments and vicissitudes. Merely being alive is enjoyable up to the point that problems which destroy tranquility arise. Reversing the Cyrenaic doctrine, Epicurus ascribed greater value to spiritual or mental than to physical pleasures, pointing out, furthermore, that spiritual or mental pain is more intense and troublesome than physical pain. The human mind may imagine and fear future pain as well as anticipate future pleasure, just as it may recollect and react to pain and pleasure experienced in the past. According to Epicurus, the superiority of spiritual over physical enjoyment makes life worth living for old people whose capacity for physical pleasure wanes, but whose zest for philosophy can always retain undiminished intensity. He contends that the fear of death, instead of being the source of mental anguish, should become a matter of indifference to us, since there is no reason to fear it while we are alive, therefore not yet within its clutch, and certainly, when death does overtake us, we can be sure of experiencing either a future life or a state in which neither fear nor anything else can be sensed. Consequently, it is nonsense to fear death. With fear of death removed, the way is opened for enjoying life. Epicurus held that the right philosophy, which includes belief in God, is necessary for a wholesome outlook on life.

Epicurean Metaphysics.   Epicurus adhered to the materialistic philosophy of Democritus in attributing to atomic structure all forms of physical and spiritual reality. The assumption that the gods exist is not essential to a rational interpretation of the universe, inasmuch as the gods themselves, like all other things, consist of corporeal entities, the physical atoms. The soul, identified by Epicurus as a composite of atoms, resides in the heart and disintegrates when physical life ends in death. All knowledge is perceptual, obtained through the senses; ideas and memories are representations of past sensations. According to Epicurus, sensory knowledge, which discloses facts, and emotions, which make it possible to distinguish between good and evil, constitute a valid criterion of truth. Consequently, a belief may be said to be true only if it is based upon a corresponding perception. All things are explicable in terms of natural causes, for from nothing, nothing comes; and the atoms which constitute reality never pass away, for they have always existed and will remain eternally.

Epicurus' numerous adherents included Metrodorus of Lampsacus (survived by Epicurus); Hermarchus of Mitylene (successor to Epicurus); Polystratus (successor to Hermarchus); Zeno of Sidon, who wrote more than four hundred books; Phaedrus (Cicero's contemporary): and T. Lucretius Carus (95–52 B.C.), author of the classic *On the Nature of Things.* Despite the wide popularity of Epicureanism in the later Roman period, its proponents lacked originality and failed to contribute any significantly new or independent thought to this school.

SKEPTICISM: THE SUSPENSION OF JUDGMENT

The many conflicting philosophical views of the diverse schools competing for the individual's attention created serious doubts in his mind and upset his mental equilibrium. With each system of thought exhibiting both strong and weak arguments, it was difficult to choose among them. Thoughtful men realized that if on any question one school had discovered the truth, then the rival schools presenting an opposing opinion would have to be regarded as mistaken. The central problem of choice remained: Which system should be accepted as the best in its point of view?

Skeptics and Eclectics.   Attempts to settle this question resulted in the establishment of the philosophical schools of Skepticism and Eclecticism. The Skeptics reasoned that by suspending judgment, refusing to accept any belief as the valid one, they could avoid a feeling of insecurity arising from possible error. The Eclectics, on the other hand, advocated a philosophical system which would bring together and integrate the best ideas of all the philosophers. Like their predecessors, both the Skeptics and the Eclectics regarded philosophy as a practical inquiry, for they were concerned primarily with ethics, the philosophy of life, a philosophy which can be implemented.

Schools of Skepticism.   Three schools of Skepticism developed in the following sequence: Pyrrhonic; Middle Academy; and Later or Sensationalistic.

The Pyrrhonic school, named after its systematizer, Pyrrho of Elis (365–275 B.C.), flourished during the time of Alexander the Great.

His principal pupil, Timon of Phlius (*c.* 325–235 B.C.), who became a noted figure in Athens, is known for his *sillography* (satirical poems directed against the dogmatic philosophers).

Pyrrhonian Skepticism was supplanted by Academic Skepticism early in the second century B.C. Academic Skepticism, which derived its name from Plato's Academy, turned the ideas of the Academy in a new direction, and is often referred to as the New Academy, or the Middle Academy. The Middle Academy, which sought to defend its own ethical theory by attacking Stoicism, was headed at first by Arcesilaus of Pitane in Aeolia (315–241 B.C.), next by Carneades of Cyrene (214–129 B.C), and then by Clitomachus (187–109 B.C.).

Later (Sensationalistic) Skepticism carried Skepticism to an extreme. Little is known about its adherents, but its chief proponents were Aenesidemus of Cnossus (early part of the first century B.C.), who taught in Alexandria, and Sextus Empiricus (*fl.* A.D. 200), its literary spokesman and author of *Outline Sketches of Pyrrhonism* and *Adversus Mathematikos.* A basis for Skepticism may be found in Socratic irony, a technique devised by Socrates (he started from the assumption that he knew nothing about the truth); a similar approach is evident during the Socratic period in Plato's dialogues, which arrive at no definite conclusions in accordance with the Socratic method.

Basic Ideas of Skepticism.   As noted above, the central idea of the early Skeptics was to avoid mental insecurity or doubt by abstaining from judgment on issues; suspension of judgment (*epoché*) became the fundamental theory of Skepticism. The policy of withholding judgment applied not only to metaphysical and logical questions, but also to value judgments pertaining to right conduct, the good, and the desirable. Thus the Skeptics developed primarily a system of ethics grounded in the principle of *epoché.* The Academic Skeptics used it as a weapon against Stoicism. Actually, the Skeptics' principle of *epoché* was comparable to the Stoics' *adiaphora,* an attitude of indifference, which similarly avoided the necessity for taking sides on controversial questions. Both *epoché* and *adiaphora* were means of escape that were used to preserve a state of mental equanimity.

Skeptics, however, disagreed with the dogmatism of the Stoics in regard to the possibility of obtaining knowledge, of attaining certainty about the ultimate truth. Since the Skeptics could not prove their philosophical conclusions, they sought to defend themselves by launching an attack against their most potent rivals, the Stoics. Timon's *sillographs*, in his work entitled *Sketches*, were an example of these attacks on Stoic dogmatism.

The Skeptics, who were called the doubters, suspenders of judgment, and inquirers, based their philosophy on the premise that since we can know nothing of ultimate reality, then such basic things are matters of indifference to us, and they must be treated as inconsequential. Therefore the only significant problems were those of everyday living—a practical view comparable to that of modern Pragmatism, except that the Skeptics go on to assert that since ultimate reality is inscrutable, a closed book, we must refrain from making judgments about it. This neutral position, which refuses to choose from conflicting interpretations of reality, becomes a shield from the vicissitudes of life, a means of preserving mental tranquility.

The Skeptics distinguished between ultimate (metaphysical) reality and appearance. (Plato made a similar distinction.) The position of Skepticism was that while ultimate truth can never be known with certainty, appearance can be known on the basis of probability. In rational thought and everyday activities, therefore, we must think and act in the light of probable consequences, not certainties, and our estimate of the degree of probability of any proposition will depend upon our previous experience as individuals with natural forces and with social tradition. We can never assert that a proposition is surely true or surely false, but only that it *appears* so to us. Timon wrote: "That a thing is sweet I do not affirm, only admit that it appears so." [1] Thus the theory of appearances (phenomena) gave the Skeptics the basis for their agnostic conclusions, a fundamental concept evolved from the Protagorean doctrine of relativity, i.e., the subjectivity of sensory knowledge.

In order to counteract the criticism that their directives were self-contradictory, Skeptics insisted that they rejected absolute truth, asserting that they "determine nothing and assent to nothing," [2] but they could not avoid the comparable criticism directed against their necessary theory of probable truth. Thus, ironically, Skepticism became its own opponent, for it was inherently self-contradictory, since, if nothing can be known, how could this alleged fact itself be known? The Academic Skeptics set forth the fundamental premise that they could know only one thing, namely, that *nothing is know-*

[1] *Ibid.*, 214.
[2] *Ibid.*

able; the Later Skeptics, seeking to avoid this dilemma, asserted that even the Skeptical premise is not known with certainty, but is merely probable knowledge. The Later Skeptics were not concerned principally with questions of logic, but in the attainment of *ataraxy* (equanimity of mind). Instead of making a vain attempt to solve inscrutable philosophical problems, they accepted them as permanent, unsolved problems, viewing them with a Stoical indifference which yielded them peace of mind. Like the Stoics, the Skeptics laid great stress upon the will, for judgment regarding the acceptance or rejection, affirmation or denial, of a doctrine is an act of will, and in this respect, Skepticism is essentially a practical philosophy, an ethic. However, Stoical emphasis upon will is applied in another context, that of an inviolate will which an individual must never surrender to anyone, because he would then become a slave to the person to whom his will capitulates; one must never allow another to break his will.

ECLECTICISM: AMALGAMATION OF THE BEST DOCTRINES AVAILABLE

The Eclectics, most of whom were Roman philosophers, including particularly Cicero (106–43 B.C.) and Seneca (A.D. 4–65), did not take refuge in Skeptical defenses to maintain a formidable philosophical position. Yet, like the Skeptics, they too developed a reactionary view seeking to establish acceptable doctrines to cope with the conflicting philosophical situation which prevailed at that time. The following four leading schools of philosophy in Athens competed for adherents: (1) the Stoa group of the Stoics; (2) the Epicurean "Philosophers of the Garden"; (3) the Academy (Platonists); and (4) the Lyceum, consisting of the Peripatetic philosophers accepting the views of Aristotle. The Skeptics supported none of these schools; in contrast the Eclectics sought truths in all of them and attempted to unify them into a single integrated philosophical system.

Cicero and Comparable Roman Philosophers. It will be recalled that the Skeptics of the Middle Academy regarded *probability* as the best criterion of truth. The Stoics preferred *consensus gentium*, that is, the universal opinion of mankind derived from the laws of nature, such as the law of self-preservation. Cicero and other Roman philosophers joined these two criteria with the concept of innate ideas (a concept which the modern philosopher Descartes later used as a foundation stone of his philosophy). In ethics, Cicero oscillated between the Stoic virtue of self-control and the

Peripatetic view of happiness as the product of satisfying purposive activity. In the field of physical science, he showed no interest. In political philosophy, he blended the ideas of Platonism, Aristotelianism, and Stoicism. (The Eclectics had revived and emphasized ancient ideas which had been neglected and underemphasized, but they actually did not contribute any important original ideas to philosophy.)

The Sextians. An attempt was made by the Sextians to synthesize the Pythagorean and Stoic philosophies. The founders of the Sextian school were the Greek philosopher Quintas Sextius (born about 70 B.C.) and his son Sotion of Alexandria (who was Seneca's teacher from A.D. 18 to 20). The Sextian philosophy centered in Pythagorean ideas (transmigration, vegetarianism, and moral self-examination) and basic Stoic ideas (individual indifference to external realities, the primacy of knowledge as a means of attaining virtue and happiness).

With the Roman and Sextian Eclectics the philosophical development emphasizing man's analysis of himself as a part of the universe —a process begun with the Sophists' teachings in the fifth century B.C.—came to an end, a turning point in the history of rational thought. The next period shifted the emphasis from the primary goal of self-evaluation and moral value to a highly systematized exploration of all the principal divisions of philosophy, including metaphysics, the philosophy of the state, the philosophy of religion, and epistemology, as well as the traditional fields of ethics and the philosophy of life. This next period is that of systematic philosophy developed through the integrated system of the intellectual giant Plato and his renowned disciple, Aristotle.

Chapter 4

Systematic Philosophy—
Plato and Aristotle

The philosophic systems of Plato and Aristotle dominated Western philosophy throughout the Middle Ages and their influence persisted into modern and contemporary times. The two philosophies have consistently contended for the allegiance of the foremost thinkers in this area of human inquiry, with Platonism most influential during the early medieval period and Aristotelian views especially significant thereafter.

PLATO

Plato (427–347 B.C.) of Athens, son of the aristocrat Ariston, was the most distinguished and gifted disciple of Socrates, under whom he studied from 407 to 399 B.C. After the death of Socrates, Plato and others withdrew to Megara, the home of Euclid, and it was then that the period of Plato's *Wanderjahre* (period of wandering) began. During this time he traveled to Cyrene, Egypt, and Asia Minor, then back to Athens; later, at about forty years of age, he sojourned to the mainland of Italy and eventually arrived in Sicily, where, as reward for his outspokenness, the tyrant Dionysius I sold him into slavery. Ransomed by his friend, Anniceris of Cyrene, Plato founded his university, the Academy, in Athens in 386 B.C. Twenty years later, he journeyed to Syracuse. After the death of Dionysius in 367 B.C. he was unable to win acceptance from the younger Dionysius for the application of Platonic ideals. As a consequence, Plato withdrew from practical affairs of state and devoted the remainder of his life to his writings in all principal fields of philosophy. He died in 347 B.C., in his eightieth year.

PLATONIC IDEALISM

Plato's theory of ideas is described as *dialectic*, based on the Socratic technique of raising questions and seeking answers constituting or leading to the acquisition of true knowledge, and thus discovering the nature of reality, the true essence of objects, and objective truth. For Plato, truth is identified with ultimate, ideal reality. This final reality (the ontologically real in metaphysics) consists of Idea or Ideal (the later designation); hence Plato's view is known as Platonic Idealism.

Objects, Classes, and Ideas. By means of dialectical argument (the technique used in Plato's *Dialogues*, written in the form of dramas in which each individual defends his philosophical views) the individual discerns the nature of an external object, the characteristics which Socrates regarded as constituting its essence and which Plato described as the common elements in a group of related objects. In modern terms, for example, H_2O is the formula representing the characteristics of water, irrespective of its particular location (e.g., in the ocean, in a vegetable, or in a human being), form, or action. Plato initially used the term *Idea* to denote the class name or species of an object, but later he changed the connotation to signify the object's permanent essence, its ultimate truth, its ontological Being, that is, its primordial existence, a prototype or archetype to which every particular object in the universe corresponds as its manifestation, i.e., as a copy or imitation of the Idea or Ideal.

Metaphysical Dualism. Thus we find in Plato as a dominant theme perfused throughout his entire philosophical system a Metaphysical Dualism of the ontologically real and the actually existent. The *Ontos* (the ontological reality) is distinguished from *phenomenon* (its manifestation) as it appears to us through sense experience. Plato asserts that the phenomenal world, which consists of *matter*, is restricted to limitations of time and space (imprisoned or locked in time and space), whereas the ontologically real world transcends space and time and is free of spatial or temporal restrictions. Time itself began with the creation of the material world but that most beautiful of all generated things—the ideal world—is eternal. At this point in Platonic theory we find a synthesis of the Protagorean doctrine of relativity and the Parmenidean doctrine of Being, a synthesis which posits the theory that sense experience provides us with merely relative truths while our understanding gives us absolute truth. Sensory phenomena are transitory experiences which Plato identified with Heraclitan flux, while the real world of conceptual knowledge transcends the sensory world and reveals reality, an ideal world of which the world of phenomenal experience is but a replica. The phenomenal world is tangible, perceived by the senses; the ideal world is intangible, conceived by the mind. In formulating this principle that human understanding or reason discerns truth, objective reality, Plato may be credited with having laid the foundations of natural science. To recapitulate: not only are there two orders of Being, namely, mind and matter—but there are also two orders of knowing, of epistemology, namely that of sensory knowledge and that of conceptual or philosophical knowledge.

Becoming and Being. The phenomenal world, which manifests itself to our senses, is a representation of the real world; it is therefore subordinate or inferior to the ontologically real, the ideal, world. Furthermore, the phenomenal world strives to correspond more and more to the ontologically real world; that is to say, the phenomenal world seeks to perfect itself by molding itself into the prescriptive pattern laid down by the ideal world. Consequently, the phenomenal, sensory world of existence is in a state of continuous development—always becoming, but never quite finished—ever striving for completeness and perfection, guided by the blue print or goal mandated by the supersensible world of ideal reality.

Thus, the Ideals of Plato become the teleological force motivating the world of the senses and impelling it to move toward its appointed end of perfect correspondence to reality. Ideals are themselves self-motivated. Every phenomenal object in the universe is fashioned with a purpose, the ideal goal which it seeks to realize. In this manner, although the phenomenal objects "participate" in, "imitate," their ideal archetypes, such diverse particular phenomena remain nevertheless distinct and separate from the corresponding universal, ideal realities. The Ideals are immaterial, immutable, eternal; the phenomena are material, perishing, transitory; and the former, like the permanent Being of Parmenides, always *is,* whereas the latter, like the flux of Heraclitus, is in a permanent state of *becoming,* yet never actually attains the desired state of completion, of permanency, of perfection. The sensory world is a mere shadow of the real world of Ideals. Since the real world is composed of Ideals, Platonic Idealism must be construed as identical with Platonic Realism.

PLATO'S PHILOSOPHY OF RELIGION

Plato's philosophy of religion is a concomitant of his metaphysical Idealism, for most fundamental idea in both fields of his philosophy is that of the good, the supreme Deity—God. The Deity, as the highest, perfect reality in the universe (Plato's term for God is *Demiurge,* Hand-Worker) is an architect world builder. But God does not create anything out of nothing; the primordial stuff constituting all the elements of the universe is identified as *materia* in

Plato's philosophy. Aristotle later referred to this basic substance as *matter*, but Plato uses the term, as we shall see, to denote extended substance which God removed from a receptacle (where it had existed in a chaotic state without form or qualitative characteristic) in order to create the universe. God, the artist, designs the cosmos out of chaos; like a master craftsman, he brings the orderly world into being by reshaping disorganized primitive matter according to the blue print of eternal Ideals. The soul (Ideals) of the newly created world unites with its body (matter); and it is the soul that gives the body beauty, order, goodness, direction, and purpose.

However, inasmuch as matter, the substance out of which God created the world, is imperfect, lacking the ideal quality of the immaterial world, the tangible world of the senses can never attain perfection. No material object is perfect, nor will it ever become perfect. Plato attributed the world's imperfection, not to God, but to the nature of the substance with which God had to work; in the same way, said Plato, a builder cannot construct a fireproof building out of combustible materials. Not even God can make a perfect world out of imperfect elements. Nevertheless, being absolutely good, God as the World Reason (Anaxagoras' *Nous*) creates objects which approximate his own perfection so far as possible—objects impelled by the Universal Reason to move forward toward the good in a teleological (purposive) striving to achieve the divine purpose. This fundamental concept of teleology (purpose) is identified with the mind of God, that highest good which is responsible for bringing the phenomenal world into existence. Plato accepted the Democritan theory of creation (including the chemical composition of the four Empedoclean elements of earth, air, fire, and water) to explain how God, the teleological principle of the universe, creates the forces of nature and establishes natural law. Let us now consider Plato's ethical theory where divine teleology is seen operating at its finest.

PLATO'S ETHICAL THEORY

Plato's ethical theory is inextricably interwoven with his ideas about the soul and immortality. According to Plato the transient sensory life of the individual, consisting of his thoughts, perceptions, and experiences which comprise his phenomenal or tangible world, ceases at death, and he then returns to existence in the ideal world, the real universe, from which he came and to which he must conform. Thus Plato's ethical theory centers in the doctrine of self-realization since the individual in the next life gradually achieves perfection, a godlike state liberated from the limitations of space and time, of corporeal existence, and of sensory (phenomenal) experiences. Man is created with a purpose, a yearning to achieve his end or goal in life, that of imitating the good, transforming himself into closer approximation to the good.

Moral Responsibility.   Man's soul finds itself in that strange intermediary position of being a member of two worlds, i.e., the material world of sense perception and the spiritual world of ideal reality, but the soul is actually supersensible and belongs to the spiritual world of eternal Ideals. Plato reasoned that the soul, being eternal, must have had a pre-existence in the ideal world where it learned about the eternal Ideals. The individual now living in the sensory world—barred from the ideal world—can recollect the great Ideals in the form of faint reminiscences, a dim awareness of the divine world of ontological reality. Plato accepted the Pythagorean theory of transmigration and held that the soul, besides originating in the ideal world, also must return to it, owing to its eternal nature and to the inexorable law whereby it attains moral self-realization—the reward of reaching a godlike state. Just as the universe has a soul, a *Cosmic Spirit*—the *Nous* of Anaxagoras—so does man, who is in fact a miniature replica of the universe; the universe may be regarded as a macrocosm, and man as a microcosm. Furthermore, just as evil forces in the universe combat the good, so do evil forces within man impede his attainment of the good. Man's moral task, therefore, is that of attaining as much good as possible. Anyone who understands what is good will be drawn to it; thus knowledge impels man to yearn for a godlike condition, to strive to become like him. This identification with the good is the highest Platonic virtue, namely *holiness*, an attribute which Plato later merged with the virtue *justice*. The successful effort to become like God rewards man with the highest state of blessedness—perfect happiness.

Resemblance to God, then, is the ethical end of man. Like Socrates, Plato maintained that knowledge of the ideal good is necessary in order to become good, but, unlike Socrates, he emphasized the role of the freedom of the *will*, insisting that evil actions must be attributed, not to God, but to man's failure to live up to his responsibility.

A Hierarchy of Pleasures.   Plato asserted that since God is the creator of nature, then it is as good as it can possibly be made. At the same time, however, he posited a threefold classification of pleasures: (1) the *sensual* pleasures, which he regarded as base,

(2) the *sensuous* pleasures which comprise an intermediate grade of good, and (3) the *ideal* pleasures, which are spiritual and supremely worthy, for they conform to the nature of God.

Man's sexual desire is an example of the first, or inferior, class of pleasures; admiration of beauty as an attribute of womanhood is an example of the second, or intermediate, class of pleasures; and intellectual (Platonic) love for a woman's soul is an example of the third, or superior, class of pleasures.

Even as any object of the ideal world has its inferior counterpart in the sense world, so the third class of pleasure, ideal love, has its correlative in the form of the first, or physical love. In fact, physical love is but a lower type of animal imitation of pure or ideal love (philosophical love). The intellectual love of one mind for another, of one person for another (far above the level of sexual desire), constitutes Platonic love.

Plato held that aesthetic or artistic experience is intermediate between sensual and ideal realities. A beautiful sunset is nature's attempt to actualize the prototype of beauty—ideal beauty—and the artist strives sensuously (not sensually) to realize the ideal of beauty which resides in the *noumenal world,* so-called in order to distinguish it from the phenomenal or sensory world. Ideal beauty, like other archetypes, is an eternal, immutable, ontologically real object which, though imperceptible to the senses, is understood as a concept through the rational activity of the mind. A thing becomes beautiful when it participates in the ideal of beauty. When the ideal shines through the sensible, it permeates it, renders it beautiful. Everything in the universe possesses a yearning to actualize the ideal; it is instinctive within each thing to do so. But, alas, perfection within the sense world is at best an approximation never completely attained; consequently perfection must wait for the world to come, the ideal world. Nevertheless, God created the sensory world because he preferred its existence to its nonexistence.

PLATO'S POLITICAL PHILOSOPHY

Platonic ethical theory leads directly into his social and political theory. In fact, each division of his philosophy is inextricably interwoven with the others and cannot be understood without considering their interrelationships. The role of virtue and the soul permeates his social and political philosophy. His social philosophy is essentially a social ethic, the continuation of an individual or personal ethic, because the State also is a realization of the good, or that aspect of it which Plato terms the virtue of *justice.* A good State is one in which ideal justice has been realized. A corrupt State is one deficient in justice; the degree of its imperfection varies with the degree to which it has deviated from the ideal of justice.

The Ideal of Social Justice.   According to Plato, there subsists in the realm of ultimate reality an ontologically real State, ideal in its nature; the social responsibility of a collective society is to see to the actualization of this ideal State. Thus political activity is moral endeavor; even as an individual person's happiness depends upon his virtuous achievement, the good or happiness of society is contingent upon its realization of the social ideal—justice. Plato describes his ideal State in *The Republic,* his greatest masterpiece, supplemented by discussions in his *Laws* and *Politicus.* His ideal State would be ruled either by a single, wise ruler or by an aristocracy of wise men.

The ideal State (in which justice prevails) is one in which every individual functions in his best capacity according to his natural abilities. The fact that each person contributes his talent to the State by working at tasks for which he is best suited helps to bring about harmony within society, and such harmony is regarded by Plato as identical with *justice.*

Individual Differences.   In order for social justice to prevail, individual differences must be taken into account. Moreover, justice, as perfect order or balance, must prevail not only within the State as social justice, but also within the individual as internal harmony so that he will achieve good health and happiness. Plato, noting that the ideal community depends upon balance both within and among individuals, considered the human soul to be fundamental to moral or virtuous conduct. He posited a threefold division of the soul: (1) an intellectual division (with a divine aspect situated in the head), comparable to the World Soul (World Reason), accounts for the intellectual activity of man; (2) a courageous division (with an aggressive, spirited aspect situated in the heart); and (3) an inferior, appetitive division (with an animal-like aspect situated in the liver). The first, or rational, division is to be found only in man, not in the animal or vegetable realms, and it is this soul which achieves immortality. (Note that in Plato's *Phaedrus* all three aspects of the soul are described as pre-existing, but in his *Timaeus* only the first is immortal and the other two belong to the mortal sphere, the body.) The second, or courageous, aspect of the soul is characteristic of animal existence, reflected often in an irascible temperament or in an aggressive disposition which takes the form of courage; it is found not only in man but also in "nobler" animals, and in this respect each soul from man downward can be graded in a descending order. It is true that beings other than man possess souls, but only man's soul is immortal.

When each of the three divisions of the soul attains its state of perfection, it displays a concomitant virtue: for the rational division, the virtue of *wisdom;* for the spirited division, will power, that is, the virtue of *courage;* and for the appetitive division, the capacity of self-control, that is, the virtue of *moderation.* Virtue, according to Plato, is identical with *excellence,* something both taught and innate. Although every person possesses all three aspects of the soul with their concomitant virtuous qualities, the degree of virtue varies among individuals.

Such individual differences are attributed to the fact that nature is aristocratic and apportions to men varying amounts of innate ability. Consequently, some men may excel over others because of superior intellectual power. Some may possess or acquire virtue through natural endowment, others through philosophical education. Nevertheless, Plato felt that the masses are incapable of that true philosophical understanding which nature has reserved for the aristocratic few.

Three Social Classes. The State is based upon the ethical ideal of training citizens to become virtuous. Virtue ought to be desired for its own sake, not for sake of reward or punishment, because it is the soul's state of health and beauty, that from which happiness arises. Since virtuous conduct should be an end in itself, said Plato, it is better to suffer injustice than to inflict injustice upon others. Moreover, individuals vary in the kind of virtue they possess, and each person's characteristic virtue determines his place and function in society, his social class. Men of wisdom, who are trained in philosophical reasoning, are the *guardians;* they fill the ruling posts in government and serve as the administrators of State affairs. Men of courage (or valor) become *warriors,* unselfishly bound to duty, who defend the State, protecting it from foreign enemies as well as from those citizens who would break the law and thereby disrupt order and justice. The masses are the *artisans,* whose obligation it is to exercise self-control over their appetites, and hold their bodies ready for obedient service; they must obey the laws of the State and abide by the rule of their leaders. It is the artisans, motivated by the need for satisfying their appetites, who manufacture the material goods in the State by working in trades, industry, and commercial activities that provide for the daily needs of the body. All three classes must work, not for individual goals, but for the *common* welfare—the realization of the true and the good—the ideal State in which justice prevails.

Competitive Education. The class to which an individual belongs will depend upon his natural ability, his attainment in virtue. Everyone, therefore, must be educated in order to disclose to which of the three classes he properly belongs. Education is provided for all of the citizens of the State. In this respect, Plato's republic is democratic, since each person has an equal opportunity for proving himself—for attaining the highest stations in life. The highest positions go to the best qualified. Education during the first years of childhood emphasizes care of the body; from three to six years of age, the emphasis shifts to the narration of myths (religion was important to Plato); from seven to ten years, to gymnastics; from ten to thirteen years, to reading and writing; from fourteen to sixteen years, to poetry and music; from sixteen to eighteen years, to mathematics; and from eighteen to twenty years, to military drill. The sifting process commences at this time: those of scientific and philosophical talent remain in school for additional education, while those of a valorous disposition join the warrior class. Another sifting process occurs at the age of thirty, on completion of more intensive, abstract, and advanced studies in science and philosophy. One's ability for dialectic, for over-all comprehension, that is, for a synoptic grasp of abstract relations, is evaluated. The more promising students continue their studies until the age of thirty-five, while others are given assignments in public office, but of a more practical nature. Those who remain in school are trained in dialectic; from the age of thirty to fifty years, these advanced students assume positions of highest authority requiring the keenest philosophical ability; their contemplation of the good is implemented in, or rather realized in, the State.

Philosophers as Leaders. Plato was convinced that there would be no hope for the State until the time came that kings became philosophers or philosophers kings. The *philosopher-king* seemed to him to be the appropriate ruler, one who would be capable of achieving the good State. Ideally, the State should be governed by the philosophically astute, namely, men who are *both good and wise*. Such a State could be either a monarchy ruled by one good philosophically trained man interested in actualizing the ideal State or by an aristocracy of the best men (of relatively equal ability) ruling as a senate. Whether the ruler be a single monarch or a group of aristocrats, the choice of rulers will depend upon the natural endowments of available individuals who have proved themselves to be the best qualified by means of educational competition.

These leaders in an ideal State can possess nothing of their own, neither property nor family, but must live together in a community where wives and children are held in common to insure against corruption, bribery, or nepotism in the government. It is especially important, in order to achieve the good State, for the elite philosophers to mate with women of comparable ability and similar education—a necessary procedure to produce children who will become the best qualified for positions of highest responsibility in the State.

Forms of Government. Plato realized that the ideal State may not always be attainable and that imperfect forms of government may often be inevitable. He listed the alternative forms and ranked them in order of their worth as follows, in descending order: *timocracy*, the rule of a person whom the people wish to honor— usually a military leader; *oligarchy*, the rule of a few wealthy persons interested chiefly in material goods—the government is entrusted to those who are honored for their wealth; *democracy*, government by the masses, usually the lower classes, who promote freedom, equality, and the abolition of class and natural distinction; and, finally, *tyranny*, the most perverse form of government in which there is a complete miscarriage of justice, evil is supreme, and a single base person commands all others for sake of his unjust and selfish interests.

Some of the foregoing ideas in *The Republic* were modified in two of Plato's later works: in the *Laws*, he gave up the advocacy of communistic sharing of family and property; and in the *Politicus*, he substituted a political monarch for the philosopher-king, stipulating, however, that the monarch, though not restricted by laws, must be wise enough and good enough to do whatever is necessary to achieve the ideal State. An evil monarch could easily circumvent any laws, whereas a wise and good monarch could be a law unto himself for the benefit of the community as a whole. In the *Politicus*, furthermore, Plato contrasted three forms of government with their respective defective forms. Thus, an evil correlative of monarchy is tyranny, that of aristocracy is oligarchy, and that of democracy is mob rule. These comparisons between good and evil forms of government gave Aristotle, Plato's most gifted disciple, some of his basic ideas of political philosophy.

ARISTOTLE

Aristotle of Stagira in Thrace (384–322 B.C.), son of the physician Nicomachus, became Plato's student at eighteen years of age and studied with him for twenty years. Shortly afterward (in 343 B.C.) he became tutor for three years of the thirteen-year-old Alexander who was to rule the world as Alexander the Great. After Alexander's acquisition of the throne, Aristotle, having severed relationship with the Platonists, in 335 B.C. founded his own school, the *Lyceum* or *Peripatetic School* of philosophers. Lyceum was the name of the gymnasium (dedicated to the Lycian Apollo) in which the members met, and the philosophers of the school were called Peripatetics (from the Greek word meaning to walk about) because of Aristotle's custom of lecturing and discussing philosophical issues as he and his disciples promenaded along the shady walks. His tenure as head of the Lyceum lasted only twelve years, ending in 323 B.C. (the year Alexander died) when the civil authorities accused him of impiety for allegedly having deified the tyrant Hermias. Aristotle, recalling the fate of Socrates, fled from Athens to Chalcis in Euboea, where at the age of sixty-three he died of a stomach ailment.

For two thousand years Aristotle has been accorded the title of *the philosopher*, reflecting the common view of this most gifted of Plato's disciples as the greatest of all philosophers. His influence has permeated the work of scientists and philosophers throughout the ages; in philosophy it has profoundly affected the chief tenets of Stoicism, Epicureanism, Neo-Platonism, Gnosticism, and Scholasticism—in fact, all the philosophical systems developed by medieval and modern thinkers, such as Aquinas, Leibniz, Descartes, Kant, Hegel, Hartmann, and a vast number of other contributors to the history of philosophy.

ARISTOTELIAN LOGIC

Aristotle's work on logic is found in his *Organon* (meaning the method or organ of investigation), which consists of a number of his writings: *On Interpretation*, about the structure of a logical proposition; *Prior Analytics*, the doctrine of the syllogism; *Posterior Analytics*, the logic of science and the applications of the syllogism; *Topics*, the logic of argument based on probable truths; and *Sophistical Tests*, dealing with logical fallacies. He advised students to familiarize themselves with the two volumes of the *Analytics* before studying his metaphysical doctrines set forth in his *First Philosophy*, or *Metaphysics*.

Aristotle divided philosophy into *theoretical, practical* and *poetic* divisions. Theoretical (abstract) philosophy he subdivided into mathematics, physics, and metaphysics. Practical philosophy deals with the practice or application of theory, as in ethics and politics. Poetic philosophy analyzes the aesthetics (elements of beauty) in, and emotional reactions to, art, poetry, and drama. Aristotle did not include logic as a division of philosophy, for he intended it to be used as a method of finding truths rather than as a compendium of truths. He regarded logic as a preparatory study for students of philosophy proper.

Aristotle understood truth to mean the agreement of knowledge with reality; truth exists when the mind's mental representations (ideas) correspond with things in the objective world. On the other hand, error (falsehood) occurs when our judgment (the combination of ideas in the mind) does not accord with the genuine relationships among things in the outer world. "Affirming nonexistence of the existent, or existence of the nonexistent, is falsehood; but affirming existence of the existent, and nonexistence of the nonexistent, is truth."

Two Forms of Logical Inference. Logic is essentially a method of drawing correct *inferences*. There are, said Aristotle, two principal forms of logical inference. The first form, the *syllogism*, enables one to draw inferences by reasoning from the universal (a principle) to the particular (an individual case or instance), i.e., by *deduction;* the second form, *induction*, proceeds in the opposite direction, enabling one to reason from particular instances to a universal (a principle or law of science). Genuine proof results when valid inferences are drawn from true or ultimate premises (self-evident propositions), or from premises which are based upon true or self-evident propositions—ultimate statements or axioms that must be taken for granted because they cannot or need not be proved.

Logical reasoning makes us certain that our conclusions are true, and thus provides us with accepted scientific proofs of universally valid propositions or statements. *Scientific inference* thus consists of conclusions based on true and certain principles or premises. Another form of reasoning is *dialectical inference,* whereby conclusions are drawn from apparent, not certain or self-evident, data; such conclusions are useful only as tentative inferences. Aristotle described a third means of arriving at conclusions, namely, sophistical inference, which results in false assumptions because it is based on erroneous premises. He defined inference as the derivation of new knowledge from known information and hypotheses.

Two Fundamental Laws.   Aristotle propounded as two fundamental laws of logic the *principle of contradiction* (that a proposition cannot be both true and false) and the *principle of the excluded middle* (that a proposition must be either true or false). Man's reason immediately apprehends such principles, even prior to and quite apart from any knowledge about the facts of sense experience.

Fundamental principles cannot be proved because they constitute ultimate truths which are used in order to prove all other propositions. In order to prove a statement one must refer to a more general, broad, and certain proposition as the basis for the statement. When one appeals to the most fundamental, ultimate, general truths, there are no broader truths than these, and therefore they must be accepted without proof as certain, undeniable axioms. For this reason the fundamental truths of science must be accepted as self-evident principles which can be used to prove all other propositions.

Classes of Objects.   It will be recalled that correct definitions were regarded by Socrates as essential to understanding and knowledge, for the attempt to define what an object is leads to deeper inquiry about its nature. Aristotle held that definitions can be based either upon immediate knowledge or upon inductive knowledge. To define an object one must first identify the general class (genus) to which it belongs and then add all the distinctive, specific qualities or properties which make it a member of its species (differentiae). Thus an object is adequately defined when its specific characteristics shared by all members of its species are combined with the qualities shared by all members of its genus or general class. Aristotle pointed out, furthermore, that a general or universal concept is classifiable with more general concepts, and these with still more general concepts until at last one arrives at final or ultimate concepts.

The Categories.   Aristotle listed the following ten ultimate concepts, which he called the *categories:* (1) substance; (2) quantity; (3) quality (4) relation; (5) location (in respect to place); (6) time; (7) position (in respect to posture); (8) possession; (9) active; and (10) passive. Although the categories relate to forms of existence and thought (for they are statements about that which exists), nevertheless they also correspond to the parts of speech. Some authorities believe that the categories characterize or classify substance on the basis of its specific qualities; for example, when substance makes its appearance, it always has a definite relationship to a place, a time, and a given amount of its characteristic quality. Aristotle regarded substance as the essence of a thing, and the other categories as its determining accidents. He used his list of categories only as a means of identifying ultimate classes or *genera*.

Essence and Accident. He identified the truth about a thing as its essence (the ontologically real Being, or the ideal reality of which Plato spoke). Its accidental characteristics (contrasted with its essential nature) merely accompany the object and if they cease to be attached to it, nevertheless the object will retain its essence or essential character, for they are not a necessary aspect of its nature. The normal human body, for example, has two arms but, obviously, the loss of his arms in an accident does not make an individual nonhuman, for the two limbs are merely "accidental" characteristics, not essential to the definition of a member of the species. On the other hand, according to Aristotle some of the accidental aspects of an object necessarily follow from its nature; thus it is essential that a triangle possess three angles, and it is accidental but still necessary as a matter of logical inference that the sum of its angles must always be equal to two right angles. The freakish variations of individuals in nature were explained by Aristotle in terms of accidents; although an individual member of a class may deviate from its characteristics, the class as a whole must abide by the laws of its nature—must remain in accord with its essence. Aristotle's theory of individual variations is strikingly similar to the theories of the modern physicists Bohr and Heisenberg regarding the indeterminacy of matter.

ARISTOTELIAN METAPHYSICS

Aristotle referred to his metaphysical writings as the *First Philosophy*, first in the sense that he was here dealing with first principles. His volume under this title analyzes the nature of ultimate reality, including the doctrines of natural theology. The title *Metaphysics* was contributed by Andronicus of Rhodes, systematizer of Aristotle's works, who, with the assistance of Tyrannion the grammarian, collated the published writings of the philosopher approximately midway in the first century B.C. Andronicus described the *First Philosophy* as a set of principles which come "after" or "beyond" physics (in Greek, *ta meta ta physika*) and identified them with those writings of Aristotle which were placed after the physics volume in Aristotle's library. Eventually, however, the term *metaphysics* became well-established in the history of philosophy as signifying that branch of philosophical inquiry which goes beyond physical events or substances and is hence metaphysical. This definite organization of subject matter into a division of philosophy as metaphysics must be attributed to two factors: (1) the nature of the topics which Aristotle discussed in his *First Philosophy*—namely, ultimate or metaphysical reality, including the study of ontology (the study of Being), epistemology (the theory of knowledge), and natural theology (the genesis or cause of the world, and the existence of God); and (2) the teachings of the Scholastics and later philosophers who regarded metaphysics as that province which transcends the physical to enter upon the realm of the transcendental, the world beyond the senses, the spiritual universe. The German Liebnizian philosopher, Christian Wolff, developed the modern view of metaphysics as consisting of four disciplines: ontology (the study of Being); cosmology (the study of the orderly universe); psychology (the rational study of the soul); and rational theology (natural, rather than revealed, theology).

As we have seen, the ancient Greek philosophers persistently attempted to solve the paradox inherent in permanence and change as characteristics of reality. If an object is permanently real, how can it become something different? How can anything remain itself, while at the same time it is developing, growing, changing into something else? If the laws of nature make ultimate reality permanent and unchanging, how can we explain the appearance of motion and change? On the other hand, if the laws of nature compel all things to move and change, how could there be anything ultimate, fixed, and permanent, such as the real objects undergoing change?

Universals within Particulars. Plato sought to resolve the issue by positing a dualism wherein the eternal ideals serve as guiding principles and possess inherent patterns that correspond to the things we sense. All things in nature (phenomena) develop from one stage to another, at all times imitating or corresponding to the ideals. Aristotle objected to this kind of sharp separation between two distinct worlds—the world of ideals and the world of natural objects perceived by the individual. He preferred the Empiricist view that the ideas postulated by Plato constitute the essence of the objects of sensory perception. The ultimate, ideal reality (Plato's Ideas) unfolds itself in the phenomenal world—the world around us which we know through sense experience.

For Plato, the sense world realized itself by imitating the ideal world, whereas for Aristotle, the Platonic Ideals realize themselves through the phenomenal world. For Aristotle, Plato's universals (Ideals) were always to be found in particulars (empirical objects). Plato's ontologically real object—Ideal—was given the term *essence* by Aristotle; at other times he called it *form, intelligible essence,* or *notional essence.* Whereas for Plato, the essence (ideal object) is actually independent of particular things, for Aristotle essence is real only when it is actualized, that is, only as it realizes itself in phenomenal objects and therein takes on some appearance detectable by sense experience. In this manner, Aristotle solved the age-old metaphysical problem of the antithesis of Heraclitan objects in a state of multiplicity and flux with the Parmenidean motionless one Being. For Aristotle, all nature everywhere is seeking to realize itself, to develop its potentialities into actualities, to realize its possibilities, as the seed of a rose does when it comes into the beauty of full flower, or the seed of man does from his inception to the full flower of manhood. Everything seeks to realize its *essence.*

Relationship of Form to Matter. Thus the basic problem confronting Aristotle was that of explaining the relationship between *form* (essence) and *matter* (substance); it was necessary to find a principle or natural process impelling matter to take on some definite form, or, from the reverse point of view, enabling form to become actual in matter. The idea of a rose becomes real, is perfected, when it achieves actuality in the material substance, the rose itself; similarly matter or substance exists only when it takes on some form, some design. The natural world is dynamic, not static, for it is a beautiful active process wherein the material world takes on some form or design, and is thus constantly perfecting itself.

Matter *qua* matter, said Aristotle, would be devoid of shape or form if it had no design; it would be in a chaotic unformed state. Brute matter, if it could be in such a state, would possess merely potentiality, the possibility of becoming something, and, unless it were activated, it would remain in that dormant state of nonexistence. Matter that has not yet been actualized, has not acquired a form or design, is not in Being; such "pure matter" would have to be considered dead, lacking activity, possessing only potency, the possibility of becoming activated. Matter cannot act spontaneously, cannot move itself, but must be acted upon, must depend upon something else to motivate it into becoming an actuality from its latent state of mere possibility. Matter in its "original" condition, then, is in a state of want or deprivation in the sense that it needs to be realized through the action of something else upon it—some force or principle that will move it from its state of merely potential perfection toward the actualization or realization of its nature. The principle whereby each essence within (or ideal form of) the phenomenon realizes itself is *entelechy*, the Greek term used by Aristotle to signify inner purpose, end, or completion. Since all matter possesses entelechy, it follows that there is no unformed matter (or matterless form). The form in matter (its essence) is merely the possibility of matter for becoming actualized; when this potentiality in matter (its essence) becomes actualized, then it is perfected, or, which is the same thing, it becomes real—realized. The cosmic processes of the world are, therefore, the essences in phenomena realizing themselves by virtue of entelechy. Thus change or motion is simply the transition of objects from a state of potentiality to one of reality or actuality.

With the Aristotelian concept of entelechy, the teleological concept of the world reaches its epitome as a philosophical principle. Each aspect of the world, as well as the world as a whole, is seen as unfolding in accordance with its appointed purpose. According to Aristotle, *nature makes nothing in vain*, for all that God creates is done with a purpose. God has seen to it that matter everywhere is internally formed, designed for its respective objective. The goal of each object, therefore, is to realize its decreed end.

The Four Causes. The *causes* which contribute to the formation of matter in order that it may attain its end—a state of perfection—are four in number, and these four causes are regarded by Aristotle as first principles found in every realm of reality. They constitute the basic principles of his *First Philosophy* (metaphysics), namely: (1) *matter or substance* (the material cause); (2) *form or essence* (the formal cause); (3) *motion* (the efficient cause); and (4) *end* (the final or teleological cause). Each individual object, truly real in its own right, is teleologically determined according to the self-realizing form within it. The essence or substance within each thing actualizes itself by virtue of the form which it possesses, that is, the nature which inheres within it. The four causes are the principles by which each thing is governed as it undergoes this process of development, of being perfected, from potential to actual reality. To illustrate: In making a bronze statue, the *material cause* would consist of the bronze metal which is used, and the *efficient cause* would be the energy, the forces, expended to change bronze from one state to another; but merely to alter the bronze from one condition to another is insufficient, for the sculptor must change it from the state in which it is found (perhaps a chaotic one) to one which has the desired shape or form according to the conceptual archetype or plan which he has in mind—the *formal cause*. Finally, the statue must be utilized for the purpose for which it was originally intended (for example, to beautify a building or park), and this would be its teleological or *final cause*. Thus the four causes constitute the principles by which each particular thing is changed from its original potential state of unformed matter to one of full realization or perfection. (The idea of the material cause will be recognized as identical with the mechanical explanation of nature advanced by Democritus, while the other three causes may be regarded as part of Plato's teleological explanation of nature as the unfolding of a common purpose.)

ARISTOTELIAN PHILOSOPHY OF RELIGION

According to Aristotle, the imperfections in nature are due to matter, the substance which needs to be formed into its perfected state. Matter also accounts for the individuality of things, i.e., the fact that each thing is different from every other thing (therefore, no two trees can be exactly alike). The inability of matter (mere potentiality) fully to realize its form results in imperfection; the specific manner in which each material object develops or actualizes itself accounts for the individual differences in things, for, to repeat, no two things can be identical.

Degrees of Reality. The work of a sculptor illustrates how the material nature of an object accounts for its imperfection. The sculptor cannot fully achieve his ideal archetype if he must work with excessively hard or brittle material. As in his case, so throughout nature, the failure to attain a worthy end, perfection, is inherent in the very nature of matter itself. The more material a thing is, the more imperfect it is, while the more form it has actualized, the more perfect it becomes. According to the relative degree of form or actuality an object has, the greater is its reality, and the higher it is placed upon a scale of relative values. Non-living material objects (such as minerals) would be lowest on such a graded scale since they are the closest approximation to "brute matter." Next on the ascending scale of nature is vegetative life—the first form of living things; higher than vegetative life is animal life; still higher on the scale is human life, which is more ideal than the subhuman forms; and, finally, at the summit is God, who is *pure form, pure act,* devoid of all potentiality (materiality).

God as Pure Form.   Throughout the universe, said Aristotle, the universal ideal is found in particular things (sense objects); without knowledge of the particular facts, their universal principle cannot be known. Knowledge is fundamentally a process for abstracting ideal essences from individual substances. In the case of God, however, owing to the immaterial nature of God, there is no distinction between universal and particular aspects.

God as pure form or pure act, is perfect; that is, he wants nothing, does not need to perfect or actualize himself, being fully perfected or completely actualized. God is absolute spirit, completely immaterial, whereas all other objects in the world are comprised of both form and matter. God (complete actuality) is the *unmoved mover,* who motivates the universe as its cause, designer, and purpose. As such, he is pure thought (*Nous*), a mind that possesses only itself as its content. Material objects in realizing themselves move toward their divine origin, and in this way become perfected; in the case of man, his highest nature (his soul)—his intellectual or rational aspect— finds its perfection in the contemplation of God, that is, in becoming like God in the life of the mind (not of the sensual body); but in the case of God, he needs to do nothing to further perfect himself, for he is completely actualized. God's activity consists of thought, the activity of the mind. As pure act, his life consists of self-contemplation, thought about thought, absolute self-consciousness. This state of God's existence is completely eternal blessedness, and, as man draws closer to this state of contemplative existence, he, too, attains his highest happiness.

Thus we find that Plato's idea of the good, the highest of Platonic ideals (God), the prime mover which motivates all things to their end or purpose for being, becomes Aristotle's prime mover or pure form which motivates all things to their designed end, namely, Aristotle's Deity. Each material object, designed by God, moves toward God himself in its striving and longing for perfection; to attain perfection each thing must comply with its propulsion toward God, a way of action and a goal for which it was initially created. Consequently, God is loved by all things in the universe, and everything seeks to become like him in order to find its beauty, happiness, and state of perfection or complete realization. Aristotle's postulate that

God is absolute mind (pure spirit), completely devoid of corporeality, a spiritual being transcendent and apart from the universe, shows his point of view to have been that of unmistakable *monotheism*.

Aristotle's argument for the existence of God is both teleological (argument from design) and cosmological, or, more accurately, aetiological (argument from first cause). The form and pattern which material objects possess imply design. The world and the things within it are designed in such a fashion as to achieve the predetermined objective of their existence. The movements which things undergo are not mere irrational transitions from one state to another; they constitute motivated activity from a potential condition to the final state of actualization of their possibilities. All motion is goal-directed. God and nature do nothing in vain. The purposeful transition from potentiality to realization requires two factors: a motivating agency which causes the transition; and an original design pointed toward the specific purpose of self-realization. Even in the lowest of animals there is something of the divine, something admirable, purposeful, and beautiful. The motivation of all things, the first mover, is provided by pure energy in contrast to mere potential energy possessed by man—and the possibility of becoming something.

According to Aristotle, therefore, the prime mover must be free from potentiality; he must be perfectly actualized, eternal, pure, incorporeal form. As immaterial form, he must be simple in the sense of being composed of no parts and without plurality. As such he is pure spirit. Although he motivates all things, he himself is unmoved, and he causes things to be moved by the attraction which all things have for him (God) as the sole purpose of their creation and existence. The end of each thing is its good, and each thing has within it a tendency (love) toward realizing its respective end or good. The degree of perfection of a thing is directly proportional to its direct influence or progress toward God. But God did not create the world as a new entity—for matter is eternal, unbegun, unending. He designed the order of the universe from all eternity. As the actual principle basic to all purposive activity in the universe, he determines the goal, method, and teleological course of everything that exists.

Immortality. Aristotle believed not only in a monotheistic God but also in the immortality of the human soul. Unlike other substances, such as vegetation or non-human forms of life, man possesses a completely incorporeal and immortal soul. By its very nature the soul of man is immortal; that is, it existed before birth and will survive death. Aristotle regarded the souls of man and those of sub-human beings as a vital force, but he insisted that the soul (vital force) of plants merely functions as a constructive force, while that of animals possesses the characteristics of sense, desire, and animation. He further held that only in human beings these characteristics shared with the lower species are co-ordinated by reason—the rational soul. The human soul is the entelechy (the fully realized potentiality) of the physical body, whereas the body is only a potential aspect, a basis for self-realization.

Two Entelechies of the Soul.   Aristotle attributed a double entelechy to the human soul. The first entelechy is that aspect of the human mind which accumulates knowledge from sense experiences. This passive soul is a *tabula rasa* mind, a blank tablet upon which the various senses register the indelible perceptions which each individual acquires during his lifetime. This aspect of the soul, depending upon organic sensations of the body for its proper functioning, is therefore not eternal, but is subject to conditioning (outside influences) and akin to the soul of other animals. The second entelechy —the rational soul—is both man's motivating principle and his purpose for living; the body functions in order to fulfill the soul's ends. Man's lower (vegetative and animal) nature is co-ordinated by reason, his rational soul. Whereas the passive soul is governed by external forces, the rational soul is an active force which controls other things, and it is this second entelechy of the soul (the intellectual soul) which is eternal, existing before birth and after death. While both aspects of the soul (the first and second entelechies) are realized potentialities, speculative knowledge (thinking) belongs to the second aspect, while only passive or rote knowledge belongs to the first. The second soul, however, is still not perfect. Even though it possesses the self-conscious ability to manifest its own essence, nevertheless it is unlike God's mind, which is solely engaged in self-contemplation. Heaven, according to Aristotle, is a place of perfection, order, permanency, while earth is necessarily in a state of imperfection and multifarious transitoriness.

ARISTOTELIAN ETHICS

Aristotle's teleological conclusions are set forth most comprehensively in his writings on ethical theory. A concept fundamental to his ethical philosophy states that God and nature do nothing in vain, that everything in the universe has been created to achieve a purpose, has been designed to perform the given function or type of activity for which it was fashioned. Although this principle governs all forms of animal life, it is particularly evident in human beings. Thus, every organ in man as in other animals was created to fulfill a definite objective, and the end or goal of each organ consists of its activity. Each organ has a purpose conducive to its own good; and the performance of its proper activity results in its own good. In the case of man, the goal of actions (which are directed toward his greatest good) is *happiness*.

Virtue as Rational Activity. As the nourishing vegetative soul in plants is a vital activity which brings it into the beauties of its full flower, and the animal soul finds expression in the activities of sense, appetite, and animation for its fulfillment, so the happiness of man (which is sufficient evidence that his activity is proper for him) is contingent upon the soul's rational (virtuous) activity. The function of man's highest nature, his rational soul, is to live a well-ordered life in which every phase of man responds to his rational dictates in the sense that his lower nature behaves in conformity to reason. Thus virtue comprises essentially the use of one's ability to act purposefully in conformity with one's intellectual insight. Virtue means the application of intelligence to practical situations and concrete actions. Therefore, virtue depends upon both the possession and the practical exercise of intelligence so that the rational life of the individual will become his habitual mode of behavior, his characteristic trait or disposition.

Since virtue involves both intelligence and practical action, Aristotle suggested that there are two corresponding types of virtuous activity: dianoetic—the proper functioning of rational thought; and practical or ethical—action directed by desire, by the free will of the individual.

The dianoetic virtues are those of (1) reason; (2) science; (3) art; and (4) practical intelligence (prudence and understanding). The quality of wisdom is closely associated with these four dianoetic virtues and imbues with its power the rational activities of mankind in art, science, and logic. The dianoetic virtues are used for creative and technically proficient arts as well as for the exercise of practical wisdom (contingent knowledge) in everyday living; the other aspect of dianoetic virtues produces intuitive reasoning and scientific knowledge or truths which are logically necessary.

The practical or ethical virtues require the correct channeling of and control over desire, bending the individual's conduct to the dictates of his free will; moral conduct, therefore, depends upon free desire—freedom of the will. It is true, said Aristotle, that man's inner lack of knowledge, as well as external restraints, may prevent him from performing free, moral actions, but certainly whenever no such obstacles confront him, the individual can deliberately and intelligently choose and follow a proper course of moral action.

The Principle of Moderation. Although the right act is always virtuous, the mere isolated performance of the right act does not make one virtuous. When the right action is performed regularly until it becomes imbedded within the personality as a habit, then virtue has been instilled. The virtuous or right act is a mean between two extremes. Aristotle strongly urges *moderation* in all things, for the immoderate act is immoral or vicious. Extremes are always evil, whether it be the extreme of deficiency or that of excess. Between two extremes, a virtue will be found. When one cannot hold to the dead center of a mean, then he is advised to lean to the side of the lesser evil, to choose the lesser of the two evils. One extreme choice will always be less evil than its opposite—for example, if the virtue is courage and the two extremes are cowardice and foolhardiness (rashness or recklessness), it will be best to choose cowardice in preference to foolhardiness if the ideal virtue, courage, is at the moment impossible. Every true virtue, as a mean between extremes, impels man to live in harmony with reason, to live a rational life. The moderate, right act means doing the right thing to the right person, at the right time, to the right extent, with the right purpose, in the right manner. Thus, right doing is not within the reach of everyone, but only of the one equipped with the knowledge and ability to make the correct choice and discovering the truth—just as not everyone can be expected to find the exact center of a circle.

In addition to courage (with its corresponding vices of cowardice and rashness) Aristotle listed the virtues of *temperance* (the vices are intemperance and insensibility); two virtues concerned with financial matters, namely, *liberality* (the vices are meanness and prodigality) and *magnificence* (the vices are niggardliness and vulgarity); two virtues concerned with honor, namely, *magnanimity* (the vices are humility and vanity) and *ambition* (the vices are lack of ambition and overaggressiveness, or lack of restraint in wrongfully seeking what is not rightfully owned); the virtue concerned with anger, namely, *gentleness* (the vices are indifference and irascibility); three virtues concerned with social intercourse, namely, *friendliness* (the vices are churlishness and obsequiousness), *truthfulness* (the vices are false modesty and boastfulness), and *wittiness* (the vices are boorishness and buffoonery).

Aristotle discussed three kinds of friendship: (1) friendship of people with whom one finds pleasure; (2) friendship of people who prove to be of some practical use to us; and (3) good and perfect friendship which is superior to the other two types because it includes all their values. Only moral persons are capable of the third, noble type of friendship. Notwithstanding the high regard in which Aristotle holds friendship (even asserting that life is hardly worth living without it), he gives precedence to truth over friendship, and he reminds us that we should honor truth more than loyal friendship. Therefore Aristotle considered Plato dear, but truth dearer still.

A *quasi* virtue is *modesty* (the vices are bashfulness—or timidity —and shamelessness).

Finally, there is the virtue of *justice*, which concerns itself with the proper recognition of the rights of others in the light of the principle of equality. Note that Aristotle begins with the virtue of courage (which pertains to self-preservation) and ends with justice (which is necessary for the preservation of the group, the ethical foundation of the good and durable State). Justice means respect for the rights of individuals. Justice is thus the sum of all the virtues.

Personal and Social Ethics. Virtues are the expressions of a well-ordered life, one which accords with reason. The individual should live a life of reason in order to achieve happiness. Since everything, including man, is made with a purpose, whatever tends to thwart or frustrate one's predetermined purpose will bring frustration and misery, whereas whatever tends to fulfill it will produce that happiness which is a supreme goal. Man's chief purpose (that of his rational soul) is to perform the functions of his mind. Although the satisfaction of man's lower (vegetative and animal) nature brings some lesser degree of happiness, nevertheless, the exercise of reason, in its fullest flowering, results in the highest and finest form of happiness—a blessed life. Conditions which frustrate the mind of man reduce him to the worst state of misery, while, on the contrary, conditions which help his mind, in all its innate potentialities, to fully develop for his self-realization, bring about his highest good as well as his perfection, the ultimate and supreme end of man—*eudaemonia* (happiness in the sense of well-being, a good or pleasant state of mind).

Thus Aristotle's personal ethics develops into social ethics—his social or political philosophy. Consideration of the virtue, justice, leads us to deal with the problems of political philosophy, the basis for which, with Aristotle, is the conception of the State as a moral idea—its purpose being to diffuse perfect virtue throughout the lives of its citizens. His social or political philosophy is therefore a logical complement of his personal ethics.

ARISTOTLE'S SOCIAL AND POLITICAL PHILOSOPHY

For Aristotle, the basic function of the State is to extricate man from the crude natural condition in which he finds himself and to guide him into the civilized culture of an ethical and intellectual life, an accomplishment wrought through the finer arts. Thus the goal of the State is good living, a life of happiness based upon virtue. Outside of the State, the perfected moral life is an impossibility inasmuch as man is a *political or social animal* by nature. In order for man to fulfill himself, he must activate his social nature, an exercise which requires an existence within some society. As a complement to man's needs, the State also must be considered the instrument whereby man may attain his goal; consequently, the purpose of the State is that of ethical training for the benefit of its citizens. Just as the highest virtue for the individual is intellectual activity, so the highest duty of society is that of achieving and making the proper use of a state of peace. Man's natural condition is not one of belligerency, as the Spartans taught, but one of peace. Aristotle, commenting on the failure of Sparta, which he attributed to its military education and bellicose way of life, said that the Spartans, ever geared for war and not for peace, in times of peace rusted as a sword in a scabbard.

Six Forms of Government. Aristotle tended to favor a monarchical form of government—not a government based upon the divine right of kings, but rather a government under the leadership of the one person who is by nature and education best qualified for the task of governing. He added the qualification, however, that the particular form of government is not crucial, provided the public interest, not any private interest, be made the major concern of the rulers. Any form of government is good whose primary consideration is public welfare, and, conversely, any government which is principally concerned with the private gain of its officials is a degenerate or corrupt form. The varieties of government discussed by Aristotle are the same as described in Plato's *Politicus;* Aristotle enumerates six of them—monarchy, aristocracy, polity, tyranny, oligarchy, and democracy. The first three forms of government are good because in them the rulers are primarily interested in the common welfare of the citizens, but the other three forms are defective because in them the rulers seek their own personal profit as the first order of business.

Aristotle pointed out that each good form of government has its corresponding corrupt form. *Monarchy,* rule by one man interested in the good of the State as a whole, corresponds to a corrupt form, *tyranny,* to which it degenerates when the monarch's interests turn to selfish ends and he deteriorates into a despot. Aristocracy, rule by the best people (the most capable through natural endowment and education and always limited to a few persons, the intellectual elite) often degenerates into the corrupt form, *oligarchy,* the rule of a few whose chief objective is not the good of the citizens but their own financial advancement. The third form of government, *polity,* or *constitutional government,* means rule by the masses of citizens who comprise the State; sovereignty rests with the corporate citizenry who govern themselves under law protected by a constitution. A polity can be degraded into democracy, that is, rule by the great masses of people who are not principally interested in the common good inasmuch as each individual is concerned mainly about his personal gain. The form of good government which should be chosen by any particular State should depend upon the social situation prevailing at the time. Nevertheless, the preferred form will be that which establishes control by either one intellectually and morally superior person (monarchy) or by a few such persons (aristocracy). The best specific laws for any State will vary with the form of government selected.

Excluded Classes. Women, children, and slaves, being considered inferior, are excluded from government. Aristotle regarded slavery as natural, and therefore condoned it. Although he did not justify the practice of seizing slaves by conquest, he regarded the slave as an individual who by natural disposition, lacking intellectual acumen, prefers to obey rather than to command, to follow rather than to think for himself. His complement, the master, prefers to think and act for himself, to issue orders and to assume responsibility. The two together compose a fine team in which the happiness of each is augmented, but unhappiness must result if they live apart or fail to work harmoniously in their respective, natural roles.

Children should be provided with proper *education in virtue,* enabling them to become responsible citizens whose concern will be for the common good rather than for egoistic interests. The subjects that should be taught in elementary school are grammar, gymnastics, music, and drawing.

Moderation in Government. The principle of moderation must be observed in all phases of the State; it must be moderate in size and population, in climate, in the number of slaves, tradesmen, and soldiers, and even in the source of power in government so that the middle class will be dominant. Aristotle pointed out that even if the middle class does not dominate, owing to its being outnumbered by either the upper or the lower class, it may still swing the balance of power by casting its lot with one of the other two classes, and thereby through coalescence exert a decisive influence in the affairs of State. Moderation must also characterize the character and disposition of the citizens; the preferred constituency would represent a blend of spirited and courageous Europeans with the intellectually alert and inventive Asiatics. Happily, said Aristotle, the Hellenes enjoy such a synthesis, whereas the other regions are subject to deficiencies which may later prove to be the cause of their downfall.

ARISTOTLE'S AESTHETICS

Aristotle's aesthetics is closely related to his ethics and his political philosophy, for all of his philosophies are eminently practical and demand action rather than mere theorizing. Aristotle's aesthetic theory is found in his *Rhetoric* and *Poetics*. His theory of art, which is contained in his *Poetics*, emphasizes the idea that all art is *imitation*. The purpose of art is to stimulate man's emotions in such a manner that he will thereby be able to find a release from emotional stress and regain his poise and serenity.

According to Aristotle the study of any art, considered as a technical skill, provides human beings with the knowledge and understanding they need in order to practice the principles governing that particular art. Such technical training is necessary to complement the individual's natural talents and abilities. Amusements and recreational activities are imitative arts, releasing pent-up pressures which put a strain upon the soul (personality). Aristotle called this relaxation *catharsis,* a purification of the soul by relieving or healing it of its intense passions. Not only the undesirable feelings (as in Freudian psychoanalysis), but all the other intense feelings of the individual become quiescent and relaxed. Art is based on imitation, the mimicking of objects possessing more than average beauty; by copying the essence or form rather than the individual object as such, the artist idealizes the objects of his art and thus creates a beautiful finished product. All beauty possesses a certain greatness and orderliness.

Tragedy, too, is an imitative art; it imitates events of utmost gravity by using beautiful language augmented by meter and song. Music, painting, and poetry are similar forms of artistic expression. Prerequisites of proper tragedy include a serious theme, lessons of moral rectitude, and aesthetic tastefulness. Like all other forms of art, tragedy is cathartic; through sympathy with the characters, the audience obtains relief from fear and grief, and the playgoer's soul, liberated from its tumultuous emotions, regains its tranquility.

The foregoing discussion of Aristotle's aesthetics rings down the curtain on the golden age of Hellenic philosophy. Virtually the entire body of philosophy which followed for the next two millennia was dominated by the theories of Plato and Aristotle, and may therefore be regarded as a form either of Neo-Platonism (which often included attempts to synthesize Platonic and Aristotelian doctrines) or of Neo-Aristotelianism. The principal philosophical doctrines during the remainder of the ancient period (until about A.D. 500) and those during the first period of the Middle Ages (until about A.D. 1200) were marked by an emphasis upon Neo-Platonism. Thereafter, at least until the mid-fifteenth century, Neo-Aristotelian philosophy alone was universally accepted. Even in early modern times, Aristotle's logic, inductive methods, and other doctrines remained extremely influential.

Chapter 5

The Religious Problem

During the early Christian Era, two major systems of thought were dominant, namely, *Christianity* and *Neo-Platonism*. Alexandria was the geographical center of Neo-Platonist philosophy; some Neo-Platonists were Christians who tried to adapt philosophy as a basis for Christian theology. The world at that time was confronted by a dualistic conflict between a perishable earthly world of sensual pleasure, intoxicating to the senses, and a supersensuous world of a divine nature which offered a proper, loftier form of enjoyment. There was a pressing need for profound, authoritative doctrines concerning man's beliefs, faith, and salvation. It was at this time that men began to seek certainty and salvation in a spiritual world that they accepted as transcending the realm of sense experience.

Seneca, Epictetus, and Marcus Aurelius had transposed the philosophy of Stoicism into one of redemptive deliverance, one of salvation; Demonax had performed the same service for Cynicism. The religious movement of some *Neo-Platonists* and the philosophy of the *Patristics* rose to the occasion to meet the demand of the times for ethical and religious salvation. Both groups were principally concerned with the religious problem of salvation; furthermore, both sought to establish scientific and philosophical bases for their conviction that the human soul was in need of redemption. Each school was faced with the problem of ethical and religious salvation. The period of theological metaphysics was now under way, its chief characteristic being a religious interpretation of Plato's philosophy. The two great rival theories of the time were those of the contemporaries Plotinus, the non-Christian philosopher, and Origen, the Christian theologian. Both men were the disciples of *Ammonius Saccus* (reputed founder of Neo-Platonism), and both defended the following ideas: matter is the product of spirit, and phenomena are essentially spiritual—theories of spiritual monism; there is a dualism between spirit and matter that poses a moral problem; the sense world is evil and alien to God; the soul's salvation requires that it extricate itself from matter and return to pure spirit from which it initially came. It may be said that ancient philosophy ended with the attempt of the Neo-Platonists and Patristics to spiritualize the world.

The Christian Neo-Platonists were divided among themselves in their interpretation of God's nature. Some, such as Justin and the Gnostics, respected the views of the Jewish Neo-Platonist theologian Philo, who argued that no specific qualities should be predicated of God because they are all too delimiting. Philo regarded God as exalted above all human understanding, hence as infinite, incomprehensible, nameless, and transcending human knowledge, and he insisted that the most that can be asserted of God is what he is not— a philosophy of religion called *negative theology*. Similarly, for Plotinus, God as the One, preceding all thought and Being, is infinite, formless, and transcends the sense world as well as the intellect of man; as such, he is neither conscious nor active, but a transcendent primordial Being above mind, yet he is the cause of thought, Being, the Platonic ideal good, and the end (Aristotelian *Nous*) of all. In strong sympathy with the Neo-Platonists, but in intellectual disagreement with their doctrine of the Deity, many of the Christian philosophers conceived of God as a spiritual personality, not in the Hellenistic sense of a finite Being but as an infinite Being bearing a personal relationship to man, his creation, and as a Being whose personality finds its image in man, God's heir by divine sonship. Whereas non-Christian Neo-Platonists viewed personality merely as a transitory product of life, hence ultimately impersonal, the Christians regarded persons and interpersonal relationships as the very essence of reality. Nevertheless, both groups were faced with a problem of dualism: that of the opposition of God as moral spirit to the world as immoral matter, a moral dualism between good and evil, between a good heavenly God and the evil world of matter, between godly and satanic forces. To these fundamental religious problems regarding salvation, the Neo-Platonists and the Patristics addressed themselves; the most influential of the former group was Plotinus, and of the latter, Origen.

ORIGINS OF NEO-PLATONISM

Neo-Platonism is the philosophy developed by those philosophers of the early Christian Era who sought to synthesize Platonic and Aristotelian ideas with Oriental thought. It had its birth in Alexandria (the nexus of Hellenistic and Judeo-Christian philosophy) where there was a trend toward the formation of religions grounded upon Hellenistic thought. Neo-Platonism, essentially a religious philosophy accepting as its fundamental principle the doctrine of the transcendence of God, was the logical continuation of Neo-Pythagoreanism and Middle-Platonism. As a philosophy, it was eclectic, combining the ideas of Platonism, Aristotelianism, Neo-Pythagoreanism, and Stoicism, with a strong bent toward Platonism, as evidenced by its slogan, "Back to Plato."

The reputed founder of the Alexandrian school of Neo-Platonism was Ammonius Saccas (A.D. 175–250), who left no writings; but the true founder and the chief proponent of the school was his student Plotinus (A.D. 204–269), its first articulate systematizer. An important disciple of Ammonius, Origen Adamantius (*d*. A.D. 254), adapted Neo-Platonism as a philosophical foundation for Christian theology. Another notable member of this school was Tryrian Porphyry (*c*. A.D. 230–300). A second branch of the Alexandrian school was founded in Syria by Jamblichus of Chalcis in Coele-Syria (*d*. A.D. 330), who had been a student of Porphyry. A third wing of the school was founded in Athens by Plutarch (*d*. after A.D. 430). Successors to Plutarch in the Athenian school were his disciples Syrianus and Proclus (A.D. 411–485).

PLOTINUS

Neo-Platonism was first systematically developed by Plotinus (born in Lycopolis in Egypt, and educated under Ammonius Saccas in Alexandria). In A.D. 244, at the age of forty, in Rome, Plotinus began to teach his philosophy. He wrote his first works at fifty years of age (in A.D. 253); they were revised, arranged, and edited by his disciple Porphyry, who published them in six *Enneads* (a title indicating that each of the six books has nine chapters, with a total of fifty-four brief treatises). The six *Enneads* discuss the following subjects in sequence: (1) living being and the nature of man; (2) the heavens and two kinds of matter; (3) the cosmos; (4) the soul; (5) the *Nous* and First Being; and (6) the existent and the good or the One (including human and divine freedom).

God as a Transcendent Principle. The principal doctrine of Plotinus stated that there is but the one exalted God, exalted by Plotinus even over the *Nous*, as Aristotle understood the term. The original Being, God, is indescribable; that is, we cannot ascribe qualities which characterize him. The most that we can do is assert, without any descriptive substratum, that he is a supreme power, such as the final cause, the cosmic force, or the highest spiritual, creative Being. He is the absolute unity synthesizing the antithesis of thought and Being (mind and substance). In fact, even the use of such terms as *cosmic force* and *spiritual Being* may give an inaccurate impression of the view of Plotinus, who preferred to think of God as an impersonal *It* (like the *One* of Parmenides), a transcendent principle who creates the universe out of himself in a process which is timeless and eternal. Although present in all objects of creation, he is distinct from them, and God, as the One, supreme, is above and before all things, hence not merely a pantheistic force. According to Plotinus, then, God cannot be categorized, cannot be classified as spiritual, material, soul substance, or in any other category, but must be regarded as One who, without possessing specific attributes, yet creates all things and is superior to everything originated by him.

God's Relationship to the Universe. God is the absolute permanent One, as Parmenides taught, but the universe as his creation comprises a changeable plurality, as Heraclitus taught; thus Plotinus effected a synthesis between these two systems of philosophy. God's relationship to the world may be compared superficially to the relationship between light and the real objects reflected by light. But Plotinus interpreted the physical and spiritual universe as the by-product of the One, or God, embracing Anaxagoras' *Nous*, as well as Plato's concepts of the good, Ideas, substance, and matter as emanations from God, and Aristotle's interpretation of the *Nous* as imbued with entelechy, as teleological in nature. Thus to Plotinus the *Nous* is a suprasensible object which includes the Platonic Ideas; the Ideas are immanent in the *Nous*. Since the *Nous* does not reflect the truth as its image but the truth is inherent in it, it can never be subject to error. The Ideas, inasmuch as they are immanent in the *Nous*, are similarly not subject to error. The soul, however, being a product of the *Nous*, is only its image, and hence is fallible.

The soul, as a mediator, points in two directions: toward its by-product the *Nous*, and toward the material substances which the soul has also created. Thus, corporeal things are only an extension of the soul, just as a line is but an extension of a point. Plotinus held that the soul has a double aspect: an ideal, indivisible element; and a divisible element constituting the material world. Like ultimate reality, however, the soul is itself an immaterial substance, Actually, the body is contained within the soul, not vice versa. Since there are innumerable material things, each contained within its corresponding soul, there must be many individual souls. The soul of the entire universe is the supreme World Soul, and, unlike Platonic universal Ideals, the individual souls are simply aspects of the World Soul. In fact, according to Plotinus, each soul is diffused as a principle activating the entire body, the latter being its projected aspect, and the soul begets and motivates the body. However, the soul cannot be regarded as being within the body for it is superior to it and must be situated in the *Nous*, while the *Nous* in turn must be within the One or God.

Man's Relationship to God and the Universe. Plotinus contrasted the rational principle of the universe, the *Logos*, with matter; he identified the *Logos* with light as something which is real, existent, whereas matter is identical with darkness, which has no being, is nonexistent, and signifies only the absence of light. Evil is a formless thing, matter deprived of form. Matter exhibits many degrees of evil and good, ranging from mere sense objects to ideal substances which approach the goal of self-realization or perfection. The objects in sense perception are but images of the ideal forms, and sensory objects rest on a foundation which is a mere shadow of the ideal, true reality.

For Plotinus beauty means much more than mere symmetry. It involves a close relationship to the ideal reality postulated by Plato. It is a higher, superior representation of Plato's Ideas than ordinary sensory perceptions or images. Beauty is identified with higher reality as something superior to sensory images, just as form is superior to matter, the soul to the body, and it is a controlling force, just as reason and goodness govern the soul.

Plotinus analyzed the reasons for man's predicament arising from the effort to discover the truth about God and the universe. He explained that the human soul was created by God but thereafter, in response to man's desire to achieve independence and self-direction, descended into the world of material objects—thus attempting to control sensory objects and matter. In this way, man abandoned the realm of God and must now be converted, must return to him. Since man now possesses a free will, he can return to God and find both redemption and self-realization through virtue.

Plotinus defined virtues as qualities inherent in God (a Platonic concept) and also as qualities in conformity with human nature (the Stoic concept) or as actions in obedience to reason (the Aristotelian view). He grouped the virtues into three classes in order of their rank, as follows: (1) the relatively inferior or lowest virtues, namely, the civic virtues of practical wisdom, courage, temperance, and justice (identical with Plato's cardinal four virtues); (2) the purifying virtues, which enable man to achieve deliverance from sins (sins of the flesh or of material things); and (3) the highest virtues, which unite us with God and represent the supreme and ultimate goals of human life.

Man, said Plotinus, has cut himself off from God and must now return to him in order to find blessedness, the true good. He must elevate and identify himself again with the good, thus achieving the deepest satisfaction, a state of sheer ecstasy. Plotinus agreed with the Platonic view that man's reason enables him to know the Ideas which constitute reality, but he regarded rational thinking as only an intermediate stage of man's progress toward immediate contact with the good itself. The soul yearns to be godlike as an Unmoved Mover (the Aristotelian concept); nevertheless, since the soul cannot attain this supreme goal through the activity of rational thought, it must find a different road superior to such activity and it actually finds it in direct communion with God. To look upon God in this direct way, to experience this immediate ecstatic contact with and vision of God, will bring to fruition man's noblest goal, will bring him rest and perfect blessedness. Such a vision or contact is rare, reserved only for the best, most virtuous, wisest, godlike men.

The philosophy of Plotinus (especially his contempt for the material world and his conviction that the soul can be liberated through asceticism and can be transported mystically to a state of rapturous ecstasy in contact with the divine) made Neo-Platonism perfectly acceptable to Christian mystics, such as *Pseudo-Dionysius* who introduced it into the Church so effectively that it remained there nine centuries from approximately A.D. 600 to 1500. Meister Eckhart's Mysticism was grounded in Neo-Platonism. It may be said that Neo-Platonism was the wellspring from which the philosophy of Mysticism emerged.

SCHOOLS OF PATRISTIC PHILOSOPHY

Patristic philosophy was the body of philosophical doctrines accepted by the Fathers of the early Christian Church. Christian philosophy of that time is usually divided into *antenicene* and *postnicene*, the dividing line being A.D. 325, the date of the Council of Nice. The early Patristic philosophers are commonly referred to as the Apologists because they devoted most of their attention to apologetics, a philosophical defense of the Christian faith against the claims of secular philosophy and Gnosticism. An effective defense required the Apologists to merge rational philosophy with Christian doctrines based on faith.

The most influential Christian Apologist was Flavius Justin Martyr, of Sichem (*c.* A.D. 150); the second most prominent was Minucius Felix (*c.* A.D. 200). Among other eminent Apologists were Aristides; Athenagoras of Athens; Theophilus of Antioch; Melito of Sardis; and Apollinaris of Hierapolis. With the exceptions of Felix and Firmianus Lactantius (*c.* A.D. 300), who were members of the Latin school, the Apologists belonged to the Hellenic school. (Aristides' writings however, were widely available in Armenian instead of Latin or Greek.)

The African school of antenicene Patristics had two outstanding leaders: *Quintus Septimius Florens Tertullian* (A.D. 165–220), and *Arobius of Numidia* (*fl.* A.D. 290), both renowned for their anti-rationalism, their skeptical attitude toward reason, which they attempted to discredit in order to establish the supremacy of faith.

The Alexandrian school of Patristics was indebted mainly to Justin and Athenagoras. Its most distinguished leaders were Clement of Alexandria (*c.* A.D. 150–220) and Origen the Adamantine (*c.* A.D. 185–254). During the postnicene period, Christian philosophy was dominated by the most distinguished philosopher, St. Aurelius Augustine (A.D. 354?–430), although there were other notable contributors, such as St. Athanasius (A.D. 296?–373), St. Hilary of Poitiers (A.D. 315?–367), St. Basil (A.D. 329–379), St. Gregory of Nyssa (A.D. 331?–395?), and St. Cyril of Alexandria (A.D. 376?–444).

Patristic philosophy flourished during the period beginning in the second and extending well into the fifth century A.D. and culminating in a definite type of Neo-Platonism. St. Augustine, who subordinated philosophy (Platonism and Neo-Platonism) to Christian doctrine, thus laid the foundations of medieval philosophy. The dominant philosophers of the Middle Ages, the Scholastics, sought to resolve the conflict between faith and reason. Although in that conflict the adherents of Patristic faith disputed the advocates of Hellenic rational philosophy, nevertheless, in the last analysis, Patristic theology and philosophy were actually based upon fundamental concepts of Hellenic thought.

ORIGEN

Origen studied with Clement of Alexandria, then with Ammonius Saccas, founder of Neo-Platonism. Christian theology had never been integrated into a system of thought prior to Origen's work, and he may therefore be considered the founder of Christian philosophy, which he set forth on the basis of the Bible and the *Regula Fidei* (rule of faith as taught by the Church or the Church Council).

God as Eternal Creator. Attempting to defend theological beliefs which had hitherto been accepted through faith alone, Origen asserted the rational argument that God, as pure spiritual essence (in perfect unity and absolute changelessness), is not only above everything else in the universe (and all Beings) but also the eternal creator of all things. Matter is changeable and perishable, but the unchangeable God is everlasting. Although human reason cannot encompass or truly comprehend God's attributes, it can discern certain divine characteristics such as the absolute causality of God's will, or, in other words, God's eternal creativity. God's creativity must be regarded as eternal because as the eternal God he has forever been (and will continue forever to be) ceaselessly active. He disagreed sharply with the Greek philosophers (for example, Plato and Aristotle) who claimed that God is the architect that formed the world out of eternally existing matter. Origen insisted that God created matter itself, that he willed the universe into being and predetermined its nature. Not matter, then, but creativity is co-eternal with God. Owing to God's unchangeableness, and to the changeability and perishability of matter, God himself does not directly make the phenomenal world, but allocates this function to his image, the *Logos*, a second God, begotten by God.

The Logos. However, the *Logos* is not *the* God (God himself), but a subordinate divinity. This second God is the Son of God who participates in creation by bringing into being the transitory and perishable world of matter. The *Logos* is a personal copy of the Father God, though inferior to God himself. The relationship of the *Logos* to God is the same as the relationship which the Holy Spirit (or Holy Ghost) bears to the Son of God; nevertheless, one is not temporally prior to the other, for all are co-eternal. The *Logos* is the world's prototype, the idea or "blue print" according to which everything is created by edict of the divine will.

The Problem of Sin. Eventually all spiritual beings will know God as his Son does, and they will then become sons of God comparable to the *Logos*, his only begotten Son. Origen maintained that man's spirit existed prior to his body, that man became an earth creature as a consequence of his sins, but also that he and all other spiritual beings, including even Satan, will eventually find salvation, a state of divine blessedness in which each partakes of the divine essence. He held that man was made out of (or imprisoned by) material substance as punishment for sin but now has the power to achieve redemption through purification. Man's fall is attributed to misuse of his freedom of the will. Even after his fall, man still possesses the freedom to choose between good and evil. The material world is in itself good, for God created it; only man's perverted will causes him to sin and results in chaining him to substance (materiality) so that the soul is incorporated into flesh. Non-human spirits (e.g., angels, stars, and evil demons) occupy their different places or ranks in the material world.

The Origenian doctrine of freedom of the will constituted a logical means of reconciling the seemingly conflicting Christian doctrines that God is all-powerful (and all-knowing) and that sin exists (and is known by man to exist). Man, though in a fallen state, aspires through use of his free will to attain salvation, to return to his divine origin through emancipation from matter. With the assistance of the *Logos*, i.e., the sinless soul of Jesus, man (whose spirit is eternal) may progress through two ascending stages of redemption, namely, faith—whereby he achieves understanding of the sensory world through religious knowledge—and knowledge of the *Logos* until he reaches the highest state of absolute absorption into God, liberated entirely from material existence. By virtue of this combination of grace and freedom, all spirits find their perfection in the third stage of redemption. Ultimate reality consists of personalities, together with their interpersonal relationships with one another and with the infinite Person, God.

ST. AUGUSTINE

The psychical and spiritual that had displaced the material and the physical in the philosophy of Plotinus and Origen reached its full systematic development in the philosophy of Augustine. Although Augustine was a prolific writer, his philosophy did not constitute a complete, integrated system, but consisted of discussions of specific topics which commanded his attention as the occasion called for it—a fact particularly evident in his debates with philosophers whose points of view he rejected.

Augustine's Criteria of Truth. Two fundamental *criteria of truth* underlie the entire philosophy of Augustine: the first criterion is the *authority* of the Church; the second criterion is the certainty of *conscience*, that is, the absolutely certain knowledge which man actually finds in his inner experiences (memory, intellect, and will) comprising consciousness. Reason presents immediate certainty to the mind or soul (these are identical). Since man's inner consciousness as a criterion of truth may contradict some of the authoritative conclusions of the Church, the philosophy of Augustine is subject to possible inconsistency from the point of view of logic. Incongruities sometimes become evident when Church doctrines cannot logically be reconciled with the dictates of reason. Despite such occasional lack of consistency between Augustine's theology and his philosophy, his views exerted a potent influence not only upon the course of medieval thought, but even upon important trends in modern, including contemporary, philosophy.

Refutation of Skepticism; Proof of the Existence of the Soul. Notwithstanding Augustine's strong affinity for Platonic and Neo-Platonic philosophy, he severely attacked the Skeptics of the Platonic school, who, because of their doubts concerning the attainment of truth, turned to the defeatist attitude of Skepticism. Augustine held that the Skeptics are mistaken in assuming that certainty of knowledge is impossible and that man can achieve only "probable knowledge," i.e., ideas whose validity is highly probable. Since any degree of probable knowledge implies an approach toward completely certain knowledge, the assumption of probably valid truths presupposes or implies the existence and attainability of absolute truths.

Thus Augustine's arguments against Skepticism used the experience of uncertainty and doubt as a logical defense for the existence of certainty and absolute truth. If the Skeptic argues that no real objects of his sensory experience exist, nevertheless he cannot doubt the fact that his perceptions do exist. The person who doubts all truths is caught in a logical dilemma, for he must exist in order to doubt; in fact, no matter what else he doubts, he proves his own existence through the act of doubting—and he thereby establishes the absolute reality of his own soul, i.e., his own mind and spirit.

For Augustine the soul comprises the entire personality of the living individual, who becomes aware through self-consciousness not only that he is a real integrated existing person but also that he knows with absolute certainty his own activities and powers of *memory, intellect,* and *will.* Thus the individual remembers what he is doing in the very act of self-doubt; he understands or knows his immediate experience; and he can will to act or not to act as he does. Hence the three aspects of the human soul (or personality) may be described as powers of memory, intellect, and will; or as sources of idea, judgment, and will; or as activities of being, knowing, and willing. Note the corresponding three aspects in Augustine's view of God's personality, namely, omnipotence (God is all-powerful), omniscience (God is all-knowing), and absolute goodness (God practices the highest good). The creation and continuing existence of the universe must be attributed to these three qualities in God's nature. The most important aspect of the soul (or world spirit) is *will*, the faculty which enables man to live, makes his salvation possible, and is responsible for having brought the world into existence *ex nihilo* (out of nothing). The Augustinian concept of the soul as a self-conscious unity of the total personality anticipated a fundamental idea in modern philosophy. That concept assigned to the human soul a higher role and function than those which either Aristotle or the Neo-Platonists had suggested.

Ethics and Immortality. Augustine held that the soul, which is immaterial, did not exist prior to the birth of the individual human being, but that, subsequent to his birth, it possesses an immortal nature, living on into eternity. Its immortality arises from the fact that it shares in the immutable truths of the universe and thus unites its essence with the eternal processes of reason and life. It is because sin impairs these natural processes that it must be regarded as evil which is attributable not to God as the creator of all things but rather to the will of mankind. God created all things out of nothing; therefore all natural things, based upon the divine decree, are necessarily good, while any impairment of the natural processes is evil.

An evil will, said Augustine, has a deficient cause (not an efficient cause), for evil is merely the absence of good, a negative condition of privation or, in other words, a loss of good, of beauty, of happiness, of virtue. Consequently, evil cannot exist without violation of a corresponding moral good, for it is a concomitant of good. An absolute good could conceivably be achieved, but an absolute evil—evil without good—is an impossibility. Augustine's view of the relationship between good and evil can be illustrated by examples from everyday experience. Thus, injury to a person's good right arm would be an evil event, but such evil does not exist as a substance, nor could it exist in any sense without the previous existence of a healthy, uninjured arm; and after the limb has been restored to its natural state of health—goodness—then the evil state disappears; it does not shift to another place but ceases to exist.

Sin made its first appearance in the world when Adam, impelled by his own evil will and free choice, disobeyed the commandments of God. With Adam's fall from grace, his sin became the sin of all later ages of humanity. This inherited corruption of human nature therefore called for remedial action to effect the redemption of man. Divine justice demands that all mankind be punished for original sin, but God in his inscrutable wisdom, mercy, and grace has elected some men (although they are unworthy of it) to everlasting blessedness and other men to everlasting suffering. Without the aid of God's grace, man is unable to progress toward the good, for all good issues from God alone. Thus, as a result of Adam's disobedience of God's command (which occurred through the foreknowledge of God, yet was effected solely by the will of Adam), man became subject to death as his just and merited punishment. Augustine asserted, however, that there are two kinds of death: physical death when the soul abandons its body, and death of the soul when God abandons it; evildoers must face not only physical death but death of the soul as well. Augustine's conception of immortality includes both physical resurrection and eternal life for the soul.

In his infinite wisdom, God has given man a free will which man has so misused as to place him in his present predicament. The proper exercise of his free will makes it impossible for men to sin and constitutes the highest form of freedom enjoyed by the elect who have been granted salvation. Augustine's doctrine of freedom of the will and his doctrine of predestination are irreconcilable and contradictory, and the Church brought pressure to bear against his emphasis upon freedom of will and conscience.

Ethics and the Philosophy of History. Augustine's ethical theory permeates his entire philosophy of history. He held that there are two opposing realms within the world, that of the damned, evil demons, fallen angels, and the devil, and that of God, the saved, and the unfallen angels. The condemned seek wealth, power, and choices while they live on earth, warring among themselves in their struggle for illusory values. The saved, on the other hand, are those, loyal to God, who look not to this world for their kingdom, but await it in this temporal life by dwelling in the saving institution of that divine kingdom, the Church.

The divine truth or greatest good is God. Accordingly, God is the *summum bonum* for which man seeks, and for which his will strives. Once the soul or its will reaches its ultimate goal (God), then all striving ceases, and the soul is at peace in a perfect state of blessedness. The greatest virtue in this search for God and eternal truth is the love of God. The three great virtues of St. Paul—faith, hope, and love—take precedence over other virtues, both dianoetic and practical. The four cardinal virtues of Plato become aspects of the love of God: *temperance* means keeping oneself incorruptible for God; *courage* means enduring, potent love for the sake of the loved object, namely, God; *justice* means loving service to God; and *wisdom* means discriminating between good and evil, between what leads the soul to God or deters it from its loved object. Through the virtue of love, man reaches his highest state of sanctification and blessedness, that of being illumined in the highest and ultimate truth, the greatest good, by the complete subordination of his will to the infinite and ultimate Being, God. Thus, Augustine remained true to Plato and Neo-Platonism, to the mystic contemplation of the good—God.

Chapter 6

Scholasticism

→ end of antiquity

According to some historians, medieval philosophy may be said to have begun at about the time when Justinian I closed the Academy at Athens (A.D. 529). Dionysius the Areopagite, a Neo-Platonist who flourished about A.D. 500 might then be considered the first philosopher of the Middle Ages. But most scholars prefer to regard John Scotus Erigena (*c.* A.D. 810–877) as the first major philosopher of the medieval period and to designate A.D. 800, the date of Charlemagne's coronation as the start of the medieval intellectual record. They may even designate the intervening period from the fall of Rome in A.D. 476 to the founding of Charlemagne's empire in A.D. 800 as the "Dark Ages," as an era of intellectual stagnation. From the standpoint of systematic philosophy, the period prior to Charlemagne is regarded as static, a period ending when he ushered in a new era of learning in which education was entrusted to the Churchmen, the Scholastics.

The proponents of Scholasticism, the dominant philosophy during the Middle Ages, were university professors (or Schoolmen) whose philosophical system represented a continuation of the philosophy of the Christian Era. The Schoolmen were Christian philosophers; they accepted Church dogmas as the basis for their philosophical views. Since Scholasticism merely sought to justify rationally what the Church had already accepted as a foregone conclusion, the Scholastic method of inquiry was directly contrary to the free spirit of investigation characteristic of ancient Greek philosophers and secular philosophers of later times. For the Scholastics, Church dogma was infallible. Philosophy consisted of rational explanations designed to corroborate the truth of ecclesiastical doctrine.

faith first

PROBLEMS OF MEDIEVAL PHILOSOPHY

Two fundamental problems predominated in medieval philosophy, persisting both in the Platonic period (A.D. 529–1200) and in the Aristotelian period (A.D. 1200–1453): (1) the problem of universals as objective realities; (2) the problem of logical proofs for the existence of God. The Platonic view of universals assumed that the more nearly perfect a thing is, the more real it must be—that since universal ideals are perfect, they must be real entities. Particular objects are real only to the degree that they participate in or approximate the perfection of the ideal or universal. Aristotle's view that the universal ideal exists only in particular objects was the subject of heated discussion with advocates of Platonic Realism. (The issue was hotly debated during the first period of Scholastic philosophy.) On the other hand, the problem of finding logical proofs for the existence of God stimulated no such controversy, for it was a shared interest of all adherents of Church doctrines.

NEO-PLATONISM, THE FIRST
PERIOD OF MEDIEVAL PHILOSOPHY

The first period of medieval philosophy was dominated by the influence of Plato as represented in the views of the Neo-Platonists, supplemented by portions of Aristotle's *Logic*. Aristotle was relatively little known as a philosopher prior to the latter half of the twelfth century when the first great universities made their appearance (the University of Bologna, Oxford University, and the University of Paris); by that time his works had been translated from Greek into Latin, the language adopted by the academic world during the Middle Ages. The first period ended at the close of the twelfth century with the dominance of Aristotelian ideas, soon thereafter represented by the most influential of the Scholastic philosophers, St. Thomas Aquinas. Aristotelianism became the philosophy accepted by the Roman Catholic Church, albeit with enough modifications to justify renaming that philosophy Thomism.

During the Platonic period of medieval philosophy the most influential philosophers were John Scotus Erigena (*c.* 810–877), St. Anselm of Canterbury (1033–1109), Roscellinus of Amorica in Brittany (*c.* 1050–1121), and Peter Abelard (1079–1142).

JOHN SCOTUS ERIGENA

The earliest of the leading Scholastics, John Scotus Erigena, was a Scot, born and reared in Ireland. Upon the invitation of Charles the Bald, he journeyed to Paris where he served as a teacher at the court school. In his point of view regarding basic problems of philosophy, he was greatly influenced by the Neo-Platonist Dionysius the Areopagite, whose works he translated.

The Problem of Universals. As a Neo-Platonist, Scotus adhered to the theory that the universal (the class, genus, or ideal) is the essence of reality, and that each particular object is contained within the universal and is a product of the universal. This relationship between a universal and a particular object is analogous to the relationship between universal man as an ideal or as a species and an individual man, or between humanity (as the creative sources of of the species) and a specific person, such as, for example, Socrates. According to Neo-Platonic Realism, universal man (humanity) is not only the ultimately real substance (consequently the term *Realism*), but also the source from which particular things (Socrates, Plato, Aristotle, and all other individuals) originate. The more universal an object is, the more real it is; the more of humanity a particular person possesses, the more real he is. The real is the universal; the particular represents merely the process of unfolding the universal. Scholastics expressed this relationship in the popular formula, *universalia ante rem* (the universal is prior to the particular thing), which states that prior to the history of any object a universal or general ideal had to exist as the source imparting reality to the particular object. Humanity must exist as a universal before any individual human being can possibly exist. An object's essence (universal) must be a reality before the particular object can come into existence.[1] The assumption that universals exist as objective realities is the principal thesis of Scholastic Realism.

God and Negative Theology. Applying this theory of Scholastic Realism to theology, Scotus concluded that God, the supreme unity, the original Being, and the universal of all universals, has created all things by means of a logical unfolding of particulars from their universal essences. To create is simply to particularize, a process of unfolding that makes individual things out of universals—for example, a particular man out of the essence of man (the universal reality). Conversely, Scotus held that immortality is an opposite process whereby the particulars return to their universal essence, just as an individual human being returns to the common state of all humanity (universal essence). Immortality means the return of things to God, that is, their deification, so that there is complete unity of all things in God—Pantheism. The universal exists prior to the individual object, but it also exists in the particular object—thus, humanity is discernible as an ideal reality in each person.

---

[1] The antithesis of this position is found later, particularly in the philosophies of Neo-Thomism and Existentialism.

Scotus' theology was negative in the sense that it characterized God in negative terms on the ground that the infinite Deity is beyond human comprehension. Scotus predicated specific positive qualities of God, not as a literal but only as a symbolical reference. In his book, *De Divisione Naturae*, he set forth a pantheistic interpretation as consisting of four types of reality: (1) that which creates but is not created (i.e., God as creator of the world); (2) that which is created and creates (ideals or prototypes which subsist in God as primordial causes prior to the existence of particular sensory objects); (3) sensory objects confined to specific times and places—the particular things which are sensed and which have unfolded from the universal idealism in (2) above; and (4) God as the purpose or end for sake of which all particular things are created and to which all particular things return. Thus, in the logical Pantheism of John Scotus Erigena, the sensory world is portrayed as the unfolding of God, its ultimate, eternal purpose or objective being to rejoin God as creator of the universe.

The Problem of Good and Evil. According to Scotus, man's soul exhibits three aspects (sense perception, intelligent awareness, and reasoning) suggestive of the Trinity, but its true nature is inscrutable, for it is identical with the inscrutable essence of God. Man is an angel who sinned—a fallen angel—and although he remains the highest and noblest of all creatures on earth or in heaven, his sin has diminished his beauty and purity. Because man's sin depended upon his physical nature (his sensuous life dominated over his intellectual, spiritual life), he can regain perfect beauty and purity only in a future life of the spirit. Problems of material existence, such as disease, were caused by man's original sin, evil conduct which deprived man of a higher good, the complete reality of perfection. Evil, in Scotus' view, is therefore the absence of good, and punishment in hell is but a temporary, spiritual experience preceding man's eventual return to God, perfection, the highest good.

ST. ANSELM OF CANTERBURY

The Neo-Platonic Realism of John Scotus Erigena was fully developed in the philosophy of St. Anselm of Canterbury (1033–1109). (In 1078 St. Anselm became Abbot of the monastery of Bec in Normandy, and in 1093 he was appointed Archbishop of Canterbury.)

Anselm's Doctrine of Realism. The Neo-Platonic doctrine of universals (a doctrine of Realism stating that the universal or general nature of an object exists prior to the particular material thing) was utilized by Anselm in his famous *ontological argument* for the existence of God. According to this philosophy of Neo-Platonic Realism, the extent to which any object is real depends upon the degree of its universality. Inasmuch as God is the most universal Being, he is the most real of all Beings, absolutely real because all his attributes are universal. As a human being, the individual person possesses characteristics that are not general traits of mankind, but are peculiar to himself. Since there is only one universal God, however, all of God's attributes are universal. The universal quality common to all mankind does not mean that any particular individual must exist, whereas the fact that God is a universal Being means that he exists.

The Ontological Argument. Anselm's ontological argument (delineated in his book, *Proslogium*) states that since we possess an idea of a perfect Being (and we can think of nothing greater or higher), such a Being must necessarily exist because perfection implies existence. Any idea that was lacking in reality (any concept which had no objective reality of its own) would be imperfect, whereas one of the attributes of a perfect Being is actual existence (not merely an idea in any person's mind, but real existence external to any mind which happens to conceive of it). Anselm's concept of God is apparently identical with that of St. Augustine and Plato, namely, the highest good compared with which nothing superior or nobler can be conceived.

The monk Gaunilo of Marmoutier, in his book, *Liber pro Insipiente*, criticized Anselm's ontological argument on the ground that the argument did not actually prove its conclusion. For example, said Gaunilo, anyone could claim to possess an idea of an unreal object, such as a perfect island, as proof of its existence. Anselm replied that an idea of an unreal object does not prove its existence but that the idea of God does imply his existence because the idea portrays him not as an imaginary or possible object, but as a perfect, indispensable, necessary Being.

Anselm's ontological argument has been resurrected often throughout the history of philosophy. One point of view holds that the idea of God can be regarded as identical with the existence of God, in which case the argument can be accepted as valid. According to this interpretation, the ontological argument could be accepted as true by adherents of the philosophy of Plato or of Hegel, but it would not satisfy critics who consider the argument inapplicable to a personal God, such as the theistic God portrayed in the Bible.

Anselm's Cosmological Argument for God's Existence. In his work, *Monologium,* Anselm accepted the doctrine of Platonic Realism that truth, goodness, beauty, and other universals have an existence of their own independent of the individual things to which the universals may apply. Thus beauty exists irrespective of any specific beautiful object, such as a beautiful sunset. Universals exist in particular objects but they also exist apart from the particular objects in which they are found. For example, many good things exist, some of which possess a greater amount of good than others do. Such things possess only relative good, depending upon their worth, but they are not absolutely good. Inasmuch as some things possess more goodness than others do, there must be an absolute good, a standard which can be used to evaluate their comparative goodness. This absolute good is the *summum bonum* or greatest good, namely, God. Reference to a good or better quality implies God as possessing the highest or best quality.

Anselm's views concerning the attributes and activities of God as the universal reality were very similar to those of Plato and Augustine. God is constantly creating the world, saving it from oblivion through his presence, and imparting reality to all things in the universe through their participation in the ideal, universal archetypes of which they are copies. For example, a person can be just only if he shares in ideal justice as a universal eternal prototype; God himself, however, is justice itself—absolute justice, as well as absolute goodness and wisdom. As attributes of God, or identical with him, these universal ideals are similarly omnipresent and eternal.

Anselm's Theory of Satisfaction. In his significant work, *Cur Deus Homo? (Why Did God Become Man?),* Anselm formulated his *Christological theory of satisfaction,* in an attempt to reconcile the apparent inconsistency between the ideals of divine justice and divine goodness. It seemed to him that man, having sinned against the command of the eternal God, must for that reason suffer the punishment of eternal damnation, but that such a penalty, required by divine justice, would be an affront to the mercy and goodness of God. To solve this dilemma, Anselm set forth the doctrine of *representative satisfaction,* which stated that the infinitely good God as a substitute for humanity represented the human race so that man would be enabled by means of the virgin birth to free himself from the stain of original sin—a process of sacrificial suffering for which man owes gratitude to God, yet a process which also vicariously satisfies the penalty required by divine justice.

Anselm's Credo: I Believe in Order that I May Understand.
Anselm accepted St. Augustine's view that faith is the only proper basis for rational belief, a view epitomized by the famous motto, *Credo ut intelligam* (I believe in order that I may understand). For Anselm, as for St. Augustine, faith must be accepted as the absolute standard for all rational thought, in contrast to the arguments of the Patristics, who considered reason just as valid as Church doctrine as a source of truth. The authority of the Church is strengthened by acceptance of its assertion that truth is revealed to it directly by God, and that consequently the individual should unconditionally subordinate his judgment to that of the universal Church—in other words, rational philosophical thought must give way to revealed theology.

As we shall see, Anselm's student, Abelard, soon revised the credo to read: I understand in order to believe. Meanwhile, however, another Scholastic philosopher, Roscellinus, attacked the foundations of Anselmian Realism.

ROSCELLINUS—THE PHILOSOPHY OF NOMINALISM

During the second half of the eleventh century A.D. the Nominalist school of philosophy (purportedly founded by Roscellinus) propounded and obtained wide acceptance of their theory that universals are merely names designating the individual things which together constitute a group or class. These staunch antagonists of Realism insisted that a universal or absolute idea is simply a collective name for a general class of things, representing only a mere word or vocal sound (*flatus vocis*) signifying those accidents of substances, that is, those multiple characteristics, which make things members of the same class.

According to the Nominalists, reality consists of individual things, while universals are but names (for a class of things) existing only in the human mind. Thus humanity is a theoretical construction of the intellect, but each individual man is a real entity. Rejecting the doctrine of Realism—*universalia ante rem* (the universal exists before the particular thing)—Nominalism preferred the proposition, *universalia post rem* (the universal exists after the particular thing). Reality for the Nominalists is to be found in the sensory world, not in the ideal world, for the individual things are the realities observed by means of the sense organs. It should be noted that Realism was therefore rooted in Platonic doctrines, Nominalism in Aristotelian doctrines.

Because Nominalism had far-reaching implications which affected Church doctrine adversely, the theologians condemned its founder Roscellinus, who had served as a canon in Compiegne. Among the products of Nominalistic philosophy was the heresy of tritheism— the theory that the three persons in the Godhead (the Trinity) are actually three separate Gods. Furthermore, the Nominalists' theory that only the individual is real means that there could be no genuinely *catholic* or universal Church, that the Church universal is nothing but a mere name, an oral word (*flatus vocis*). Nominalism also held that the doctrine of original sin is false; since in its view individual sins alone are real, then original sin could be nothing but an artificial term communicated by the human voice. Platonic Realism, on the other hand, reserved a basic role for the universals of the Church and the doctrine of original sin and was therefore acceptable to Church authorities despite their rejection of its pantheistic concepts and its belief in universal human salvation by Christ and the immortality (universal) of all humanity.

Our next great Scholastic philosopher, Peter Abelard, attempted to develop a new approach to or middle way between the Realistic doctrine of universals and the Nominalist doctrine of particulars.

PETER ABELARD—THE PRIMACY OF REASON

Peter Abelard (1079–1142), a native of Palais, was the student of the Nominalist Roscellinus and the Realist William of Champeaux. He became the most noted philosopher during the first half of the twelfth century.

Abelard is reputed to have enjoyed a long and popular service as a teacher of philosophy in Paris, and he has been credited with the idea for the University of Paris, which was established in the twelfth century. As secret lover of Heloise, he experienced personal difficulties which impelled him to become a Benedictine monk; as a philosopher with partially Nominalist views, he was condemned for heresy (A.D. 1140) and died while on his way to Rome to defend himself.

Abelard's Rationalism. In his book, *Sic et Non*, Abelard employed a technique similar to the didactic method of Socrates, setting forth the divergent or conflicting theories of the Patristic philosophers and advocating an appeal to reason (not to faith or authority) as a proper means of arriving at the truth regarding the various issues. For each topic, he constructed a balance sheet of *pros* and *cons*. When all the facts about any topic in dispute have been presented, then in the light of the conflicting evidence, reason (as the proper criterion of truth), in this dialectical manner, must determine the conclusion which ought to be drawn; consequently, Abelard's method is that of Rationalism. Abelard's dialectical technique of analyzing issues, as used in his written works, was adopted (with some modifications) by the later Scholastics, such as Peter Lombard and St. Thomas Aquinas.

The Rationalism of Abelard impelled him to reverse the Augustinian-Anselmian dictum, *Credo ut intelligam* (I believe in order that I may understand), formulating his own view, namely, *Intelligo ut credam* (I understand in order that I may believe). Both for Anselm and for Abelard, there could be no real distinction between revealed truth and philosophical truth, for both truths are identical, but Anselm gave faith priority over reason, whereas Abelard accorded superior status to reason. Abelard argued that a doctrine is believed, not because God declares it to be correct, but only because of the dictates of reason. He asserted further that there is no sin in doubting because the person who doubts is thereby led to enquire about, and eventually to discover, the truth.

Rational Religion. Abelard's philosophical Rationalism prompted him to adopt a liberal attitude toward religion, reflected in his emphasis upon the role of free will in the realm of ethics. It was his view that Christianity had not presented new ideas but rather represented the consummation of a long process in the history of religions, that Christianity should be regarded as a democratized form of Hellenic philosophy. To Abelard the ancient Greek philosophers, such as Socrates and Plato, seemed to have been inspired Christs who had taught the basic elements of Christianity, the moral law, long before the beginnings of the Christian Era.

Abelard's Ethical Theory. Abelard considered ethics to be essentially a matter of good will. He believed that ethical conduct means action inspired by a good heart, that is, action motivated by good intentions. In other words, morality is not simply a matter of what a person actually does, the act he performs, but also the purpose or will which directs his action, the intention which motivates him. Consequently, the person who has a clear conscience can do nothing really immoral, even though his conscience (sense of morals, propriety) may be mistaken or deficient and therefore misleading. Abelard pointed out that a person whose will and conscience function harmoniously together must be regarded as virtuous because God judges him by reference not merely to his overt behavior, but rather to the motive, the spirit of good will, prompting his behavior. However, he stated further that in addition to being motivated by good will, by the individual's conscience, an overt act must also be consonant with the principles of right conduct as determined by the will and good pleasure of God. Thus Abelard drew a distinction between moral purpose or responsibility as subjective experience and moral deeds or laws as objective realities. The individual's subjective purpose and love of God impel him to obey God's moral commands, but only divine freedom (God's will) can determine the moral principles themselves, that is, the nature of the moral law.

The Doctrine of Conceptualism. Abelard formulated his doctrine of Conceptualism in an attempt to synthesize the Nominalist views of Roscellinus with the Realist views of William of Champeaux. His technique, *Sic et Non*, called for rational evaluation of both sides of an argument. His method of accepting whatever seemed reasonable in both types of doctrine constituted his own system, *Conceptualism*, a point of view later adopted by Arabian philosophers and also by leading Scholastics such as St. Thomas Aquinas, John Duns Scotus, and other Roman Catholic philosophers.

The medieval philosophers analyzed Conceptualism as a mediating doctrine consisting of a major thesis (*universalia in re*, or the universal exists in the particular object) and two related concepts, namely, the Realist proposition, *universalia ante rem* (the universal exists before the particular object) and the Nominalist proposition, *universalia post rem* (the universal exists after the particular object). For medieval philosophers, universals existed in three ways: (1) in the mind of God as ideals preceding or beyond particular things; (2) as attributes within particular objects in the world of nature; and (3) as concepts after experience with the particular objects themselves. For example, beauty might be viewed as an ideal in the mind of God; it might exist as a fundamental characteristic of an object in nature; and it might be a human concept derived from experience with beautiful objects.

The medieval philosophers were satisfied with Abelard's solution of the conflict between Nominalist and Realist points of view. In modern times, however, the issue has been revived and in contemporary philosophy there is a sharp division between Nominalist concepts of Materialism (and Positivism) and Realist concepts of Idealism.

ARISTOTELIANISM, THE SECOND
PERIOD OF MEDIEVAL PHILOSOPHY

During the second period of medieval philosophy (from 1200 to the fall of Constantinople in 1453) Abelard's Rationalism (which included Nominalist concepts reminiscent of Aristotle's views) continued to exert a predominant influence notwithstanding the fact that his philosophy had been condemned by the Church authorities. At the outset of the thirteenth century, Christian philosophers were unfamiliar with most of Aristotle's works. This situation changed when, at about the middle of the century, Robert, Bishop of Lincoln (Robert Grosseteste) translated Aristotle's *Nicomachean Ethics* into Latin. The Church had condemned Aristotle's *Physics* in 1209, his *Metaphysics* in 1215, but now translations of his works were being encouraged. In fact, Aristotle's works, which had been preserved by Arabian scholars, were acclaimed by the Church as criteria of truth which were to be accepted by all Christians just as they accepted the traditional dogma of the Church. Anyone who contradicted Aristotle was to be adjudged guilty of heresy. Arabian scholars, who interpreted Aristotelian philosophy for the Christian world, were made welcome at the court of Emperor Frederick who presented Latin translations of the great Peripatetic's works to the Universities of Bologna, Oxford, and Paris.

Important Arabian philosophers included Avicenna (Ibn Sina, 980–1037), celebrated physician and interpreter of Aristotle, and Averroes of Cordova (1126–1198), the most distinguished Arabian philosopher of the period, "the commentator of commentators," judge and physician, as well as philosopher. Another notable figure was Algazel of Bagdad (1059–1111), a philosophical Skeptic adhering to a mystical interpretation of philosophy.

During this period of medieval philosophy, a number of Jewish scholars, who derived many of their ideas from the Mohammedan philosophers, acquired considerable influence. The foremost Jewish philosopher of this period was Moses Maimonides (1135–1204), whose classic treatise, *Guide to the Perplexed*, owed much to Aristotelian works interpreted and translated by Arabian philosophers. Jewish scholars, in turn, translated Arabian philosophical writings and passed them on to the Western world.

Among the distinguished Christian philosophers in this period were Albertus Magnus (1193–1280), who taught the greatest of all Scholastics, St. Thomas Aquinas (1225–1274); John Duns Scotus

(1265–1308); William of Occam (1280–1347); and the two mystics, Bonaventura (1221–1274) and Meister Eckhart (1260–1327). Other notable figures included the Franciscan scientist, Roger Bacon (1214–1294) and the pantheistic philosopher, Nicolas of Cusa (1401–1464), known principally for his treatise *De Docta Ignorantia*. The following section will discuss the epochal contributions of St. Thomas Aquinas and the subsequent philosophies of John Duns Scotus, William of Occam, and Nicolas of Cusa.

ST. THOMAS AQUINAS—THE PHILOSOPHY OF INTELLECTUALISM

The high point of Scholastic philosophy was reached in the works of its most illustrious representative, St. Thomas Aquinas, founder of the Dominican tradition. The "angelic doctor" (emulating a number of other scholars of his day) occupied himself with listing (giving the sum of) the body of Church doctrines in his greatest work, *Summa Theologiae*.

The influence of Thomistic philosophy has continued throughout medieval and modern times. (In 1879 the encyclical *Aeterni Patris* issued by Pope Leo XIII cited the philosophy of Aquinas as the official philosophy of the Roman Catholic Church.) Thomistic philosophy owed much to Aristotelianism, especially as interpreted by Arabian philosophers, but in matters of revealed theology Aquinas was guided mainly by the teachings of St. Augustine and St. Paul.

As an eclectic philosopher, St. Thomas made use of concepts developed by many preceding philosophers which he organized as part of a philosophical system designed to establish the fundamental rationality of the world as God's revelation. He held that all created things reveal divine characteristics, that God created the world in order to reveal himself in as many ways as possible. All kinds of life, ranging from the lowest to the highest forms, from vegetation to moral beings, help to reveal God's attributes expressed in our universe, his creation. Thus nature reveals the world of grace.

The Twofold Nature of Truth. Unlike St. Augustine, St. Thomas made no sharp distinction between the natural and divine worlds, nor did he place secular society in opposition to the City of God. All creation, be it natural or supernatural, and all truth, be it revealed or rational, stem from God's personality. Nevertheless, St. Thomas recognized the fact that the supernatural world, the world of grace, is superior to the world of nature, just as revealed truth is superior to rational conclusions, and that the City of God (the

Christian Church) is superior to any secular authority. The two sources ought not to conflict, for revelation, although it is a higher source of truth, does not contradict reason. God sees to it that revealed teachings as presented by the Church never contradict the laws of logic, because such contradictions would negate the attributes of his own personality. Above all, there is an even higher source of truth than these historical revelations, namely, the mystical union by which a person gains immediate intuitive knowledge of God. St. Thomas defined truth as the agreement of an idea with its object. God's ideas are the ultimate, real objects themselves, not merely precise reproductions; therefore, God is truth *per se*.

Since all truth comes from God, the channel for its transmission is not of major consequence; i.e., it does not matter whether God conveys his truth through revelation or through reason. Consequently, unless some error has been made through faulty interpretations, faith will never conflict with reason. Some truths reach us through reason solely, such as those found in natural sciences (e.g., a modern scientist might cite the truth in the formula for hydrochloric acid); other truths become known to us solely through faith or revelation, such as the dogmas of the Church (truths about the Trinity or the Incarnation are examples of these dogmas which transcend human reason). St. Thomas added, however, that some truths are provided through both sources, revelation and reason; thus the existence of God is not merely a revealed truth, for human reason also informs us of his existence.

In this way St. Thomas synthesized the antitheses of his predecessors Anselm (who claimed that a person must first believe or have faith before he can understand) and Abelard (who insisted that it is necessary initially to understand before being able to have faith). Aquinas reconciled these opposing doctrines by accepting both propositions: *credo ut intelligam* (I believe in order that I may understand) and *intelligo ut credam* (I understand in order that I may believe).

Thomistic Metaphysics. The Thomists postulated two kinds of Being: (1) abstract and (2) essential. Abstract Being refers to abstractions, that is, to things that are devoid of any positive essence; examples of such abstractions are poverty, deafness, or other privations. Essential Being refers to any substance (or essence) which is composed of form and matter. Whereas all other things possess a dual nature (comprising both matter and form), God alone is a single essence consisting of pure form. St. Thomas said that matter is only a potential thing and must assume a particular form or shape in order to be real or actual. The innumerable Beings in the universe differ from one another because each had to acquire its own individual form in order to become real instead of merely potential Being. In this process of generation, matter unites with form; the materialization of form gives each object its individuality (*principium individualis*, the principle of individuation), by which one object (such as a person) is distinguished from another. Only God and the angels are individualized without being materialized. All imperfections are caused by materialization; but God, since he is pure form and completely spiritual, is absolutely perfect.

Matter without form, without a universal or ideal aspect, is meaningless, for it is the universal (the ideal in the particular material thing) which gives each object its essence and makes it what it is. The scientist studies this universal aspect (St. Thomas called it a *quiddity* or *whatness*) of an object in order to discover the laws of nature; thus a psychologist describes human nature in terms of man's universal characteristics, but his conclusions are based upon knowledge he has acquired about individual men, including the traits they share with all other men and the physical attributes which differentiate them from others. Only their universal characteristics (their forms) can give objects their order, meaning, and purpose.

St. Thomas regarded all human knowledge as conceptual, consisting of universal forms which constitute the essences of particular things, but he further asserted that these concepts or forms are based upon sense perceptions, that everything which exists in one's understanding must first have appeared to one's senses. He accepted Abelard's view of the relationship between universals and particulars, that is, Conceptualism (or Moderate Realism), including the Aristotelian thesis that Plato's universals can be found only in particular things which thus become actualities detectable in sense experience. For St. Thomas, too, the universal nature, the essence, of a thing exists immanently in the object itself as part of the real world, but this universal characteristic (the substantial form of an object) is also an idea or concept separated from its object when it is abstracted in the human mind. As a part of the real world, the universal essence never exists independently of its object. Yet, before nature was created, these universals (essences) existed in the mind of God as archetypes or ideas which God used in creating the universe. Thus the Moderate Realism of St. Thomas accepts Aristotle's view that universals exist in individual objects (*universalia in re*) but also asserts that universals exist in the mind of God prior to the particular objects (*universalia ante rem*) and in the mind of man (as concepts) after the particular object has been created (*universalia post rem*).

Thomistic Philosophy of Religion. Only God is pure form, complete actuality, hence immaterial and without imperfection. If God's Being were composed of matter, as human beings are, then he would not be perfect because matter is in a state of potentiality (transition) which has not yet become fully actualized. Since God is in need of nothing, and his every possibility has been fully realized, he is complete, that is, perfect.

In contrast to Plato and Aristotle, St. Thomas claimed that God created the world out of nothing (*ex nihilo*), a truth allegedly derived from revelation, inasmuch as reason proves neither that the world was eternal nor that it had a beginning. When he created the universe, God also created time so that the universe and time have coexisted from the beginning of creation. The world of matter must have been created out of nothing, for it could never have arisen out of the spiritual, immaterial nature of God. Inasmuch as God invariably chooses the good (that which his reason designates as absolutely good), this world must be the best possible world, created for the purpose of manifesting the purpose of its maker through the great variety of his creations. St. Thomas pictured the entire universe as consisting of two realms: that of nature (earthly existence) and that of grace (the heavenly world).

God is not only the first cause of the spiritual and material world, but also the final cause, that is, the purpose of its existence. All things tend to become like the Creator in beauty and goodness, approaching complete development or actualization as God intended. The absoluteness of God is found in his absolutely simple Being as a single spiritual essence (which cannot be decomposed or destroyed), in his absolute perfection (which requires no actualization since he is pure act, perfectly actualized), in his absolute intelligence (which unerringly knows all, for God makes no mistakes), in his absolute consciousness (which embraces all creation, rendering him omnipresent), and in his absolute will (which invariably chooses the good as prescribed by his infallible intellect).

Man acquires knowledge of God not only from revelation, but also from his own intellect which proves God's existence by means of reason. Although Anselm's ontological argument for God's existence is impugned by Aquinas, he does offer five arguments which he believes to be cogent and which for the most part he borrowed from

Aristotle, Augustine, and the Arabians. They are (1) the argument of motion, or first cause, (2) the argument of efficient causality, (3) the argument of possibility and necessity, (4) the argument of degrees of perfection, and (5) the argument of design or purposiveness. The first, an aetiological argument, states that God must have existed as a *first cause* because every effect requires a cause and this must have been true of the entire universe. The second argument, similarly causal, states that the material world is contingent, unable to create itself, hence requires something else, a necessary, spiritually uncreated Being to bring it into existence and impel it to continue its progress. The third argument states that there must have been a time when the world did not exist, for all things in the world are mere possibilities dependent on some other objects for their being and development; the fact that the world does exist implies that a necessary or noncontingent Being exists who was capable of creating the world. The fourth argument states that there are degrees of perfection in the world, that there must be a perfect Being as a basis for comparison who makes it possible for the relatively perfect things to exist. The fifth argument states that the presence of design in the world, the fact that objects are designed with a purpose, to function for a given end, implies the existence of an intelligent, competent designer who planned the purpose of each thing that exists. (The modern philosopher Immanuel Kant designated the first three arguments as *cosmological arguments*; the fourth is a *Platonic argument*; and the fifth is known as a *teleological argument*.)

St. Thomas attributed the immortality of man's soul to its immaterial nature; the soul is eternal by its nature, because it is pure form and, unlike material substance, is not subject to destruction. In contrast to plant and animal souls, which cannot be severed from the material to which they adhere, man's soul is pure spirit, an immaterial subsistent form which is the entelechy of the body, yet separable from matter. The intellectual soul (or that aspect of it which conceives of universals) can perform its functions without bodily or material substance and (together with the will) survives to eternity as an immortal Being. Intelligence and will comprise the essence of the soul, and these two qualities join in the individual to distinguish him from the souls of other men. The soul does not exist in a different state before the body. When the body has been properly prepared, the soul is created and infused into it.

The Thomists held that man's original sin is responsible for his need of salvation, which can be attained only through the grace of

God; but God's grace can function only if the free will of the individual assents. It is true that God knows in advance which individuals will refuse his grace, but he does not doom anyone irrevocably to damnation. God's grace is made available through the Church's sacraments. Despite the fact that some persons do choose a path which leads to eternal punishment, nevertheless the goal of all moral and religious endeavor is the attainment of universal salvation, the resurrection of soul and body.

Thomistic Ethical Theory. The ethical theory of St. Thomas may be regarded as a Christian interpretation of Aristotelian ethics. Its fundamental premise states that God created everything for a definite purpose. Inasmuch as the end which God prescribed for creatures is good, it is to the benefit of all creatures to direct their lives so as to achieve his purposes for them. Since man is part of nature and is God's creation, it is the moral duty of man to realize that true nature which God has accorded him. The goal of every creature is to seek what is good for itself; and inasmuch as man's highest good is God, his ultimate objective must be to attain *the vision of God,* an accomplishment only partially attainable in this earthly life, but perfectly attainable in the life to come. Moreover, the attainment of true understanding of and communion with God may be subjectively accomplished in the present life by becoming like him as much as possible, for this is not only holiness, but goodness in the sense of a state of grace or blessedness, i.e., a state of supreme happiness resulting from the fullest possible realization of man's true self.

Nonrational beings, such as plants and animals, also seek their own good and by achieving full splendor and beauty attest to the glory of God; but man, unlike subhuman beings, possesses a free will whereby he may choose either to diverge from his true goal or to pursue it rationally. Man has yet another advantage over other animals in that he possesses intellect, which he can perfect and exercise by means of contemplation; thus he has the power to understand and think about God, his highest good, and decide upon the proper direction of his progress toward perfection, this being a holy exercise that leads to his highest blessedness. Nevertheless, man's happiest state comes with his vision of God, an accomplishment reserved for the future life since in this life he can gain only analogical (logical or rational) knowledge of God, whereas in the life to come his soul has its immediate encounter with God—that is, the beatific vision then comes to him immediately through intuition. To see God is to love him, for we cannot have an intuitional or contemplative vision of God without loving him. God, man's highest good and his life's objective, makes man a blessed Being, and blessedness always brings with it supreme happiness.

Moral actions result from intellectual deliberation and choice, so that only free rational beings are capable of morality. Rational action is good because it conforms to the dictates of God's unerring reason. The divine law, the product of God's reason, consists of the moral commandments prescribed in the Bible. In addition, some moral principles, such as the law of self-preservation, are found in nature. Since all natural laws proceed from God, they are moral edicts which call for obedience. All natural law is moral law for man to obey; to go contrary to natural law is to run counter to moral law. Human laws, those statutes enacted by men in legislative bodies, also possess moral connotations. Indirectly, these, too, emanate from God, for all earthly power exists by God's permission.

As in the case of God, whose intellect holds priority over his will (St. Thomas emphasizes intellectualism), so, too, man's intellect determines the good, while his free will chooses according to the dictates of his intelligence. St. Thomas, accepting Augustine's view, regards evil, not as a substance with its own essence, but as a lack of good or as a defective good. When a human being or any other creature responds according to his prescribed or true nature, he achieves what is truly good for him. But when he does not follow his true nature and goal, and instead wills an evil action, his deed is lacking in the correct guidance which his reason, following the divine law, could have provided. Everything seeks its own good as its aim, but when a person pursues evil, he does not truly intend it, for he mistakenly thinks it to be good for him. No one really desires evil; he misconstrues it as good for himself. St. Thomas' name for conscience is *synderesis,* that aspect of reason which judges moral issues and enjoins man to choose good and avoid evil.

St. Thomas classified sins into venial and mortal types. The *venial* are pardonable, because suitable reparations may be made, but the *mortal* cannot be pardoned, and, consequently, stain the soul. He also described three kinds of virtue: theological, ethical (or moral), and intellectual. The theological virtues are infused in us by God and have a supernatural objective; they are faith, hope, and love, but the greatest is love. The ethical virtues are identical with Plato's: temperance, courage, prudence, and justice, the highest being justice. The intellectual virtues are wisdom, science, and understanding. All virtues function for the same end, that of directing man to attain his own good, namely, God.

In agreement with Aristotle, St. Thomas claimed that the contemplative life is the highest and best, that is, the most blessed and happiest. It is this contemplative life which brings us closest to God where the soul, unhampered by the senses, can enjoy God in deep mystical contemplation. The practical life of sense experience depends on the love of man, but the life of contemplation, based upon the love of God, is superior. Self-denial of earthly goods (the ascetic life) gives one rapid access to blessedness, although the monastic ideal of poverty and celibacy is reserved for the few. But if all men were to abandon sex and procreation (a moral obligation prescribed by natural law), then it would be immoral even for the few (such as the clergy) to frustrate the procreative goal of sex. Nevertheless, man's highest good is not to be found in the present world, but in the life to come, the present life being regarded as a pilgrimage to the world to come wherein man will find his greatest good—God and eternal blessedness. Human life, then, is a procession from the world of nature to the world of grace, from want to satisfaction, from imperfection to perfection.

Thomistic Social and Political Philosophy. Accepting Aristotle's *Politics* and St. Augustine's *City of God* as guides, Aquinas described the ideal State. He agreed with Aristotle that man is a political being who seeks the fulfillment of his life in a society. The goal of the State is to achieve the common good, to establish peace and security, and to protect the people against enemies, foreign or domestic. Monarchy is the preferred form of government, but constitutional safeguards must be enforced in order to prevent deterioration into tyranny. In the good State, the aristocrats, few in number and well qualified, assist the monarch in his duties. Even a bit of democracy is allowed in that the people are permitted to choose their leader, but democracy as such is not widely practiced, for it would be contrary to nature since in nature some persons are born superior and others inferior, and consequently, some are chosen by nature to be leaders, others to be followers.

Societies are not deliberately chosen but arise out of man's need to realize more fully his true, potential nature. All societies were established by God for man's good; therefore all laws, not only natural and divine, but also human laws, those statutes enacted by men, must be obeyed since they are designed to attain human good and ultimately (directly and indirectly) emanate from God.

The monarch's rule should be consistent with the divine purpose of the State, namely, the realization of man's highest good. Since man's chief good, however, is found in the life to come—God and the concomitant blessedness arising from the vision of God—the eternal institution of the Church is superior to the temporal political institutions of society. Consequently, the Church, deputized by God as his emissary on earth, is gaining control over all earthly secular power, requiring the subordination of temporal to ecclesiastical rulers. Secular rulers must remain subservient to the Church, the superior of the two divinely established social institutions; accordingly, an excommunicated ruler no longer has any claim upon the loyalty of his subjects. (Note the repudiation of St. Augustine's contention that the State is not a divine institution, but merely a derivation of man's sinful nature. From Paul St. Thomas derived the theory that all earthly power is instituted by God.)

JOHN DUNS SCOTUS—THE PRIMACY OF WILL

John Duns Scotus, the severest critic and opponent of Thomism, denied the primacy of the intellect over the will and, on the contrary, attributed to the will decisive control over the intellect. Scotus was a master of dialectic, accorded the title of *doctor subtilis* (the subtle doctor).

Scotus was a native of Dunston in Northumberland (or perhaps Dun, in northern Ireland), became a monk of the Franciscan order, and taught at Oxford, Paris, and Cologne. Although he died in 1308, at the early age of forty-three, among the philosophers of the second period of medieval philosophy Scotus ranked second only to St. Thomas. According to some scholars, he was the most important thinker of the Middle Ages.

The Methodology of Scotus. The criterion of truth for Scotus was the authority of the Church, which he accepted as the supreme standard of philosophical reasoning. The dogma of the Church was sacred and inviolable; consequently, it enjoyed a status beyond question or debate, as the court of final appeal. Philosophy must be subordinated to theology because natural reason is incomplete unless aided by revelation. Regarding questions of faith, logic can neither prove nor disprove such issues. Nevertheless, reason and revelation need not conflict. The articles of faith or dogma, including belief in the existence of God, cannot be proved if proof means the kind of demonstrable evidence found in mathematical propositions. Scotus pointed out that reason, though powerless to establish the truth of dogmas, is equally unable to disprove them. Philosophy must then be regarded as a science, within which logic is given a scientific realm of its own; but philosophy cannot attain the highest realm, that of theology, including its many articles of faith such as beliefs in the Trinity, the Incarnation, creation, immortality, and the existence of God.

Like the modern philosopher Immanuel Kant, Scotus was chiefly a critic, the dominant characteristic of his philosophy being the criticism of the thought of other systems, particularly that of his main antagonist, St. Thomas Aquinas. On most issues, the Church favored Thomistic philosophy over Scotism. (One exception was the Scotist doctrine of the immaculate conception of the virgin birth which the Roman Catholic Church adopted.) It was St. Thomas, not Scotus, who won sainthood.

The Individualism of Scotus.   Like other great thinkers of his time, Scotus accepted the Conceptualist view that universals exist *before things* (as *forms*) in the mind of God, *in things* (as their essence in nature), and *after things* (as concepts which the mind forms by means of mental abstraction). For Scotus, however, the essence (what St. Thomas called the *quiddity* or *whatness*) or universal nature of an object (e.g., the idea of humanity applied to the nature of individual men) is displaced by an emphasis upon the *thisness* (*haecceitas*), the specific characteristics of each object—thus the personality of Socrates as an individual is emphasized, in addition to his qualities as a human being. The individual (the *thisness*) is in fact the ultimate reality, an irreducible ultimate fact which cannot be explained any further. Individuals do not owe their existence to universals or principles. The ultimate fact is that as individuals their *thisness* or reality distinguishes them from all other individuals. Scotus disagreed with St. Thomas' claim that matter is the principle which makes an object different from others similar to it. He further disagreed with St. Thomas' view that angels and souls are pure form completely devoid of matter. Scotus argued that only God is pure form since only he is completely actualized; all other Beings, including angels and all created spirits, are not completely immaterial Beings, for their potentiality is never absolutely realized. Matter, for Scotus, is the material substance of each individual object.

Scotus agreed, on the other hand, that universals must also be real in their own right, for otherwise empirical science would be either impossible or at most a compendium of logical theory formulated without the necessity of factual observation. The universals or ideas in the mind correspond to real facts in our outer world of experience, thus revealing truth (Scotus' formulation of the correspondence theory of truth). From the knowledge of particular objects, we acquire knowledge of universal principles, but in reality the ideal (or the realm of the universal) and the particular are inextricably united, for the universal is devoid of reality without the individual, and vice versa.

The Primacy of Will over Intellect. In opposition to the intellectualism of St. Thomas, Scotus maintained that both in God and in the nature of man the will holds primacy over the intellect. If this were not the case, then the will would not be genuinely free, but would be controlled by the intellect, a force extraneous to itself. Scotus held that the intellect subserves the will, not the other way around. God wills and his intellect obeys. God is not bound by the dictates of his reason, but chooses freely. God's choice becomes the moral standard and the basis for all creation. St. Thomas erred in describing this as the best possible world, for the arbitrary choice of God brought it into existence. If God so desired, he could create other things besides the present universe. Consequently, Abelard, too, erred in assuming that what God actually created is the only thing that he could have created—that what he created was inevitable.

Inasmuch as the will of God is absolutely free, then it is inscrutable; no possible reason can be found for his choices. It is precisely for this reason that logic will never be able to ascertain the reason for God's actions. All that man can do is to study the facts of nature empirically as his experience indicates them to him, and state them as facts, not as *necessary* explanations, because God could have created a different kind of universe if he had so desired. Not only the laws of science but also the laws of morality depend upon the capricious will of the divine. Thus Scotus formulated the doctrine of *accidental creation*, that it was not necessary for God to create the world the way it happens to be or to create any world at all.

According to Scotus, a thing is good because the inscrutable and absolute will of God commands it. God's will is free, not controlled by reason or anything else. Whatever God wills becomes good automatically by virtue of his willing it. For example, if God were to commit murder, then it would be good, simply because God willed it. The good is not rationally determined in God, but is willed into existence merely by being God's choice. The moral law is valid because God's will decreed it, not because reason or anything else discovered it.

The controversy between the point of view of Scotus (voluntarism) and that of St. Thomas (intellectualism) frequently reappeared, initially among the German Idealists: e.g., Schopenhauer's Panthelism (all is will) conflicted with Hegel's Panlogism (all is reason). Scotus' influence was immediate: his contemporary, the Dominican bishop William Durand of St. Pourcain abandoned Thomism and built his philosophical system on the premise, *to exist means to be an individual.* William of Occam, another of Scotus' disciples, carried Scotism to its extreme, postulating an unadulterated Nominalism, a reversion to the doctrine of Roscellinus which had lain dormant for over two centuries. Scotus' influence has continued into modern philosophy down to the present.

WILLIAM OF OCCAM

The Scholastic controversy over the doctrine of universals reached its final stage in the philosophy of William of Occam, *doctor invincibilis,* a Franciscan student of Scotus (born at Occam in the county of Surrey, England, about 1280). The *venerable inceptor* (so called by his followers) took sides in the violent conflict then in progress between Church and State. Seeking refuge from the Pope, he fled to Louis of Bavaria for protection with the proposition: "Do thou defend me by thy sword, and I will defend thee with my pen." (Sometimes referred to as the "first Protestant," he lived at the Court of Bavaria until his death in 1347.) Many of Occam's ideas were eventually taken up and systematically developed by the modern Empiricist philosopher John Locke and formed the basis for Positivism.

Occam's Terminism. Occam constructed his philosophy upon the premise that only particulars exist, that the individual, not the universal, is real. The universal is a mere abstraction, a term used to express a group of similar individuals; hence the appellation *Terminism* has been applied to this type of Nominalism. Universals are terms or conventional signs which refer to the sum of a given species. Thus, instead of describing every individual person, we can employ a word sign which refers to the entire gamut of individuals designated by the term *human being.*

The logical outcome of Occam's Nominalism was Skepticism, including scientific agnosticism, the theory that science cannot gain truth or knowledge; if scientific laws are not universal principles, but only words identifying a number of individual things, then universal laws of science do not exist. Scientists cannot study man as such but only this or that individual, nor can they generalize or apply universals to individuals as members of a class. The Skeptic asserts that it is impossible for a botanist to study a plant species as a whole, but only the characteristics of this or that individual plant, for universal characteristics do not exist. All universals are merely terms of description, not real entities existing in particular objects.

Occam, a devout Franciscan, believed that he was supporting religion by divorcing knowledge from theology, which seemed to him to be a false science. God must be accepted on the basis of faith, not proof, because theological beliefs are not subject to demonstration. He believed that through Skepticism he was opening the door to faith, which belongs to man, not to science, the province of God. But the Church condemned Occam's system, Terminism, which in fact marked the close of the Scholastic era. By opposing the Scholastic attempts to prove Christian dogma and insisting that they be accepted on faith, he left the way open for all other problems to be dealt with through the empirical data of science. Occam's ideas concerning the Deity are almost identical with those of his teacher, Scotus. God, an omnipotent Being, whose will is superior to the intellect, with boundless freedom decrees what shall come into existence either as a fact of nature or as a principle. Nothing being self-evident, we cannot through logical necessity ascertain or anticipate God's creative activity; that is, we cannot discern the reality of the world through sheer logic without the evidence of empirical data.

Occam's Razor. A universal does not exist within an object, but is merely an idea, a mental abstraction existing only in the mind. The Realists are mistaken in assuming that abstract ideas or universals exist in objects external to the mind of man. There is no justifiable reason for assuming the existence of such alleged realities. Occam's razor is the principle which states that hypothetical realities must be kept to a minimum, that the simplest explanation is the best. Abstract ideas are not essential to the existence of real objects, nor do they help to explain reality. Universals, being superfluous, must therefore be shaved, eliminated, from our interpretation of our experience.

First and Second Intentions. Occam agreed with Scotus that the reality of individual things is known to us intuitively, that their basic forms are presented to the mind of man directly and immediately (by sense experience), rather than through the instrument of *intelligibles* (ideas) or Platonic class concepts. The particular object itself, which is related to us in our experience, produces an idea which represents it in our minds. Thus a specific tree standing before me produces in my mind an idea of it when I close my eyes. We may call this relation of my mental idea to its particular object, the tree, a relation of the *first intention*. But I may have a general idea about the nature of a tree without necessarily thinking of any specific tree, and such ideas which refer to abstract classes, to ideas about things such as a tree, rather than to a specific tree, have a relation called the *second intention*. Ideas of the second intention are merely arbitrary and relate to individual ideas, but the individual ideas themselves relate directly to real individual objects.

On the basis of first and second intentions, Occam distinguished between a *real* and a *rational* science. A real science pertains directly to individual real things which are known through immediate intuition, while a rational science deals with abstract concepts, organizing and describing the immanent relations which prevail among the various abstract ideas without direct sense experience.

NICOLAS OF CUSA

The distinction between first and second intentions, as expounded in Occam's Terminism, was taken up and developed further in the philosophical system (Idealistic Nominalism) of Nicolas of Cusa (1401–1464), who held that the only true knowledge of science consists of the inner world of ideas. Such ideas, although they serve as signs denoting individual things in the external world, are nevertheless different from the individual objects which they represent. Moreover, these *ideas* exist only in the mind. Consequently, Occam's Terministic Nominalism erred in assuming that knowledge concerns the world of external objects, for the mind knows only what is contained within itself, its own ideas—conjecture and representations—not individual things, but images of individual things. Accordingly, human knowledge is based upon ideas of things, rather than the real things themselves. It is only through knowledge of these ideas (through knowledge of nonreality) that a person can know the real world. Man, by means of mental representations, mirrors the real world. One must transcend rational science to reach the inexpressible, signless, ultimate reality—that is, true Being—God.

As a Pantheist, Nicolas of Cusa believed the world to be a copy of God, but he attempted to distinguish God from the world by claiming a different essence for each. He viewed God as a unity, the harmonious synthesis of opposites in an absolutely infinite and unique being, the absolute reality by which possibilities are actualized. As a mystic, who used Nominalistic doctrines to prove that reason can never obtain knowledge of God, Nicolas held that God must be sought through immediate intuition, through an ecstatic *vision without comprehension*. He referred to this state of mind as *learned ignorance*, a state in which rational thought is transcended and ultimate reality (God) is encountered. Nicolas adhered to a *negative theology* which taught that we can discern what God is not, rather than what he is. The infinite God, transcending our knowledge of him, leaves us in a state of *learned* or *instructed ignorance*.

Nicolas of Cusa may be said to have been the last major philosopher of the medieval period (although some scholars regard him as a Renaissance philosopher), for his philosophical ideas were Scholastic and definitely of a medieval vintage. His Idealistic Nominalism represented a futile attempt to synthesize the conflicting elements of Scholasticism in order to restore it as a perfectly integrated and unified whole. That attempt marked the final disintegration of the Scholastic system and the last stage of medieval philosophy.

Chapter 7

Renaissance Philosophy

The period of Renaissance philosophy (a transition period extending roughly from the fall of Constantinople in 1453 to the beginnings of the Enlightenment in 1690) saw the rebirth of Greco-Roman culture, the revival of an independent spirit of learning, the renewal of interest in the humanities, and with the downfall of Scholasticism, the termination of the subserviency of philosophy to theology and to the authority of the Church. Philosophy developed in a natural progression free from the yoke of ecclesiastical dogmatism. Large segments of the Roman Catholic Church, stimulated by the thinking of reformers such as Martin Luther and John Calvin, attempted to substitute Biblical for Church authority. It is worth noting that seeds of the Renaissance had been sown in the philosophy of John Duns Scotus with its emphasis upon the separation of philosophy from theology, of reason from faith, of independent thought from dogma, and that, contrary to his own expectations, the movement generated by his thought led away from the Church rather than toward it.

The Renaissance may be divided into the Humanistic period, from 1453 to 1600 (that is, to the death of Giordano Bruno), and the Natural Science period, from 1600 to 1690 (that is, to the publication of Locke's *Essay on the Human Understanding* which marked the beginnings of the Enlightenment). Philosophy during the Humanistic period was *man-centered,* emphasizing the place of man in the universe, while that during the Natural Science period was *cosmos-centered.* In both periods, philosophers turned their attention from theological studies of heaven, the life to come, God, the Church, and supernatural things to the study of man and nature, the earthly needs of man, nature's relationship to man, and scientific methodology. Even the language of the Church, Latin, was discarded by the academic world for the various national languages, as the power of the Church declined. Rome was losing mastery over the Church as new centers of religion appeared in Wittenberg (with

Martin Luther and Philip Melanchthon), Geneva (with John Calvin), and London.

Scientific inquiry developed in all directions. While the universities of Paris and Oxford remained as great centers of learning, new institutions were established in Vienna, Heidelberg, Prague, and throughout Italy as well as Protestant Germany. Although for a time the Renaissance in Italy was impeded by the Counter-Reformation led by Church authorities, nevertheless, there as in Germany the Humanistic trend had a profound influence. During the seventeenth century the scientific point of view became dominant in England, France, and the Netherlands. Both groups, the Humanists and the scientists, accepted new points of view—new methods of inquiry, new knowledge, new standards for the new man in his new universe. There was a difference in their approach and emphasis, for the Humanists sought to revive Hellenic culture, while the scientists relied mainly upon empirical observation and rational methods of discovery.

Leading Humanists included Leonardo da Vinci (1452–1519), Pico della Mirandola (1463–1494), Niccolo Machiavelli (1469–1527), Nicolas Copernicus (1473–1543), Thomas More (1478–1535), Martin Luther (1483–1546), Theophrastus of Hohenheim (Paracelsus) (1493–1541), Philip Melanchthon (1497–1560), John Calvin (1509–1564), Giordano Bruno (1548–1600), Tommaso Campanella (1568–1639), and Jacob Boehme (1575–1624).

Among the most influential philosophers adhering to the strictly scientific school were Galileo Galilei (1564–1642), Francis Bacon (1561–1626), Hugo Grotius (1583–1620), Thomas Hobbes (1588–1679), and Isaac Newton (1642–1727).

The great philosopher René Descartes (1596–1650) was a contemporary of these Humanist and scientific philosophers of the Renaissance, but his approach differed markedly from theirs, and he is acknowledged to be the father of modern philosophy. In fact, some scholars fix the period of modern philosophy as beginning in the seventeenth century with Descartes' teachings, particularly his *Meditations on the First Philosophy* (1641). The other major philosophies during the Renaissance placed their primary emphasis upon either or both of two kinds of law: civil or juridical law and natural law; the former embraces social and political philosophy, the latter, scientific method and natural philosophy (or the philosophy of science).

SOCIAL AND POLITICAL PHILOSOPHY OF THE RENAISSANCE

Among the most significant writings on social and political problems (the philosophy of civil or juridical law) during the Renaissance were Machiavelli's *The Prince* (completed in 1513) and his *The Discourses* (1532); More's *Utopia* (1518); Francis Bacon's *New Atlantis* (1623); Campanella's *City of the Sun* (1623); and Hobbes' *Leviathan* (1651). The works of More, Bacon, and Campanella clearly reflected the influence of Plato's writings, particularly his *The Republic;* Machiavelli and Hobbes also adopted Plato's thesis that social arrangements should be founded upon the nature of man.

NICCOLO MACHIAVELLI

Machiavelli, the most important political philosopher of the Italian Renaissance, had a notable political career (1494–1512), including service as Secretary of the Chancellery of the Council of Ten at Florence before turning to a new career as author of significant works on law and politics.

The Prince. The book for which Machiavelli is best known, *The Prince*, was dedicated to Lorenzo II in the futile hope of regaining lost favor with the Medici family. The book described the activities of Caesar Borgia and his father Pope Alexander VI, and attested to the corrupt practices common in Renaissance Italy. It offered a philosophical justification for the low moral standards prevalent at that time and a practical guide to unscrupulous rulers who wished to gain or retain power over the masses.

Machiavellianism, as this philosophy is opprobriously termed, states that in politics *the end justifies the means*, any means, no matter how deceitful, lawless, or unscrupulous. If a person successfully achieves highest political power, then it is of little consequence how he achieved it, because the masses, who allow themselves to be deceived, will then obey and respect their ruler. The only sin consists of failure to achieve political power, for the person who fails can be destroyed. Machiavelli, like the modern philosopher Nietzsche, admired power as an end in itself, to be achieved without regard to moral standards or ethical character.

Machiavelli held that a wise ruler will eliminate those who assisted him in gaining his superior position, for these persons will know the evil techniques employed by the ruler and could be a threat to his dominion. The ruler must have the characteristics of a fox (in order to outwit his opponents with cunning and stealth) and a lion (in order to intimidate his enemies). He must also disseminate a public image of himself as a man of high dignity, virile (without any hint of effeminacy), and endowed with a maximum of the following five virtues: mercy, faith, integrity, humanity, and religion. It is not necessary that he possess any of these qualities, but he must give a convincing impression that he is virtuous. In fact, if he were to be truly virtuous, he would court disaster. The masses, being gullible, can readily be hoodwinked into believing the ruler's noble image of himself. The few wise persons among them, those who may see through the false veneer of virtue to the evil personality of the ruler, will not dare to revolt against him owing to their paucity of numbers as well as to the military and police protecting the ruler, with whom, indeed, the people always prefer to side. The prince should maintain his popularity among the masses by making public appearances at festivals and shows, and granting awards to persons who excel in the arts. He must personally bestow favors on others, but he will delegate to others those actions that will be resented by the masses, for in this way the ruler will win the support of the multitude while they will blame their troubles upon other officials whom the ruler can promptly dismiss and thereby gain still more favor with the people. Since most people wish to live in peace, the ruler must publicly advocate peaceful policies, but since his military forces will prefer war because of the opportunity for them to obtain more promotions and awards, he must make more militant speeches to them. The ruler may make whatever promises he may deem fit to the people, but he need not fulfill them for two reasons: first, he can always find excuses which the gullible masses will accept; and second, he is justified in breaking faith with his people because they are themselves corrupt. In brief, the end justifies the means.

The Discourses. Machiavelli stated that the political philosophy set forth in *The Prince* is not applicable in a State where the citizens are good, but only where they are corrupt. For a society of virtuous persons, he recommends a quite different system, a republic instead of the tyranny espoused in *The Prince*. In *The Discourses on the First Decade of Living* he described the democratic republic, a society of free people, as superior to any other form of government. In such a State, the rulers must obtain the people's consent. The task of those in government is to establish cohesiveness, stability, and an organic unity, which will assure the survival of the State. Military power will also guarantee social survival, for the conduct of a nation in wartime tests the state of its health. A national religion is also desirable as a means of solidifying the masses. But the weaker virtues, the Christian virtues of humility and pacificism, are undesirable because they threaten the military strength of a nation. The people need to develop their will to survive, and they must employ ruthless measures when necessary. Decadence and corruption destroy civilizations, whereas rejuvenation and power cause new ones to arise.

SIR THOMAS MORE

Perhaps the most outstanding philosopher in England during the Humanistic period of the Renaissance was Sir Thomas More, an Oxford-educated lawyer whose experience in Parliament and as Chancellor of England contributed to his qualifications for leadership in the field of political philosophy. His famous work, *Utopia* (1518), related the experiences of Raphael Hythloday, a sailor who inadvertently found an island in the south seas, named Utopia (Noplace). Returning home, Hythloday recounted his adventures on the island, describing the customs, institutions, and moral standards which he had observed.

Many of the practices were reminiscent of Platonic ideas on social and political questions; for example, Communism was in vogue, as advocated by Plato in *The Republic*. These islanders owned everything in common. Private property had been abolished in favor of equality, for the sake of the public good. The homes in which people lived were changed every decade to prevent them from developing a sense of ownership. The clothing was prescribed so that there would be one uniform style for men, another for women, a third for married individuals, and another for the unmarried, without a change of clothing either for fashions or for seasons. Each family was held responsible for making its own clothes.

The workday consisted of only six hours, three of them to be scheduled before dinner and three after dinner, this arrangement made possible because no one was idle, and there were no indolent rich to be waited upon. Everyone retired at eight o'clock and enjoyed eight hours of sleep. One hour after supper was given over to recreation, and morning lectures were made available to those who wished to attend. There were forty or more workers on each farm, supervised by an old and wise couple as master and mistress. The society was patriarchal, the father being the head of the household, which included his married sons and their families.

The maintenance of peace was a basic goal. Wars, when necessary, were to be waged by employing mercenaries. Violent occupations, such as hunting and killing for food, were carried on by slaves, two of whom were employed for this purpose on each farm. (Slaves were persons who had been condemned to death either in Utopia or in some other land, but who preferred to live as bondmen instead of facing execution for their crimes.) War was regarded as justifiable for three reasons only: (1) to defend one's homeland against an invader; (2) to liberate an ally from invading aggressors; and (3) to emancipate an oppressed people from tyranny.

On learning that Christ had repudiated private property, Hythloday attempted with considerable success to convert the inhabitants to Christianity. Although the few atheists on the island were denied citizenship, a variety of religions were practiced there, and each was tolerated. The small number of priests on the island (including male and female priests) were accorded honor, but had no power. The female priests were aged widows; the male priests were considered holy but not very wise.

FRANCIS BACON

About a century after More wrote his *Utopia*, another great English philosopher portrayed the ideal life of people living on an imaginary island. This philosopher, Francis Bacon (1561–1626), was educated in the law at Trinity College of Cambridge University and, like More, became Lord Chancellor of England. Bacon, however, was convicted of bribery and sentenced to life imprisonment. After serving a brief period of his sentence, he was released, retiring to his home in St. Albans where he devoted himself to philosophy. His Utopian work on political philosophy, *The New Atlantis* (1623), which was the product of a lifetime of wide political experience, was completed four years prior to his death.

Bacon's *New Atlantis* (this island was situated in the south seas of the Austral continent) was inhabited by people who sought increased productivity through scientific advancement. The imaginary community attempted to put into practice many of Plato's political ideas. In a college in New Atlantis, the members of the community sought to discover new truths and principles, to find the true causes of things, including the causes of disease, to prolong life and cure illnesses, and to create new inventions, new scientific techniques, and new methods of agriculture. The research work was carried on by twelve students comprising the intellectual aristocracy of the island; but the island was ruled by a wise and competent monarch. From this center the fruits of learning were disseminated throughout the world, the main purpose of trade and contact with foreign lands being to spread the "light" (enlightenment). The people on the island were interested in communistic sharing, but they emphasized sharing of knowledge rather than property; they encouraged foreign trade and commerce as a means of exchanging knowledge, and they took care to prevent corrupting ideas or influences from infiltrating their homeland. They believed that civilization progresses through science, which unites man with his fellows and with God, and that science will enable man to discover natural laws, follow them, and thus control nature itself.

Bacon's *New Atlantis* gained immediate influence, reflected, for example, in the fact that the college of science which he suggested led eventually to the founding of the Royal Society and other centers of learning.

THOMAS CAMPANELLA

A third Utopian philosopher reflecting Platonic influence was Thomas Campanella (1568–1639), an Italian patriot and native of Calabria who in his youth entered the Dominican order. Despite the intercession of the pope in his behalf, he was imprisoned for twenty-seven years by the Spanish Inquisition, during which time he wrote *The City of the Sun* (1623), the work for which he is best known. Compelled to leave Rome on his release from prison, he went to Paris, where he was befriended by Richelieu, the king granted him a pension of 3,000 livres, and the Sorbonne vouched for the orthodoxy of his writings.

Campanella's social philosophy was decidedly communistic, more so than that of his two Utopian predecessors. His story told about a Genoa sea captain on a distant island who was led to the City of the Sun, a city where no person received more than he deserved or more than his needs required. Neither poverty nor financial wealth—the two main evils—existed. According to Campanella, poverty makes men liars, thieves, and worse, while riches make them wanton, boastful, deceptive, insolent, and slanderous. On the island there was no ownership of private property, no private houses. Manual labor was considered honorable; there was no place for slavery, no place for a priesthood, no place for nobility. Every man was motivated by love of country to perform the work for which he was qualified and prepared. The rulers were persons who had the best academic and practical education. Nothing was left to chance. Thus, in choosing people to enter upon a vocation, or even in selecting a marriage partner, the character of each individual and the consequences of each decision were carefully studied. Four hours of daily work was sufficient to support the community since all adults worked and there were no idle rich. In this socialistic land there were no tyrannical or hereditary rulers, not even an established religion, but only a Christian ethics based on reason and natural law. Essential tasks of government were entrusted to learned persons elected by the people.

THOMAS HOBBES

Thomas Hobbes (1588–1679) ranks with Francis Bacon as the most important British philosopher prior to the time of John Locke. He wrote his great political treatise, *The Leviathan* (1651), in France, hoping that it would please Charles II, who on the contrary was displeased with the work inasmuch as it advocated the replacement of any government unable to provide peace and safety for the citizens. The book also antagonized Roman Catholics, for one section included a trenchant criticism of the Church. Hobbes subordinated the Church to the State. The king was to decide upon a State religion, but even that decision could be only a temporary legal procedure, for the permanent or true religion was to be reserved for the Last Judgment.

Although Hobbes agreed with Plato's *Republic* in basing political theory upon the nature of man, he developed his own philosophy of materialism, the belief that ultimate reality consists exclusively of inert extended substances: "whatever exists is matter, and whatever changes is motion." Implied in Hobbes' Materialism is the doctrine which was later to be termed *epiphenomenalism*, the theory that mental or spiritual entities are not realities in their own right but merely by-products of matter which perish when their material base is destroyed. Consequently, the soul or mind is simply body in motion, the activity of a physiological system. A ultilitarian in spirit, Hobbes accepted only pragmatic or useful points of views; consequently he accepted religion as only a practical instrument or means, denying the validity of theology as a science of God.

Hobbes pointed out that man, like other animals, is made of body in motion, that his will is a physical force, that he has the same natural right as other animals to kill or be killed so that the strongest will prevail in accordance with nature's law: *might makes right,* for in a state of nature whatever comports with natural law is moral. A different kind of morality comes into being only when men enact laws and agree to obey them for sake of self-preservation —the first law of nature.

Hobbes' theories constitute a "selfish system of ethics." Since men in groups are roughly equal in power, despite individual differences, war places everyone's life in jeopardy. Moreover, weaker persons could use cunning or ingenious weapons to subdue or kill their stronger opponents. Wise men therefore seek to preserve peace, as, for example, by means of a social compact in which each person relinquishes his natural right, the right to kill, harm, or steal from others, provided that the others are willing to reciprocate. This *social contract,* as a form of civil law, restricts the natural liberties of all persons through mutual agreement.

Hobbes regarded the social contract as a negative statement of the Golden Rule: do not do to another what you do not want him to do to you. Thus, men who obey the first law of nature, the law of self-preservation (effected by means of reciprocal self-limitation), go on to practice the second law of nature, the Golden Rule. With these natural laws as a basis, Hobbes formulated thirteen additional laws conducive to a democratic society—as, for example, laws of arbitration, equity, mediation, common ownership, equality, and justice.

Who will guarantee that the members of a society will live up to their social contract? Hobbes asserted that only the Leviathan could insure adherence to the contract. Such authority might be vested in a mortal god or sovereign power, a reigning monarch, who seized control and ruled by force; or it might be vested in a government (by one man or an assembly) instituted by and responsible to the will of the people. The ruler who depends upon seizure and force is entitled to reign only as long as he is able to prevent anyone else from displacing him. Nevertheless, every ruler (Leviathan) is above the law and need not obey it, for he is not a party to the social contract but simply sees to it that his subjects live up to the contract which they have mutually agreed to obey. It is his duty to punish those who transgress the laws of the land.

Hobbes' concept of the social contract had a powerful influence upon the political philosophers of the modern era, including Immanuel Kant and other Western philosophers down to contemporary times.

NATURAL LAW AND
THE PHILOSOPHY OF SCIENCE

Bacon and Hobbes not only were major philosophers in the social and political fields, but also contributed profoundly to the philosophy of science emphasized during the period 1600–1690. Another luminary of that period was Galileo Galilei (1564–1642). Since Hobbes' point of view has been set forth in our discussion of his political theories, the remainder of this section will be devoted to Bacon and Galileo as exponents of scientific method—the inductive method whereby the accumulation and interpretation of specific facts led to the discovery of a universal principle or law of nature. It was their objective to substitute the inductive method for the Aristotelian syllogism and the deductive method of the Scholastic philosophers.

FRANCIS BACON

Bacon was convinced that by means of induction he could open new paths for scientific advancement. In his *Novum Organum* (1620) designed to replace Aristotle's *Organon* as a guide to knowledge, Bacon argued that the sophistries and errors of the past were due to four classes of *Idols*, the Greek term for *false forms*. The Idols are: (1) Idols of the Tribe—defects in the nature of human nature itself, compelling the individual to distort natural phenomena as if they appeared in a false mirror; (2) Idols of the Cave—defects in the experience and background of the individual so that he views nature in a biased way; (3) Idols of the Market Place—defects arising from imperfect and unsuitable communication among men; and (4) Idols of the Theatre—defects attributable to the false ideas and methods of past philosophers whose views lead men into the wrong paths of inquiry.

Bacon's formulation of the inductive method was not limited to the mere enumeration or summation of instances, to the collection of particular objects of the same kind. His three basic principles of induction, eventually incorporated into John Stuart Mill's canons for determining causes scientifically, were as follows: (1) *The Table of Essence or Presence*—stating that when the form of a particular group of similar objects is correctly educed, then a quality concomitant with the form will always be found when the form is present. Thus, when heat (as a cause) is present, warmth (as an effect) will be present. This principle was the forerunner of Mill's Method of Agreement. (2) *The Table of Deviation or of Absence of Proximity* —stating that if the true form of an object is removed, then its quality invariably disappears also. Thus, when heat is absent, warmth will be absent. All negative instances (exceptions) must be taken into consideration. This method anticipated Mill's Method of Difference. (3) *The Table of Degrees or Comparative Instances*— stating that if the true form is increased, the characteristic quality will be proportionately increased, but that if the true form is decreased, the quality will be concomitantly decreased. Thus an increase in heat will increase warmth, while a decrease in heat will decrease warmth. This principle became Mill's Method of Concomitant Variations.

True knowledge is a great asset, for, according to Bacon, "knowledge is power," and the practical utility of scientific knowledge is immense. Through science nature may be brought under man's control, and those social or natural conditions harmful to man ameliorated. The day of the rule of man over nature must come. Man's salvation is to be found in knowledge.

SCIENTIFIC METHOD OF GALILEO, KEPLER, AND NEWTON

Francis Bacon's passionate desire for utility and the practical application of knowledge, blinded him to the vast theoretical value of mathematics. Consequently, he lost sight of the enormous significance which mathematics held for the symbolic understanding of the cosmic order. This achievement was left to Galileo Galilei (1564–1642), the last of the Italians (with the exception of Giambattista Vico, who died in 1744) to achieve great prominence in philosophy prior to the twentieth century. Lack of progress in Italy has been attributed to opposition from the Inquisition, which condemned Galileo privately in 1616, and publicly in 1633.

Galileo, who had served as mathematician and philosopher in the court at Tuscany, taught at the universities of Padua and Pisa. His *mathematical theory of motion*, which represented a decisive advance over Bacon's method of inquiry, grew out of his use of empirical Pythagoreanism, i.e., the application of mathematical to empirical facts about motion. Although Leonardo da Vinci (1452–1519) had noted the problem of finding a mathematical symbolic expression for the cosmic order, it was Johann Kepler (1571–1630) who actually solved the problem by setting forth the necessary mathematical formulae based on the method of induction and thus delineating the laws of planetary motion. Galileo's inductive method was a great success, for it established a constant mathematical relationship applied to a group or entire series of phenomena which remained constantly the same and subject to mathematical measurement; that is, he discovered the laws of change. Whereas *forms* were the objects sought in Bacon's method of induction, Galileo, through his method of analysis, sought the mathematical relationships controlling the simplest, most fundamental phenomena of motion. To his method of induction or analysis, Galileo added a second step, that of the method of deduction or *synthesis*. This second method is not to be confused with the Aristotelian method of syllogistic deduction, but is a method of composition, of synthesis, or of *mathematical deduction*. This second method proved fruitful in determining the movement of astral bodies which could not be observed in an experimental laboratory.

Galileo had taken the laws of nature and placed them in a universal mathematical form; he had composed an ideal construction of them, i.e., a rational principle. He was enabled thus to resolve the age-old problem of the ancient Greeks regarding Being and Becoming; he was successful in applying the principle of Plato and Democritus to Becoming (the changes occurring in nature). Thus, the world is indebted to Galileo for correcting the vagaries of Empiricism by means of mathematical calculations, replacing the sterile Pythagorean number philosophy of the Humanistic period with an empirically valid mathematical theory. Galileo has also been credited, along with Bacon, for John Stuart Mill's Principle of Concomitant Variations. Furthermore, it was Galileo who postulated the law of falling bodies which Isaac Newton (1642–1727) explained as the law of inertia— the first law of motion. Newton, born the year after the death of Galileo, developed combined mathematical and mechanical explanations for the data observed in everyday experience, demanding use of the analytic method prior to the synthetic method. (The analytic method draws conclusions from experiments and observations, whereas the synthetic method attempts to predict phenomena which will result from given causes.)

The preceding discussion of Renaissance philosophy has actually taken us into the era of modern thought; the two periods, Renaissance and modern, cannot be divided satisfactorily along intellectual lines, but must be regarded as one period merging into another.

Renaissance philosophy merged gradually into modern thought, for the Renaissance constituted an era of transition without clear-cut lines of demarcation. For this reason some scholars may even include the philosophy of the Renaissance within the period of modern philosophy. For our purposes, however, modern philosophy may be said to begin with Descartes, who continued the methodology of the Natural Science period of the Renaissance and inaugurated a new era of philosophy as the acknowledged father of modern metaphysics.

Chapter 8

The Continental Rationalists

Modern philosophy may be said to have begun early in the seventeenth century with the work of the Continental Rationalists, the first of whom, Descartes, initiated a long series of attempts to construct comprehensive, integrated systems of philosophy. The seventeenth-century Continental Rationalists were followed by the eighteenth-century philosophers of the Enlightenment (starting with the British Empiricists, continuing in the works of Immanuel Kant, and culminating in publication of his *Critique of Pure Reason* in 1781). The German Idealists dominated in philosophy during the nineteenth century and their influence has extended into contemporary philosophy.

The Rationalist philosophy of Renaissance Continental Europe held that truth is derived from reason, that reason is superior to as well as independent of sense experience, and that knowledge is deducible from *a priori* concepts or necessary ideas. This point of view continued in Germany during the period of the Enlightenment, as reflected in the Rationalism of Hegel. In Great Britain, however, Empiricism (the theory that knowledge depends upon experience) flourished and, during the period of the Enlightenment, clashed directly with the Rationalism of Continental Europe, especially Cartesianism. Eventually the German Idealists, such as Kant, tried to merge and synthesize the Rationalist and Empiricist positions. Thus the Kantian synthesis concluded that valid knowledge is a fusion of understanding (Rationalism) and perceptions (Empiricism).

The new Rationalist emphasis in philosophy received its greatest impetus from the works of three great philosophers: René Descartes (1596–1650), a French Roman Catholic; Benedict Spinoza (1632–1677), a Dutch Jew; and Gottfried Wilhelm Leibniz (1646–1716), a German Protestant. Other notable thinkers of the time were the Cartesian Occasionalists, Arnold Geulincx (1625–1669) and Nicole Malebranche (1688–1715); the mystical Cartesian Skeptic, Blaise

Pascal (1623–1662); and the great systematizer of the philosophy of Leibniz, Christian Wolff (1679–1754).

RENÉ DESCARTES

René Descartes (1596–1650), France's most eminent philosopher, was born in La Haye, Touraine. He was trained in Scholastic philosophy under the tutelege of the Jesuits in La Flèche. Here he also studied mathematics, in which he distinguished himself by founding analytical geometry. From 1629 to 1649 he lived in the Netherlands, where he wrote his chief works: *Discourse on Method* (1637); *Meditations on the First Philosophy* (1641); *Principles of Philosophy* (1644); and the two posthumously published works, *The Passions of the Soul* (written during 1646–1649, and published in 1650) and *The World* (written during 1630–1632 and published in 1664). Notwithstanding his being a Catholic, Descartes' books were placed upon the *Index* by the Roman Catholic Church. Oxford University prohibited the teaching of his philosophy.

Cartesian Methodology and Epistemology. Cartesian (this term for the philosophy of Descartes was derived from the Latin form of his name, *Cartesius*) methodology represented an attempt on the part of Descartes to continue the pursuit of a method which the Natural Science period of philosophy had initiated during the second period of the Renaissance. To Bacon's inductive technique and to Galileo's deductive method, Descartes added his absolute principle of universalizing mathematics, applying it to all disciplines. Descartes explained this point of view in his *A Discourse on the Method of Rightly Conducting and Seeking Truth in the Sciences.*

Rationalism and the Geometric Method. The Cartesian method was that of Rationalism, the attempt to discover truth through the use of reason. From self-evident (axiomatic) truths, which he termed innate ideas, Descartes claimed to have deduced on the basis of rational necessity all other truths. Basically, this was the system of mathematics, of geometric method, applied to the problems of philosophy.

The Cartesian Criterion of Truth. For Descartes, then, the only valid criterion of truth was reason as an immediate intuitive certainty comparable to a person's knowledge of himself—self-consciousness. Rational knowledge is like the mind's indubitable and clear knowledge of its own existence. Whatever is as *clear and distinct* as the mind's consciousness of self must be true. The Rationalism of Descartes was founded upon a belief in the elementary truths of consciousness, which are axiomatic to the mind of man (innate ideas inherent in his personality) and provide him with immediate and rational proof. On the other hand, alleged truths which appear to come from the outer world to our senses are unclear and indistinct, hence unreliable, and we can never know whether or not they correspond to real objects. Innate ideas are clear and distinct, unmuddied by the senses; as such they are true ideas derived from our own nature. Hence, Descartes held that *reason, defined as the innate intuition of clear and distinct ideas,* is the only valid criterion of truth.

Cartesian Rules. Cartesian methodology included four principles or rules: (1) Never accept anything as true which is not known clearly and distinctly to be true. (2) Subdivide complex problems into as many simpler parts as necessary in order to arrive at a satisfactory solution. (3) Arrange ideas in an orderly sequence from the simplest to the more and more complex, with due regard, however, for the natural sequence of events. (4) Take into account the most detailed points or facts and make certain that nothing is omitted.

Cartesian Maxims and Ethics. Descartes, aware that these four principles could not be immediately implemented, suggested that the following practical rules of everyday conduct be regularly practiced: (1) obey the laws and customs of the nation, your religious faith, and your family tradition, and avoid extremes of behavior; (2) stand by the convictions you have formed and be resolute in the course of action you have chosen; (3) adapt yourself and your ambitions to your environment and fortune, instead of defying them; and (4) carefully choose the life work which will be best for you. These rules of conduct reflect Aristotelian and Stoic influences. In fact, Descartes in his *Passions of the Soul,* presented an ethical theory which includes Aristotelian elements. He listed six fundamental emotions (admiration, love, hate, desire, joy, and sadness) from which all other passions are derived. He held that the most nearly perfect or highest emotion is the intellectual love of God, that happiness arises from consciousness of perfection, and that we are virtuous insofar as our reason remains in control of our passions.

Cartesian Opinions. Descartes expressed reactions to the academic disciplines, such as eloquence, poetry, and mathematics, with all of which he was delighted. Theology gained his reverence as an open road to heaven for the ignorant and learned alike. He felt that the revealed truths of theology transcend human reason. But in regard to philosophy, he had little to say except that it lacked any shred of certainty, that all its propositions were subject to dispute. The sciences, too, since they were based upon philosophical principles, seemed to him lacking in their foundations, hence worthy neither of honor nor of cultivation. He condemned the attempt to use science as a means of bettering one's fortune. Finally, like Socrates, he "resolved no longer to seek any other science than knowledge of myself, or of the great book of the world."

The Cartesian Method of Doubt. A skeptical point of view permeates Descartes' *Meditations on the First Philosophy*, but his was not a negative attitude toward the possibility of all knowledge; instead, it reflected an obsession with the need for absolute certainty to counteract the faulty rationalism of the Scholastics, who had arrived at highly dubious or improbable conclusions. Descartes insisted that every idea must be subjected to doubt until its truth or falsity can be demonstrated with the same perfect certainty as a mathematical proof—absolute certainty derived from axiomatic or self-evident truths innately imbedded in the mind at birth without the necessity of sense experience. Ideas based on mere probability, which is inferred from sense perceptions, do not qualify as genuine knowledge.

The Cartesian Cogito. His search for mathematical certainty in metaphysics led Descartes to formulate his famous philosophical proof of the existence of the soul. That proof became the starting point and basic premise of his entire philosophical system.

Descartes attempted to prove existence of the soul by establishing its indubitability. Even if a person denied his own state of consciousness, his own act of thinking, the denial itself would prove that he exists as a thinking Being. One could deny anything else, but not the fact that he doubts or denies a given proposition. For example, Descartes could not prove the existence of his own hands, for they might be hallucinatory or dream objects. But the act of doubting could not be denied; if it were merely an act of dreaming, even then he would still have to exist and think in order to dream. He concluded that everything is subject to doubt except the fact of doubting itself, and that, since doubting is an aspect of thinking, thought itself is the one indubitable undeniable experience. The doubt that one exists is an act of thinking which proves one's existence. Thus, to doubt is to think, and to think is to exist. Accordingly, every time a person doubts, he thereby demonstrates his own Being as a person. Descartes argued ingeniously that even if a person's thoughts were not voluntary acts but were merely ideas imposed upon them by a god or by a diabolical Being in order to deceive him, nevertheless, as soon as the thinker says to himself, "Cogito, ergo sum" ("I think, therefore I exist"), he knows with absolute certainty that he exists. The denial of his own existence would involve a person in a self-contradictory statement impossible for him to believe, for he would have to exist in order to deny his existence.

Innate Ideas.   The Cartesian *Cogito* which proves the existence of the soul beyond all doubt is one example of an innate idea, that is, an idea with which we are born, an idea which does not require sense experience as a basis for its validity. Mathematical axioms are self-evident and do not require factual proof; the same is true of innate ideas, axioms imbedded in the mind at birth. While ideas in general are images or copies of objects of the external world created by sense perceptions, innate ideas have always been internal as part of the self, derived from one's own nature.

They are eternal truths. The innate idea that one's soul exists does not have to be proved by experience external to one's own inner consciousness, and the same is true of other innate ideas. Descartes listed the following innate ideas: (1) God, who is as innate to me as my own soul; (2) *ex nihilo nihil fit* (out of nothing nothing comes), the principle that it is impossible that a thing can originate out of nothing, i.e., the principle that every effect must have a cause; (3) the principle of the impossibility that the same thing can both exist and not exist at one and the same time; (4) the idea that whatever is done can never be undone; and (5) the innate idea of the soul, namely, that when I think, I cannot be nonexistent as long as I am thinking.

Proofs of God's Existence.   Descartes offered two arguments for the existence of God: (1) as an innate idea of an infinite Being, an infinite idea which no finite Being could possibly create; (2) as a perfect Being whose perfection proves his existence.

Descartes explained the first argument as follows: "There only remains, therefore, the idea of God, in which I must consider whether there is anything that cannot be supposed to originate with myself. By the name God, I understand a substance infinite (eternal, immutable), independent, all-knowing, all-powerful, and by which I myself, and every other thing that exists, if any such there be were created. But these properties are so great and excellent, that the more attentively I consider them the less I feel persuaded that the idea I have of them owes its origin to myself alone. And thus it is absolutely necessary to conclude, from all that I have before said, that God exists: for though the idea of substance be in my mind owing to this, that I myself am a substance, I should not, however, have the idea of an infinite substance, seeing I am a finite being, unless it were given me by some substance in reality infinite." [1]

The second argument is comparable to Anselm's ontological argument for God's existence. Descartes pointed out that just as the essence of a geometric figure follows from its definition, so God's existence follows from the clear idea of his Being. From the essence of a triangle, one concludes that the sum of its angles are equal to its two right angles. In the same way we may say that God's existence follows from his essence, because by God is meant an absolutely perfect Being, and perfection necessarily implies existence; since God's existence cannot be divorced from his essence, then he must necessarily exist. The act of defining God as real and perfect implies an existent Being. Thus even the simple possibility of thinking about God's Being is sufficient proof of his existence.

Note that the second argument rests upon the Rationalist criterion of truth, namely, that those propositions are both certain and true which present themselves clearly and distinctly to reason or man's consciousness. In precisely this same manner the truths of mathematics are demonstrated.

Metaphysical Dualism and Cartesian Mechanism. Ultimate or ontological reality, according to Descartes, consists of substance. In his *Principles of Philosophy* he defined substance as "a thing which exists in such a way as to stand in need of nothing beyond itself." There exists only one absolutely independent substance, namely God, all other substance being his creation. However, although God and his creations are both substances, they are not substances in the same sense, for "the term substance does not apply to God and the creatures univocally," but is an equivocal term used in two different senses.

It is in reference to created substances, man and the universe, that Cartesian Metaphysical Dualism applies. That is to say, the ultimate universe is composed of two distinct and independently

---

[1] *Meditations of the First Philosophy*, meditation III.

separate entities: mind and matter, or soul substance and corporeal substance (thinking substance and bodily substance). Each substance has but one principal attribute: thinking is the chief attribute of mind; and extension is the prime attribute of body (i.e., bodies occupy space). Whatever attribute a corporeal body has is some mode of an extended thing, and whatever attribute mind or soul has is some mode of thinking. Corporeal substance has the quality of filling space, spatiality, while thinking substance (soul, mind) has the quality of (non-spatial) consciousness. Whatever exists must be either one or the other, and whatever is not conscious must be spatial, and vice versa, so that everything is either body or mind, spatial or conscious.

According to Descartes, body and mind are both finite, depending upon God for existence, whereas God, the infinite Being, needs nothing else for his existence; he is absolute, uncreated, independent, and infinite. Furthermore, it is the veracity of God which guarantees that our knowledge of what is axiomatic (clear and distinct) is true, and it is his veracity which assures us that the external world which is known by our senses is not a fiction, but a genuine reality. If there were no God, or if there were a devil controlling the universe, then our external world might merely be no more than a nightmare, a fanciful unreal thing.

All physical extended substance operates in accordance with the law of mechanics and functions like a machine. The body of each animal, like all other physical things, is a machine without a soul. The sum total of all the motion occurring in the world is always constant; it neither increases nor diminishes. All forces exerted upon bodies are external, and one of these external forces can be the cause of the body's destruction and death. Soul substance, however, is unaffected by external or mechanical causes, hence is immortal by nature, inasmuch as nothing can cause its demise.

Descartes was confronted with the serious problem facing every Metaphysical Dualist, namely, the problem of interaction. If body and mind are completely different entities, the one taking up space, extended, and the other unextended (immaterial, spaceless), then the question arises: At what point do they interact? How is it possible for a three-dimensional object to make contact with a non-dimensional substance? Descartes, unable to offer a suitable answer, placed the nexus of these two substances in the pineal gland, which is an appendage of the brain. He knew that the brain had much to do with mental life and surmised that the crossover of these two completely unrelated substances took place in this brain organ which he identified as the seat of the soul. But he failed to explain what happens when the pineal gland atrophies as it does in the human being during adolescence. How does interaction then continue? The logical inference from this problem was drawn by the Cartesian Occasionalists.

CARTESIAN SOLUTIONS

As noted above, Cartesian Metaphysical Dualism confronted serious difficulty in attempting to explain interaction between two completely heterogeneous substances. It had denied to bodily substance any spiritual quality and to mind any extension. How, then, was it possible for the mind to influence the body, or vice versa? When one wills his arm to be raised, it is raised, and yet on the premise of Cartesian Dualism, the mind cannot even know its body, much less be the cause of bodily movements.

Geulincx and Malebranche: The Doctrine of Occasionalism. It remained for the followers of Descartes, principally Arnold Geulincx and Nicolas Malebranche, to propose a logical solution to this problem. Their thinking combined Cartesian Dualism with the Neo-Platonic world of Ideas in God. These men were called Occasionalists because of their theory that on those occasions when the body interacts with the mind, or the mind with the body, it is a divine agency that brings about the necessary changes. At such times God's will modifies the acts of thinking substance to comport with changes in bodily substance. In this way God creates in the soul an idea corresponding to bodily change. Also, whenever a person wills that his body respond to the dictates of his thought, God intervenes and motivates the body to act in accordance with that person's will. It may be noted that Benedict Spinoza, the most famous of the Continental Rationalists to follow Descartes, found it intellectually impossible to subscribe to the doctrine of Occasionalism; instead, reverting to a form of Dualism of mind and body, he sought to resolve the issue by appeal to a Metaphysical Monism which identified mind and body as two attributes of one and the same substance. With Spinoza, the three substances of Descartes (God, mind, and body) were reduced to one, namely, God (Pantheism).

The Mysticism of Blaise Pascal. Another attempt to solve the problem of Cartesian Dualism was made by Blaise Pascal (1623–1662), a fellow countryman of Descartes, in his *Provincial Letters*

(1656) and *Pensées* (1670). Pascal was a mathematician and physicist who associated himself with the reformers of the Roman Catholic Church—the Jansenists of Port Royal who adhered to St. Augustine's philosophy.

Pascal is known principally for his Mysticism which he founded upon Skepticism. Accepting the Metaphysical Dualism of Descartes with its inherent nonteleological or mechanistic view of nature, he concluded that the reason or purpose of things cannot be known. Furthermore, man cannot prove immortality or the existence of God, nor can science or philosophy produce mathematical certainty or proof.

On the basis of this Skepticism, the only approach a person may take toward theology is a practical one; man must remain content with the dictates not of reason but of his heart, for the heart has its reasons which the mind does not know. Man is motivated not by the intellect, but by the heart's directions. True, God's existence cannot be proved, but neither is proof desirable. What is called for is an exercise of faith, the faith that God exists. Pascal's argument for God, termed a *religious wager*, confronts man with a forced option, that of believing in his existence or denying it. Either you accept God's existence or you do not; there is no other alternative, since the agnostic (the noncommittal position of a person who asserts that he does not know whether or not God exists) in practice either affirms or denies God's existence. If you cast your lot on the side of God, then you have nothing to lose in this life and everything to gain in the life after death, but if you deny God's reality, then you jeopardize yourself for all eternity should the case turn out to be in God's favor. The gambling odds are one out of two, a fifty-fifty chance. (Pascal was quite familiar with gambling).

The entire argument rests on the assumption that God (if he exists) would punish the deceased individual who had refused to believe while living—that a man's inability to believe in God in the light of the evidence which we have of him in the present life justifies his eternal damnation.

BENEDICT SPINOZA

Benedict Spinoza (1632–1677), a Jewish philosopher, reasoning that he could be equally as blessed in Latin as in Hebrew, changed his name from Baruch (Hebrew for *blessed*) to the Latin, Benedict, as a result of his excommunication in 1656 from the Jewish synagogue. Spinoza's parents were crypto-Jews (Jews converted to Christianity by force during the Spanish Inquisition, yet remaining Jews in spirit) who fled Portugal for Holland (where Benedict was born) because the Union of Utrecht had decreed freedom of religion.

Benedict was trained by rabbis in a Hebrew school where he came under the tutelege of Saul Morteira and Manasseh ben Israel, the most eminent scholars of the Jewish community. (It is known that in 1670 Spinoza lived at Rijnsburg, situated not far from Amsterdam and Leyden; for a few years prior to his death, he lived in The Hague.) Having attained considerable renown for his ideas, he was offered the chair of philosophy at Heidelberg University in 1673, which he refused because he cherished absolute freedom of thought in his pursuit of philosophical truth. He earned his living by grinding lenses and giving private instruction as a tutor.

Only two of Spinoza's writings were published during his lifetime: *Renati des Cartes Principiorum Philosophiae* (1663), and the *Tractatus Theologico-Politicus* (1670). Three additional works appeared in the year of his death: the *Ethics*, which brought him universal fame in the annals of philosophy; his treatise, *On the Improvement of the Understanding;* and his *Political Treatise.*

Spinoza's Geometrical Method. In his methodology Spinoza was influenced by Francis Bacon and Descartes. In Bacon's *Novum Organum* he found inspiration for a new method of analysis which could be applied to the laws of human conduct as well as to the laws governing the processes of nature. The deductive, mathematical method of Descartes inspired him to construct a philosophical system patterned after geometrical principles and based on his thesis that both human nature and the natural world are governed (in the same way as geometrical figures) by fixed scientific laws. "I will therefore write about human beings as though I were concerned with lines and planes and solids," he wrote. And that, he most certainly did, for his *magnum opus, The Ethics,* reads like a mathematical treatise, like Euclid's geometry. From a base of definitions and axioms, he proceeded carefully to deduce propositions with appropriate scholia and corollaries, then finally concluded each with Q.E.D. (*quod erat demonstrandum*—which was to be demonstrated). By means of the geometrical method, by mathematical demonstration, Spinoza expected to establish the flawless accuracy and absolute proof of his philosophical ideas.

To the Rationalism of Descartes he added a new theory of coherence, the belief that all true ideas are ultimately interrelated in an integrated systematic whole which comprises absolute or metaphysical reality. Beginning with true ideas, which he termed "adequate ideas," he sought their interrelationship with all other true ideas, a relationship which is infinite in its various combinations. Spinoza emphasized that this system of ideas must necessarily be infinite because the ultimate reality to which it refers is God himself, the infinitely ontological real substance of which the particular manifestations of the world as we observe them are merely modes, or modifications. To understand the world in its correct logical structure we must view it *sub specie aeternitatis*—under the aspect of the eternal; that is, we must see its logical structure as an integrated whole, or apprehend the logical relationship of one object to everything else, to the ultimate substance—God. The ultimate universe is one infinitely enormous integrated logical structure, and the world of nature functions like a machine governed by unavoidable, irreversible laws. For Spinoza the cause-effect relationship is not a temporal one in the sense that a cause must precede its effect; all causes are logically connected with effects through active principles—that is, they are necessary causes like those in geometry where mathematical necessity determines the outcome or effect (as in the case of the triangle, in which a necessary cause consists of its having three sides). "Nothing in the universe is contingent," wrote Spinoza, "but all things are conditioned to exist and operate in a particular manner by the necessity of the divine nature." [1]

Pantheism and the Problem of Evil. In a logico-mathematical sense, God is the cause of the universe. As *natura naturans*, God is the universal principle, causing the world of nature to exist, while the particular transitory phenomenal manifestations of nature about us are *natura naturata*. Spinoza identified absolute reality with perfection, and he regarded particular objects as finite things. Ultimately, then, error and evil do not exist, nor can either possibly exist, for ultimate reality is God and God is ultimate reality (a basic concept of Pantheism). In God, there is neither error nor evil. Error is a confused idea, which is not logically integrated with or related to the whole; in other words, it is a partial view of the whole, one which is not viewed *sub specie aeternitatis* (under the aspect of the eternal). This same misunderstanding occurs regard-

---

[1] *Ethics* (1677), tr. R. H. M. Elwes, Part I, Proposition 29.

ing the nature of evil, inasmuch as the ultimately real is God, and he is good. Since the sum total of nature is God, and God is good, evil does not exist, and that which men designate as evil is so designated merely through ignorance, through the inability to see reality in its entirety (as a unified good entity) with each of its components a necessary aspect of it. Miracles, defined as the disruption of the logical processes of nature, do not exist; such disorder would not imply the existence of a good God, but if the description were sufficiently disorderly or disorganized, would imply the existence of a diabolical Being.

Spinoza defined God as a Being absolutely infinite, necessarily existent (the ontological argument), and identical with the ultimate stuff or substance of the world. He described substance as "that which is in itself, and is conceived through itself: in other words, that of which a conception can be formed independently of any other conception." But of these infinite attributes of God (or substance) we have knowledge of only two: mind and matter. Since ultimate reality (substance), as humans know it, is both thought and extension, God is a thinking thing and also an extended thing, for these are the only divine attributes known to man, who must remain ignorant about the infinity of God. (Note here Spinoza's adherence to a negative theology.)

Spinoza held that an affirmative answer to the question, Does anything exist? proves the existence of God since, by definition, God consists of everything that exists and everything that exists is God. It is God who, through his existence and power, creates the essence of things and thus brings them into existence, not as transitory phenomena but as ultimate reality, infinite, within the realm of permanent, divine substance. As for the human being, it is his essence (his essential humanity) that is immortal (including his intellect which, as part of God's infinite intellect, understands things under the aspect of eternity); through intellectual love of God, man becomes immortal. "The human mind cannot be absolutely destroyed with the body, but there remains of it something which is eternal." [1]

Thus for Spinoza God is the eternal, infinite substance, the essence of reality; outside of God, no other substance is conceivable. "Whatever is, is in God, and without God nothing can be, or be conceived." [2] Thus Spinoza's Pantheism and Metaphysical Monism

---

[1] *Ibid.*, Part V, Proposition 23.
[2] *Ibid.*, Part I, Proposition 15.

are complete. Since nothing is external to God, he is the indwelling, not the transient or external, cause of things. Everything consists of God, his eternal and infinite attributes, together with their finite modifications and the infinite relationships among his attributes. The following schematic presents Spinoza's metaphysical ideas as an integrated system.

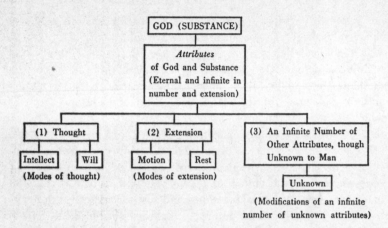

Psychophysical Parallelism. Descartes, in separating thinking substance (mind) from extended substance (body) as two distinctly different substances, had encountered difficulty in accounting for the interactions which take place between mind and body. For Spinoza, only like can affect like, and two distinctly different ultimate substances could not affect each other. Consequently, he sought to resolve the mind-body problem by uniting the two as one and the same substance. Each is merely an aspect, an attribute, of substance. Substance is the ultimate ontological reality. Thus when any effect is taking place in either mind or body, it is actually one and the same substance itself that is being affected, which in turn affects every one of its attributes. Ideas and things parallel each other by being only aspects of a basic substance. "The order and connection of ideas is the same as the order and connection of things." [1] The two parallel each other in every respect. However, the "body cannot determine mind to think, neither can mind determine body to motion or rest." [2] Wherever there is body, mind will always accompany it. Everything has a mental aspect (the

---

[1] *Ibid.*, Part II, Proposition 7.
[2] *Ibid.*, Part III, Proposition 3.

doctrine of Panpsychism) and mind and body operate parallel to each other so that whatever affects the one automatically affects the other (the doctrine of Psychophysical Parallelism). In stating that ideas and matter (mind and body) obey the same chain of causes, Spinoza anticipated by three centuries the current concepts of psychosomatic medicine, and he similarly contributed the basis for present trends in abnormal psychology through his insistence that all things, even the ravings of an irrational person, can be explained by means of reason and necessary causes (a view which Freud accepted).

Spinoza's Ethical Theory. Spinoza regarded God as the *summum bonum* (greatest good), and the actual knowing or understanding of him as the supreme virtue. Any possessor of this supreme virtue needs no further reward; such understanding is his reward, because virtue and blessedness are one and the same. Blessedness is found in love toward God, not an emotional love, but an intellectual love derived from man's highest form of cognition, from his intuitive knowledge or scientific intuition. For Spinoza, opinion (or imagination) and reason are inferior forms of knowledge compared with intellectual, intuitive knowledge of God which embraces understanding of the whole universe. The intellect is not static but dynamic; when man understands the laws of his personality, for instance, he gains immediate control over his emotions. Willing is only a form of thinking and thought is the only means of motivating action. Even God does not act according to freedom of the will, but according to the direction of his intellect. Consequently, the infinite mind of God could not have instituted a world different from the present one, since his infinite intellect guided him to create the world as it is.

When our intellect guides us aright, then it is aligned with nature, and our actions harmonize with the reality of things. Since nature and God are one, then the moral and the natural are the same. Thus, man should act for his own self-preservation because it is a natural law. The more one understands of reality, the more he understands God. The intellectual love of God, then, is man's goal. Man, by subordinating his spirit to natural necessity, finds perfect peace.

GOTTFRIED WILHELM LEIBNIZ

Gottfried Wilhelm Leibniz (1646–1716), the third great Rationalist in Continental Europe, was a native of Leipzig, where his father had been a professor of philosophy. He studied law at Leipzig University, entering at fifteen years of age, but the University in 1666 refused to confer the doctorate because of his youth. (Immediately thereafter he received the Doctor of Laws degree at Altorf University in Nuremberg.) During some years of service for the Elector of Mainz, Leibniz journeyed on diplomatic missions to Paris, where he met Arnauld, Malebranche, and Christian Huygens, and became familiar with the philosophy of Descartes, and to Holland, where he became acquainted with Spinoza, who gave him excerpts from the yet unpublished *Ethics*. He was greatly influenced not only by these two famous contemporaries but also by his intensive studies of the philosophies of Aristotle, Aquinas, John Duns Scotus, Francis Bacon, and Hobbes. Only a few of his writings were published during his lifetime (including his dissertation, *Individuation*, in 1663, and his impressive *Theodicy*, in 1710). Among other significant writings delineating his philosophical system were: *Discourse on Metaphysics* (1690); *New System of Nature* (1695); *New Essays on the Human Understanding* (1704); *Monadology* (1714); *Principles of Nature and Grace* (1714); his correspondence with Arnauld; and his correspondence with Clarke.

Leibnizian Teleology and Mechanism. Although he was an adherent of and major contributor to the philosophy of Rationalism, Leibniz modified that point of view in an effort to make a place for Empiricist ideas, thus setting the stage for the synthesis later formulated by Immanuel Kant. Leibniz tried also to reconcile Cartesian mechanistic views of nature with Aristotelian teleological views. Further, he attempted to build a bridge between scientific and theological methods of inquiry.

According to Leibniz, the universe is teleological because it realizes the goals set forth by God, but it is also mechanical because physical nature operates like a mechanism impelled and controlled by specific, efficient causes even though its course leads to an ultimate, predetermined purpose. The mechanics of nature and the phenomena we observe are simply the effective means of fulfilling God's purposes (the principle of fitness). In fact, the laws of physics and the principles of mechanics are dependent upon God's objectives, for they require the direction of a supreme intelligence. This conclusion represented an attempt to synthesize the Cartesian doctrine of mechanism with the Aristotelian doctrine of entelechies.

Methodology and Epistemology. Leibniz agreed with Hobbes that philosophers should use words as accurately and logically as mathematicians use numbers. From Raymond Lully he got the idea of a thought machine, a system of logic using symbols or letters instead of subject terms and predicate terms, so that symbols would represent precise truths, thus making metaphysics an exact science like mathematics. His views in this field initiated the study of what eventually became the science of mathematical (or symbolic) logic. Leibniz, himself the creator of the mathematical calculus, believed that his symbolic language would become a universal language or linguistic calculus.

As a Rationalist he was fascinated with the ideal and exact form which mathematics assumed in proceeding by logical necessity from one principle to another (as two plus two equals four by logical necessity), yet he had also accepted empirical experiences as brute facts of life. The ideal or the logically necessary, in the form of principles, and the empirically factual, in the form of brute sense data, could not be reconciled or brought together into a unified whole. He admitted that the rational world and the empirical world stand antithetically opposed to each other; each must be understood in the light of its own logic, because each has its own truth peculiar to itself.

Leibniz drew a sharp distinction between the two classes of truth, referring to the truths of reason as *a priori* or innate knowledge prior to and independent of experience, and to the truths of fact as *a posteriori* or knowledge acquired from experience during a limited period of time, not from logical or mathematical reasoning. Truths of reason are necessary permanent truths because their opposites are impossible to conceive. (Thus, the three angles of a triangle must always equal two right angles.) Truths of fact, which come and go, are merely empirical data or occurrences whose opposites are imaginable because they are accidental, not necessary, truths. (For example, although all snow is white, it is possible to imagine it as red. Only in God's mind can there by an analysis of empirical facts so complete that their opposites cannot be conceived.) For both classes of truth, however, there is only one identical criterion by which they are known to be valid, namely, the Rationalist's criterion of clear and distinct ideas (not mere sensory experiences) in the mind.

Leibniz explained that each class of truths is governed by a principle; truths of reason must comply with the *principle of contradiction,* and truths of fact must comply with the *principle of sufficient reason.* Truths of reason are necessary truths which can be proved *a priori;* truths of fact are empirical data which (responding to the *principle of contingency*) can be most reasonably explained by reference to all the conditions in which they are found. According to the principle of sufficient reason, *"nothing happens without a reason,"* that is, nothing ever happens without its being possible for him who "should sufficiently understand things, to give a reason sufficient to determine why it is so and not otherwise." [1] (Since God does nothing without a reason, everything in the physical world has some explicable reason for being.) According to the principle of contradiction, anything self-contradictory is necessarily false and its opposite is necessarily true.

The world of nature responds to Leibniz' *law of continuity,* which states that "everything goes by steps in nature, and nothing by leaps." There exists a gradual connection between various species, a continuous series of intermediate beings. The facts of reality form an enormous integrated and coherent system of development. This principle holds true not merely in biology but in physics and elsewhere. The fine variations, gradations, and changes in nature are imperceptible to our senses. Leibniz, expounding this law of continuity, pointed out that motion never begins with maximum force from a point at rest, but proceeds in an uninterrupted series of regularly progressive changes; it does not stop abruptly, but ceases gradually. (If an egg stopped abruptly in falling it would not have time to break; breakage requires gradual stopping.) Leibniz' principle states that there are no gaps in nature, no great or sudden changes.

Leibniz' Metaphysics and Monadology.   Substance had been regarded by Leibniz' predecessors merely as extended or inert matter, whereas he considered it to be a vital, dynamic activity comprising immaterial and nonspatial force; for Leibniz space and time were merely phenomenal things (appearances) and not genuine (or ultimate) realities. He called the ultimate entities *monads,* the ultimate stuff out of which even the atoms were made. He agreed with Hobbes that only bodies and bodies in motion existed, but only in the sense 'that all bodies are ultimate quantums of force, active entities; the essential nature of all bodies is force. It is true that, as manifested to our senses, force (activity) occupies space and exists in time, but these properties are only an effect of its basic nature. The real substance of the universe transcends physical qualities and

---

[1] Wilhelm Leibniz, *The Principles of Nature and Grace, Based on Reason* (1714).

hence is *meta*physical. Since it views all reality as based upon force or activity, Leibniz' system of philosophy is defined as Panpsychism —and also, since the life principle is central therein, is often referred to as Vitalism.

Leibniz used the term *monad* (Greek for *unity* or *oneness*) to denote the activity or force constituting the essence of substance. Each monad exists in its own right as an independent Being unlike all other monads in the universe; hence in this sense Leibniz was an Individualist philosopher. He held that the monads, as the ultimate real elements of the universe, are infinite in number, a theory which made him a Metaphysical Pluralist. These independent monads are always active, but they do not contact or affect one another. They are individual, conscious, active, alive, and range in quality from the lowest type (matter) through the higher types (souls or mind) up to the highest of all (God, who is responsible for all the rest). Each monad has a thought life or inner activity, for its nature is not physical, but mental or spiritual. Thus the ultimate substance of the world is a cosmic force, an immanent activity. Leibniz defined substance as "a being capable of action." Existence is action; *to be is to be active.* The monad changes in appearance because its inner desire or drive impels it to pass from one phenomenal representation to another, and good and evil are the fundamental values in the laws governing purpose and desire.

Leibniz pictured each monad as a living and perpetual mirror of all the other monads since each represents the entire universe; therefore to know one monad thoroughly is to know the world. Inasmuch as the monads are self-contained (have no windows), each cannot lose any of its inherent force nor gain force from outside itself. Consequently, cause (understood as force) does not really exist, and the body cannot exert any causal influence on the soul, nor can the soul in any way affect or interact with the body.

Doctrine of Preëstablished Harmony.   Leibniz rejected Descartes' theory of interaction between mind and body in the region of the pineal gland, and he offered his explanation of the mind-body problem that differed from Spinoza's Psychophysical Parallelism. According to Leibniz, mind and body do not interact at all; they merely appear to do so. Each monad is given a characteristic nature by the central monad, God. Because God has created the essence of every other monad with its own peculiar nature (so that, despite its changing appearance, it does not interfere with or conflict with other monads), the monads and the entire universe obey

the principle of Preëstablished Harmony. Leibniz compared Preëstablished Harmony with the concomitant actions of two clocks
or watches which are in complete agreement with each other, each
keeping perfect time in unison. Descartes attempted to explain this
parallel activity by assuming interaction among real substances.
The Occasionalists assumed that God's will intercedes and causes
every reaction between mind and body. But Leibniz' principle of
Preëstablished Harmony stated that God had created mind and body
so perfectly in advance that all actions of all substances (monads)
occur in perfect unison, just as the most skillfully made clocks will
keep perfect time together without being connected.

Leibniz' Philosophy of Religion.   According to Leibniz, God
is the supreme monad and pure activity responsible for the entire
universe: God designed monads so that they would function in
Preëstablished Harmony, arranged the monads so that they (the
world) would work in conformity with the laws of nature, and
created human beings out of indestructible monads in such an order
that the soul of man would be immortal, while at the same time
each personality would differ from all others. Inasmuch as monads
are force, they are spiritual (immaterial) in nature, not extended.
Their spatial character is merely phenomenal, not real. Hence the
soul of man is immaterial and eternal, transcending the unreal phenomena known to us as time and space.

Unlike man, God's Being is eternal truth, absolute necessity, hence
is governed according to the law of contradiction. Finite souls
(men) are contingent Beings, hence are governed by the principle
of sufficient reason. That is to say, man is not an absolute or necessary Being, but is conditioned, dependent upon another Being for
his existence, as is the case with the world at large. Leibniz attributed the contingent nature of the world to the will of God. This
world could have been otherwise, if God had so chosen; he selected
this one from among the infinite possibilities open to him, creating
a universe with the best characteristics of variety, order, arrangements, places, times, knowledge, goodness, happiness, and powers.
(Note that Leibniz agreed with John Duns Scotus about the arbitrary
will of God.) Being omniscient, God knew what the best possible
world would be; being good, he willed it; and being omnipotent,
he possessed the power to bring it into existence. For Leibniz, this
is the *best possible world* from the standpoint of its ingredients,
all of which are indispensable. God decided that a world of free-

dom, even allowing man to choose evil at times, would be better than a world without freedom of the will. The fact that there is much more of good than of evil in the world justified its creation. Leibniz agreed that, if the universe had not been worth creating, God would not have created it.

Empiricism vs. Rationalism. When Descartes' concept of innate ideas was attacked by other philosophers (such as John Locke, who had accepted ancient Greek and medieval Scholastic views of the human mind as a "blank tablet" or *tabula rasa*), Leibniz came to his rescue. He pointed out that necessary truths, such as those found in mathematics, can be proved only from principles implanted in the mind—that is, innate ideas. In the animal kingdom, only man, he said, therefore possesses scientific knowledge, the reason being the existence in the human mind of something necessary for scientific knowledge which is absent in the brute. The opponents of the concept of innate ideas who assert that "there is nothing in the intellect which was not previously in the senses" are right, said Leibniz, "provided we make the reservation, except the intellect itself." This insight formed the basis for Kantian Idealism, which constituted (as we shall see) a synthesis of Rationalism and Empiricism.

LEIBNIZIANISM

Of the important interpreters and popularizers of Leibniz' philosophy, two of the most influential were Christian Wolff and Gotthold Ephraim Lessing.

The Leibniz-Wolffian School. Christian Wolff (1679–1754), a professor at Halle and Marburg, who systematized the philosophy of Leibniz, is credited with the traditional fourfold division of metaphysics: (1) ontology, the study of ultimate Being or existence; (2) cosmology, the study of the orderly universe as a whole; (3) rational psychology, the study of the soul from a nonempirical standpoint; and (4) natural theology, the study of the nature and existence of God.

Wolff developed an eclectic view integrating with the Leibnizian system various elements of Aristotelian, Scholastic, Cartesian, and Empiricist philosophies. The Leibniz-Wolffian philosophy became dominant in Germany prior to Kantianism, and even Kant was greatly influenced by it. Although practically all the philosophers of the German Enlightenment fell under his influence, Wolff's contributions were limited (so far as original ideas were concerned) mainly to his division of science into rational and empirical types and his attempt to weave empirical facts into Leibniz' Rationalism.

Lessing and the German Romantic Movement. Gotthold Ephraim Lessing (1729–1781) championed the concept of individual development as a central theme of Leibnizian philosophy and thereby gave impetus to German Romanticism, a phase of German Idealism transitional (1775 to 1815) between the Kantian and Hegelian periods of dominance.

Lessing regarded religion as a living relationship between man and God. Without revelation, religion is impossible. He viewed the history of religions as a series of revelations by which God educates the human race. Revelation makes progress in progressive stages possible and is thus related to the entire human race in the same way that education is related to the individual man.

Lessing's chief contributions must be attributed to his critical (rather than his creative) abilities, his profound historical sense, and his unquenchable thirst for truth and spiritual growth. Truth he regarded as a goal, not a possession. A man's worth must be evaluated in terms of the honest pains which he endures in acquiring it, not in mere possession, and each stage of human accomplishment in the pursuit of truth must be regarded as a tentative starting point for further unceasing effort. This point of view characterized the German Romantic movement in which the principal thinkers included the Schlegel brothers (August W., 1767–1845, and Friedrich, 1772–1829), Novalis (1772–1801), Jacob Fries (1773–1843), and Friedrich W. J. Schelling (1775–1854). The Romanticists sought reality in subjectivity (subjective methods), valued most highly good will and sentiment, and adhered to an idealistic point of view. During the Storm and Stress period (1775 to 1787) Romanticism lapsed into Sentimentalism, as in Rousseau's philosophy which turned attention in the direction of self-study by the individual and an awareness of the limitations of reason.

Chapter 9

The British Empiricists

Continental Rationalism set forth a primary thesis of early modern philosophy that knowledge is derived from reason, that the intellect always has at its disposal certain principles of reasoning or innate ideas—in other words that true knowledge is inborn, not acquired. This philosophy of Rationalism encountered opposition from the British Empiricists, who held that no innate knowledge exists and that whatever knowledge man possesses he has acquired either during the natal period or thereafter.

The chief proponent of this mode of thinking was the Englishman, John Locke (1632–1704), who, with the publication of his most important work, *An Essay concerning Human Understanding*, in 1690, ushered in a new era of thought, the Enlightenment. Locke's influence sowed the seeds of the French philosophy of Sensationalism, the religious philosophy of Deism, the ethics of Utilitarianism, the psychology of Associationism, and the epistemology of Empiricism, most especially the latter philosophy which was further developed by the Irish Idealist George Berkeley (1685–1753) and by Scotland's most distinguished philosopher David Hume (1711–1776).

JOHN LOCKE'S METAPHYSICAL AGNOSTICISM

John Locke, a native of Wrington (near Bristol), England, was educated at Oxford and held several high positions in government. Besides his most influential work, *An Essay concerning Human Understanding*, he wrote *Letters on Toleration* (1685–89), *Two Treatises on Civil Government* (1689), *Some Thoughts on Education* (1693), *The Reasonableness of Christianity* (1695), and the posthumously published work, *Of the Conduct of the Understanding*.

Denial of Innate Ideas. In his *An Essay concerning Human Understanding*, an essay comprising four books, Locke began his argument by pointing out that while it is true that innate ideas are universally accepted by mankind, such universal agreement does not prove them to be innate. Moreover, the axiomatic principles of logic,

153

such as the principle of identity ("Whatever is, is") and the principle of contradiction ("It is impossible for the same thing to be and not to be") are not even known to some children and to idiots, and consequently could not have been imprinted upon the mind at birth. The dubious assertion that reason merely discovers or discloses these ideas does not prove them to be innate. Even moral principles, such as the principle of justice or the Golden Rule, are not innate, for they require proof. Nor is conscience any proof of the innateness of moral rules. Furthermore, the idea of God is not innate.

The Mind—A *Tabula Rasa* (Blank Tablet). According to Locke, in the process of gaining knowledge, only the mental faculty (or power) is innate, whereas the actual knowledge itself is acquired. Knowledge is imprinted upon the mind by sensations, which impress themselves upon the mind as if it were a *tabula rasa,* a blank tablet or "white paper void of all characters, without any ideas." All ideas (all materials used in reasoning and knowing) come from experience; hence Locke's philosophy is called Empiricism. There are two kinds of experience, external and internal, and two corresponding avenues of knowledge: (1) sensations provide us with ideas emanating from external experience (from objects outside ourselves); (2) inner reflection also provides ideas as part of the world within us. Our understanding receives ideas in the same way that a blackboard receives chalk marks imprinted upon it. Sense experience presents sensible qualities to the mind, such as yellowness, heat, softness, sweetness; the mind, reflecting on these activities and states, receives a second set of ideas, as in perception, thinking, doubting, believing, reasoning, knowing, and willing. Only after the mind acquires sense experience may it have these reflections and ideas dealing with its inner sensory operations.

Simple and Complex Ideas. Locke distinguished between simple ideas and complex ideas, the latter being abstractions from or combinations of the former.

Simple ideas, which come to us either through sense experience or through reflection, consist of four types: (1) those which we receive from one sense only, such as ideas of color, sound, taste, touch, and smell; (2) those which we obtain from two or more senses combined, such as ideas of space, extension, figure, rest, and motion; (3) those which we obtain by reflection only, comprising ideas created by our *power of thinking* (which is called the understanding) and our *power of volition* (which is called the will), examples of these powers or faculties being remembering, discerning, reasoning, judging, knowing, and believing; (4) those which we obtain from both sensation and reflection, namely, ideas of pleasure, pain, power, existence, and unity.

Simple ideas can be repeated, compared, and united to form an infinite variety of complex ideas. God is one example of a complex idea, resulting from an enlargement upon our simple ideas of existence, time, knowledge, power, etc. The mind has the power to know some things and then to combine and multiply them to infinity. Inasmuch as Locke reduced abstract ideas (complex ideas) to the data of sensation, he must be regarded as a Nominalist, and his Nominalist point of view was accepted by the majority of other British philosophers.

Primary and Secondary Qualities. Locke distinguished sharply between ideas (simple or complex) and objective reality, the external world which the ideas designate. Ideas are within us, whereas real things are outside of us and possess the powers or qualities which excite our ideas. These powers or qualities include primary and secondary types.

The primary qualities of objects are their real qualities, inhering in and inseparable from the objects themselves. When we say that we experience primary qualities, our ideas are actually only copies of the qualities themselves, mental forms or pictures corresponding to the external things-in-themselves as they really exist. Examples of primary qualities are solidity, extension, figure, motion, rest, and number, all of which excite or produce similar forms or ideas in our minds.

The objects themselves also produce in us those sensations that are not in the objects at all but constitute the secondary qualities which we associate with them. Examples of these secondary qualities are color, sound, smell, taste, and sound. A red stone really occupies space (a primary quality) but it only seems to be red (a secondary quality) because we see redness through our sense of vision.

Locke also postulated a third quality of objects to explain how they can cause changes in the primary qualities of other objects, just as the sun has the power to "make wax white, and fire to make lead fluid." In other words any object can so change or affect other things that we will sense them differently from the way we did before.

Note that Locke attributed cause-and-effect relationships to powers residing in external objects themselves: one object has a power which causes changes in other objects and in perceptions or ideas of them. (This cause-effect relationship was later denied by the Skeptical Empiricist, Hume.)

Metaphysical Agnosticism. The complex ideas (combinations of simple ideas) are classified into three types: (1) modes, or ideas (roundness, motion, hardness) which depend upon substances; (2) relations, that is, comparisons between one idea and other ideas (Locke defined truth as this kind of association or relation among things whereby they agree or disagree with one another); and (3) substances, or bodies themselves, the particular things, which subsist by themselves and provide the basis for the primary and secondary qualities we experience.

Locke's assumption that substances exist as things-in-themselves (irrespective of their specific qualities of extension, color, etc.) posed a fundamental metaphysical problem still with us today. If a basic substance or power exists and is real, what is its nature? What is the substratum underlying and producing the qualities which we call substance? Locke confessed that he was unable to answer this question—he called substance an "I-know-not-what" thing—and must therefore be classed as a metaphysical agnostic, adhering to the doctrine that the nature of ultimate reality cannot be proved or known. We know only the accidents or qualities associated with a substance, but the substance itself remains inscrutable, and even the idea of a substance is merely an unprovable assumption.

Epistemology and the Degrees of Knowledge. Locke identified the knowledge of truth with the perception of agreement or disagreement between ideas. There are four types of such agreement or disagreement. (1) The principle of identity states that an idea agrees with itself and that two distinct ideas disagree with each other ("What is, is" and "It is impossible for the same thing to be and not to be"). Thus, *blue is not yellow* is a truth of identity. (2) There may be a relation between two ideas. Thus, *two triangles upon equal bases between two parallels are equal* is a truth of relation. (3) There may be a necessary connection (or coexisting qualities) invariably accompanying an object. Thus, *gold is yellow and of a certain weight* and *iron is susceptible of magnetic attraction* are truths of necessary connection. (4) An idea of an object as real may agree with the fact that the object exists. Thus, the idea of God as real agrees with the fact that he exists. Locke also believed that truth is a relationship among ideas or words as mental or verbal propositions, and he is for this reason classed as a Terminist.

He classified knowledge into three degrees or levels: intuitive, demonstrative, and sensitive. Intuitive knowledge consists of immediate awareness of agreement or disagreement between two ideas; for example, we have an immediate, indubitable knowledge of our own existence. If we know that we doubt, then we know (as Descartes had asserted) that we must exist in order to doubt. Demonstrative knowledge consists of understanding (by means of reasoning) of the logical relationships among ideas; examples are the deductive conclusions of mathematics, as in the analysis of relationships (arriving at proofs) among geometric figures or propositions. Sensitive knowledge consists of those perceptions of or conclusions about particular objects which we accept as probable facts but not as certain truths about the external world; thus, if we notice repeatedly that a certain event precedes a given result, we conclude that there is probably a cause-effect relationship between them.

Proof of the Existence of God. Locke's argument for the existence of God is mainly cosmological with epistemological elements. Locke did not accept Descartes' concept of God as an innately known idea, although he held that man does have an intuitive, certain knowledge of God's existence. He believed that, since we are aware of the world as a complex of causes and powers, we must logically conclude that there is an original, supreme source of all causes and powers, namely, God. Surely, nature could not have existed eternally and could not have come out of nothing; it must have been brought into existence by an eternal thinking (cogitative) Being, for senseless matter could never produce the sense experience, perception, and thoughts that exist in the universe. The world of ideas does not function willy-nilly, in any way we please, but depends upon the thinking that ends in the world itself; and the thinking, the ideas, in the universe depends upon a supreme thinking source corresponding to our idea of the Divine Being.

Locke's Ethics and Political Philosophy. Since there are no innate ideas, moral, religious, and political values must be regarded as products of experience, but these values must obey the will of God (as expressed in natural law), the laws and ethical policies upon which men agree (as the basis for social contracts or constitutional governments), and the established traditions, customs, and opinions of mankind. As a Utilitarian, moreover, Locke believed that happiness is the greatest good and that obedience to the moral law results in happiness.

Locke's political theory (set forth in 1690 in his *Two Treatises of Government*) defended the doctrines of human liberty and human rights against absolutism and attempted to harmonize libertarian ideals with the necessity for civil law and order. Men are born free and equal, for in a state of nature they were familiar only with natural laws and knew nothing about government or manmade legal standards. When a society developed, the members entered into a compact or social contract whereby they delegated to selected officers certain powers set forth in their constitution. Government is therefore a system based upon and always subject to the mutual consent and joint decisions of the citizens.

GEORGE BERKELEY'S METAPHYSICAL IDEALISM

Ireland's most brilliant philosopher, George Berkeley (1685–1753), was a bishop of the Anglican Church who has been credited with founding the philosophy of Objective Immaterialism, a form of Idealism based on the theory that the real universe is solely phenomenal and nonmaterial in nature. Among his principal philosophical writings are *A New Theory of Vision* (1709); *A Treatise concerning the Principles of Human Knowledge* (1710); *Three Dialogues between Hylas and Philonous* (1713); *Alciphron, the Minute Philosopher* (1732); and *Siris: A Chain of Philosophical Reflections* (1744).

Berkeleyan Idealism. Berkeley developed an extreme Nominalist view that abstract ideas do not exist, that the essence or reality of everything in the universe consists in its being perceived —excepting those personal spiritual beings (man and God) who function as the agents of perception. Matter is a fiction, a nonexistent entity. The physical universe does not exist independently, but only insofar as it is perceived in the mind of God and (to some extent) in the minds of men. According to Berkeley, God determines causes and effects by means of his divine will and thus establishes order and regularity among phenomena; and the system of order in the universe and therefore in our experience (Berkeley accepted Locke's Empiricist emphasis on sense experience) proves the existence of God.

In other words, the world consists of only two kinds of things: (1) those which actively sense, perceive, and experience; (2) those which are passively sensed, perceived, and experienced. But both kinds of objects are basically the same in that they are equally spiritual, sensitive, immaterial substances capable of being experienced. A stone exists and is real only because it is capable of affecting our senses so that we have an idea of it, feel its hardness and see its color and shape. If no one, not even God, experiences a given object, then it cannot possibly exist. Before a thing can truly exist, it must first be capable of being subject to experience, that is, it must be experienceable. However, for a thing to be experienced, there must necessarily be a mind capable of actively experiencing, for the experienced object is passive, and only in this capacity of passive existence can it be implanted upon the mind. A thing cannot exist in its own right independently of a mind; it requires a mind that will provide the ground of its existence.

This does not mean that when I leave my room the objects of my sense perception disappear because no one is in the room to perceive them, but it does mean that if they are incapable of being experienced, then they no longer exist. Their potentiality for being perceived once again when I enter the room depends upon the fact that they are experienceable, as well as being actually experienced by God. The fact that God experiences all objects renders them potentially perceptible to our human minds even if they are not as yet actually experienced by us. (For example, the far side of the North Star is seen by God and is potentially perceptible to me although I cannot see it now.)

Objects are never experienced as having any material substance. When I look at the book on my desk, it does not somehow leave the top of my desk and enter into my consciousness. The only book which I experience is the sensation of seeing a book, a psychological image in my sense perception. This sensate book which appears in my perception is immaterial, spiritual; that is, it consists of the same ingredients as my sensation.

Berkeley is not a *solipsist*, who believes that he alone exists and the external world is merely the subjective world of his own inner experiences, a dream world. It should be noted that solipsism is a self-refuting doctrine inasmuch as the solipsist seeks to prove the truth of his theory to other persons who, according to his doctrine, presumably do not exist. The world is real, for if it were not real, we could not experience it. Imaginations are subjective, but the world of sense is objective. However, its objectivity consists of sensitivity. If the outer world had no sense effect upon us, then it would be incapable of being experienced, hence would not exist. It is only because objects are made of the same stuff as our experience that we can sense them. We cannot walk through a wall, and if we should try we would experience its pressure and perhaps a painful sensation. This proves that the wall is objectively real, but its reality is composed of the stuff of sense experience— not material substance, but spiritual substance. If it were composed of matter, then we would not be able to experience it, because the only object capable of entering our experience (our personal consciousness) must be sensitive substance, not insensitive matter. If there were any such thing as insensitive matter, we would never be able to experience it, for our minds are equipped only to experience ideal perceptions, the images of sense found in sensations. Spirit (that which perceives), either that of man or God, is the only genuine substance, and no other *substratum*, no unthinking substance, exists. Although substance possesses an independent existence, only the substance of God is absolute and of the highest form or significance.

God and the Doctrine of Divine Arbitrariness. We have seen that for Berkeley the real things in the universe are ideas imprinted upon our senses, and the creator of those ideas is God. If we do not experience certain external objects, they can still exist, but only because the omniscient and omnipresent mind of God is eternally perceiving them. Consequently, without God, the objects of sense experience would not exist in the first place, nor would there be finite minds like ours experiencing them.

Berkeley's doctrine of divine arbitrariness is a twofold argument for the existence of God: first, the things we perceive are more vivid than those we merely imagine or dream about—and this is due to the fact that an absolutely powerful Spirit, God's mind, is activating them; second, the things we perceive do not obey our personal wills (as our imaginations or reveries do) but resist our wishes, for they obey the will and laws of God, whose will is indeed arbitrary only in the sense that we cannot predict his divine mind *a priori*. It is only by means of repeated experience that we can discern the regular activity arising from the nature of things, that is, from the will of God. Berkeley agreed with the Scotists that God could have chosen any other set of natural laws to govern the universe if he had so desired. The only necessary connection between a so-called "cause" and its effect is not causal at all, but only a matter of sequence or order in time. We assume that there is a given cause-and-effect relationship merely because we happen to experience things invariably working together. Whenever we experience the cause, the effect accompanies it with regularity, not through any logical necessity, but in a sequence.

Laws of nature, then, are simply the habitual ways in which God wills things to behave; hence natural laws are God's habits, not things which are perceptible to the senses. The fact of the regularity of nature, the fact of natural laws, is evidence of the existence of God—a supreme mind operative in a world which is not of our own making.

DAVID HUME'S METAPHYSICAL SKEPTICISM

David Hume (1711–1776), a native of Edinburgh and educated in law at the university there, has often been acclaimed as Great Britain's foremost philosopher. Among his influential writings are his greatest work, *A Treatise on Human Nature* (1739); *An Enquiry concerning Human Understanding* (1748); *A Dissertation on the Passions* (1751); *An Enquiry concerning the Principles of Morals* (1751, considered by Hume to be his finest work); *Essays, Moral, Political, and Literary* (1741); *The Natural History of Religion* (1755); *Autobiography* (1777); and *Dialogues concerning Natural Religion* (1779, posthumously).

Hume's Epistemology: Empiricism and Skepticism. The intellectual heritage of British Empiricism passed from Locke to Berkeley to Hume. Locke had denied the existence of innate ideas; Berkeley had denied the validity of any ideas abstracted from sensory experience; and now Hume asserted that the only knowledge we can possess consists of a mere sequence of ideas—perceptions, or assumptions—none of which can be proved to be true. All knowledge is therefore restricted to mental states or experiences; of those only can we be certain. Hume was a thoroughgoing Skeptic concerning the possibility of achieving certainty. He challenged all alleged truths except those of mathematics and the immediate intuitive awareness of our sense experiences. We know that time and space exist, for our sense experiences occur at specific times and in definite places; and we are aware of our sensations as impressions tied together by contiguity (or association) among ideas.

Berkeley had retained the idea of a spiritual agent or substance as the mind which produces sensations and ideas, but Hume saw no necessity for any such substance. Hume held that the soul is nothing but a set or sequence of ideas, "a bundle of perceptions." He did not deem it necessary to explain how there could be such ideas and experiences without a mind or agent to produce them. Just as an object, such as a cherry, consists only of certain sensory qualities (sweetness, for example) so the individual himself consists, not of a soul which creates experiences, but only of a series of mental activities.

Hume formulated three laws whereby perceptions are associated or connected with one another: (1) the principle of resemblance (a picture impels us to think about the original); (2) the principle of contiguity (mention of one room in a building impels us to think about another); and (3) the principle of cause and effect (when we think about a wound, we also think about the subsequent pain).

In addition, he analyzed the various functions of human understanding and classified them into (1) relationships among ideas, and (2) relationships among facts. The former involve mathematical propositions (e.g., three times five equals fifteen); they are true and certain whether or not the things they refer to exist in nature. The latter—relationships among facts—cannot be proved exclusively by reasoning, but must be assumed on the basis of sense experience; thus the fact that the sun will rise tomorrow is a proposition based on previous sense impressions, and it is conceivable that the world could end today or that the sun will not rise tomorrow.

Since Hume denied the existence of ultimate reality (substance), he was known as a Metaphysical Nihilist, and because he asserted the existence only of the phenomena of sense, he was considered a *Phenomenalist* (or *Panphenomenalist,* inasmuch as he reduced even the self to a complex of ideas instead of a spiritual substance). Today the theory that there is no genuine substance or ultimate reality beyond the phenomena of sense is a central concept of Positivism; hence Hume may also be labelled a Positivist, but that term was not current in his day. He was a Skeptic in metaphysics because of his fundamental thesis that man cannot know ultimate reality or achieve any knowledge beyond a mere awareness of phenomenal, sensory images.

For Hume, there was no such thing as a true cause-and-effect relationship. Thus, in his view, we have learned to associate friction with heat (in our association among ideas), but we are mistaken if we assume that friction causes the heat or possesses any power which must inevitably produce heat. There is merely repetition of two incidents so that the effect habitually attends the cause but is not a necessary consequence of it. Hume's statement regarding causal relations revolutionized subsequent philosophical thought.

Hume's Ethical Theory. As an Ethical Subjectivist, Hume adhered to the theory that morality consists of principles or values which the individual formulates for himself as a matter of personal opinion. Hume, furthermore, was a Social Subjectivist, inasmuch as he also believed that moral values are based upon the opinions of a particular society. Moral principles are relative to (determined by and varying with) public opinion. Those ethical standards which the group approve are called moral, while those which the group disapproves are regarded as immoral. Whereas moral sentiments are held in common and are widely approved because they enhance the social good, immoral attitudes are egoistic, detrimental, and antisocial. Therefore, according to Hume, not logic nor reason, but sentiment becomes the foundation of morality. The individual may choose to approve and accept a specific ethical attitude or moral feeling, or he may find it disagreeable and reject it. He decides what is to be moral conduct for him. But Hume felt that the best judge of morality would be the disinterested spectator, the innocent bystander who, not being involved in the social situation, could coldly examine the society and ascertain what its people as a whole approve or disapprove. Whatever receives social approbation is moral and whatever encounters widespread disapproval is immoral.

Hume's Philosophy of Religion. Hume's Skepticism carried over into his philosophy of religion. He had rejected the idea of absolute matter, the concept of the soul as a substance, the validity of scientific law, and the view of moral principles as objective realities. Now he applied to religious ideas the same characteristic of relativity as in the case of ethical standards; he rejected Berkeley's assertion of the metaphysical reality of spiritual things and denied all possibility of certainty in religious doctrines which, he said, must be based on mere probability at best. He denied the existence of miracles. He held that the world could have existed throughout eternity, requiring no first cause, although he believed that we could attribute its order and design to an architect if we so preferred. However, he insisted that such an architect would have to be held responsible for natural evil; consequently, the problem of evil would remain unresolved unless a finite, limited God were to be accepted as the alleged architect of the universe, a God who, if he were perfectly good, must also be impotent to eliminate all evil in nature. In other words, according to Hume, any assumed deity would have to be limited either as to his goodness or as to his power.

THOMAS REID AND THE COMMON SENSE SCHOOL

It remained for another Scot, Thomas Reid (1710–1796) to become the most influential opponent of Hume's Skepticism. Reid was the founder of the Common Sense school of Scottish philosophy. Among other notable adherents of the Common Sense school were Dugald Stewart (1753–1828) and Thomas Brown (1778–1820), both professors at the University of Edinburgh. Of lesser importance were two philosophers, namely, James Beattie (1753–1803) and James Oswald (*d.* 1793), who became well known because their views were cited by Immanuel Kant in his works.

The philosophers of the Common Sense school accepted the Empiricist view that knowledge is acquired through sense experience, but they rejected Locke's contention that ideas in the mind must be separated from the external objects which the ideas represent. The Common Sense philosophers asserted that the individual knows the real objects in the universe by means of direct, immediate perceptions of them, that the sense impressions are not images or copies but contacts with the realities themselves. Today this view of reality is known as Naïve Realism: the reality itself, the object, is exactly what it appears to the senses to be; somehow, sense experience is immediately connected with the sensed object which possesses an existence of its own, independent of our experience of it. We therefore know intuitively, by means of common sense, that objects exist, and they exist whether or not anyone experiences them. Thus, although all our ideas are derived either from sensation or from reflection (as Locke had asserted), Berkeley erred in reducing real substances to the status of mere ideas, or spiritual substance, and Hume had erred in relegating real objects to the "limbo of nonexistence."

The Common Sense school, with its Metaphysical Realism, has only historical value for contemporary philosophy except that some of its ideas have been accepted in part by American and British advocates of Neorealism. The efforts of the Common Sense school to repudiate Humean Skepticism had little success, in contrast to the decisive influence of the Kantian synthesis of Empiricism and Rationalism.

PHILOSOPHERS OF THE FRENCH ENLIGHTENMENT

Practically all the philosophers who founded their philosophical positions upon Locke's Empiricism may be regarded as philosophers of the French Enlightenment. It was Locke's epistemology which contributed most to subsequent philosophical systems, but when his Empiricist ideas reached the French intellectual elite, they accepted more than his epistemological idea; some of them, such as Voltaire, were greatly influenced by his social and political philosophy as well.

Voltaire. *François Marie Arouet* (1694–1778), whose pen name was *Voltaire,* deeply admired British institutions and particularly the philosophy of Empiricism which he effectively propagated in France. Voltaire fought for the cause of individual freedom against the authority of Church and State, accepting many of John Locke's political, social, and epistemological views. He agreed with the Deists, such as John Toland (1670–1722), and with Isaac Newton that the presence of order and design in the cosmos justifies a belief in God. (The Deists sought to formulate a rational religion based on Descartes' concept of a mechanical universe, Newton's laws of physics, the Copernican theory of the planets, and John Locke's view of experience as the only valid foundation of knowledge.)

Voltaire, who believed in a finite God, with powers so limited that they could not eliminate the evils in nature, opposed religious institutions as such and in particular accused the Roman Catholic Church in France of persecution, superstition, and deceit. He himself accepted the theory that mankind has a free will to choose its course of action, although he later modified this view, admitting that what a man apparently freely chooses must have been made necessary by his background of experience. Although he fought for political liberty and civil rights he opposed democracy as a system run by the ignorant rabble, and he preferred an enlightened monarchy.

The French Encyclopaedists. Dennis Diderot (1713–1784) and Jean Le Rond D'Alembert (1717–1783) were the principal editors of an extraordinary multiple work, the *French Encyclopaedia,* to which Voltaire contributed numerous articles. The twenty-eight volumes in this encyclopaedia included a great variety of contributions from Skeptics, Materialists, and atheists (such as Dietrich von Holbach) as well as the Deists. Summarizing the scholarship and rational thought of the time, the encyclopaedia, which followed Francis Bacon's classification of scientific disciplines, had a profound influence on political, social, and cultural trends in France and in many other countries during the eighteenth and early nineteenth centuries.

French Sensationalism. A group of French philosophers, adhering generally to Locke's Empiricism, developed theories of consciousness and related concepts classifiable under the heading of French Sensationalism. In this group were Condillac, Helvétius, La Mettrie, and Holbach.

CONDILLAC. Étienne Bonnot de Condillac (1715–1780) outlined his system of Sensationalism in his *Treatise on Sensations* (1754). Condillac was an extreme Empiricist who regarded all consciousness (mental functions) as merely transformed sensations. Even internal reflection is a perception which originates in external sense perception; consequently, higher thought processes are no more than sense transformations. The mind is so completely passive that should its first sensation be that of the scent of a rose, then at that point of time the entire personality would be nothing more than the scent of a rose. The soul is composed entirely of sensations, and we lack any knowledge of its real substance. Condillac interpreted desire as simply the recollection of previous sensations of pleasure experienced by the soul. Secondary qualities (such as color, sound, and odor) are subjective sensations, whereas extension is a quality of the things themselves in the outer world. Despite his Sensationalist point of view, however, he was not a Materialist, because (taking his lead again from Locke) he denied the possibility that matter could ever be able to think or feel. He believed that feeling and thought imply the existence of a substratum, providing a unity or unified relationship between object and subject.

HELVÉTIUS. Claude Adrien Helvétius (1715–1771) patterned his philosophy after Condillac's Sensationalism. He emphasized a thesis of egoistic Hedonism, based upon the theory that the mind initially is a blank tablet whose desires arise from experiences of pleasure and pain. Unlike the Deists and those who adopted a rational ethics of nature, he preferred to accept the theological morality of the Church.

LA METTRIE. Julian Offrai de La Mettrie (1709–1751) was a Materialist noted primarily for his *L'homme machine* (1748), a work based upon the mechanistic psychology (or physiology) of

Descartes. In this book he set forth the hypothesis that all animals are merely machines, including man as the human machine. His conclusions were based upon his observations of the similarities in the physiology of the plants, animals, and human beings. He considered physical substance to be the fundamental reality, concluding that since spiritual functions are profoundly affected by the condition of the body, the soul must perish at the same time as the body. La Mettrie condemned ethics that preached abstinence, for he advocated a maximum of sensual enjoyment as the proper goal for mankind.

HOLBACH. Dietrich von Holbach (1723–1789), a German philosopher who lived in France, wrote in French his *System of Nature* (1770), which set forth materialistic doctrines similar to those of La Mettrie. Attributing the functions of the mind to brain activity, he asserted that all human behavior is mechanical and that the soul consists entirely of the epiphenomena resulting from, or identified with, bodily functions. He repudiated the belief in God and immortality, and advocated that man return to those moral principles which guided him in a state of nature, prior to his corruption by the customs and institutions of civilization.

ROUSSEAU. Jean Jacques Rousseau (1712–1778) succeeded Voltaire as the paramount philosopher of the French Enlightenment. He had early come under the influence of Voltaire's point of view, but later became its vigorous opponent, especially in political philosophy when he rejected Voltaire's defense of constitutional monarchy and advocated equal rights for all citizens under a democratic scheme of social control.

Rousseau condemned Hobbes' theory that man is innately corrupt, insisting, on the contrary, upon the natural goodness of human nature. Man is born both innocent and good, as well as free and equal. Only the corrupting influence of civilization is responsible for current evils, which can be eliminated completely by developing and guiding the individual's natural feelings and impulses. In his famous work, *Émile* (1762) Rousseau showed how, if artificial methods of education were eliminated, a child's innate tenderness and powers could be developed in a wholesome manner and with full respect for the rights and welfare of others. The child should be taught to follow the dictates of his own heart, his nobler emotions, to obey religious inspiration, and always to express in action his sympathy for other people. Rousseau appealed therefore, not to any rational or intellectual basis for conduct, but to each person's natural feelings and sentiments, which, he believed, would lead mankind along the paths of morality and religion. He affirmed the belief in God and immortality.

Rousseau outlined his principles of social reform in his classic *The Social Contract* (1762), which set forth a well reasoned justification for a democratic form of government. The State is a political organization based upon a social contract which its citizens have entered into by virtue of their innate inalienable rights to freedom and equality, and their power of self-determination. Man, said he, "is born free, and everywhere he is found in chains." Since civilization is responsible for this condition of affairs, we must return to the simplicities of nature to determine the most natural mode of the State. In nature we find a paradigm, namely the family, the most natural form of the basic social unit. In a family there is neither slavery nor inequality, and the State should follow its example. Free and equal men with inalienable wills have a right to institute a State through mutual agreement, by engaging in a social contract, for sovereignty rests solely with the people. Decisions are made democratically by vote; however, a person must not vote for selfish advantage but only for the common good. Rousseau distinguished sharply between a collection of selfish individual votes (which he termed the *will of all*) and the majority vote (which he termed the *general will*) cast by individuals concerned for the welfare of the nation as a whole, the common good. People are good, and therefore will vote for the good: "*the people are never corrupted,* though often deceived and it is only then that they seem to will what is evil." Only when the general will prevails does a democracy thrive. Sovereign power rests with the people, owing to their inalienable will. The people may confer power on elected officials, but never will they surrender their right of sovereignty.

Rousseau's influence was considerable, particularly in political philosophy and educational theory. In the field of education, his ideas were adopted by Basedow, Pestalozzi, and Froebel, and his influence has continued into contemporary times. In political theory, his views were implemented in the *Declaration of the Rights of Man* (1789). In Germany, his ideas were reflected in the works of leading thinkers such as Kant, Schiller, Goethe, and Herder. Kant testified that he had held the masses in contempt as an ignorant rabble until Rousseau's arguments in behalf of political democracy impelled him to change his mind.

Chapter 10

The German Idealists

We have noted that the dominance of Continental Rationalism in philosophy was followed by that of British Empiricism during the Enlightenment, beginning with Locke's *An Essay concerning Human Understanding* in 1690 and culminating in Hume's complete Skepticism. The social and political ideas of Locke were reflected in the philosophy of Voltaire, the French Sensationalists and Materialists, and Rousseau; and in America, his ideas had an impact upon the framers of the United States Constitution. Leibniz had introduced new interpretations and modifications of Locke's Empiricism. But the major departure in the history of philosophy came with the work of Immanuel Kant, whose *Critique of Pure Reason* (1781) marked the end of the period of the Enlightenment and initiated a new era of critical philosophy, namely, German Idealism.

Kantian Idealism constituted a synthesis of Continental Rationalism and British Empiricism. Kant combined the Rationalists' thesis that truth is attainable through sheer reason with the opposing thesis of the British Empiricists that valid knowledge can be acquired through sense experience.

KANT'S TRANSCENDENTAL IDEALISM

Immanuel Kant (1724–1804), a native of Königsberg in Prussia, was educated at Königsberg University, which became famous as a center of philosophy through his long tenure on its faculty. Kant had been profoundly influenced by the works of Leibniz, Newton, and Hume, as well as (to a lesser degree) by Rousseau, Voltaire, and the British Deists and Intuitionists. Publication of his *Critique of Pure Reason* in 1781 initiated a new era in philosophical thought.

His most significant writings, in addition to the *Critique of Pure Reason*, were his *Critique of Practical Reason* (1788), *Critique of Judgment* (1790), *Prolegomena to Every Future System of Metaphysic* (1783), *Religion within the Limits of Pure Reason* (1784),

Fundamental Principles of the Metaphysics of Morals (1785), and *Eternal Peace* (1795). The first three works developed the foundations of his philosophy, expounding his *transcendental method* as applied to epistemology (in the *Critique of Pure Reason*), ethics (in the *Critique of Practical Reason*), and aesthetics (in the *Critique of Judgment*).

All three critiques analyze the *a priori* aspects of the mind, i.e., mental functions prior to sense experience. Kant realized that it would be necessary, first, to explore the nature of the mind itself, and second, to trace the connections between its *a priori* nature and its *a posteriori* sense impressions in order to unite or synthesize these two aspects of mental activity.

Kant's Epistemological Problem. In his *Critique of Pure Reason* Kant delved into the fundamental epistemological question, "How are *a priori* synthetic judgments possible?" In other words, how can we explain the possibility of scientific knowledge, or, more precisely, that relationship between cause and effect which enables the mind to grasp scientific truths?

It will be recalled that David Hume had negated the laws of causation as unverifiable by means of sense experience, reducing cause-effect relationships to the status of mere habitual assumptions. Kant was unable to cope with the Humean problem on the basis of Cartesian Rationalism, but he was inspired by Leibniz' reference to the human mind as an active process, as something more than sense impressions. The idea that the intellect possesses a character and powers of its own, he felt, would enable him to prove that scientific laws, particularly the Newtonian laws he admired, are valid demonstrable truths. His analysis divided the process of attaining knowledge into three stages: (1) the transcendental aesthetic; (2) the transcendental analytic; and (3) the transcendental dialectic. Instead of choosing between the Rationalist view that knowledge is derived from innate ideas and the Empiricist view that its source is sense experience, Kant analyzed the nature of the act of knowing, and he concluded that both the mind endowed with *a priori* perceptions and the sensory impressions must unite to yield scientific (or valid) knowledge.

Kantian Synthetic Philosophy. Kant therefore insisted that the concepts of time and space must be minor modes of mental experience prior to sensations and that these concepts must act upon and combine with the sensations; both *a posteriori* and *a priori* elements are essential, for without sensibility no object would be perceptible, whereas without understanding (in terms of time and space relationships) no object could be conceived. To quote from the *Critique of Pure Reason:* "Thoughts without content are empty, perceptions without conceptions are blind . . . Understanding can perceive nothing, the senses can think nothing. Knowledge arises only from their united action."

The Transcendental Aesthetic. The first stage in the process of attaining knowledge, the transcendental aesthetic, is the basic stage that synthesizes sense experience through the concepts of time and space. The mind acts upon sensory impressions, applying time and space relations to them, just as a machine works upon and refines raw materials as one step in making a finished product. In this first stage of the process of knowing, time and space are *a priori,* prior to and independent of all sense experiences, not real objects of the external world but ideal, internal creations of the mind. All sense impressions are channelled through these mental creations, the concepts of time and space, before the mind goes on to the second stage, the transcendental analytic.

The Transcendental Analytic. In the second stage, that of the transcendental analytic, the human understanding changes perceptions (which have passed through the stage of being subjected to time and space) into conceptions or ideas possessing analytical unity. The mind now applies to experience certain categories of thought, namely: (1) quantity—unity, plurality, and totality; (2) quality—reality, negation, and limitation; (3) relation—inherence and subsistence, or substance and accidents, causality and dependence, or cause and effect, and community, or reciprocity, between the active and the passive; and (4) modality—possibility-impossibility, existence-nonexistence, and necessity-contingency. Without the categories we would be unable to think at all. The categories of the transcendental analytic enable us to think scientifically, to think in terms of quantity, cause and effect, and other relationships.

The cause-and-effect relationship is fundamental to scientific thinking. Hume had proved that cause-and-effect relations are not objectively real, do not exist in the outer world. He had shown that causal relations are merely habitual or customary assumptions applied to phenomena. How then could the laws of science, which depend upon laws of cause and effect, be regarded as valid? Kant attempted to solve this problem by assuming that, just as time and space are *a priori* mental creations, not objective realities but subjective conceptual applications, so, too, cause-effect relationships and scientific law are subjective aspects and *a priori* categories of the human understanding. In no sense, therefore, are laws of physics inherent in nature; they are only modes of thought shaping the interpretation of phenomena on their way from sense experience through the processes of reasoning. The categories of human understanding make possible our *a priori* synthetic judgments as valid laws describing the workings of nature. The mind *a priori* imposes these laws upon nature as both necessary and universal; by means of its ability to synthesize, the mind demonstrates that it is creative, that it is not a passive *tabula rasa*. Here, then, the imposition of conceptual categories marks a limit beyond which genuinely valid (scientific) knowledge cannot go. Any further judgments, apart from the use of the categories, would be mere guesswork and invalid dogma. But the mind is not satisfied with this partial explanation of the process of attaining knowledge. Kant assumed a third stage of thinking—in which the mind attempts to arrive at a more adequate, comprehensive grasp of reality—the stage of the transcendental dialectic.

The Transcendental Dialectic.   The human mind seeks complete knowledge, a coherent understanding of the entire universe. Since it does not possess sufficient sensory information to acquire knowledge about the entire universe, it tries to go beyond this kind of sense experience in order to discern ultimate reality. Man's experience provides him with phenomena only, yet his mind informs him that there is an ultimate ontological reality, a real "thing-in-itself" (a noumenon) which produces (or forms the substratum for) each phenomenon. But the human mind is not equipped to sense ultimate reality, the *thing-in-itself*, because man cannot transcend the bounds of his experience. Inasmuch as things-in-themselves cannot be subjected to experience because they are non-sensuous, then he must forever remain content to be agnostic regarding the ultimate reality (the ontologically real nature) of the universe. Because Kant reasoned that the metaphysically real is beyond the reach of human knowledge, his system is one of Metaphysical Agnosticism or Agnostic Realism.

In effect, Kant postulated three kinds of reality: (1) the world of phenomena, from which all our sense experience comes, the world we live in and perceive; (2) the world of understanding, in which we discern all our scientific knowledge and the laws of science; and (3) the ultimately real world, which transcends all our ability to sense it, a supersensible world which must remain unknowable to the human mind.

Although the ultimate reality is unknowable, the mind attempts to discover and describe its nature. The real or supersensible world, that transcendent sphere which is beyond experience, is thus a *reconstruction* of the mind. The mind of man takes whatever content it receives (through its percepts and concepts), then reproduces what it believes to be the real world. Thus the real world is an ideal reconstruction in the mind of man, a replica of what he believes the real world is like. "The world is my representation," wrote Kant. This real or noumenal world of man is not "an object of sense, but is thought, by pure understanding alone, as a thing in itself."

The mind, dissatisfied with incomplete knowledge, errs in applying its categories as a means of achieving perfect knowledge of the entire universe. Eventually man realizes the futility of this method, and he attempts to create ideas about the universe which transcend the bounds of experience and in this way to unify knowledge into an integrated coherent whole. Here is the third stage, that of the transcendental dialectic; these ideas of reason (or pure conceptions of reason) "are not mere fictions," said Kant, "but spring from the very nature of reason itself, and therefore stand in a necessary relation to the whole use of understanding. . . . They are transcendent, inasmuch as they overleap the limits of all experience." Their function is to "guide understanding to clearer and wider knowledge. . . . The sole aim of pure reason is absolute totality of synthesis." These "ideals of pure reason," as Kant referred to them, possess regulative value; they serve as a *heuristic or regulative principle* of pure reason, and reflect the highest stage of synthesis of the understanding, that stage or form called *reason* in the transcendental dialectic. Their regulative value consists in attempting to grasp the totality of conditions by connecting particular phenomena with the whole of experience for the sake of a systematic and unified body of knowledge. For example, "the ideal of the Supreme Being is therefore nothing but a *regulative principle* of reason, telling us to view all connection in the world as if it proceeded from an all-sufficient necessary cause." It is impossible to arrive at the ultimate reality of the universe because phenomena are endless and the accumulation of phenomena is interminable; the task cannot be fully accomplished by reason, which must deal with insoluble problems and transcendental illusions accepted by reason as if they were settled truths.

When reason attempts to evaluate these illusions, then contradictions or antithetical ideas result; Kant called these the antinomies, that is, two contradictory inferences, correctly reasoned from principles, both of which are regarded as true. Antinomies are not logically fallacious. Kant maintained that antinomies result from the reason's attempt to apply the categories of the understanding to the absolute, to the transcendent, whereas the categories are applicable only to empirical experience. Kant set forth four antinomies of reason or conflicts between transcendental ideas; each thesis is accompanied by its antithesis as follows:

THESIS	ANTITHESIS
(1) The world has a beginning in time, and is enclosed within limits of space.	(1) The world has no beginning in time, and no limits in space, but is infinite with regard to both time and space.
(2) Every composite substance in the world is made up of simple parts, and nothing whatever exists but the simple, or that which is composed out of the simple.	(2) No composite thing in the world is made up of simple parts, nor does anything simple exist anywhere in the world.
(3) Causality in conformity with laws of nature is not the only causality, from which all the phenomena of the world can be derived. To explain those phenomena it is necessary to suppose that there is also a free causality.	(3) There is no freedom, but all that comes to be in the world takes place entirely in accordance with laws of nature.
(4) There exists an absolutely necessary being, which belongs to the world either as a part or as the cause of it.	(4) There nowhere exists an absolute necessary being, either in the world, or outside of the world as its cause.

Each antinomy has its corresponding category: the first antinomy relates to the quantity of the world; the second, to the quality of the world; the third to causal relation of the world; and the fourth to the modality of the world, i.e., to the question whether or not the world requires an absolutely necessary being.

The Ideals of Reason. Kant recognized three ideals of reason: (1) the soul; (2) the ultimate world or reality; and (3) God. These three ideals constitute the forms of reason in the same way that the categories are the *a priori* forms of the understanding, or space and time are the *a priori* forms of sense perception. Neither sense experience (perception) nor the understanding provides information about God, the soul, or the ontological nature of the universe because they are limited to the data of experience; but reason transcends the bounds of sensory experience and extends into the supersensuous, the unknowable, and thus provides us with unprovable conceptions or knowledge which man would otherwise be unable to acquire. Unlike empirical knowledge, which is relational and partial, in the natural sciences, reason (dissatisfied with such incomplete knowledge) strives to formulate unrelated and unconditional conceptions in order that it may grasp the whole of reality. Reason should be used therefore as a controlling principle which sets up an ideal of perfect knowledge even though it is unprovable. "The supreme Being is for purely speculative reason a mere ideal, but still a perfectly faultless ideal, which completes and crowns the whole of human knowledge."

Because the ideals of reason (the soul, the ultimate world, and God) transcend the bounds of experience, they are eternally unknowable by the human mind, and we must be forever agnostic as to their existence and nature. Nevertheless, granted that we cannot prove the existence of these three ideals of reason, it is equally true that no one will ever be able to disprove them either. Kant stated that he had "limited all that we can know to mere phenomena," and had therefore "found it necessary to deny knowledge of God, freedom, and immortality, in order to find a place for faith."

Kant's Ethical Theory. The *Critique of Practical Reason* is concerned with the proper role and objects of the human will. Just as the *Critique of Pure Reason* analyzed speculative reason and established its freedom from the impurities of empirical elements, so this critique on practical reason similarly used *a priori* intuition, independent of empirical experience, to delve into the functions of reason in matters pertaining to the autonomous will, that is, to moral laws of voluntary action. Kant also developed some of his principles of ethics in *The Fundamental Principles of the Metaphysics of Morals* (1785); *Religion within the Limits of Pure Reason* (1784); *Doctrine of Virtue* (1797); and *Doctrine of Rights* (1797).

Moral Law. The main purpose of Kant's system of ethics was to formulate moral laws as those necessary and universal objects of the human will which must be accepted as valid for everyone. Kant concluded that there are moral laws which he described as the *categorical imperative,* constituting moral commands which every person is bound to obey irrespective of the particular circumstances confronting him. The individual must will to obey the moral law without exception. Right is right and must be done even under the most extreme conditions. "Let justice be done though the heavens fall."

We know what is morally right *a priori,* by intuition, without having to consider practical circumstances. Indeed, the facts in a situation have no bearing upon the moral law, which must govern all conduct despite either the consequences which may follow from obeying the law or the conditions under which it is obeyed. The moral law does not depend upon what we want, desire, like, or love; it is a statement of what we *ought* to will. Kant asserted that "I ought" implies "I can"; if the categorical imperative obligates the will to obey a moral command, it must necessarily follow that the individual has the power to carry out the obligation. What is not within one's power to do, can never be a moral obligation.

Duty. According to Kant, duty represents the individual's obligation to obey the categorical imperative by choosing the morally right action which may or may not correspond to his feelings or to legal prescriptions. A person may feel one way, yet be obligated by duty to act another way. Since he cannot always control his emotions, he cannot make them agree with his moral duty on all occasions. Duty is a matter of free choice of the right course of conduct. In order to be moral, a man must act from duty, and not merely according to duty (mere legality). He must respond to moral action out of a respect for moral law, and not mechanically carry out an act which outwardly has the appearance of duty, without being prompted from duty. He may be unable to love his neighbor like a mother, but he can follow the Biblical injunction to love him in the sense that he can show good will toward him.

Ethical Intuitionism. Kant was an Ethical Intuitionist inasmuch as he believed that moral right may be determined without considering the circumstances of (or the possible consequences resulting from) the action to be carried out. Moral right is known *a priori* without the aid of external facts of experience; it is discerned within the mind by means of a rational, autonomous will. According to Kant, it is not any act with its attending consequences which is good or bad, but only what is *willed.* Only the will, not actions and their ensuing consequences, may be good or evil.

Nature of the Categorical Imperative. The moral command

which every person has the duty to obey—the categorical imperative—allows of no exceptions. It is universal, so that whatever is
morally right for one person to do, is right for all, and whatever
is morally wrong for him is wrong for all. Kant's maxim is a philosophical version of the Golden Rule: "Act only on that maxim
whereby you can at the same time will that it should become a
universal law."

Consider an example of the categorical imperative. It might
seem wise or prudent to break a promise because other people
might be harmed if you kept your promise. But do you have a
moral right to break a promise? Not according to Kant's categorical imperative, for that principle states that your action must be
universally applicable, and surely you would not wish everyone to
have the moral right to break promises whenever he so desires. It
is therefore your duty to keep your promise, just as you would
expect others to keep their pledges. The categorical imperative is
a moral law binding upon every person so that what is right for
one is right for all humanity: you must "act as if the maxim from
which you act were to become through your will a universal law
of nature."

Dignity and the Kingdom of Ends.   Kant portrayed man as
an autonomous being who respects the moral law which he must
practice and therefore as a personality having infinite intrinsic
worth or dignity. Everything else in the world has an exchange
value, a price for which the owner is willing to sell his property,
but man alone possesses self-direction and dignity, for he is price-
less, and any man who sells himself, his freedom of choice, is
short-changed. Even the angels would be inferior to man if they
were deprived of their moral will, their free choice of action in
pursuit of a morally valid goal.

> *"With all his failings, man is still*
> *Better than angels void of will."*

It is because man possesses dignity and belongs to a "kingdom of
ends" that he must never be used as a mere object of utility, but
must be treated as an end in himself. If man errs or sins, nevertheless the moral law within him, and his personality as the foun-
tainhead of moral value, must be regarded as holy.

Kant's Philosophy of Religion.   For Kant, self-determination, the autonomy of the rational will, is the indispensable condition of all morality. Without self-direction, morality would be

impossible. The individual's power of will, his freedom to make a choice among alternative actions, is its own uncaused cause. Without freedom, morality would not exist. Freedom of the will is expressed by the moral consciousness: "thou canst, for thou oughtest."

The moral consciousness reflects the reality of three necessary, supersensuous things-in-themselves: (1) freedom of the will; (2) the immortality of the soul; and (3) the existing Supreme Being, God. These three are known to us, not by means of demonstrative proofs, but through practical reason; they are necessary assumptions based upon the *a priori* moral law of the categorical imperative.

Man must be free to make moral choices. In addition, he must assume his own immortality, for the moral law could not possibly be fulfilled within the limits of a single lifetime; the complete, perfect performance of one's moral duty, based upon the never-ending process of self-understanding and self-direction, requires an eternity. Immortality therefore "results from the practically necessary condition of a duration adequate to the complete fulfillment of the moral law." Finally, since only God can insure human achievement of the supreme good, the existence of God is a necessary postulate of practical reason.

For Kant, the *summum bonum*, man's greatest good, is *virtue combined with happiness*. The moral person ought to be the one who is happy, but on earth a person's happiness is not necessarily commensurate with his goodness. Consequently there must be a God who will see that the virtuous man finds in a future life the happiness which he rightfully deserves and did not find upon earth; without such an eventual justice, morality would lose all significance. Nevertheless, Kant insisted that even in this earthly existence, man must be motivated toward moral conduct, not by the expectation of happiness, but only out of duty—reverence for the moral law. Duty is for duty's sake, not for the sake of happiness. The goal of personal ethics is twofold: (1) it is the individual's duty to attain his own perfection; and (2) it is his duty to seek the happiness of others.

In conclusion it may be said that pure practical reason (the choice of conduct by the free will) has primacy over pure speculative reason (theory about reality) in matters of cognition and proof. Speculative reason is subordinate to practical reason because "all interest is ultimately practical, and even that of speculative reason is conditional, and it is only in the practical employment of reason that it is complete." Moral good possesses primacy over science. Speculative reason must be subordinate to practical reason in order to prevent reason from contradicting itself; that is, the concepts of freedom of the will, immortality, and the existence of God are admitted by practical reason, but these concepts affect human experience far beyond the sphere of theory and cognition. Since practical reason must be accepted as the primary element in man's life, he must realize the real existence and significance of the three postulates.

Kant's Social and Political Philosophy. Kant's *Eternal Peace* (1795) set forth those main principles of his social and political philosophy which seemed to him to constitute the basis for lasting peace among the peoples of the world. He advocated the formation of a World State, a federated republic of free States comparable in many respects to the United Nations. Irrespective of their membership in national political organizations, all individuals would participate in the World State as citizens thereof possessing cosmopolitan rights and privileges. A system of international law, designed to govern the relationships among the various States, would include the following provisions: (1) Any treaties to preserve world peace must contain no secret terms or reservations. (2) No State shall subjugate or control any other State, and each shall remain free and independent. (3) Standing armies shall be abolished. (4) Each nation shall avoid the use of borrowed funds as an instrument of its foreign policy. (5) No State shall prevent other States from carrying out their constitution and laws. (6) States at war with each other shall be prohibited from using those methods and instruments of war which will make peace negotiations impossible.

Kant repudiated the political philosophy of Machiavelli as a form of political sophistry. Instead he urged statesmen to follow certain moral principles based upon his categorical imperative. According to Kant, there need be no contradiction between moral and political principles, which should be perfectly compatible. Not only must the politician obey the moral law, the categorical imperative, but the public has the right to know the facts about his activities.

Kant rejected Plato's thesis that there will be no hope for a good State unless kings become philosophers or philosophers become kings. He suggested instead that philosophers should not attempt to rule, but should serve as counsellors, advising the ruler as disinterested observers. As such, they will exercise good judgment (so often distorted by the possession of power) and will be best qualified to analyze political conditions and needs clearly and objectively.

FICHTE'S SUBJECTIVE IDEALISM

Johann Gottlieb Fichte (1762–1814) studied theology in preparation for the ministry but worked as a private tutor until 1794 when he was appointed to the faculty of the University of Jena, then the chief intellectual center of Germany. He became founder and leader of the new school of German Idealism which formulated a philosophy of the absolute—a point of view based upon theology and designed to reform practical affairs as well as philosophy and science. From 1809 to 1814 he lectured as professor of philosophy in the then newly founded University of Berlin.

Among his most influential writings are: *Criticism of All Revelation* (1792); *The Science of Knowledge* (1794–1795), his most famous work; *Foundation of Natural Rights* (1796); *The Vocation of Man* (1800); *The Doctrine of Religion* (1806); and *Speeches to the German Nation* (1808).

The Background of Fichtean Idealism. Fichte's philosophy shows a marked dependence upon the philosophy of Kant and Spinoza. From Kant it borrowed the idea of a moral order in nature and from Spinoza the idea of the unity of the universe (Metaphysical Monism). Fichte synthesized these two ideas into a Philosophical Monism centering in the moral will as the activating principle of the world. His point of view contributed much to the philosophy of Hegel (as in the Hegelian dialectic of thesis, antithesis, and synthesis) and Schopenhauer (as reflected in the latter's analysis of the will). Fichte's influence has persisted in modern philosophy; Hegelians were attracted to the absolutist aspects of his philosophy, disciples of Schopenhauer to his emphasis upon freedom of the will as man's essential nature, and contemporary Existentialists to concepts strikingly reminiscent of his form of Idealism.

Fichte's Dialectical Method. Fichte regarded the fact of consciousness as the key to understanding of reality, as reflected in the assertion, "I think" (*Cogito*). The conscious mind (self-consciousness) creates both the objects (the real) and the knowledge (the ideal) by which the objects become known. This view is identical with Berkeley's idea, "to be is to be perceived"; an object cannot exist unless a percipient experiences it. The world is a rational, unified system directed toward a purpose and therefore it is not a mere machine controlled by definite causes. Reason is a real entity or power which performs purposeful acts, and which includes self-consciousness as well as knowledge of the universe as a unified whole. Reason interprets the world by means of the *dialectical method,* a logical system for comprehending the universe as a rational unit. The fundamental "deed-act" is self-consciousness, an absolute first principle which can neither be proved nor predetermined by specific causes. As the basic principle of human knowledge, self-consciousness is the means of searching for the Absolute. The philosopher's search for the truth begins with a *demand* calling for fulfillment, namely, "Think thyself!" It is the sole and fundamental task of philosophy to clarify what is involved in this act of self-analysis. As reason performs its function, it encounters problems of choice or contradictions between the deed-act which actually occurs and the deed-act which reason would logically expect to occur. As reason attempts to solve these problems or contradictions, it creates new ones. In this dialectic, reason thus utilizes three rational principles—thesis, antithesis, and synthesis—to interpret the nature and goals of the universe. A thesis or first conclusion fails to provide an adequate solution and gives rise to a similarly inadequate antithesis; the synthesis combines thesis with antithesis in a dialectic logic of reason.

It was Kant who raised the question, "How are synthetic judgments *a priori* possible?" Fichte's answer is that the dialectical method makes them possible through its synthesis uniting opposing principles, namely, the Ego and the Non-Ego. The thesis is the Ego; the antithesis is the Non-Ego; and the synthesis is the Ego and Non-Ego united. But the dialectical process, like moral progress, is endless, for each synthesis, in turn, becomes a new thesis which joins its corresponding antithesis in a new synthesis to repeat the never-ending process. The original thesis (the starting point) is the person and his own consciousness (the Ego); the antithesis is the object of his consciousness, that is, sense phenomena (the Non-Ego); and the synthesis is the unification of these two opposites into subject-object (Ego and Non-Ego). This dialectical process continues until the Absolute, the universal Ego, has been attained.

Fichte's dialectical method owed much to the influence of Spinoza's Metaphysical Monism, which required that the entire universe be understood as a unified, infinite composite and that all things therein be viewed from the standpoint of eternity. The dialectical method became the basis for Hegelian philosophy and was commonly referred to as the Hegelian dialectic. The same kind of synthesis is today being used widely by scholars specializing in the philosophy of history as they attempt to interpret the record of man's intellectual and cultural attainments. In our preceding discussions we have utilized the same dialectic method in designating Continental Rationalism as the thesis of modern philosophy, British Empiricism as the antithesis, and the German philosophy of Kant as the synthesis; then we drew out of the Kantian synthesis an analysis of post-Kantian German Idealism, which became a new and higher thesis (German Rationalism) and reached its highest point in Hegelian philosophy. (As we shall see, the antithesis to Hegelian philosophy developed in the views of many post-Hegelian philosophers in direct opposition to Hegelian Absolutism.)

Subjective Idealism. Fichte sought to perfect Kant's philosophical system by synthesizing pure reason with practical reason (speculative reason with moral reason, theory with practice, or reason with the will). He built upon Kant's "transcendental unity of apperception" the concept of Ego or self-consciousness as the basis for his principle, "I think"—comparable to the *Cogito* of Descartes. To Fichte the Ego became the *a priori* means of combining the various Kantian categories with the moral law, the categorical imperative, thereby synthesizing the two elements into a single system. Thus, Fichte synthesized into a single unity Kant's fundamental views set forth in his *Critiques* of *Pure Reason* and *Practical Reason. A priori* reasoning and Idealism seemed to him to be the only valid approach to philosophy. Even the so-called "material substance" and extension must be regarded as spiritual and purposive in nature.

According to Fichte, ultimate reality is the moral Ego, pure will, active reason, the good. The Being posited by Parmenides, the ontologically real, exists only for the sake of doing, and whatever exists must be understood in the light of what ought to be. We do not strive for Being, but for what ought to be, namely, the fulfillment of our duty. Being, *per se,* has no value, for as substance or matter it is merely appearance, phenomena. Its value consists of its manifestation of pure will, which is the thing-in-itself, i.e., the ultimate and absolute reality. As Aristotle taught, it is this activity through the universal force or will that impels all objects in nature to realize their potential, their true ends. The existence of objects can be understood only in terms of their contribution to what ought to be, i.e., to the realization of the moral world order. Consequently, to be valid a philosophy must begin with the assumption that Being is nothing, that duty is absolutely everything. Anyone who considers the phenomenal world apart from its intelligible essence will find it to be unintelligible and insubstantial. Nature must be explained on the basis of teleology; events are not made necessary by causes, but, on the contrary, everything is motivated by its own purpose. The Ego, as the uncaused, spontaneous act of self-consciousness, posits itself and also the Non-Ego or sensory, phenomenal world which must be guided by practical reason. The self-consciousness of the Ego constitutes knowledge, which includes the sensory phenomena, as Berkeley contended in his statement, *Esse* is *percipe* (to exist is to be perceived). In this Berkeleyan sense, the subject makes the object, as expressed in the fundamental thesis of Subjective Idealism. All of nature as it is known to us consists only of illusory sense material which reflects the on-going moral reality, the goal or duty, of the entire universe. Institutions, such as laws, can participate in the fulfillment of moral duty, for they control and harmonize conflicting personalities which would otherwise be unable to realize their moral purpose. In fact the entire phenomenal world is simply the stuff of duty structured in sensory form as the Non-Ego which seeks to realize itself. "There is a moral order of the world" and therefore the individual must act according to his duty and conscience.

The world order, the essence of things and their supreme principle, is freedom, the highest reality superior even to truth. Indeed, the free will which creates itself (realizes itself) is the truest of all realities; and time itself, like all phenomena, serves merely as a means of self-realization by the free will, the latter being the essence of the moral world order. Fichte believed in the primacy of practical reason, subordinating theoretical reason to the will. In his view, therefore, reason serves moral objectives, and in so doing it unites in a synthesis with the will. Rational thought and the will act together in man and aid him to attain self-realization through self-assertion, through the struggle of his Ego against the Non-Ego or phenomenal (sensory) world which threatens to lead him astray from the moral goal.

Fichte held that self-realization through the freedom of the will is achieved gradually, in stages, in a divine process whereby God constitutes or regulates the moral order of the universe, representing universal duty. God is the universal Ego, the free universal moral process, the world-creating activity. Fichte agreed with Kant that man's moral progress continues throughout eternity.

SCHELLING, SCHILLER, AND SCHLEIERMACHER

Closely related to Kantian and Fichtean philosophies are Schelling's Transcendental Idealism, Schiller's Aesthetic Idealism, and Schleiermacher's Identity of Thought and Being—three points of view which may be regarded as new interpretations of Transcendental Idealism and Subjective Idealism.

Schelling's Transcendental Idealism. Friedrich Wilhelm Joseph Schelling (1775–1854) taught philosophy at Jena, Munich, Berlin, and other German universities. He competed unsuccessfully with Hegel for popularity and prestige, exerting some influence upon Hegel but never approaching the latter's eminence. Schelling's early writings comprise his *negative philosophy,* including his *Philosophy of Nature* (1797); *The World-Soul* (1798); *Transcendental Idealism* (1800); *System of Identity* (1801); *Bruno* (1802); *The Method of Academic Study* (1803); and *Philosophy and Religion* (1804). His later writings represent a positive philosophy and include *The Essence of Human Freedom* (1809); *On the Divinity of Samothrace* (1816); and *Philosophy of Mythology and Revelation* (lectures published by his son).

Schelling's Idealism, borrowing much from Kant and Fichte, posited the Ego and the world as two poles of one and the same absolute reality. Unable to accept Fichte's theory that nature is the product of the absolute Ego and serves merely as the material utilized in the fulfillment of moral duty, Schelling contended that nature is the visible form of spirit, and that, conversely, spirit is the invisible form of nature. He interpreted nature as the Ego in the process of becoming, as the outward expression of a mind actively at work. It is true, said Schelling, that objective reason at first manifests itself in nature as materialistic and then strives to attain conscious expression, but the mind encompasses a greater reality than reason or conscious intelligence; as a spiritual entity it also encompasses forces which are instinctive, unconscious, and purposive. Creative energy, which is the source of everything, is the absolute Ego, an all-pervading World Spirit.

Mind and nature, subject and object, are ultimately the same reality. Whereas Spinoza advocated the doctrine of psychophysical parallelism which portrayed all objects as being either material or mental, but not both, Schelling regarded all phenomena as both ideal and real, as both thought and being—the two are identical. Differences between matter and mind are only apparent, not real, whereas the Absolute or Real is indifferent to such distinctions, just as a magnet is indifferent to the varying strengths of its opposing poles. Schelling's concept of the Absolute as an identity devoid of any differences was rejected by Hegel, who called it "the midnight in which all cows are black."

For Schelling, Absolute Reality consists of creative energy evolving through stages as mind and as matter and at present at its highest level, namely, self-consciousness. The same creative energy manifested in human self-consciousness, freedom, and will is operative everywhere else in the universe—on the unconscious level of sense perception, in the instincts of animals, in gravitational forces, in chemical activity, and in organic growth. Although mind is found in each and all of these entities, the basic creative energy takes the form of blind, unconscious impulse when it acts on a subconscious level, and it becomes completely free and rational when it attains the level of self-consciousness familiar to human experience. Thus the creative spirit in the universe produces nature itself and realizes the goal of self-consciousness when it reaches the evolutionary level of mankind.

Objects in nature represent mind, intelligence, but only in a three-dimensional state when they remain unconscious of their activity. Consequently, nature is but a material manifestation of reason, which, in man, becomes conscious of itself.

On the high level of self-conscious activity attained by mankind, art constitutes the highest stage of development and consciously imitates the creative activity of the Absolute. Therefore, in his creative art, man becomes conscious of the activity of the Absolute, while the Absolute is at the same time conscious of itself, of its own creative energy. Creative art supersedes even morality as the highest function of man, and it constitutes life's basic reality. Thus, it was in the realm of aesthetics that Schelling found a synthesis of the world of sense phenomena with the world of mind or man's moral spirit.

But the aesthetic activity is not limited to either the sensory objects or the moral spirit. The sensuous and the supersensuous are synthesized in beauty so that the highest goal of mankind attains complete fruition in the aesthetic experience. The philosophy of mind reaches its climax in aesthetic reason; hence art supplants logic as the mode by which reason develops, and art becomes the goal of reason. God is the supreme creative artist, and the world is his artistic creation and highest expression. Man attains the fullest realization of his Ego (self) through artistic activity inasmuch as his aesthetic activity transcends both the moral will and his physical sense experience and reaches into the sphere of the divine. Man's noblest endeavor is therefore art, the aesthetic life, not morality. His supreme goal is attainable through aesthetic reason, a concept which Schelling obtained from Schiller who prized it as a spontaneous, ideal play activity. In fact, Schelling's idea of aesthetic reason was based primarily upon Schiller's Aesthetic Idealism.

Schiller's Aesthetic Idealism. Johann Christoph Friedrich Schiller (1759–1805), the German poet, defined beauty as "freedom in phenomenal appearance," because artistic beauty is the free expression of the artist. In artistic creation, the "play impulse" unfolds itself. Only when man plays is he truly man. It is art that refines man's temper, feeling, and sensuous purposes, impelling his moral will to emerge and develop itself effectively, for art destroys the sensuous will, thereby giving free reign to the moral will. When man encounters the beautiful, he undergoes refinement: his uncouthness vanishes, and he is awakened to a higher vocation. Art is both the means and the end of education; it generates the fruits of science and morality. Through art man attains beauty and his beautiful soul (*schöne Seele*) is liberated from the moral conflict (expounded in Kantian ethical theory) between duty and inclination, for a truly beautiful soul is imbued with the desire to fulfill the moral law.

Schleiermacher's Identity of Thought and Being. In another aspect of his philosophy, Schelling had been influenced by the ideas of Friedrich Daniel Ernst Schleiermacher (1768–1834), distinguished teacher of philosophy at the University of Berlin. Schiller had rejected Kant's view of morality as the highest religious activity and had accorded primacy to art, subordinating ethical to aesthetic values. Schleiermacher, however, rejected both views and set forth his own thesis that a mystical awareness or feeling is the highest religious activity.

According to Schleiermacher, God is the "identity of thought and Being," the goal of all learning and knowledge. The aim of all knowledge is to synthesize in human consciousness this "identity of thought and Being." He pointed out that, in human consciousness, the two are not identified as one, but exist as separate entities. In human experience, thought is regarded as concepts, as ideal factors, as intellectual functions, whereas Being is regarded as real, as a composite of perceptions, of organic entities. This division by the human mind has resulted in the dichotomous cleavage of subject matter into physics and ethics, that is, into theory and practice—into formal factors which tend toward understanding and material factors which tend toward action.

Only in the Absolute are the two aspects of knowledge disclosed as one, as God. Since knowledge is always divided in human consciousness, whereas the Absolute (the identity of thought and Being) is not in reality divided at all, scientific knowledge or philosophy can never acquire a true knowledge of God. Philosophy must always remain in a perpetual state of becoming, a state of dialectic, because man's partial, limited knowledge is always in a state of flux.

Inasmuch as it is impossible for us to know God, we cannot pattern our ethical life by referring to his nature or to any of his characteristics, powers, or actions. Consequently, for Schleiermacher the highest religious activity has nothing to do with knowledge or ethics; it consists of communion with God in which Being and consciousness are seen to be identical. The highest form of human activity is to be found only in the closest relationship to God, a communion with God based upon a pious feeling, that is, a feeling of absolute dependence upon God as the divine reality which cannot be fully explored by human thought. God is the infinite World-Ground, i.e., the underlying basis of reality, or the reason, the cause, and the explanation of everything else in the universe. God, as the object of mystical feeling, transcends both human knowledge and the will of man. Thus, in the uniqueness of his religious awareness, a mystical experience, man finds his God as the "identity of thought and Being." Because of this fact, theology becomes a special science with its own data, and it is independent of and transcends philosophy and science. Both Schleiermacher and Schelling interpreted God as the identity of thought and Being.

HEGEL'S ABSOLUTE IDEALISM

Georg Wilhelm Friedrich Hegel (1770–1831), along with Kant the greatest of the German Idealists, developed the most systematic and comprehensive philosophy of modern times, justifying his title of *the* philosopher of this era. Hegel, a native of Stuttgart, studied philosophy and theology at the national university in Tübingen, where he came into frequent contact with Schelling, who recommended him for appointment to the faculty of Jena University. Later he became professor of philosophy at Heidelberg University and, in 1818, succeeded Fichte at the University of Berlin. Among his important works were: *Phenomenology of Mind* (1807); *Science of Logic* (1812–1816); *Encyclopedia of Philosophy* (1817); and *Philosophy of Right* (or *Philosophy of Law*) (1821). (Many of his lectures in various fields of philosophy were published posthumously by his students.) Owing to the complexity of his philosophical system, he often was unable to find words which would have a single precise meaning expressing his ideas and for this reason he had to use the same word to convey several meanings. The student of Hegel must therefore be careful to pinpoint the exact connotation of a Hegelian term.

Hegel's Logical Idealism.   Hegel sought to synthesize the ontology of the ancient Greeks (particularly the theories of Aristotle) with Kantianism. Some of his views may be traced to the influence of Heraclitus, Fichte, Schelling, and Spinoza. In fact, notwithstanding its revolutionary emphasis, the Hegelian system represents largely a synthesis of other philosophies. Kant had set a precedent for such syntheses when he successfully combined the conceptual (rational) world of ideas with the phenomenal world of perception as the basis for valid knowledge. Similarly, Hegel set out to synthesize *all* opposites to arrive at truth, bringing together in his synthesis the epistemology of human reason with the metaphysical cosmos and arriving at the conclusion that "what exists is reason." For Hegel, "What is real is rational—what is rational is real." Thus he united thought and reality into one Absolute which is both rational and real.

To clear the way for his system of Absolute Idealism, Hegel analyzed and rejected Spinoza's concept of Absolute Substance, which he regarded as a mere nonentity or "nothingness," and Schelling's view based on the Identity of Indifference. It seemed to Hegel that Spinoza and Schelling had abstracted from substance so many of its characteristics that it became a concept devoid of all quality and meaning. If every possible characteristic is removed from substance, then it is reduced to a sheer nullity. Beginning with Descartes, all modern metaphysics had moved in this direction. Descartes reduced substance to the status of an insensitive object of the understanding—that which could not be experienced by the senses. At the end of his discussion of substance, Locke emptied it of all characteristics except the mystic one which he called the unknown ("I-know-not-what"). Berkeley identified it with spiritual phenomena, the stuff of experience. Hume eliminated substance altogether. Kant agreed with Locke that it was an unknowable thing-in-itself. Fichte reverted to Berkeley's point of view that substance is a spiritual entity. Spinoza's concept of substance as an abstract universal was rejected by Hegel, who compared this Absolute with the lion's den of Aesop's fable. When Schelling went even beyond Spinoza in abstracting definite qualities from substance, Hegel compared his principle of the Identity of Indifference to the blackness of all cows at midnight.

It was Hegel's task to reverse the trend in philosophy by turning from abstraction to its opposite, concretion. He accepted Fichte's view of the Absolute as spiritual, but to Hegel the Absolute Reality appeared to be a concrete universal entity—not an abstracted reality, but instead a universal which includes within itself every concrete phenomenal object. Whereas for Kant, phenomena are merely the mode in which the things-in-themselves (Absolute Reality) represent themselves to the human individual, for Hegel phenomena are the genuine externalization of the Absolute Spirit in objective nature; that is to say, they are real facts in the objective world, not mere images as his predecessors had assumed.

The True is the Whole. As noted above, Hegel believed that a person who keeps abstracting qualities from concrete objects will eventually produce total abstraction, which means only a nullity or nothingness; consequently, he concluded that the directly opposite activity of discerning the relationship among concrete realities— among all concrete objects in the universe considered as an integrated whole—would uncover genuine rational truth. Hegel used *abstract* and *concrete* as important technical terms with specific meanings: he used *abstract* to refer to the isolation or severance of parts from the whole repeatedly until no further abstraction is possible and the result is complete isolation of every part into a state of nothingness.

Isolated facts or factors—*moments,* as Hegel often refers to them —may be presented in formally correct statements, but they can never constitute the truth because "the truth is the whole." Only when we consider all factors (*momentums*) as forming an organic whole, may we claim to possess the truth. The truth therefore is an integrated unity. Accordingly, Hegel's theory of truth (which is at the same time a criterion of truth) is referred to as the *organic theory of truth*, or the *organic theory of reality*. For Hegel, reality is a Gestalt in which the whole is greater than the sum of its parts. Truth is not static, but dynamic. Abstractions, which are replete with contradictions, need to be synthesized into a coherent whole. The coherent whole is rational—for "the rational is real, and the real is rational."

Phenomena (the facts of nature), as *moments* or factors in an organic whole, are progressing in an evolutionary process according to the course prescribed by reason, which Hegel terms the *Welt Geist*—the World Spirit. The world's unfolding or progressive development is directed by the Reason or *Logos* of the cosmos, that is, by the Spirit of the Absolute. This World Spirit, comparable to the Aristotelian entelechy, actualizes the progress of nature in its evolutionary unfolding.

To determine the truth about animate Beings or inanimate objects, it is necessary to discover the concrete relationship of each entity to the whole, its precise relationship to everything in the universe, that is, to the Absolute. This goal can be achieved by means of a logical process or method, the Hegelian dialectic.

The Hegelian Dialectic.   Since the Rationalists depended upon the static logic developed by Aristotle, instead of dialectical logic, they formed more and more abstractions until they reached the limit of abstractions—the point of nothingness. For this reason Hegel's *Logic* identifies "Being" (Parmenides and his followers had stripped it down by the process of abstraction) with "Nothing." "Being and Nought are empty abstractions." Having denied the reality of anything except pure Parmenidean Being, the philosopher is left with nothingness, for he can no longer think of it as a concrete thing. Hegel agreed with Heraclitus that everything is changing from one concrete state to another; therefore, "Becoming is the fundamental feature of all existence." Life activity occurs as part of this stream or process of change—of Becoming—and Mind is a higher form of Becoming. Nothing is at a standstill, for everything develops by means of the dialectical process. Whatever is absolutely still (in the sense that there is no active process) is nonexistent; thus it is that a completely abstracted Being and Nothing are identical.

Being and Nothing are thesis and antithesis, respectively. As such, each is a *momentum* (Hegel borrowed this term from the science of mechanics), and both are contending but reciprocally dependent forces whose mutual contradiction forms an equation. Thus these momentums—Being $=$ Nothing, and Being $+$ Nothing —account for all instances of Existence.

The *Hegelian dialectic* is a dynamic logic which finds truth through a series of triads: thesis, antithesis, and synthesis. Every thesis, if it is to have any meaning, will find it in its antithesis: every fact will be understood only when related to its opposites, to those things which the thesis is not. Only by pointing out the many relationships of any one object to other objects can we establish the truth about that object. A thesis is any starting point (any momentum) one chooses and carries with it its own antithesis, owing to the Hegelian principle of *negativity* (a cosmic law). If we assume any idea to be true, we will encounter its opposite—its contradiction. If we relate or unite the idea to its opposite, we discover a different truth about them which transcends their previous separate meanings. In setting forth this law of the dialectic, of consciousness, Hegel was agreeing with Spinoza's dictum that "all determination is negation," for the true meaning of a thesis is to be found in its antithesis, in their reciprocal relationships.

All theses or moments "are related to that which they are not. It is this negative relation which defines them." Because of this principle of negativity, the opposites (thesis and antithesis), as a result of their opposition, their clash, are reconciled; they enter into a higher unity, a synthesis. Any synthetic truth involves two contradictory ideas taken up (*aufgehoben*) and "reconciled" in the dialectic logic which reminds us of Aristotle's conclusion that virtue and truth are a mean between opposing extremes or contradictory possibilities. Hegel applied this approach to all relationships in the universe; to find the truth, we must view all possible dialectical opposites together as if they formed a coherent organic and integrated whole.

The dialectic of triads (thesis, antithesis, and the resulting synthesis) continues indefinitely as a logical process until one arrives at the Absolute. The process of approaching the Absolute is the same as that of synthesizing opposites, but each synthesis of opposites now becomes a *new* thesis which, by the principle of negativity, comes into relation to its opposite (its antithesis) in such a way as to gain fuller meaning. These two opposites then unite to form another new and greater synthesis, which then becomes the starting point, the thesis, of a still newer triad. When the dialectic has exhausted all potential applications of which it is capable (having related each thesis to every one of its antitheses) it reveals the whole, unified, absolute truth. The truth is the whole system comprising all possible relationships in the universe, but actually, since nature is an unfolding process of the World Spirit, the task of uniting thesis and antithesis into synthesis persists indefinitely.

Basic Concepts of Hegel's Absolute Idealism. To repeat, Hegel's philosophical system is one in which everything is established in triadic units, and each triad finds its specific relationship to the Absolute. Hegel's system can be shown in a "schema of trinities," in which each trinity will have its thesis (fixed position), its antithesis (negation), and its synthesis (sublation or reconciliation). This schema of triads represents every possible way in which the mind of man can think of reality so as to weave its particular factors or momentums into a unified and integrated system. Each element in the triad is but a moment or factor which finds its truth or value only when synthesized or connected with the rest, the Absolute, the whole. Both reality and mind are fundamentally characterized by contradictions and antitheses. Consequently, the unfolding of reality as well as the unfolding of logical thought entail these conflicting aspects which we can describe as movement and change. Variant phenomena rise up and perish, a process which in itself constitutes their reality. The nature of truth is movement. Within the Absolute, all is change and there is conflict between contradictory factors; yet, within the Absolute, too, all is permanent, in the sense that it forms an interrelated, logical whole.

The Absolute, identical with the divine Idea (similar to Plato's concept of the highest principle) or God, is outside of time and therefore comprises the universe in its potential state, awaiting further evolutionary development. The Spirit or Mind (the *Geist*) constitutes the divine Idea actualized through evolution, the biological, social, and historical unfolding of the world. Thus it is that the Mind, in its aspects both of freedom and of self-consciousness, fulfills its own potentiality. For Hegel, as for Plato, the Idea is creative since the rational is equated with the real. Just as mechanical necessity is the true nature of matter, so freedom is the essence of reason.

THE HEGELIAN SYSTEM

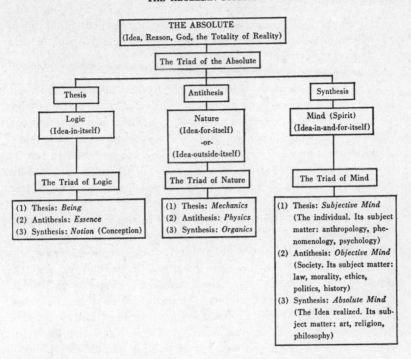

Hegel's Absolute Idea (God) assumes three forms: the Idea-in-itself; the Idea-for-itself; and the Idea-in-and-for-itself. Each of these forms of the Absolute Idea has its own triadic stages or aspects.

THE IDEA-IN-ITSELF. The universal concepts referred to as Ideas-in-themselves are those logical, rational Ideas which form the basis and precede the physical forms known to us as the world of nature. The Absolute Idea is here in its ideal, ultimate form, and hence justifies Hegel's conclusion that all true philosophy is ultimately Ideal, the system of Idealism. It is identical with logic as a process consisting of a thesis (Being, or the ontologically real), an antithesis (Essence, or Negation whereby Being attains its status of phenomena), and a synthesis of Being and Essence, termed the Notion or Concept, representing substance as an independent force or power. The Notion evolves into a triad: (1) Subjective Notion (which develops into its own triad of *conceptions per se, judgments,* and *syllogisms* as a synthesis of these two); (2) Objective

Notion (which develops into the three factors or momentums of mechanism, chemism, and their synthesis, teleology); and (3) the Idea (the synthesis of Subjective and Objective Notion, unifying each concept and its corresponding reality). The individual forces or momentums of the Idea are Life, Cognition, and Absolute Idea as all-pervasive truth.

THE IDEA-FOR-ITSELF. The Idea-for-itself refers to the application or realization of the Absolute Idea in forms manifested to our senses so that they appear as specific individual objects. It is what we know as finite spirits and physical nature, that is, man and the world in which he lives. It is the conscious or mental representation of God's activity in the world. Nature is reason in unconscious form; it is the spatial and temporal character of the Idea or God. The forms of nature, of the Idea-for-itself, are analyzed in our physical and organic sciences.

THE IDEA-IN-AND-FOR-ITSELF. The Idea-in-and-for-itself (Mind or Spirit) is a synthesis of the preceding two forms of reality; it is consciousness which ceases to manifest itself in those forms and returns to itself. It accomplishes this result in three ways: (1) rational activity by the subjective individual (Subjective Mind); (2) rational activity by society (Objective Mind); and (3) rational activity by Absolute Mind, the Idea actualized. Let us examine further this triad of rational activity, which forms the basis for Hegel's systems of ethical, social, and political philosophy, philosophy of history, aesthetics, and philosophy of religion.

SUBJECTIVE MIND. Subjective Mind represents the individual as one who creates abstractions and is independent of society or culture; its components or modes of expression are: (1) the soul in its most rudimentary stage, providing the subject matter for the science of anthropology; (2) consciousness, comprising the world of phenomena (at this stage, the soul is conscious of objects presented to it as the subject); (3) the mind or intellect, in all aspects studied by the science of psychology, this being the synthesis of the preceding two factors—the highest or truth-finding phase of Subjective Mind. The first component (the soul) deals with the relationship of the Subjective Mind to the body; the second (consciousness) manifests spiritual experience by means of reflection, conscious awareness, perception, understanding, and reason; and the third (mind or intellect) expresses itself in the form of intelligence, will, and moral choice.

OBJECTIVE MIND. The Objective Mind reflects the free will as it develops in three areas of experience: (1) legal, abstract, or formal right as an implementation of freedom; (2) morality, in which the will evaluates itself and sets its own standards, a process of conscience; and (3) social ethics, pertaining to the family, society, and the State. The self-conscious moral judgment and action of the Objective Mind are realized in the State insofar as the State puts the ethical Idea into practice.

ABSOLUTE MIND. Absolute Spirit or Absolute Mind is the synthesis of Subjective Mind and Objective Mind. Subjective Mind is restricted to inner experience, whereas Objective Mind goes to the opposite extreme (for example, the State is not a conscious Being but exists as a reality in the objective world). In Absolute Mind the subjective and objective realities unite; it is only by way of the synthesis (the Absolute Mind) that human beings can be consciously aware of Absolute Reality. The Absolute Mind expresses itself in three forms: (1) art, whereby the Absolute assumes a sensuous form (the Absolute in sensuous experience is beauty); (2) religion, which presents absolute truth as representations in consciousness (the synthesis or unity of man with the divine is experienced through the medium of worship and religious experience); and (3) philosophy, as the highest form and the synthesis of art and religion (philosophy discerns absolute truth in pure form without the necessity of representations). Absolute Mind expresses itself in art as sense perception, in religion as imaginative representation, and in philosophy as conceptual appearance (including a view of all other forms of Absolute Reality).

Hegel's Ethical, Social, and Political Philosophy. Hegel's ethical, social, and political philosophy belongs to the province of Objective Mind (or Objective Spirit). By the principle of negativity, personal morality develops as the antithesis of a person's abstract rights. One's right in abstract form is formulated by Hegel as a general law: "Be a person and respect others as persons." One possesses this right by virtue of the fact that he is a person, that is, a self-conscious Being who is self-determined, hence infinite. Persons have rights over things, but not vice versa, because things are means to personal satisfactions; they are not ends in themselves.

TRIAD OF RIGHTS. A person's rights consist of the triad: (1) property rights, (2) right of contract, and (3) right to redress of wrongs (torts and crimes). His legal rights are created by the will; they represent freedom in practice, the objectification of universal will (the rational will). The will creates three classes of property rights applied to: (1) the act of possession of the object, (2) the use of the object, and (3) the right of relinquishing the object. The right of contract makes possible the voluntary transfer of property from one person to another. Wrongs (torts and crimes) consist of voluntary acts which are contrary to the universal will (to the rational will or the law of right). Accordingly, acts of bad faith, such as fraud, are wrong. Unpremeditated wrong is a lesser degree of wrong than fraud. Crime is the greatest degree of wrong, and punishment for crime is justified because it restores rights and vindicates justice.

MORALITY. The personal conscience of the individual, as he distinguishes between good and evil, is an inner state of the will in which the Ego fulfills its own freedom by making a moral choice. Thus morality is purely subjective, coming into existence only through a moral choice (between goodness and wickedness) which constitutes a synthesis of the individual's purpose in regard to his property rights and his relationships to others.

Moral action is action in accord with the universal rational will. Since reason is identical with the universal will, all rational acts of the will must be universal and morally good. The irrational will, which makes the individual's life self-contradictory, leads him to seek evil, capricious goals. It is his conscience that enables the individual to live in a rational way, in accord with the universal will, and thus to follow the principles of universal reason, the law of moral goodness.

SOCIAL ETHICS AND POLITICAL PHILOSOPHY. Hegel referred to social ethics as a synthesis of abstract objective right and subjective individual morality. In his view, social ethics evolves in three stages: (1) the family, (2) society, and (3) the State. Ethical substance (morality in action) functions through synthesis of moral subjectivity and moral objectivity. To be fully realized in practice, however, ethical substance must be applied dialectically to the three institutions.

In the first institution (thesis), the family, love unites two individuals in marriage, and the two personalities become one. The family is regarded as a single entity, not as a composite of independent persons. An individual finds his real nature and Being only in others—first, in his mate, and then in the greater society, namely the family, the community, and the State. The wider his relationships, and the more he relates himself to others, the more satisfying and complete will his life be as compared with his previously incomplete (partial) existence. An individual is only potentially a whole person, for his true personality develops through association with the family, community, and State. Hegel wrote that "the individual is not a real person unless related to other persons."

In his dialectical analysis of social ethics, Hegel held that society is the antithesis of the family, which is disrupted when its members marry and start their own families. This process establishes a community (society) of independent persons who nevertheless are dependent upon one another in many ways. Civic institutions perform a triad of social functions: they provide for the basic work satisfactions and wants (needs) of individuals, they administer justice to protect property, and they maintain in the common interest police forces and Corporations (associations in which like-minded people may pursue common goals). The family and the business enterprise or Corporation are the ethical basis for the State. Skilled employees work in the Corporation for common rational limited ends, rather than merely personal motives or requirements.

THE STATE. The transition from the sphere of social ethics to that of political philosophy occurs by way of the Corporation, which, despite its own limited end, cannot realize its full potentiality until it moves toward the accomplishment of the universal purpose of the State. Hegel's dialectical analysis passes from the social functions of the Corporation to those of the State as the synthesis of the family and society. As such a synthesis, "the State is the realization of the ethical idea. . . . The true State is the ethical whole and the realization of freedom. . . . The State is the march of God through the world. . . . The State is an organism. . . . The State is real, and its reality consists in the interest of the whole being realized in particular ends. . . . The State is the world which the spirit has made for itself. . . . One often speaks of the wisdom of God in nature, but one must not believe that the physical world of nature is higher than the world of spirit. Just as spirit is superior to nature, so is the State superior to the physical life. We must therefore worship the State as the manifestation of the divine on earth." [1]

The State as the most universal form of man is a rational self-

---

[1] Georg Hegel, *The Philosophy of Right*, tr. J. Loewenberg in *Hegel Selections* (New York: Charles Scribner's Sons, 1929), chap. x, "The Philosophy of Law."

conscious ethical force expressing and implementing universal reason.

The three aspects of the State are reflected in (1) its constitution or internal polity; (2) international law; and (3) world history. THE CONSTITUTION. Hegel recommended a constitutional monarchy as the preferred type of political organization, namely because the monarch, as the one person acting as agent for the State, exercises sovereignty only because he is fulfilling the universal will (or universal reason) and is not acting capriciously, like a despot. The ruler is merely executor and implements the purpose of the World Spirit. It is not his personal will which is being executed, but the universal will or the march of the World Spirit in history. His decisions are mere formalities. "In a well-ordered monarchy the law alone has objective power to which the monarch has but to affix the subjective 'I will.' "

The constitution then, is but the expression of the World Spirit, not of the subjective decisions of the people, and, like the State, is an organism in process of growth, an actualization of the Idea. The legislators merely pass laws which carry out the terms of the developing constitution and thus the aims of the World Spirit.

INTERNATIONAL LAW. Within a State the individual is subordinate, but the State itself is not subordinate to other States. Each State is an organic unity, independent and sovereign, and so it remains even when at war with another. Unlike individual persons, who must subject their individual wills to the universal will as determined by the State, the State is subject only to its own arbitrary will. An agreement between States simply carries out a consensus of their individual wills, as in treaties fulfilling their right to enter into contracts. Since there is no authority superior to that of the individual States, and since there is no potent international or world authority, Hegel concluded that disputes between States must be resolved by war. He dismissed Kant's espousal of eternal peace as a mere dream. Hegel glorified war, stating that "there is an ethical element in war. . . . By it the ethical health of the nations is preserved and their finite aims uprooted. . . . War protects the people from the corruption which an everlasting peace would bring upon it." According to the Hegelian dialectic, progress comes only through conflict, the clash of opposing forces. Consequently, peace means stagnation, whereas conflict insures progress. Moreover, the State must not be isolated, for it has no real individuality unless related to other States.

WORLD HISTORY. Since the State is independent, in the absence of control by international courts or a world political organization, final decisions can be made only by the World Spirit, which (as world history) is the supreme tribunal and judge over all nations. "The higher judge is the universal and absolute Spirit alone—the World Spirit." What actually happens to a State or a people represents the final judgment as to the worth of a national policy or course of action. For Hegel, world history constitutes the world's court of justice.

Hegel's Philosophy of History. Each State represents and embodies some phase of the Absolute Idea as the latter expresses itself in temporal events. The predominant nation in any epoch of world history represents the dominant phase of the Idea, which courses through history as the World Spirit (*Welt Geist*). The successive dominant phases represented by the peoples outstanding during their respective eras constitute universal or world history. Thus, world history and political history are substantially identical; they represent the stream of historical events directed by the free activity of reason. Therefore the course of world history is not determined by chance or caprice; it is an unfolding of reason, of Idea developing rationally.

Freedom is an idea which, through external and phenomenal means, actualizes itself in accordance with the Ideal of reason. The idea of freedom, which is integral to God's will, reflects his purpose and work as the sources of world history.

Hegel's point of view is highly optimistic because it assumes a world created by God, rationally constructed, with a rational goal (the Absolute Idea, God) and course of action (historical events) and progressing toward its goal. This assumption that God is at the helm of the world led Hegel to believe that "whatever is, is right. . . . This Good, this Reason, in its most concrete form, is God. God governs the world."

Hegel's Aesthetics. As noted above, the Mind or Spirit (the Idea-in-and-for-itself) manifests itself in the rational activity of the individual (Subjective Spirit), in the rational activity of society (Objective Spirit), and in the rational activity of the Absolute Mind which synthesizes the individual and social activity. Individuals become aware of the Absolute Mind through art, religion, and philosophy, each of which is a mode of apprehending Absolute Truth. (Religion is a higher mode than art, while philosophy is the highest mode.) According to Hegel, beauty is essentially the Absolute Idea shining through to the sense world. The artist combines the spiritual content and the sensuous form of his art. The sensuous form must be such as to make evident the spiritual essence of his creation. Although beauty is to be found in plants and animals other than man, the human being is capable of creating forms of beauty superior to those existing in nature. The fact that his art reveals inner spiritual reality is most apparent in music and poetry, which do not merely imitate nature but, as Aristotle pointed out, express moral values and purify the emotions.

The history of the fine arts displays a triadic development. (1) The Symbolic type of art, in which the form dominates over the spiritual content, suggests a meaning without adequately expressing it; it is abstract and vague. Symbolic art is typified by the art of the Orient "with its endless quest, its inner struggle, its sphinx-like mystery, and its sublimity." (2) The Classical type of art (typified by the art of the ancient Greeks) embodies an equal or well-balanced proportion of form and spirit. The Classical ideal, uniting form and spirit into an integrated whole, is realized both as a visionary good and as a genuine fact in the world. The form of the spiritual ideal provides fullest expression of meaning in perfect accord. (3) The Romantic type of art, in which the spirit predominates over form, is a higher means of expression than the other two modes of art because it represents reality in its truest form—Spirit. The content of Romantic art is the inner spiritual world. All three modes of expression however, are correctly regarded as true art because they express the ideal of beauty, a spiritual ideal, in sensuous form.

Hegel designated architecture as fundamentally Symbolic art and sculpture as Classical art; he also referred to architecture as External art and to sculpture as Objective art, as well as to painting, music, and poetry as Romantic art, stating that they are all subjective arts of the soul. The specific arts are the "universal types of the self-unfolding idea of beauty." But the "history of the world will require its evolution of countless ages" for the self-developing spirit of beauty to attain its fullest external realization of the ideal of beauty. The appearance and historical development of art in the world are necessitated by the *notion;* that is, they are the logical and rational course taken by the spirit in history.

Hegel's Philosophy of Religion.   In religion, the Absolute Idea no longer manifests itself in sensuous form, but in representation, i.e., in pure thought couched in imagery and in pictorial or figurative contemplation. Hegel assumed that, as in other areas of experience, religion, too, has developed historically in three stages of unfolding the Absolute Idea: (1) natural religions, those religions of the Orient which conceive of God as a substance of nature or as a form of magic; (2) religions of spiritual individuality, those religions which view God as subject, such as the Jewish religion (the religion of sublimity), the ancient Greek religion (the religion of beauty), and the Roman religion (the religion of utility); (3) the absolute religion, namely, Christianity. Christianity is the absolute religion owing to its having absolute truth for its content. It is consonant with the Hegelian System: identical in content, but differing in form. The Christian Trinity had God the Father as the Hegelian concept of Logic or Absolute Idea, God the Son as the world of nature, and the Holy Spirit as unfolding historical reality in the form of self-conscious Mind, all operating within or through the institutions of the Christian Church.

Religion is only the intermediate stage between art and philosophy, and it is in philosophy that we approach closest to the Absolute, God. The Absolute is depicted in sensuous form in art, and in representation (imagery or figurative thought) in religion, whereas in philosophy the Absolute is purely conceptual and is apprehended as pure thought, as pure reason, as the universal. In philosophy, thought and content become one and the same, for both are thought—conceptual. In philosophy, knowledge of the Absolute Idea is unique in and for itself—Idea. Hegel united the agent and object of knowledge, for both what is known and that which knows are identical, the Idea, which is therefore subject and object, making the final synthesis of world history complete in one unified whole.

In conclusion, it should be noted that the Hegelian system, with reason as its sole reality, finds a place for every particular concrete reality (all instances of truth), as sublated *momentums* in the dialectical development of the whole, as the activity of reason occurring within the Absolute.

NEO-HEGELIANISM

After Hegel's death in 1831, his followers divided into two factions: (1) the Hegelian Right, which was the conservative element of religious-minded philosophers who regarded Hegel's views as consistent with Christianity, opposed pantheistic interpretations of the Hegelian system, stressed the importance of personality as a metaphysical entity, and developed a philosophical basis for theism; and (2) the Hegelian Left, which was the radical element, young Hegelians, most of whom espoused Materialism. The Hegelian Right included philosophers such as Göschel, K. Rosenkranz, J. E. Erdmann, and I. H. Fichte (son of the famous philosopher). The Hegelian Left included David Friedrich Strauss, Ludwig Feuerbach, and (somewhat later) Karl Marx and Friedrich Engels. Another group of Hegelians (among them Kuno Fischer, F. K. A. Schwegler, and Erdmann) distinguished themselves as historians of philosophy.

The Hegelian Left.   In the history of philosophy, the Hegelian Left was much more influential than the Hegelian Right. David Friedrich Strauss (1808–1874), in his *Life of Jesus* (1835), sought to prove that the Gospel story is neither literal history nor intentional fiction, but a myth inspired by the times and by the enormous impression which Jesus made upon the Gospel writers. Strauss contended that, instead of portraying Jesus as a historical force, the Scriptures tell about Christ as envisioned by true believers in the meaning of the story. On the other hand, Ludwig Feuerbach (1804–1872), notwithstanding his studies with Hegel, turned toward Materialism and considered himself to be an atheist. He taught that "man is what he eats." According to Feuerbach, only objects of sense (not those of reason) are real, man's highest good being sensuous enjoyment—pleasure. Although he introduced the doctrine of philosophical egoism (the theory that only the individual and his senses, the "I," is absolute), he believed that only in society could man achieve his greatest good. Feuerbach had a great influence on Karl Marx.

In *The Essence of Christianity* (1841), Feuerbach set forth his philosophy of Humanism. The basic phenomenon of religion is the *theogonic wish,* the principle or impetus which brings God into existence. Man cannot transcend his own nature; consequently his conceptions reflect his anthropomorphic personality. Man creates absolute reality out of his subjectivity, then proclaims his faith in that which he has projected, namely, his beliefs. Thus, religious values, including belief in God, are merely the projection of man's subjective nature and ideals. God is created out of human imagination. Feuerbach's *theory of the wish* makes God the fulfillment of man's wishes. Without man, God cannot exist, for man is God. To become man is to create God; God is an extension of man's nature. "Man has his highest being, his God, in himself."

Herbart's Opposing Views. Johann Friedrich Herbart (1776–1841), whose philosophy represented a reaction against Hegelianism, was a Realist in the modern sense of the term as used by Neorealists—that is, he believed that objects exist independently of the mind which thinks them or the consciousness which experiences them. Herbart's method was that of analysis, whereby he sought to explain the mechanics of the world. Herbart's views largely destroyed the Faculty School of Psychology which held that the human mind consists of separate powers or faculties each amenable to education and development. For Herbart consciousness is an aggregate of mental states which arise from the soul's encounter with external reality. These constituents of consciousness (ideas) provide us with our knowledge. An idea is said to be on the threshold of consciousness at that level from which it enters consciousness; below that level, it is an impulse. According to Herbart's theory of apperceptive mass, a person's past experiences play an important role in his formation of new mental associations. New learning is often dependent upon or integrated with that which has passed into the subconscious. Although Herbart was unable to develop a metaphysical system satisfactory to the majority of philosophers, his point of view found wide acceptance by others, particularly educators and psychologists. (Of far greater significance in philosophy were the works of the Socialist interpreters of Hegelianism, namely, Marx and Engels.) (See page 246.)

Neo-Hegelians in the Twentieth Century. At the turn of the twentieth century, a group of British and American thinkers, whose philosophy of Idealism and adoption of the Hegelian dialectic gave them a common bond, became known as Neo-Hegelians. The leaders in this group were: among the British, Edward Caird (1835–1908), Thomas Hill Green (1836–1882), Francis Herbert Bradley (1846–1924), Bernard Bosanquet (1848–1923), and John M. E. McTaggart (1866–1925); among the Americans, William Torrey Harris (1835–1908), Josiah Royce (1855–1916), James E. Creighton (1861–1924), and Mary W. Calkins (1863–1930).

Other Neo-Hegelians in this century have included the German philosopher, Wilhelm Dilthey (1833–1911); the Canadian philosopher, John Watson (1847–1939); and the Italian philosophers, Benedetto Croce (1866–1952) and Giovanni Gentile (1875–1944). Moreover, Hegel's system has greatly influenced a number of philosophers who did not adhere to the major tenets of Hegelian Idealism, men of quite diverse views, such as Wilhelm Windelband (1848–

1915) who applied the Hegelian dialectic to the history of philosophy, Karl Marx (Dialectical Materialist), Søren Kierkegaard (Existentialist), Samuel Alexander (Neorealist and Evolutionary Naturalist), Alfred North Whitehead (Panpsychist and Organismic philosopher), and John Dewey (Pragmatist).

The distinguishing feature of Absolute Idealism is that it identifies reality with the Absolute, i.e., the whole of reality, the world, Hegel's System. The nature of the Absolute is in one of its aspects ideal, spiritual, mental; it includes not merely objects of sense, but all real objects whether they be those of value or objects of thought. The Absolute is a coherent whole in which the unity of all things is to be found; consequently, whatever is real must be an aspect of the System of the Absolute. For F. H. Bradley, author of *Appearance and Reality* (1893, 1896), "The Absolute *is* its appearances, it really is all and every one of them." The Neo-Hegelian Absolutists agree that the Absolute is not a remote object, but an all-encompassing reality, a totality which is everywhere present and constantly in touch with each and all of us.

ARTHUR SCHOPENHAUER

Arthur Schopenhauer (1788–1860), native of Danzig, studied at the University of Göttingen and also at Jena, where he received his doctoral degree in 1813, submitting as his dissertation *The Fourfold Root of the Principle of Sufficient Reason*. His principal work, *The World as Will and Idea* (1818), reflects the marked influence of Plato and Kant.

Schopenhauer opposed Hegelianism as a system of Rational Optimism. (By coincidence, at the University of Berlin, he competed unsuccessfully with Hegel to attract students to his classes.) His pessimistic philosophical views may have had some basis in an unhappy family life; it is said that hereditary insanity afflicted both sides of his family tree, and he himself became a neurotic bachelor who lived alone with his dog. He submitted his essay, *The Basis of Morality* (1840), in a prize contest, but although it was the only manuscript presented, it nevertheless proved unacceptable. His reputation for sexual overindulgence became a source of guilt and shame. During most of his lifetime, his philosophy encountered mainly antagonism among scholars—as well as among the German populace who, discouraged by the economic depression following the Napoleonic wars and by the abortive revolution of 1848 were at first in no mood to accept his pessimistic outlook. During the last years of his life, however, Schopenhauer was a quite popular figure in intellectual circles, and it became fashionable to be pessimistic and to believe in Schopenhauerianism.

Schopenhauer's Metaphysics. Whereas Hegel believed reality to be rational, and a perfectly rational world may seem to justify a philosophy of Optimism, the pessimist Schopenhauer took the opposite position, viewing reality as a blind irrational will and life as evil. In contrast to Hegel's belief that phenomena are concretely real, Schopenhauer regarded them as mere illusions.

Schopenhauer divided the world into the two entities of idea (representation) and will. The world known to us in sense experiences, that is, the phenomenal world, consists of ideas or representations. The world of ultimate reality, the ontologically real (or what Kant called the thing-in-itself), is the will. The phenomenal world is merely an image; it mirrors the will, the real world. The world which the individual senses is merely an idea within him: "The world is my idea." It is made of the substance of idea, as Berkeley claimed. Nothing objective can possibly exist without a subject who experiences it. "All that exists, exists only for the subject," and there is "no object without a subject." Nevertheless, Schopenhauer, like Berkeley, rejected the solipsistic theory of egoism (the theory that I alone exist and that the only world is my own subjective state of existence). He concluded that the physical world of individual things must be simply an illusion (*maya*) or mere appearance (phenomenon). The basic substance (or essence) of phenomena, the real world, is the will. Kant was mistaken, wrote Schopenhauer, in assuming the ultimately real world to be unknowable, for it is knowable—and it is known as the will. The Kantian thing-in-itself is the will. Since he believed that both idea and will are of the nature of mind, Schopenhauer was an Idealist, but he made a sharp distinction between the mode of action of the two types of Ideal Substance. The will, which is knowable to us through immediate awareness (intuition), is perfectly free in its action, but the phenomenal world of the idea is not free but is governed by necessity and follows a course prescribed by four principles of sufficient reason. According to Schopenhauer, phenomena are subject to the following four principles: (1) the principle of sufficient reason of Becoming, whereby every phenomenon must have a cause; (2) the principle of sufficient reason of knowledge, whereby logical judgments must be based on proper grounds; (3) the principle of sufficient reason of Being, whereby objects of sense must occupy space and time, and we

sense them as such by *a priori* intuitions (as given); (4) the principle of sufficient reason of action, whereby every act must have a
dynamic motive of power behind it. In contrast to all phenomena,
which are thus controlled by laws, the will acts only in complete
freedom. Consequently, the will cannot be rationally explained, nor
does it respond to reason; it is motivated solely by its own caprice.
Furthermore, the will is permanent, whereas phenomena are merely
the transitory, overt manifestations of the will.

Schopenhauer held that individual sensory phenomena possess a
universal character and are really copies of Ideas in the Platonic
sense. These Platonic universal Ideas are intermediate between the
will and the individual phenomena which it creates and directs.
Every physical object depends upon the Universal, the Idea, and is
also a mental image of the Idea. But for Schopenhauer the Ideas
are not ontological realities, for only the will is reality, the Kantian
thing-in-itself. Schopenhauer's recognition of ultimate reality as
volition synthesized Platonic Ideas with Kantian things-in-themselves.
Thus, he postulated three aspects of Being: (1) phenomena—particular physical objects which are ideal in nature; (2) Platonic Ideas,
the original unchanging forms to which phenomena respond in accordance with the principle of sufficient reason; and (3) the one
universal will. All three elements of reality are ideal in their nature.

Schopenhauerian Pessimism. Hegel's view of the World
Spirit as a rational force was optimistic in the sense that reason
could always control events and enable man to organize, clarify,
and explain experience and look forward to solutions of problems.
But Schopenhauer believed in a nonrational will to which reason is
subordinated, in fact a will that functions capriciously and controls
reason, which thus merely attempts to justify (rationalize) the un-
restrained actions of the will.

The will expresses itself in the three spheres of physical, vegetative
(or animal), and human nature. In each case it is a force, a nonrational urge, drive, or instinct. In the sphere of physical phenomena,
the will manifests itself in the form of gravitational forces, electrical
impulses, or chemical forces; in the sphere of animal nature, instinctive impulses are added; and in the sphere of human nature, conscious desire is joined to the other forces of the will. Where the force
is of a conscious nature, then there is suffering. Since man is aware
of his insatiable desires, wants, and needs, his suffering is most acute
and poignant, and it is worst of all among highly intelligent persons,

whose unhappiness is compounded by understanding of their own plight.

Schopenhauer's concept of suffering corresponds to the modern psychologist's idea of frustration. The conscious will, he said, by "its hindrance through an obstacle which places itself between it and its temporary aim we call suffering, and, on the other hand, its attainment of the end satisfaction, well-being, happiness." Schopenhauer's outlook on life was bleakly pessimistic because he insisted that there is no final end to striving and that, consequently, "there is no measure and end of suffering."

Desires, wrote Schopenhauer, can never be fully satisfied; even when we partially satisfy some, we are tortured with a dozen others which frustrate us. Moreover, when we think we have satisfied one, we simply find that the feeling of satisfaction soon dies away, and our spirits long for other things in life. Immediately after we satisfy our heart's desire, we find that we are bored again.

For example, sexual satisfaction is followed by a feeling of boredom in a repeated succession of fulfilled desire and new desire, never by a lasting or constant sense of happiness. The will cares nothing about sex needs of the individual; it provides for perpetuation of the species, for reproduction resulting from blind, irrational urges and not as an intelligently designed activity of a rational will; the will is a capricious, "willful," dynamic drive. It cares nothing at all for the individual, but only for the race. It forces a person to remain alive even when there is nothing for which to live. It impels him to live and suffer another day even when there is no hope or promise of any pleasant future prospects. It is "like the alms which the beggar receives from life today that he may hunger again on the morrow." For all men, irrespective of their status, the essence of life is misery and frustration. In fact, compared with the poor, the wealthy are worse off, for they have exhausted the supply of pleasurable things to try, new experiences to enjoy; in despair they go from town to town in desperation, hoping to discover some new interest to end their intense boredom. The upshot of the matter is that life is essentially painful and unfulfilling—a waste of effort. Schopenhauer concluded that "human life must be some kind of mistake." If it were not for the intensity of the drive of sex, no one would bring a child (or wish a child to be born) into this world. "For the greatest crime of man is that he ever was born," agreed Schopenhauer with Calderon, citing the very fact of birth as man's original sin. Leibniz was in error; ours is the worst of possible worlds. Schopenhauer was an atheist, asserting that this mad world could not possibly have an author, since, if it did, its God would set it in order.

According to Schopenhauer, the active work of the world is not ethically good but evil, while happiness is a passive or negative state consisting merely of the momentary absence of evil and suffering. For example, pervasive brutality in the animal kingdom indicates the preponderance of evil in the universe, for one animal's pleasure in devouring another is not commensurate with the pain suffered by the victim. He pointed out that the creative arts, such as painting, drama, and poetry, correctly portray the fact that pain and evil are the mode, with happiness as a mere brief interlude. Thus drama may often depict life as one struggle after another, a fight for happiness, an endless striving in which the hero surmounts a thousand obstacles to attain his goal, but after he has succeeded, and has married the heroine, the story must end and the stage curtains must be drawn; for if the story were permitted to continue, then it would become evident that not happiness but continued disappointment, failure, and misery would result from new difficulties which would bring repeated strife and pain—the actual experiences of life.

Suicide provides no escape from evil because the will is indestructible and continues into eternity. Living organisms, including the human body, are only manifestations of the will, which survives death. Schopenhauer set forth a doctrine of *palingenesis*, which states that the blind irrational will is perpetually reborn and persists in reincarnated form. Thus, there is no assurance that an individual will be annihilated by death. "Suicide is not the end; death is not absolute annihilation." Moreover, suicide is wrong because it prevents attainment of our highest goal—moral freedom. Man, therefore, faces a dilemma: he cannot become nothing; he must endure pain. His life is more than a disappointment; it is a form of deception; and all human beings born into this world are condemned—not to death, but to life.

Schopenhauer's Doctrine of Salvation. What then must we do to be saved from evil inherent in existence? Schopenhauer asserted that there are three means of salvation: aesthetic, ethical, and religious.

AESTHETIC SALVATION. Schopenhauer held that the contemplation of Platonic Ideas transports us above the storms of passion to a higher plane of existence, one in which desire is absent. On this level of cognition, the individual's intellectual concentration upon

Platonic ideals liberates him from servitude to animal desire, to the dictates of the will. During this period of such contemplation he becomes a timeless, spaceless, knowing person devoid of specific desires and therefore free of pain and unhappiness. Unfortunately, however, he cannot remain forever in that state of pure contemplation (Plato's ideal world), but has to return to "mundane" things, to phenomenal reality and to subjection by the will as it expresses itself once more in the form of desires and frustrations.

Schopenhauer's aesthetic theory assumes that the creative artist communicates pure knowledge (Plato's Ideas) to us through his works, as in sculpture, painting, music, and poetry. The Platonic Idea is the object of art. The consumer of art, as he gains awareness of Ideas which reflect reality (the will), experiences a concomitant effect of release from striving, stress, and frustration. "Knowledge of the whole, of the nature of the thing-in-itself . . . becomes a *quieter* of all and every volition." Art, stemming from Platonic Ideas, is a reproduction of them in phenomenal form; "it is the true mirror of the world and life." The artistic genius reveals the Platonic archetypes.

Man finds release from misery by becoming lost in aesthetic experiences. Especially through epic poetry and music, man experiences a world of "pure knowing free from will, which certainly, as a matter of fact, is the only pure happiness . . . but this happiness cannot fill a whole life, but is only possible at moments." Music is more than the reproduction of Platonic Ideas; it actually reveals the will as the thing-in-itself. "The momentary cessation of all volition, which takes place whenever we give ourselves up to aesthetic contemplation, as pure will-less subjects of knowledge, the correlative of the Idea, is one of the principal elements in our pleasure in the beautiful." [1]

ETHICAL SALVATION. Our original sin is in being born as individual phenomenal manifestations of the will with its accompanying egoistic desires. Our aim in life and its greatest good is "a final satisfaction of the will, after which no new desire could arise." Ethically, this is accomplished by crushing egoistic desire through love and sympathy. Immorality finds its root in egoism, but through compassionate sympathy we become one with the sufferer, and thereby are assured of virtue and blessedness, and are on the direct road

---

[1] *The World as Will and Idea* (1818), tr. by R. B. Haldane and J. Kemp (1884–86).

to salvation. Sex is selfishness, while "all love is sympathy," a pure and disinterested love of all persons. Such compassionate love directs us to salvation because it leads to the surrender of the will to live. Sex love, and all love which is not sympathy, is selfishness, while "all true and pure love is sympathy." Thus, love and sympathy are identical. From this source, not only all goodness, benevolence, justice, virtue, and nobility of character spring, but eventually there arises the denial of the will to live—permanent happiness.

RELIGIOUS SALVATION. The most effective means of bringing about the denial of the will is to live in accordance with asceticism. Christians, Hindus, and Buddhists achieve this goal by fasting, chastisement, constant privation, suffering, and self-renunciation. Such action constitutes holiness, the mortification of the self through asceticism, enabling us gradually to destroy the will. Eventually, the ascetic will "exist only as a pure, knowing being, the undimmed mirror of the world. Nothing can trouble him more, nothing can move him, for he has cut all the thousand cords of will which hold us bound to the world, and, as desire, fear, envy, anger, drag us hither and thither in constant pain." To such a man, life is an illusion to which he must be indifferent.

The highest ethical achievement of man is not to reject life, but to repudiate desire and thus to gain complete deliverance from the will and to pass into the state of Nirvana, that state of nothingness in which there is no birth, age, sickness, or death. In this state, restless striving ceases, and perfect peace and a tranquil spirit are found. With the passing of the will, the world also passes away, and only nothingness remains, for where there is no will, everything is abolished. "No will: no idea, no world." The conduct and contemplative life of the saints ushers us into Nirvana, a peaceful condition utterly devoid of strife, purpose, or action.

Schopenhauer's Influence. The Schopenhauer philosophy of extreme Pessimism, perhaps rooted in events of his neurotic life, was limited in that it failed to take into account sufficiently the positive values of reality, such as successful achievement and happiness, and it exaggerated those evil aspects which are seen to be evil only in the light of contrasting good. Moreover, the final solution suggested proved to be completely negative, unclear, and almost mystical in its reference to nothingness as the ideal state. Nevertheless, Schopenhauer's central ideas about the irrational forces of the universe and his recognition of the creative arts as sources of relief and happiness commanded the attention of many later philosophers and raised challenging issues in modern philosophy. Some notable philosophers turned his negative views in a more positive direction. Thus, Nietzsche made the will a positive force of life-affirmation; and Albert Schweitzer transformed the negative will into an optimistic will reflecting the ideal of reverence for life.

EDUARD HARTMANN

A synthesis of Hegelian Optimism and Schopenhauerian Pessimism was formulated by Eduard von Hartmann (1842–1906) in his *Philosophy of the Unconscious* (1869). He attempted to reconcile the two opposing Idealistic schools of Rationalism and Irrationalism by ascribing the essential characteristics of both idea and will to the World Spirit, the unconscious, as the true reality of the universe. He meant his concept of the unconscious to replace the great variety of interpretations, such as Schelling's and Schopenhauer's ideas of the will, as well as the assumptions of other philosophers regarding vital forces, entelechies, and momentums. Hartmann accepted a pessimistic outlook but modified it by finding some truth in Leibniz' view of the world as the best of all possible worlds, while admitting that, despite the elements of good in nature, the over-all situation is so bad that it would have been preferable not to have any world at all.

Hartmann believed that there have been three stages of metaphysical development: the unconscious, cosmic, and perfectly conscious stages.

In the first stage, that of the *unconscious,* the genesis of the world separated the previously united will and idea. The world consisted of immaterial substances, atoms of force; the ultimate controlling power was that of the unconscious will, which made possible the emergence of moral value, history, and men of genius.

In the second or *cosmic stage,* conscious life originated, enabling mankind to strive toward happiness and ideal goals, two mutually incompatible ends. This is our present stage. The unconscious will is irrational in its creative activity; consequently, civilization and culture advance, and so does human misery. Pessimism accompanies evolution, and must continue to increase until the world ends. Suicide would be both futile and cowardly. The race must hold together until universal discontent reaches a maximum.

In the third and last stage, the will will be nullified, and suffering will end. Civilization should direct its attention to the goal of salvation, the ethical task of saving the will through the denial of illusions (by the action of the conscious reason in exposing and dispelling illusions) and thus redeeming the will from the misery of existence. The philosopher, as one who opposes the will, values reason, and he wins control over the will by conscious and rational thinking.

The individual human being similarly passes through three stages from childhood to youth and then to the philosophical maturity of manhood. In the first stage, he seeks happiness; in the second, he prizes the rewards of heaven; but in the third, he turns his efforts to the building of a heaven on earth. Thus, Hegel's view finally triumphs over Schopenhauer's, and Hartmann's philosophy becomes an evolutionary Optimism.

NEO-KANTIANISM
AND THE MARBURG AND BADEN SCHOOLS

Classical German Idealism (the philosophy of Fichte, Schelling, and Hegel) and Schopenhauerian Idealism had explored problems which Kant had designated as beyond the limits of knowledge. Kant had claimed that ultimate reality is unknowable, that only the phenomenal world is the proper subject matter of knowledge. In other words, only scientific knowledge is valid or genuine. The German Idealists, from the time immediately following Kant to the time of Schopenhauer, set forth ideas about the ontologically real, even to the extent of stating the nature of the Kantian thing-in-itself.

A reaction against these claims of German Idealism set in as a movement (with the battle cry, *Back to Kant!*) led by Otto Liebmann (1840–1912) and Friedrich Albert Lange (1828–1875). The teachings of such Neo-Kantian philosophers resulted in German Positivism, based on the theory that science alone provides legitimate knowledge, that any attempt to transcend the boundaries of science as a path to metaphysical truth is unwarranted and dogmatic. Kantian epistemological theory required adherence to the doctrine that knowledge is attainable only in regard to phenomenal objects. This view that knowledge of ultimate reality is impossible implies to many philosophers the nonexistence of metaphysical or ontological Being. Thus Lange declared that religious and metaphysical beliefs have practical value only, that they cannot be substantiated theoretically, but are merely products of a "constructive instinct."

The Marburg School. A number of philosophers at the University of Marburg attempted to counteract the *Back to Kant* movement and became known as the *Marburg school.* The group was founded by Hermann Cohen (1842–1918); other leaders included

Paul Natorp (1854–1924), Cohen's student and associate, and Rudolf Stammler (1856–1938). Cohen formulated a concept of "cultural consciousness," uniting science, ethics, and art. In his *Kant's Theory of Experience* (1871), he sought to establish the primacy of the laws of thought, asserting that the only reality which is knowable is that which thought posits; object and subject are both creations of thought, so that to be and to be thought are identical. Nature is not the object of scientific inquiry, for it provides no truths to the human mind, and man can do nothing but think about reality with the methods of science. Paul Natorp advocated a program of "idealistic Socialism," in which the individual would be subordinate to the State. Ethics, as shared values, would be the bond uniting individual wills within a community. A person's true interests would be dependent upon society, which gives him his cultural and creative values. Rudolf Stammler concentrated upon the philosophy of law, interpreted from the point of view of the Marburg school.

The Baden School. The founder of the Baden school (located in Baden, Germany, and sometimes called the Southwest German school or the Freiburg school) was the distinguished historian of philosophy, Wilhelm Windelband (1848–1915). Associated with Windelband were Heinrich Rickert (1863–1936), Ernst Troeltsch (1865–1923), and Hugo Münsterberg (1863–1916). Münsterberg later came to the United States to teach at Harvard University.

Windelband regarded philosophy as a normative study, a science concerned with three types of universal values: (1) logic, (2) ethics, and (3) aesthetics. Each of these studies represents an ideal; the first represents an ideal of thought, the second an ideal of willing, and the third an ideal of feeling. None of these ideal norms is subject to proof, for we cannot establish proof of logical axioms, moral laws, or aesthetic norms. The validity of these normative values is postulated upon the universal acceptability of each and the inherent purpose of each: the purpose or goal of thought is truth, that of the will is goodness, and that of feeling is beauty. The entire matter presupposes universal purpose which must be accepted upon faith, but universal validity (a general logical consciousness) applies to all values and is equated with truth. Windelband, like Hegel, assumed that philosophical thought evolved in a logical development, and he wrote his celebrated *History of Philosophy* (1878–1892) from the standpoint of the logical progression of ideas.

Bauch and Vaihinger. *Bruno Bauch* (1877–1942) attempted to synthesize the views of the Marburg and Baden schools. A comparable attempt was made by the influential Hans Vaihinger (1852–1933), who in his *Philosophy of "As If,"* identified his position as Positivistic Idealism or Idealistic Positivism, which presented a synthesis of Idealism and Positivism. His position reflected some of the views of American Pragmatism combined with ideas of Bentham in his *Theory of Fictions* (see page 216). Vaihinger claimed that ideas which are incapable of theoretical proof (such as God and the moral world order) may possess practical value. We cannot find any absolute truths, but, for the sake of our own well-being, we must live *as if* God, freedom of will, and moral laws really exist; these values are essential and they possess vital practical utility.

Chapter 11

British Utilitarianism

British empirical philosophy reached its climax in the works of David Hume, who wrote his *Treatise of Human Nature* in 1737. The next great British philosophical work appeared about a half-century later (1789) when Jeremy Bentham (1748–1832), founder of British Utilitarianism, wrote his *Introduction to the Principles of Morals and Legislation.* Other leaders of the Utilitarians included Bentham's disciple James Mill (1773–1836); John Stuart Mill (1806–1873), the illustrious son of James Mill; and Henry Sidgwick (1838–1900), famed educator at Cambridge University.

Utilitarianism obtained its empirical foundations from the ideas of Paley, Hume, and Comte. The British philosopher William Paley (1743–1805), whose *Moral Philosophy* was used in England as a text for fifty years, defined virtue as "seeking the happiness of mankind, in obedience to the will of God, and for the sake of lasting happiness." Hume contributed many ideas: his belief in Phenomenalism, his concept of utility as a moral good, and his theory of the association of ideas. Auguste Comte (1798–1857) wrote convincing arguments for Positivist views, such as those of Metaphysical Skepticism—the beliefs that things-in-themselves cannot be known and that knowledge is restricted to sensations. The amalgamation of these ideas formed the basis of Utilitarianism, an essentially British philosophy of the nineteenth century. It defined virtue in terms of utility (the enhancement of the happiness of man), expressed in the formula, "the greatest happiness of the greatest number," as the proper goal of society.

JEREMY BENTHAM

The Utilitarians were Skeptics or Positivists on metaphysical, ethical and religious questions. They advocated the intellectual and social independence of individuals, defended civil liberties, and declared their belief in democratic ideals. All such values, however, were regarded merely as steps toward the fundamental goal of universal happiness, not as absolute truths. Bentham avowed his faith in the democratic rights of man (such as those we value today as inalienable natural rights), but he considered them to be only fictions necessary for the successful conduct of civil life. In *The Theory of Fictions* (1832), he asserted that "the word *right* is the name of a fictitious entity; one of those objects the existence of which is feigned for the purpose of discourse—but a fiction so necessary that without it human discourse could not be carried on." The term *fiction* referred to widely accepted values, not to deceptive statements; he regarded the community as "a fictitious body, composed of the individual persons who are considered as constituting as it were its members. The interest of the community, then, is . . . the sum of interests of the several members who compose it."

Bentham became best known for his *An Introduction to the Principles of Morals and Legislation* (1789, 1823), in which he discussed utility as the greatest happiness principle, that is, as means to achieve "the greatest happiness of the greatest number." Universal happiness is the common good. He defined utility as "that property in any object whereby it tends to produce benefit, advantage, pleasure, good, or happiness." These synonymous terms are applicable either to individuals or to the community as a whole.

Bentham rejected Kant's view of duty or conscience as the criterion of moral value, of good and evil. According to Bentham, only pleasure (and avoidance of pain) can be accepted as a proper measure or criterion of right conduct, for any person who experiences pleasure must admit that he likes it—that it is good. Although approval of the individual's egoistic pleasure as a goal might seem to encourage disregard for the interests and pleasures of other people, Bentham argued that certain painful consequences would punish excessive or indiscriminate selfishness. He cited four types of penalty: (1) physical—overindulgence becomes stale or nauseating; (2) political—imprisonment may await any pleasure-seeker who transgresses upon the rights of others; (3) moral or popular—public opinion may censor, condemn, or ostracize the evildoer; and (4) religious—God may punish the seeker of excessive or antisocial pleasures.

Bentham devised a Hedonistic Calculus, a method of determining which of alternative actions would be preferable because of the amount of pleasure to be anticipated. The Hedonistic Calculus consists of seven quantities of pleasure to be taken into account in the evaluation of conduct: (1) intensity—how intense is the pleasure in question? (2) duration—how long can a certain pleasure be expected to last? (3) certainty—how much can we depend upon a certain experience to produce the expected pleasure? (4) propinquity or remoteness—how immediate or remote is the anticipated pleasure? (5) fecundity—how many future pleasures will result, and will each pleasure terminate in pain? (6) purity—how free is the pleasure from painful elements? (7) extent—how many other persons can share the pleasure?

Although Bentham admitted that his system is egoistic and individual, he pointed out that the individual and egoistic interests are shared because the pleasure and interests of one person coincide with those of others. Consequently, he advocated application of a democratic principle, expressed in the motto, "everybody to count for one, nobody for more than one."

JAMES MILL

James Mill's principal contribution to Utilitarian philosophy, *Analysis of the Phenomena of the Human Mind* (1829), set forth his theory of the "association of ideas," which David Hartley (1705–1757) and David Hume had also advocated, based on the psychological principle of contiguity. He maintained that the content of consciousness is organized into an association of ideas, which is initially a simple type of relationship but eventually becomes highly complex. He sought to show that Bentham's value theory was grounded on the principle of the association of ideas, that morality arises either from the association of actions with pleasure, pain, praise, and blame or from the expectation of these consequences.

The views of James Mill, and thus some of the principal ideas of Bentham and the Utilitarian group, had a great influence on David Ricardo (1772–1823), who explored new paths in political economy, and on Thomas Malthus (1766–1834), the famed contributor to the study of population and social problems.

JOHN STUART MILL

Utilitarianism reached its maximum development in the works of James Mill's son, John Stuart Mill, who combined into a single system the basic principles of British Empiricism and of French Positivism (as formulated by Auguste Comte). In his celebrated *A System of Logic* (1843), John Stuart Mill delineated the foundations of inductive logic and scientific method. He applied principles of Empiricism to scientific method interpreted as a system of inductive logic, rounding out and perfecting Francis Bacon's inductive technique and advocating induction as a new approach to problem-solving that would supersede the Aristotelian method of deductive logic.

Principles of Inductive Reasoning. Mill contended that all reasoning is essentially inductive, that we reason at first from particular instances and then generalize upon them. "Induction is the process by which we conclude that what is true of certain individuals of a class, is true of the whole class, or that what is true at certain times will be true in similar circumstances at all times." To generalize that "all men are mortal" is merely to state that every man we have observed is like the others, and hence we classify them all as belonging to a general or universal class—as belonging both to the class of man and to the class of mortal beings. According to Mill, the syllogism contributes nothing new to our knowledge because its premises state what we already know through induction.

Mill believed that these universals or common characteristics by which objects are classified are real *kinds*, as he termed them. Phenomena with common characteristics belong to real kinds. (He agreed with the Phenomenalistic views of Berkeley, Hume, and Comte.) Our knowledge of them, however, is limited to experience —induction.

At the same time, Mill believed in real causes. All phenomena are subject to cause-and-effect relationships. As Hume had noted, a cause means the presence of a uniformity in the behavior of phenomena; it is not a metaphysical reality transcending the realm of ideas. Mill's Positivism (or Phenomenalism) was apparent at this point, for he believed that the most that can be said about metaphysical substances is that they are *permanent possibilities of sensation.* In his *Examination of Sir William Hamilton's Philosophy* (1865), he defined matter as the "permanent possibility of sensation," and stated that nothing else can be asserted of the Kantian thing-in-itself. As to whether or not the soul or Ego is a real spiritual principle of unity in the universe, or merely (as Hume suggested) a bundle of perceptions, he remained in doubt. He defined mind as a sequence of feelings occurring in consciousness, but could not decide whether these feelings are capable of being aware of themselves as well as of their past and future experiences—an affirmative answer would imply the presence of an Ego or personality besides the sequence or bundle of self-conscious feelings.

Mill presented five canons or methods for discriminating between superstitions and genuine knowledge of the causes (or effects) resulting from observed uniformities in nature:

(1) *Method of Agreement:* If two or more instances of the phenomenon under investigation have only one circumstance in common, the circumstance in which alone all the instances agree is the cause (or effect) of the given phenomenon.

(2) *Method of Difference:* If an instance in which the phenomenon under investigation occurs, and an instance in which it does not occur, have every circumstance save one in common, that one occurring only in the former, the circumstance in which alone the two instances differ is the effect, or cause, or a necessary part of the cause, of the phenomenon.

(3) *Joint Method of Agreement and Difference:* If two or more instances in which the phenomenon occurs have only one circumstance in common, while two or more instances in which it does not occur have nothing in common save the absence of that circumstance, the circumstance in which alone the two sets of instances differ, is the effect, or cause, or a necessary part of the cause, of the phenomenon.

(4) *Method of Residues:* Subduct from any phenomenon such part as is known by previous inductions to be the effect of certain antecedents, and the residue of the phenomenon is the effect of the remaining antecedents.

(5) *Method of Concomitant Variations:* Whatever phenomenon varies in any manner whenever another phenomenon varies in some particular, is either a cause or an effect of that phenomenon, or is connected with it through some fact of causation.

These principles of induction are possible only because of the presence of uniformity in nature. Mill applied his belief in induction so widely that he regarded even mathematical propositions as empirically derived, asserting that mathematical necessity is simply psychological necessity—arising from the association of ideas.

Mill's Ethical and Socio-Political Philosophy. Mill's ethical theory, elaborated in *Utilitarianism* (1863) as a modified form of Benthamism, differed sharply from Bentham's interpretation of the nature of pleasure. Bentham insisted upon Quantitative Hedonism, the theory that pleasures are of one kind only, namely, physical or sensual, the only difference among pleasures being one of quantity measurable by the Hedonistic Calculus. Mill contended that pleasures differ in kind as well as in amount; qualitative distinctions among pleasures could make slight amounts of high-quality pleasures much more valuable than large amounts of qualitatively inferior pleasures. Mill's ethical theory of Qualitative Hedonism is contrasted with Bentham's Quantitative Hedonism. On Bentham's theory it would be better to be a happy pig than a miserable human being, because the pig can sense physical pleasure. But Mill argued that "it is better to be a human being dissatisfied than a pig satisfied; better to be Socrates dissatisfied than a fool satisfied." According to Mill, there is a qualitative pleasure (value) in just being human that surpasses any of the pleasures experienced by inferior beings. As to who makes the decisions, that matter rests with the person who has experienced both pleasures, then expresses his preference. In the case of the pig and man, the decision must be left to man, who is cognizant of animal pleasure, whereas the pig is ignorant of human values. In the case of the euphoric idiot, the decision rests with the intelligent person. It may be that the fool, believing that his life is the happier one, would not exchange places with the enlightened person. The intelligent person may also be quite convinced that the idiot is happier than he himself is, but would nevertheless prefer to remain intelligent though unhappy; here the qualitative value of intelligence offsets the quantitative value of idiotic pleasures.

Mill's defense of Utilitarianism involved a fallacy of reasoning. He asserted that "the only proof capable of being given that an object is visible, is that people actually see it. . . . And so of the other sources of our experience. In like manner, I apprehend, the sole evidence it is possible to produce that anything is desirable, is that people do actually desire it." The error involved in this argument is known as the figure of speech fallacy. Mill assumed that the suffix *-able* connotes the same thing in each instance of its use, but it does not. Visible may mean that people actually do see an object, but the word *desirable* denotes evaluation (not fact), the assumption that something ought to be desired irrespective of its actually being desired. A physician's advice to a patient may be highly desirable even though the patient listening to it may actually experience unpleasant nausea instead of desire.

Although agreeing with most of Bentham's views on ethics, Mill replaced Bentham's four moral sanctions of conduct with two: (1) internal (conscience and duty); and (2) external (fear of displeasing God and man, or the hope of winning their favor). He believed in Utilitarianism as the scientific formulation of the Golden Rule of Jesus. Justice is a sentiment, the essence of which is equality, which enables us to achieve the general good, the greatest happiness of the greatest number.

In his essay *On Liberty* (1859), Mill advocated laissez-faire individualism, including freedom of competition as well as freedom of belief, freedom to unite, and freedom of taste; he qualified all these freedoms with the proviso that an individual's liberties must not injure others or transgress upon their rights. He stood firmly for unlimited freedom of expression as a means of discovering truth, insisting that freedom of conscience and the right to publish one's beliefs on any subject whatever must be permitted.

Mill's Philosophy of Religion. Mill's religious views were set forth in three essays appearing as a posthumously published book entitled *Nature, the Utility of Religion and Theism* (1874). As a theistic finitist, believing in a good God who is involved with a world not of his own making, Mill felt that a benevolent Deity fashions or designs the world but is not responsible for its creation, and that his inability to recreate the universe indicates a limitation in divine power rather than a limitation in divine goodness. Granted that the world includes evil, we must conclude that God lacks either the power to revamp it or the will to do so. Mill preferred to believe in a good God with limitations on his power.

Rejecting the ontological (Anselmic and Cartesian) arguments and the aetiological (first-cause) argument for the existence of God, Mill nevertheless respected the teleological argument, for he felt that Darwin's doctrine of natural selection failed to provide an adequate explanation of the order and design in the universe.

Mill rejected Materialism, which he considered a false doctrine of the nature of substance. He held that the material world is composed of "permanent possibilities of sensations" and that this fact justifies a belief in human immortality. God possesses both the desire and the power to make immortal beings. Even on the question of miracles, Mill kept an open mind, stating that Hume had not disproved the existence of miracles but had merely shown that their protagonists had offered insufficient proof of their occurrence.

HENRY SIDGWICK

Sidgwick attempted to synthesize Utilitarianism with Kantian principles of ethics because he thought that this would be the only way to solve the basic problem of egoistic individualism in Utilitarianism. He maintained that there is no reason for a Utilitarian to be concerned with anyone's happiness but his own, because that is the only happiness he could possibly experience. In consequence, however, the problem of justice and concern for other people arises.

One solution suggested itself to Sidgwick, namely, that of combining Kant's theory of duty (based on the categorical imperative known intuitively) with the Utilitarian principle of the greatest happiness for the greatest number. Sidgwick argued that another's happiness will become as important to us as our own as soon as we accept the Kantian theory that what is right for one is right for all. We are therefore duty-bound to enhance the happiness of others, even though such action may sometimes call for self-sacrifice —an eventuality inconsistent with Bentham's views of Utilitarian principles.

In his first book, *The Methods of Ethics* (1874), which brought him immediate distinction, Sidgwick defined his system of Universalistic Hedonism as "the ethical theory that the conduct which, under any given circumstances, is objectively right is that which will produce the greatest amount of happiness on the whole: that is, taking into account all whose happiness is affected by the conduct."

HASTINGS RASHDALL AND GEORGE EDWARD MOORE

At the beginning of the twentieth century, Utilitarianism assumed Idealistic characteristics, and came to be known as Ideal Utilitarianism. This modified system was exemplified in the ethical theories of two British philosophers: (1) George Edward Moore (1873–1958), a Neorealist who set forth his theory in *Principia Ethica* (1903) and *Ethics* (1912); and (2) Hastings Rashdall (1859–1924), a Personal Idealist who elaborated his position in another important work, *The Theory of Good and Evil* (1907).

These men believed that morally right acts are not limited to conduct which gives pleasure, but consist of conduct which produces the best possible consequences. Moore argued that if we hold strictly to pleasure as the sole criterion of what is good, then it would follow that a drunkard pleased with breaking crockery is experiencing a pleasure as valuable as that of "a man who is fully realizing all that is exquisite in the tragedy of King Lear, provided only the mere quantity of pleasure in both cases is the same." Similarly, Rashdall (who coined the term Ideal Utilitarianism), attempting to synthesize Utilitarianism and Idealism, pointed out that "the right action is always that which . . . will produce the greatest amount of good upon the whole." Thus, contemporary Utilitarianism can be said to have joined the ranks with Idealistic philosophies.

Chapter 12

Evolutionary Naturalism

Another philosophy which found its strongest impetus in Great Britain is that of Evolutionary Naturalism. Although its leading figures were the British scientist Charles Robert Darwin (1809–1882) and the British philosopher Herbert Spencer (1820–1903), a number of other eminent philosophers, both within and beyond the British Isles, contributed to its development. Some aspects of this philosophy may be traced back to Hegel's theory of cosmic evolution. We shall see that Friedrich Nietzsche (1844–1900) applied the concept of evolution to ethical theory, Karl Marx adapted it to his socio-political philosophy, Thomas Henry Huxley (1825–1895) humanized it, Henri Bergson (1859–1941) became one of its most influential exponents, and Samuel Alexander (1859–1938) developed it into his novel theory of emergent evolution.

Philosophical Naturalism is based on the theory that all phenomena may adequately be explained by means of physical laws. Although Evolutionary Naturalism provides a foundation principle for Materialism, there is an important difference between the two philosophies, for Evolutionary Naturalism goes further in evaluating nature, to which it attributes a teleology, that is, a cosmic purpose. Evolutionary Naturalists assume that vital forces (distinct from physical or chemical forces) operate in the universe. Some of these philosophers, including Bergson, consider these vital forces to be autonomous powers which determine their own course or direction as they react to their own laws and thus become a "law unto themselves."

LAMARCK

The theory of evolution, which can be traced back as far as the ancient Greek philosophers, received its initial modern impetus from the work of the French zoologist Jean de Lamarck (1744–1829), who in 1809 presented his pioneering theory of evolution in opposition to the traditional concept that each species of living organisms was specially created in its finished form.

Lamarck believed that all forms of life undergo structural changes when individual members repeatedly use their organs to cope with the changing environment and that the modified characteristics thus acquired by the individual are passed on to their offspring. (Conversely, disuse would cause an organ to atrophy and disappear instead of being transmitted to offspring.) The celebrated British philosopher Herbert Spencer preferred Lamarck's theory to that of Darwin, who argued that, not use or disuse, but the struggle for survival is the decisive factor—that there is a process of natural selection whereby those individuals best fitted to overcome obstacles survive so that their superior characteristics are inherited by succeeding generations.

DARWIN

Charles Darwin, in his *The Origin of Species* (1859) and *The Descent of Man* (1871), presented an abundance of evidence to support his widely accepted theory of evolution. As noted above, his doctrine of natural selection (or survival of the fittest) attributed the evolution of a species to the individual member's struggle for survival and the inheritance of the survivors' superior qualities by their offspring.

The Mechanism of Natural Selection. Darwin explained the existence of the struggle for survival by pointing out that organisms in a species increase their numbers at a rate faster than the maximum which would allow sufficient food to be obtained by all the members. In the attempt to continue living, those individuals best fitted to cope with the environment survive. Thus the fittest survive and transmit their most successful or advantageous characteristics to the next generation; but the latter will include among them many individuals who by chance vary slightly from their elders and transmit like variations to their offspring. In this way, the superior characteristics of the fittest are inherited. Tiny variations also accumulate in the members so that they eventually evolve into a superior species.

Darwin's theory of evolution explained the design or purpose evident in organic life by reference to the mechanical laws of nature and the process of natural selection. His views therefore contradicted earlier concepts which attributed the specific design and purposeful functions of organs to God, the divine designer.

He agreed with Hegel as to the necessity for a historical perspective in order to understand the nature of things. He concluded that man (as a more advanced type of organism) must be understood in the light of his animal ancestry—the higher species in terms of the lower. Recent critics have cited the apparent success of the morally most worthy species as a weakness in Darwin's theory, and some have claimed that only a Cosmic Mind (God) could account for the continuous progress toward ethically more valuable forms of organic life as differentiated from mere survival. Darwin himself drifted toward agnosticism, stating that in the absence of evidence he would have to suspend judgment on the existence of a divine Being.

Darwin's Ethical Theory. Darwin accepted the theory of Ethical Intuitionism that ethical principles are innate. He attributed morality to the action of an inborn conscience, which impressed him as the most important difference between man and the lower animals. Conscience has its seat in the *social instincts,* from which are derived parental and filial affections and the enjoyment of fellowship with other members of society. While man differs from his animal ancestry, the difference is one only of degree, for he does not differ in kind from other species in the animal kingdom, and like them always behaves in accordance with the physical and mechanical laws of nature.

Darwin's ethical theory of Evolutionary Naturalism differed from Hedonism in that Darwin conceived of the general good, not as happiness, but as "full vigor and health," as a perfected state of the human faculties. Happiness is a secondary consideration; the "general good or welfare of the community" is of primary importance.

He believed that the process of natural selection probably explains the development of virtues or moral standards, which are perhaps founded upon inherited instincts of sympathy for others or upon rational ways of thinking. A conflict between certain antisocial instincts (such as revenge or aggressive hatred) and the individual's conscience often produces a sense of guilt. On the other hand, instinctive sympathy for others encourages man to develop his noblest social drive, i.e., humaneness and compassion for other living creatures, which keeps his selfish thoughts and actions in check. Thus man rises from the low level of animal selfishness to the moral heights of the Golden Rule.

HERBERT SPENCER

Spencer has been considered a co-founder with Darwin of modern evolutionary theory. Firstly, he developed as a central doctrine the agnosticism which Darwin referred to only incidentally. Secondly, he emulated Hegel in elaborating upon a theory of cosmic evolution, the difference being that with Hegel evolution is the unfolding of the self-revealing World Spirit, whereas with Spencer evolution is a process of natural changes governed by law and manifesting a mystic force which he considered beyond man's comprehension. In some respects, Spencer's Unknowable (his term for the cosmic force) was very much like Schelling's Absolute. As an Agnostic Realist, he accepted the reality of the Unknowable, but claimed that it transcends our senses, and that we can never know it because all our knowledge (which is limited to sensory objects, or phenomena) consists of relationships or comparisons among things and there is nothing to which we can relate or compare the Unknowable. (Within the scope of human knowledge he assumed three levels: the lowest kind, or un-unified knowledge; partially unified knowledge or science; and completely unified knowledge, or philosophy.)

Spencer's Fundamental Thesis. Spencer adhered to the belief in God as the ultimate reality, but also as the unknowable divine source of all things, this being the main concept of his Agnostic Realism. Although we can conclude from empirical facts and our experience that God exists as an unconditioned unitary Being, nevertheless he remains Unknowable, owing to his real (rather than phenomenal) nature. We know that God exists, but we cannot discover specific facts about his powers or characteristics. Spencer believed that God manifests himself in phenomena as the basic reality or force behind them as they occur in accordance with the laws of evolution. He defined evolution as "an integration of matter and concomitant dissipation of motion; during which the matter passes from an indefinite, incoherent homogeneity to a definite, coherent heterogeneity; and during which the retained motion undergoes a parallel transformation."

Spencer's fundamental thesis is that the entire universe develops from relative simplicity to complexity as it seeks to establish equilibrium of all its forces, both mechanical and vital; but as soon as the universal forces achieve equilibrium, they become dissipated

or redistributed again and return to an unbalanced state, as ultimate forces. This dynamic process repeats itself, creating higher
forms of reality, such as new compounds and systems, just as an
organism composed of cells has achieved a higher and better integrated organization than any of its individual cells. (A highly
developed system may, however, succumb to resisting forces, lose
all equilibrium, and dissolve.)

This view of evolution is based upon a number of presuppositions: (1) the indestructibility of matter; (2) the continuity of
motion; and (3) the persistence of force. These presuppositions
may be said to imply (1) force that is unchangeable in quantity;
(2) force that cannot be created out of nothing or disintegrate
into nothing; (3) the law that everything moves along the lines
of least resistance; (4) the assumption that the law of the continuous redistribution of matter and motion holds good for every
change in nature; and (5) the assumption that everything in
existence is subject to the law of the entire cycle of changes (a
loss of motion, followed by integration and eventually by a gain
of motion with resulting disintegration). "Evolution is always an
integration of matter and dissipation of motion. . . . This change
in the arrangement of matter is accompanied by a parallel change
in the arrangement of motion."

Spencer's System of Ethics. Spencer defined life as "the continuous adjustment of internal relations to external relations." The
organized community, or society, is a means of adaptation to the
natural environment. When men as individuals and as groups discover better or preferred ways of doing things, and modify their
ideas and emotions accordingly, the new methods and ways of thinking become habitual and are passed on to subsequent generations
as innate or *a priori* principles. Thus the successful new habits of
conduct and modes of thought and emotion become permanent
features of the species, whereas unsatisfactory techniques are discarded. Spencer agreed with Lamarck that mathematical and ethical
principles which have become *a priori* and innate were originally
experimental trial-and-error techniques of earlier generations. Eventually those principles of proven utilitarian value were constantly
used and passed on to succeeding generations until they became
well established as innate characteristics of a subsequent generation. Spencer asserted that, since the races of mankind have had
different backgrounds of learning, they must differ from one another in moral, mathematical, and other innate abilities. Accord-

ing to Spencer, savages are morally inferior to Europeans because of this factor—a conclusion contrary to modern scientific evidence that any race of people given proper education will have the capacity to match the standards and achievements of other races.

Spencer's system of ethics is based on social relationships, a major thesis being that the individual has a much better chance to survive in a society than he has if he tries to live alone. Consequently, those ethical values are perpetuated which make the survival of society possible. Justice, courage, and sympathy have persisted as innate moral principles because they protected society and contributed to social survival and through constant use became acquired characteristics transmitted, as Lamarck had claimed, to succeeding generations.

Moral behavior, which is conducive to "the greatest breadth, length and completeness of life," has a number of characteristics: (1) it enables us to adjust to our environment; (2) it is "relatively more evolved conduct" (that is, conduct which has aided in self-preservation and racial evolution in contrast to evil conduct which is destructive to both the individual and the race); and (3) good conduct is pleasurable, whereas evil conduct has painful consequences.

Spencer was neither a pessimist nor an optimist, but a meliorist, for he believed that the good in the world outweighs the evil, and that mankind can improve individual nature and social relationships.

FRIEDRICH NIETZSCHE

Nietzsche's philosophy is basically one of value theory—a philosophy calling for "a revaluation of all values." According to Nietzsche, the Judeo-Christian system of moral ideals constitutes an inversion of natural life-giving instinctive values, and it should be replaced by returning to nature's values, which are identical with the ideals of a master race. This point of view represented what were accepted by Nietzsche as the inevitable implications of Darwinism, which advocated the maximal development and expression of animal instincts, of which the primary instinct, said Nietzsche, is the "will to power." Nietzsche rejected the traditional concept (as taught by Jesus, Schopenhauer, and Darwin, too) that sympathy is the proper foundation for moral values.

The Will to Power. For Judeo-Christian values, such as humility, Nietzsche substituted an ethics of power, the principle that might makes right, as a logical consequence of Darwin's statement as to the survival of the fittest, because the best-fitted individuals desire not merely to survive but to acquire power over others. Instead of accepting the social instinct (praised by Darwin) as a guide to conduct, Nietzsche advocated egoism and rugged individualism—competitive striving to fulfill egoistic instincts and achieve personal advancement.

Master Morality and Slave Morality. In his *Genealogy of Morals* (1887) Nietzsche traced the development of two types of morality accompanying two corresponding cultures: (1) the *master morality* of aristocratic races of men (such as the Romans) who lived in freedom and held others in subjection, and (2) the *slave morality* of men (such as the Jews) who for many generations lived in slavery or subjection to the aristocratic class. (He regarded Christianity as a religious system which merely accepted and spread the moral values of Judaism.)

The aristocrats, said Nietzsche, have become rulers through the exercise of their natural superior abilities and aggressive instincts or drives. They prize highly the sex instinct and the will to power. They do not conceal or restrain their aggressive motives but express them in overt action, as, for example, in using force to subdue opponents. Since they give full vent to their aggressive drives, they do not hold a grudge against enemies but readily forgive them. In fact, they find nothing to forgive since they harbor no ill-feeling which might require forgiveness, and, as true aristocrats and superior persons, can love even those who do them harm. They welcome open combat and realize that it develops personality, that they learn much from their enemies; they do not consider either side evil but only superior or inferior.

On the other hand, members of the enslaved or subjected class have adopted an ethical code emanating from resentment at their inability to combat the aristocratic class on equal terms. To withstand the power of the superior class, the slaves have had to resort to insidious and devious tactics. They have promoted democracy, effeminate standards, and the principle of equality in order to bring the naturally superior aristocrat down to their own debased level. They have contrived elaborate religions which they have attempted to impose upon others, the purpose being to control them by using the concept of sin and evil and the services of priests who pose as God's spokesmen and demand obedience from the superior aristocrats. These inferior peoples repress all life-giving instincts, which they consider evil; they demean the sex instinct and teach humility instead of respect for power. Their every act expresses their repressed resentment.

The Superman. In his *Thus Spake Zarathustra* (1883–1885) Nietzsche described his ideal man, the Superman, whom he contrasted to the average man of the common herd. The Superman, who is "beyond good and evil," creates his own set of values, rejecting any other so-called "moral world order." As an individualist, the Superman towers over and has utter contempt for the common herd, condemning its slave morality, its conventional behavior, its virtues of meekness and pity, and its cowardly attempts to avoid war and other challenging life situations. Rejecting the belief in God and immortality and assuming that "God is dead," he insists that man must fend for himself instead of depending upon such beliefs. Nietzsche concluded that no living person had yet reached the level of Superman, for all men are too much alike and the greatest among them "all-too-human."

The Doctrine of Eternal Recurrence. The Evolutionary Naturalism developed by Nietzsche divided the evolutionary process into cosmic cycles; according to this theory, any existing set of conditions will recur repeatedly in completed cycles of events. The theory is based upon the assumption that time is of infinite duration, but that the possible combinations and arrangements of matter are limited in time. The forces at work which were responsible for past happenings continue and result in cyclical recurrences of the same persons and events. This doctrine may have a practical value for the individual in that the possibility of such recurrent cycles may constitute a consoling substitute for his hope of immortality.

THOMAS HENRY HUXLEY

The ethical theory of Thomas Henry Huxley (1825–1895), another of the British Evolutionary Naturalists, contrasted sharply with the Nietzschean point of view. In his *Evolution and Ethics* (1894) Huxley described two processes in nature: (1) the cosmic process of natural evolution; and (2) the ethical process of human evolution. Inasmuch as the two processes conflict, man's moral progress may run counter to cosmic change. For Huxley the moral goal is not survival of the fittest, but the education of as many persons as possible so that they will become worthy of survival. Huxley rejected Nietzschean individualism as naïve in view of the fact that men achieve better progress in a society than they could possibly hope to achieve by struggling against nature as isolated individuals. He agreed with Darwin and Spencer that *sympathy* is an important moral quality innate in man.

Man's Relationship to Nature. Asserting that the ethical is superior to the cosmic process, Huxley pointed out that the lower (cosmic) process obeys the law of the survival of the fittest, whereas the higher (ethical) process is guided by the principle that the morally worthy ought to survive by right. The survival of the fittest, interpreted as a moral goal, seemed to him to result in absurd consequences—for example, the perpetuation of lichens, diatoms, and microscopic organisms as if they were the best fitted (in the Nietzschean sense) to survive. On the contrary, what forms of life are morally worth preserving is determined by human intuition, not by cosmic forces, and it is man's intelligence that warns him to curb his egoistic instincts and to subordinate them to the ideal of making mankind more worthy to survive.

Man must not imitate but combat nature, for nature is non-moral. He often acts contrary to nature to control natural forces (also using his intelligence as a means of understanding the world), even to the extent of improving the evolutionary process as he does in horticulture, by eliminating conditions which necessitate a constant struggle for survival and by improving upon his natural environment. Man can also use his intelligence as a means of improving his ethical goals, replacing animal instincts with higher forms of motivation.

Agnosticism. Claiming that genuine knowledge consists only of facts verifiable by the natural sciences, Huxley pointed out that neither Metaphysical Materialism nor Spiritualistic Idealism is scientifically verifiable. Hence, on questions about the existence of God (ontology) man must remain an agnostic. Agnosticism (the term was coined by Huxley in 1889 in his essay *Agnosticism*) is a doctrine stating that neither the existence of God nor the character of ultimate reality is knowable. Atheism denies God's existence, whereas agnosticism neither affirms nor denies it. The agnostics are not always in agreement as to the scope of their other doctrine. Thus, Spencer believed in the existence of God but denied the possibility of human knowledge of specific divine characteristics; Huxley, on the contrary, claimed that we have no right to assert the truth or falsity of any assertion without sufficient relevant evidence and certainly should not require others to accept our unsubstantiated beliefs.

Huxley also introduced the philosophical concept of epiphenom-enalism—the belief that consciousness and mental phenomena are dependent upon and produced by physical processes, but that the converse is never the case. It was his view that the mind is only a by-product of the body, and that, with the body's demise, the mind inevitably perishes.

HENRI BERGSON

The French biologist and philosopher Henri Bergson, undoubtedly the most influential exponent of the evolutionary school during contemporary times, developed a philosophical system which achieved the status of being a distinct school of thought known as *Vitalism* or *Bergsonian Voluntarism*, attracting distinguished adherents, particularly in France and Latin America. His most celebrated work was *Creative Evolution* (1907), but others of major importance included *Time and Free Will* (his doctoral dissertation, 1889), *Matter and Memory* (1896), and *The Two Sources of Morality and Religion* (1932).

Vitalism, Intuitionism, and Real Duration. A central thesis of Bergson's Vitalism states that life is an autonomous function controlled by its own laws instead of the laws of physics and chemistry. In sharp opposition to many other philosophies, Vitalism maintains that the laws of physics and chemistry will never adequately explain life, for the reason that life is not material. Furthermore, reason itself is unable to explain life processes because its rational activity cannot go beyond the mechanistic explanations based on physico-chemical laws, whereas life and consciousness, being independent of physico-chemical laws, cannot be understood completely by means of logical, scientific, or mathematical analyses.

Attempts to arrive at logical explanations of reality are ineffective because reality is always in a state of becoming and never stationary or at rest; we cannot measure it mathematically or understand it by using logic that is necessarily static. Whatever reality does is unpredictable, for it is forever creating new characteristics and even new laws as yet unknown to science. Reality, in *real duration*, is in a state of constant evolutionary change. Its chief constituent quality is a vital impulse (*élan vital*) comprehended as life or consciousness—a quality which can be understood only by means of man's intuition. Man's intellect can grasp nothing except static truths, but his intuition can discern the ever changing life process itself.

The *vital impulse in real duration* makes its way through the universe, which it keeps changing in accordance with non-physical laws, just as an artist creates new and better (and unpredictable) works. The precise direction (or evolution) of the future world remains unpredictable, but in the past the *élan vital* has directed world evolution away from instinct to intelligence, and away from both of these to intuition (a self-conscious, instinctive, superior mode of comprehension). The creative process is still advancing toward higher levels, and it may even attain the goal of human immortality. Bergson referred to the world as "a machine for the making of gods," for nothing is beyond the capacity of the *élan vital* to accomplish.

Neither physical laws nor any teleological concept can be used to explain the creative activity of the cosmic process. The future course of that activity cannot be revealed by recourse to logic or scientific inquiry and laws, nor can it be restricted to any given end or purpose, for the *élan vital* is perfectly free, depicting itself (like a creative artist) as it presses onward into the unpredictable universe still to come.

Bergson's Ethical Theory. Bergson postulated two types of morality: (1) closed and (2) open. Closed morality refers to a compulsive form of behavior, i.e., rote (or instinctive) conduct which conforms to the prevailing conventions in a particular society; the individual yields to social pressures and forms the habit of obeying traditional moral standards of the community. Open morality refers to a preferred or ideal form of behavior motivated or directed by no one but the free individual himself and best exemplified in the life histories of heroes and saints, those who blaze new trails for mankind. It is a dynamic morality, guided by inspiration and intuition, on a higher level than the closed form of rigid, static, externally imposed system. Moral decisions worked out by rational planning or by intelligent reasoning may be regarded as intermediate between the compulsory or closed and ideal or open types of morality.

Bergson's Philosophy of Religion. Dualism permeates every phase of Bergson's philosophy: in his metaphysics, a dualism of mind and matter; in his epistemology, a dualism of intelligence and intuition (or intelligence and instinct); and in his ethical theory, a dualism of open and closed morality. In his philosophy of religion we find another dualism of *static religion* and *dynamic religion*.

Static religion is a set of myths devised by human intelligence as a means of defense against the depressing experiences of life. For example, man creates myths which help him to cope with impending death. Only the human being creates religious myths, for he alone knows of his susceptibility to serious illness or immanent death, whereas subhuman species live out their lives in complete tranquility as if they were indestructible and eternal. Man, fearful of the future, attempts to combat his fate by constructing the myths of religion and immersing himself in selfish enterprises instead of devoting himself to the common good or the welfare of others.

Dynamic religion consists of beliefs, prompted by the vital impulse (*élan vital*), which are based upon the identification of the human will with that of the divine, uniting the two in a mystical union. As in the mystical experiences of St. Paul and St. Francis, the soul hearkens to a voice and an indefinable presence, and therein finds boundless joy in oneness with God. With indivisible love, the mystic embraces humanity, blazes new trails for mankind to follow, institutes spiritual reforms, and enlightens us as to the existence of God and immortality. The mystic teaches us how to become gods, for the "essential function of the universe . . . is [that of] a machine for the making of gods." In Bergson's *Creative Evolution*, we are told that the nature of God is love, but in his *The Two Sources of Morality and Religion*, we are told that divine love is God himself, that through creative love the world came into being, that the world is a manifestation of God's love.

SAMUEL ALEXANDER

Samuel Alexander (1859–1938), the last of the Evolutionary Naturalists considered in this chapter, was born in Sydney, Australia, studied at the Universities of Melbourne and Oxford, and taught philosophy at Manchester University from 1893 until his retirement in 1924. He is known principally for his *Space, Time, and Deity* (1920), a two-volume work setting forth in detail his theory of emergent evolution.

Alexander's Neorealism. Alexander accepted the Neorealist view that objects of knowledge and of sense experience are externally real in their own right and not dependent upon consciousness for their existence. Furthermore, whenever an organism is conscious of any objects whatever, it is *compresent* with those objects, which, moreover, are not affected by the organism but exist independently of it. Thus, if I become conscious of a house before me, the house is itself a real entity unaffected by my consciousness of it. This Neorealist thesis is directly contrary to the claim of the Idealist school that objects cannot exist independently of consciousness—that wherever there is an object, a subject must also be present.

Alexander held that consciousness of an object merely gives the viewer a certain perspective of it, and that shifting his position will change his perspective of the object because it occupies a certain point in space and a certain instant in time which to him are imperceptible. At any rate, the viewer perceives a given perspective or a genuine portion of the object, not merely a mental image or copy of it.

Alexander carried his Realism to extremes, insisting that even illusions are genuinely real objects uncreated by the human mind. He asserted that the mind never creates anything new, but simply rearranges things, even if they be only imaginary ones, for they too are independent of the mind. Novelty is simply a matter of rearrangement; this is also true of the mind itself, which is an emergent, that is, a novel organization emerging out of existing things.

In epistemology, Alexander distinguished between the contemplation and the enjoyment of objects. When the mind contemplates objects external to it, the objects are compresent with it in perception, memory, etc., for the mind is no more than the body compresent with its surrounding objects in consciousness. When the mind enjoys its experience of an object, changes take place in the inner life of the mind, resulting in reactions of pleasure, grief, and other mental activities, including self-contemplation which is identical with the Cartesian concept of *Cogito* or of self-consciousness. In other words, contemplation consists of the act of perceiving the qualities of an object, whereas enjoyment refers to mental awareness of inner physiological activity. Perceptions are made up of neurological activity combined with the qualities of the objects being perceived. Alexander concluded that immediate sense experience consists of *sensa*, that is, real objects which are compresent with the individual who is conscious of them. In fact, he extended his theory to include, in addition to perception, the so-called "mental" objects in memory, imagination, etc., as real entities compresent with the mind—not as mere subjective creations, but as real objects in consciousness.

Alexander's Metaphysics. The ultimate or ontologically real, said Alexander, is space-time, a concept comparable to Bergson's notion of real duration and to Einstein's idea of space-time in his theory of relativity. Alexander used the term to express the fact that "space is full of time and time is full of space," that both space and time are real and must always be conceived together as *primordial reality*. One is inconceivable without the other. Time consists of an infinity of instants, while space consists of an infinity of points. Time and space each has its own dimensions; time has but one, yet its single dimension infuses every aspect of space, which, on the other hand, consists of "spatial points" that exist only in time. Consequently, the cosmos as a whole and all its contents are never static, but constantly in motion within space-time. Nothing remains absolutely at rest, for all things are in a state of perpetual transition.

Although he thus linked matter inseparably with motion, Alexander believed that matter must ultimately be regarded as consisting of point-instants, and that mind, too, finds its ultimate reality in space-time, the primordial reality of all that exists. Minds occupy space transpiring in time. He applied the term *categories* to those characteristics which all things possess in common. Categories are properties in space-time, necessarily inherent, as *a priori* and universal entities, in every space-time object. The primary category is motion, the basic prerequisite of all other categories. The four major categories are: identity or diversity; existence or being; relation; and order. Subordinate categories are: substance; casualty; reciprocity; quantity; intensity; number; and whole and parts. Without the categories, science would be impossible, since the categories are responsible for the existence of law and regularity in the world.

Alexander's Emergent Evolution. Whatever exists must *a priori* be subject to space-time and the categories; that is, space-time and the categories apply to every object in the universe. However, as evolution progresses, and new emergents appear, they may possess qualities in addition to the listed categories. Life is an emergent with novel qualities peculiar to itself which cannot be entirely traced to the categories, for its unique properties are emergents, qualities unique to itself alone and not found in inorganic matter or other low forms of being. It is therefore impossible to predict from the presence of low forms of being, such as the inorganic forms, the types of higher forms, such as living organisms, which may emerge during the next stage of evolution. It is clear, however, that organic objects consist of nothing but matter on a higher level of organization.

Alexander stated that there have been five levels of emergent evolution: the first level was the primordial stage of *space-time and the categories;* the second level saw the development of *primary qualities* through multiple sense perceptions; the third level was that of *secondary qualities* experienced through perception by one sensory organ (although such perceptions are sensory qualities, they are nevertheless real); the fourth level is that of *life;* and the fifth level is that of *mind.* Mind is an object, not of contemplation as Descartes thought, but of inward enjoyment.

When, sometime in the future, the next (sixth) level of emergent evolution appears (the level described by Alexander as that of *Deity*), then in contrast to our capacity merely to enjoy the qualities in mental experience, the Super Being or Deity will have the power to contemplate them.

Alexander's Philosophy of Religion.　In Alexander's philosophy of religion, known as Religious Naturalism, God is portrayed as the source in nature of the power to support or produce values. Alexander drew a distinction between God and Deity. God is the entire universe, whereas Deity is the next stage of emergence in the process of evolution. God as the entire universe necessarily encompasses Deity, the latter being the new emergent level toward which the process of world evolution advances. Human beings represent the highest stage of evolution; as organisms possessing minds, they are superior to other forms of organic life. Deity, representing the next emergent level toward which man strives, is a higher emergent being than man. In fact, Alexander used the term *Deity* to denote each higher stage of emergent evolution; hence, in this sense man is Deity which the living organisms devoid of minds strive to emulate.

Although he sometimes appeared to define Deity as referring to the mind of God, Alexander generally portrayed God as identical with the world as a whole and Deity as the *nisus* or urge within nature toward the next higher stage of evolution, that is, as the new emergent which is about to come into being, an entity achieving a level of existence superior to the present. Precisely what the novel emergent quality, Deity, will be, cannot be discerned, for, although the world progresses teleologically, nevertheless, what the *nisus toward Deity* will produce as Deity remains indeterminate.

Alexander was not a pantheist, even though Pantheism also identifies God with the whole of reality. On the contrary, he was a theist, stating that individual persons possess their own being and private consciousness. In this sense, man is not simply a part of God, but an organism capable of co-operating with God in the further progress of the universe. It is presently an error, said Alexander, to attribute evil to Deity, for Deity has not yet even come into existence. Man should co-operate with God in ushering Deity into existence; therefore in this respect man is responsible for the nature of Deity. He should realize that evil is part of the make-up of the world, and he should co-operate with God to convert it into good.

According to Alexander, freedom of the will may be interpreted in two senses: (1) as an activity that is merely not subject to compulsion by extraneous forces; (2) as the expression of an integrated self-directing person acting in a purposeful coherent way in order to serve not only his own interests but also those of society. In the second interpretation, freedom of the will refers to a form of ethical self-determination characteristic of a good person. Man thinks he is a free and entirely self-directing organism, but to Deity situated on a higher level of emergent evolution, it would be clear that man's conduct is actually predetermined. In the same way, lower organisms might seem to be self-directing, yet man knows that they are directed by external forces.

Alexander's Value Theory. In *Beauty and Other Forms of Value* (1933), Alexander set forth his theory that values do not exist independently of the individual, but constitute a relationship between subject and object, between man and the object which he values. Value is a quality in the object *per se;* it is an objective relationship judged by objective standards and based upon the principle of coherence, that is, upon agreement among people willing to accept it as valid.

Accepting truth, beauty, and goodness as the three greatest values in life (those designated in Plato's philosophy) Alexander also advocated loyalty to lesser, practical values such as the preservation of one's health and everyday interests. He defined truth as reality known to mind. Although he acknowledged the pragmatic criterion of truth, he preferred the coherence theory, since he viewed the world of reality as a coherent whole, concluding that truth must be the coherent ordering of reality as the mind understands it, for truth does not exist apart from the mind's knowing it, nor does the mind create it. In other words, truth consists of the mind's contemplation of external reality. He defined beauty as an interaction between the mind and each object which it considers beautiful. The mind is to a certain extent subject to a kind of illusion when it imputes beauty and value to objects, as, for example, when it interprets a painting as if it had three dimensions. He defined good in two ways: as a moral good opposed to immorality; and as anything that wards off natural evils. In the first sense, the good person is one who integrates and controls his impulses for sake of the best interests both of himself and of society. In the second sense, whatever enhances man's welfare or happiness is good. Goodness thus consists of modifications in the environment in order to aid the mind in the pursuit of its basic values and purposes.

The discussion of Samuel Alexander's philosophy of Emergent Evolution has completed our analysis of the major philosophical systems of Evolutionary Naturalism. In addition to the noted philosophers whose contributions have been reviewed, others of lesser importance who adhere to this school of thought should be mentioned: C. Lloyd Morgan (1852–1936), whose *Emergent Evolution* (1922–1923) has been compared to the works of Alexander; Roy Wood Sellars (1880–   ), an American whose *Evolutionary Naturalism* (1922) delineated a kindred philosophy; and John Fiske (1842–1901), known as an American popularizer of Herbert Spencer's philosophy and author of the celebrated works, *Outline of Cosmic Philosophy* (1874) and *Through Nature to God* (1899). It should be noted that a number of these philosophers belong to more than a single school of philosophical thought. Usually this classification in more than one school is attributable to the fact that a particular phase of a philosopher's views may be consistent with one philosophical system while the bulk of his ideas belong to one or several other systems. Thus the Utilitarian philosopher John Stuart Mill was in certain respects a Positivist under the influence of Comtean views; the Evolutionary Naturalist, Herbert Spencer, was Utilitarian in much of his ethical theory; Samuel Alexander was a Neorealist as well as an adherent of Evolutionary Naturalism; and G. E. Moore developed a form of Ideal Utilitarianism in ethics while adhering to Neorealism in metaphysics. Obviously great caution must be exercised in any attempt to classify such modern philosophers as members of specific schools of philosophy.

Chapter 13

Classical Positivism

The founder of Classical Positivism, Auguste Comte (1798–1857), ranks among the four greatest French philosophers. The principal source of inspiration for his ideas came from Claude Henri de Rouvroy, Comte de Saint-Simon (1760–1825), who was his teacher at the École Polytechnique. Saint-Simon was an advanced social thinker who favored the French and American revolutions, seeking a reorganization of society which would improve the lot of the worker by means of social and scientific progress in accordance with the tenets of positive philosophy. He envisioned a proletariat society in which all would work for the sake of the benefit of humanity. This goal would be effected by transferring earthly power from the nobility and the military class to the manufacturing classes.

COMTE'S POSITIVISM

With this background of education, Comte set out to develop his system of Positivism designed to revamp society for the sake of all classes, believing that his system would guarantee international peace and avoid economic dissension. Society's salvation was to be contingent upon scientific knowledge. Theology would have to be displaced by positive science, and a "Religion of Humanity" would replace sectism and denominationalism. Comte's goal was the wedding of positive philosophy with the "great power," namely, the proletariat.

The Principle of the Three Stages. Like Hegel and other philosophers, Comte also sought a "natural law of the history of society," believing that society is governed by laws. His views and the principles he set forth earned him the title of founder of sociology. He called attention to man's intellectual development as it unfolds historically, individually, and socially. He claimed that man's intellectual development has passed through three important ascending stages: (1) the theological stage, (2) the metaphysical stage, and (3) the positive stage.

In the theological stage, man's thinking is characterized chiefly by anthropomorphism, attributing human qualities to natural objects and to Deity, that is, to things which are not human. Man was predisposed to fetishism, to animism (ascribing souls to inanimate objects), and to belief in spirits or ghosts; he tried to explain natural phenomena as under the control of spiritual forces, accepting the polytheistic belief in a plurality of gods, each supreme in his particular sphere—e.g., the god of death decides whether any person shall live or die. It was Comte's view that as man progresses through the theological stage, he eventually arrives at a higher level of sophistication and accepts the monotheistic belief in a single God dominating all processes in nature.

In the second stage of the intellectual development of man, the metaphysical stage, he gives up his faith in spirits as the source and explanation of natural phenomena and adopts a new faith in impersonal forces such as gravity, or in theories about cause-and-effect or being-and-essence relationships. Leading thinkers at this stage of human intellectual evolution adhere to a belief in the reality of the Kantian things-in-themselves, an ultimate reality which transcends all phenomenal experience.

In the third and final stage of human progress, the positive stage, man gives up metaphysical explanations involving theories about possible forces or essences (ultimate reality) behind phenomena. He limits himself to positive knowledge and feels quite confident about ascertained facts since these are specific data subject to demonstrable conditions and constitute a factual source out of which experimentally verifiable laws may be derived.

Principles of Scientific Positivism. Comte's Positivism is in agreement with Hume's Phenomenalism in one important respect: both state that metaphysical causes or substances are not real, that only the facts of sense phenomena exist. All knowledge is relative; nothing except this principle of relative truth is absolute. According to Comte, "general facts" or what we term "laws," describing regularity of occurrence, is the only valid scientific explanation of events and the only kind of knowledge from which we can derive practical benefits. For Positivism, anything real or certain must also be useful.

Comte believed that it would be possible to list the individual sciences in order of their complexity, from the simplest to the most complex, that the complex sciences would be seen to depend upon simpler ones, and that the more complex sciences would appear later than the simpler ones related to them. He constructed a hierarchy of the sciences on this basis as follows: mathematics, astronomy, physics, chemistry, biology (which includes psychology), and sociology, the latter being the most complex and dependent upon the preceding ones for understanding. As the sciences become more complex, they advance nearer and nearer to the positive stage.

Comte pointed out that each science has its own governing laws, so that the laws of sociology, for example, cannot be reduced to those of chemistry. Each deals with its own special kind of phenomena and subject matter. He regarded Materialism as an impossible doctrine, inasmuch as none of the life sciences, such as biology, can be fully understood in terms of physical sciences, such as physics. On the ground that biological evolution was limited to external features or characteristics which did not permanently alter the character of the human race, Comte rejected the Lamarckian hypothesis.

Comte's Humanism. In his *A General View of Positivism* (1848), which was subsequently published as the first volume of his *Positive Polity* (1851–1854), Comte seems to have expounded ideas he had attributed to the theological state of human development, with the qualification, however, that he never accepted a belief in a theistic God, but preferred instead Religious Humanism based on the theory that God is humanity (or the Great Being, *le Grand Être,* as he termed it).

Each of us, said Comte, will find not only our religion and our God but our immortality as well, in the whole of humanity. The individual dies, but humanity lives on. For us to attain immortality, it is necessary to survive in the memory of those who follow us by living in a manner worthy of remembrance. A person's good influence will continue after him and become part of surviving humanity.

Our worship, too, must be dedicated to humanity. Our hymns must be sung to the highest object of devotion, to a humanity which is the composite of all noble souls from every age. Our saints are those who have rendered important services to mankind. These men become our sources of inspiration, and we are obligated to keep them in remembrance. Comte even suggested a Positivist calendar in which each month would include a day celebrating the name of a person who has rendered great service to humanity. Comte's religion of Humanism had overtones of Roman Catholicism, as in its doctrines concerning saints and the status of women. His proposed social and religious reforms were to be implemented through application of the "affective principle," the ideals prompted by human feeling. Comte had once taught the primacy of the intellect over feeling, but later he concluded that the heart must always be the dominant influence and formulated a triune principle: *"L'amour pour principe, l'ordre pour base, le progrès pour but"* (Love for the principle, order for the basis, progress for the end).

CLASSICAL POSITIVISM AFTER COMTE

Classical Positivism after the time of Comte received a strong impetus from the teachings of Ernst Mach (1838–1916), professor of physics at the University of Prague who later (in 1895) was appointed to the newly created post of professor of the philosophy of science at the University of Vienna. He is known principally for his *The Science of Mechanics* (1883) and *Analysis of Sensations* (1886), both of which reflect the Phenomenalist views of Hume and Comte.

Mach's Conception of Scientific Law. For Mach, the entire world including the personality or self, consists of phenomena. Physical things and sensations are characterized by their phenomenal nature. The laws of science are mere signs or symbols expressing the order which prevails among the phenomena in human experience— economical ways in which man identifies and describes events that recur regularly without having to recapitulate each instance of occurrence. For Mach a scientific law is a condensed statement about repetitive experienced facts. Scientific concepts (such as force and energy) are but useful fictions, names, or signs representing complexes of phenomena or sensations. There is no such thing as ultimate reality; only the constant flow of sensation-complexes exists. The Ego (self) is a group or complex of sensations. Sensations are the basic facts of both psychology and physics, treated in psychology as subjective data (arising from bodily experience), in physics as objective data. Mach did not mean to imply that the body produces sensations, but rather to point out that the body itself is a complex of sensations, as are all other objects in nature.

Mach rejected the Kantian concept of the thing-in-itself. He agreed with Kantian ideas, however, concerning the reality of sensory phenomena, which, he insisted, encompass the whole of true knowledge. Since so-called "metaphysical realities" are assumed to go beyond the boundaries of sense experience, they must be considered *non*sense, nonexistent. Scientific knowledge and scientific law are of more than merely economic value; they possess pragmatic value when directed by the will (voluntarism) for the enhancement of everyday practical living (Pragmatism). Scientific observation, in identifying thought with what is actually observed in experience (phenomena), becomes useful for purposes of adaptation and natural selection. Mach argued that the world should be viewed as the product of evolutionary development.

Avenarius, Poincaré, and Pearson. Leading Positivists whose point of view is similar to Mach's in many respects include Richard Avenarius (1843–1896), Jules Henri Poincaré (1854–1912) and Karl Pearson (1857–1936). Avenarius is well known for his *Critique of Pure Experience* (1888) and his *Der menschliche Weltbegriff* (1891), works designed to expound a scientific philosophy based on purely experiential data, especially on the universal experience of mankind. He hoped to found a symbolic language for philosophy comparable to the language of mathematical signs. Poincaré, renowned French mathematician and physicist, regarded scientific laws as merely convenient conventions, not susceptible to proof. Notwithstanding his insistence upon the classification of all scientific hypotheses as mere conventions, however, Poincaré declared that all theories must nevertheless be co-ordinated by being self-consistent as well as being compatible with the facts of sense experience. He presented this position in *Science and Hypothesis* (1902). Pearson in his *Grammar of Science* (1892) expounded theories much like those of Mach concerning the experiential basis and pragmatic values of scientific law and method.

Chapter 14

Dialectical Materialism:
Marxian Communism

Dialectical Materialism, in its wider sense, refers to the entire system of philosophy founded by Karl Marx (1818–1883); in a narrower sense, it refers particularly to his metaphysics or that theory of reality which underlies Marxism, the social philosophy known as Communism or Communistic Socialism. According to Marx, his is the only type of Socialism that could be considered scientific. In Soviet Russia, Dialectical Materialism, called *Diamat,* has achieved the highest prestige, comparable to that of a religion in other societies, and it is taught by specially trained teachers. (The word *Diamat* combines the first three letters in *dialectical* with the initial three letters in *materialism.*)

Dialectical Materialism is a synthesis, uniting aspects of the dialectic of Hegel with certain materialistic doctrines of Feuerbach. In fact, Marx was deeply indebted to these two philosophers for many ideas of his own system, even though he wrote a disparaging comment about their influence: "The philosophers have only *interpreted* the world in various ways; the point, however, is to *change* it." For some important doctrines he was also heavily indebted to the Positivism of Auguste Comte, the Positivism and Evolutionary Naturalism of Herbert Spencer, the Evolutionary Naturalism of Charles Darwin, and David Ricardo's *labor theory of value* which became the fundamental thesis of Marx' major work, *Das Kapital* (1867, 1885, 1895). He was also influenced by some of the ideas of the economists Adam Smith and Thomas Robert Malthus.

MARX AND THE MARXISTS

Karl Heinrich Marx (1818–1883) was educated at the Universities of Bonn, Berlin, and Jena, receiving a Ph.D. degree from the University of Jena in 1841. Early in his academic career he came under the influence of Hegelian philosophy and of the left-wing "Young Hegelians." He became a journalist and edited the *Rheinische Zeitung,* the *Deutschfranzösische-Jahrbücher,* and the *Neue rheinische*

Zeitung, respectively. In addition to *Das Kapital,* he wrote an epochal revolutionary pamphlet, *Manifesto of the Communist Party* (1848), in collaboration with Friedrich Engels (1820–1895), the son of a wealthy German textile manufacturer. The two men participated in the revolution of 1848. Among other significant writings of Marx are the following: *Contribution to the Critique of Hegel's Philosophy of Right* (1844); *Theses on Feuerbach* (1845); *The Poverty of Philosophy* (1847); *Contribution to the Critique of Political Economy* (1859); *Critique of the Gotha Program* (1875); and (in collaboration with Engels) *The German Ideology* (1845–1846).

In addition to Marx and Engels, other leading proponents of Marxism were Nikolai Lenin (Vladimir Ilich Ulyanov, 1870–1924), whose most important philosophical writings were *Materialism and Empirio-Criticism* (1909), and *State and Revolution* (1917); Leon Trotsky (1877–1940), author of *Literature and Revolution* (1924); and the contemporary Chinese leader, Mao Tse-tung (1893–   ), whose works (five volumes in English, four in the Chinese edition), first appeared in Peking in 1951. Mao's chief philosophical writings were *Combat Liberalism* (1937), *On Practice* (1937), *On Contradiction* (1937), and *On the Correct Handling of Contradictions among the People* (1957). Karl Kautsky (1854–1938) and Joseph Stalin (Iosif Vissarionovich Dzhugashvili, 1879–1953) also contributed numerous interpretations of Marxist doctrines and won a vast following in the Communist movement.

Principal Marxian Doctrines. The basic ideas of Dialectical Materialism and Marxian Communism may be summarized as follows: the Hegelian dialectic (applied to Communism); Historical Materialism (or economic determinism); Communism as the ownership of the means of production; abolition of private property; the labor theory of value (or "surplus value"); the inevitability of profiteering and the exploitation of labor; scientific Socialism; violent revolution; class struggle; dictatorship of the proletariat; achievement of a classless society or the withering away of the State; ten measures of social reform; religion as the opium of the masses.

The Hegelian Dialectic. Marx accepted the Hegelian dialectic, which stated that every thesis contains its own antithesis, its negation, opposite, or contradiction, and that the two conflicting forces merge to produce a synthesis, a new and greater reality. He applied this logical principle to socio-economic history. The two socio-economic classes which are antithetical to each other are the bourgeoisie (the capitalists or property-owning class) and the proletariat (the workers, who must sell their labor in order to survive). There is a constant, irreconcilable conflict between these two classes which can be resolved only when the proletariat revolts and overthrows the capitalist class, thereby establishing a classless society, a dictatorship of the proletariat. The emergent classless society, consisting only of people who work and own the means of production in common, will thus implement the philosophy and socio-economic system of Communism.

Historical Materialism. This economic interpretation of history, or, as it is sometimes called, the materialistic interpretation of history (*Historical Materialism*) is based upon the doctrine of economic determinism. Marx contended that a particular society's mode of economic production determines the nature of its culture and social structure. (Feuerbach had applied this materialistic concept to social problems and cultural evolution.) Marx traced the relevant cause-effect relationships from ancient to modern times. He noted that the chief mode of production among the ancient Greeks and Romans was replaced by feudalist methods of production during the medieval period. Feudalism and the institution of serfdom upon which it depended yielded to capitalism in the modern period when the mode of production was changed through wider use of machinery and the factory system. Marx concluded that capitalism, by its very nature, is self-destructive and hence must capitulate to Socialism, that, owing to the dialectical character of history, each historical period carries within itself the "germs of its own destruction" (Hegel's principle of negativity).

According to the doctrine of Historical Materialism, the mode of production of material goods determines the political, social, intellectual, and religious life and institutions of a given people in each era of history. "It is not the consciousness of men that determines their being, but, on the contrary, their social being that determines their consciousness." Those who own the means of production control the entire gamut of the people's culture, including their moral and religious ideas and their social and intellectual outlook. According to the doctrine of Historical Materialism, the material conditions of existence mold the ideas of the people who, mistakenly, assume that it is their ideas which shape their mode of living. The capitalists who own the means of production or control the mode of production thereby control the ideas of mankind. Thus a capitalist who runs or directs a publishing enterprise is in a position to control the ideas to which men are exposed and hence to influence and direct social and cultural developments.

Common Ownership of Means of Production. Marx defined Communism as the "common ownership of the means of production," an ideal system to be achieved by shifting control over economic resources from the capitalists to the proletariat. This transfer of property rights would bring the permanent "abolition of private property," with public ownership of all means of production, including the farms and factories, raw materials, transportation and communication facilities, and the like.

Labor Theory of Value; Exploitation of Labor. Marx noted that, since the labor of many workers is required to support a single capitalist, members of the capitalist class are parasites living at the expense of the workers who are being exploited. This assertion brings us to the principal themes of *Das Kapital,* namely, the *labor theory of value* and the *doctrine of surplus value.*

According to the labor theory of value, the price of a product is determined by the amount of labor expended on its production. Of course, a useless product possesses no value. Furthermore, the skilled worker produces a more valuable product and is entitled to higher wages than the slower worker, who receives lower wages commensurate with his speed and efficiency.

Marx defined capital as accumulated surplus value, surplus value being equal to the difference between the actual cost of manufacture of a given article and its selling price, or what is commonly known as the net profit. But Marx meant something more than technical profit when he referred to surplus value; he meant to imply the unjust procedure of profiteering by using money to earn money instead of working for such earnings. He condemned profit-making as a form of exploitation. When the capitalist accumulates wealth from surplus value, he is exploiting labor; that is, he is unjustly using other persons for his own profit. The only commodity a worker possesses is his own labor, which alone constitutes the value of whatever he produces. Marx considered the capitalist unnecessary for the production of any commodity, and hence expendable, for only the worker is indispensable. The worker sells himself at a subsistence wage instead of the proper reward which should include the surplus value—that is, the money remaining after rent, interest, subsistence wages, and other expenses have been deducted from the selling price. The capitalist is also entitled to some wages if he contributes his own labor in actual production; the evil lies in his filching the surplus value rightfully belonging to the workers. Marx noted that competition among capitalists tends to equalize profits, so that if one manufacturer makes inordinately high profits, other manufacturers will enter into competition with him, forcing profits to be reduced to a normal or average level.

Scientific Socialism: Class Struggle, Dictatorship of Proletariat, Classless Society. Consequently, an inherent class struggle or war is constantly being waged between the capitalist who exploits and the proletariat whose labor is being exploited. This conflict can be resolved only through the elimination of the capitalist (who is unnecessary for the production of goods) by force of arms, a violent revolution to overthrow the capitalist exploiters and establish the dictatorship of the proletariat. When "all workers of the world unite" in this enterprise, the two classes (the exploiters and the exploited) will cease to exist, resulting in a classless society comprising only workers, who will be guided by the Communist motto: "From each according to his abilities, to each according to his needs!" In the classless society the economic struggle between the capitalist and proletariat classes ceases as all merge into one class, the working class which is no longer subject to exploitation. In this utopian state, "pre-history ends, and history begins." Here, then, is the consummation of the ideal program of scientific Socialism.

Ten Measures of Social Reform. Marx and Engels in the *Manifesto of the Communist Party*, presented a practical plan for implementing Communist theory by calling for certain measures of social reform, as follows:

1. Abolition of property in land and application of all rents from land to public purposes.
2. A heavy progressive or graduated income tax.
3. Abolition of all right of inheritance.
4. Confiscation of property of all emigrants and rebels.
5. Centralization of credit in the hands of the State, by means of a national bank with State capital and an exclusive monopoly.
6. Centralization in State hands of the means of communication and transportation.
7. Expansion of factory systems and increased State ownership of instruments of production; State planning to bring waste lands back into cultivation and improve soils.
8. Equal obligation of all persons to perform useful work. Establishment of industrial armies, especially for agriculture.
9. Establishment of production centers combining agriculture with manufacturing; gradual abolition of the distinction between town and country through a better balanced distribution of the population.

10. Free education for all children in public schools. Abolition of child labor. Work-study programs to combine education with industrial production.

Marx and Engels regarded these measures as flexible principles which were to be implemented in different ways, depending upon prevailing conditions in each country.

Religion as the Opium of the Masses. Historical Materialism regards all events in human consciousness as physical reactions aimed at satisfying the economic and material needs of mankind; it assumes that moral, religious, and other values are epiphenomena of matter. In the Marxist view, morality is contingent upon the social class, and the social class together with its corresponding moral code is in turn the product of the mode of production.

Since man's nature is the result of historical forces, the human being changes his ideas, character, and mode of living through efforts to cope with materialistic conditions. Ideas are only by-products of matter—"matter thinks." "Human essence has no true reality." Industrial and scientific work constitutes the highest form of activity, the goal of which is the production of material goods for the enhancement of human well-being.

Marxists reject religious doctrines about spiritual values, the soul, immortality, and God, asserting that religion is an illusion, and that the illusory happiness based on it must be condemned. "Religion is the sigh of the oppressed creature, the heart of the heartless world, just as it is the spirit of a spiritless situation. It is the opium of the people." God does not create man; rather, man creates invalid religion with its mythical God. Religion functions as a police force, as a bourgeois technique to dissuade the masses from revolting by promising them a better, happier existence after death than their exploiters allow them to enjoy during their lifetime on earth.

NIKOLAI LENIN

Vladimir Ilich Ulyanov (1870–1924)—known as Nikolai Lenin because after 1900 he used the pen name N. Lenin—studied law at Kazan University and later at St. Petersburg University (in Leningrad), where he was granted his degree in 1891. As a disciple of Marx he was exiled to Siberia and later lived in various countries; in 1903 he became head of the Bolshevik party in London. Among his significant writings was his polemical work, *What the "Friends of the People" Are* (1894), attacking Populists and Idealist metaphysicians, while defending Marx' materialistic interpretation of history. He sought to show that Historical Materialism does not undermine the role of the individual in history.

In *Materialism and Empirio-Criticism* (written in 1908, published in 1909) Lenin attacked the Positivists within the ranks of Marxism who accepted the views of Mach and Avenarius. (Empirio-Criticism referred to Mach's Positivism.) He compared the views of Mach and Berkeley and condemned Machism as opening the door to Idealism and religion. The book is an attempt to define Materialism, while attacking Machism. Lenin, a staunch defender of Metaphysical Materialism, was quite dogmatic upon the subject, ignoring any evidence which might interfere with his attempt to explain all phenomena in materialistic terms. He was fully cognizant of the new physics, and quite aware of its devastating effect upon ancient Metaphysical Materialism, yet he embraced Materialism with a naïvete which should have been highly embarrassing to a philosopher, and he went so far as to attempt a materialistic interpretation of Hegelian philosophy. In his epochal *State and Revolution* (written in 1917) he elaborated upon Marx' doctrines of the dictatorship of the proletariat, the withering away of the state, and the necessity for revolution.

Lenin's is a philosophy of history, and only this limited field held his interest. Revolution was fundamental to his thought, and he referred to it as the leap, by which he meant the revolutionary leap into a social system under the dictatorship of the proletariat. (Traditionally, in metaphysics, this concept of the leap has referred to passage from matter to motion, that is, from matter to consciousness, as a kind of break in continuity. For Kierkegaard it signified a leap of faith, that is, a qualitative transition from unbelief to belief.) A dialectical transition, either in history or in science, consists of leaps, said Lenin, who contended that Hegel took refuge in Idealism because of failure to understand this essential character of such change. According to Lenin's doctrine of the self-movement of matter, matter is capable of making these leaps because it contains movement within itself. It was his theory that the dialectic, which is here essentially an identity of opposites, functions by applying a principle of negativity expressed in an inner pulsation or self-movement, an inner vitality. Lenin's theory of leaps and his emphasis on the necessity for revolutionary activity characterized him as a Neo-Marxian who had great faith in the power of philosophy not merely to explain but actually to change the world.

In epistemology, Lenin was a Naïve Realist, believing that things are in reality just as they appear to our senses. He held to the belief in the Kantian things-in-themselves, but as things-for-us, that is, as things perceived by our senses. He accepted the same criterion of truth as Marx, Engels, and other Marxists, namely, practice, ascribing validity to a Pragmatism which became an influential emphasis in philosophy not only in the Western world but also in the East, especially where it was advocated as a valid principle by Mao Tse-tung, father of Chinese Communism.

MAO TSE-TUNG

In China Mao Tse-tung (1893–   ) became the ideological, political, and military leader of the Communist party, organizing the peasants into a guerrilla army which defeated Nationalist China and established a Communist society. Two aspects of Dialectical Materialism upon which Mao placed great stress are: practice, the pragmatic element of Communism; and contradiction, which to Mao involves conflict and revolution. For Mao, the factor of contradiction must be understood in Hegelian terms to mean that without conflict (ranging from ideological controversy to war) there can be no progress: "All political power grows out of the barrel of a gun."

Pragmatic Communism. Marx had stated that philosophers merely speculate, whereas the task of man is to change the world. Similarly, Mao condemned the views of those who merely philosophize as doctrinairism and Empiricism, or doctrinaire subjectivism. He attacked the Empiricists, meaning those who draw upon their fragmentary, subjective experience for data, and he insisted that the only valid criterion of truth is man's social practice, that it is only through this pragmatic test that man gains knowledge about the external world. Verification of ideas is achieved through social practice, that is to say, through historical processes such as the class struggle, material production, and scientific experiments. Mao held that natural laws and the results of theory can be discerned only through social practice, that theory depends upon practice, and that theory is subservient to practice.

According to Mao, each act of knowing involves two stages: the first is perceptual or phenomenal, while the second is conceptual or inferential. As the individual repeatedly experiences a phenomenal object which recurs regularly in his perceptions, he makes a sudden intellectual (inductive) leap, gaining an understanding of the conceptual object and ascertaining its true essence and reality.

Contradiction. In Mao's view, the most fundamental law in Dialectical Materialism is the law of contradiction which exists in the nature of things; it is a law of the unity of opposites. This law, taken from Hegel's dialectic, implies internal contradictions in nature, society, and history. In social processes, there are two types of contradictions (conflicts): those existing between Communists and their enemies, such as the United States imperialists (as Mao called the Americans); and those existing within the Communist camp. Contradictions among the Communists may be democratically resolved by adhering to the formula: "Unity—criticism—unity." However, contradictions between Communists and capitalists can be resolved only by means of a Socialist revolution. In a Communist revolt, which grows out of a class struggle, the dictatorship of the proletariat resolves class conflicts through prosecution and repression of counter-revolutionaries at home and protection from domestic subversion and foreign intervention. Mao's staunch opposition to Liberalism (within Communism) was based on the value of using a constant ideological struggle as an effective weapon for maintaining efficiency within Communist ranks.

Chapter 15

Pragmatism

Pragmatism is essentially an American philosophy developed in the latter half of the nineteenth century, chiefly under the leadership of Charles Sanders Peirce (1839–1914), William James (1842–1910), and John Dewey (1859–1952). Among European protagonists, Ferdinand C. S. Schiller (1864–1937) in England and others, including the Marxists in Western countries, have introduced their own versions but the mainstream of Pragmatic thought stems from origins in the northeastern United States.

The term *Pragmatism* was first used by Peirce, who taught for a short period at Harvard and Johns Hopkins universities, and whose ideas were disseminated in numerous papers now comprising many volumes. In 1907, James devoted an entire volume to explaining the meaning of Pragmatism, dedicating it to John Stuart Mill "from whom I first learned the pragmatic openness of mind and whom my fancy likes to picture as our leader were he alive today." Dewey introduced the new terms *Experimentalism* and *Instrumentalism*, which seemed more characteristic of his philosophy, but he should be regarded as a successor to Peirce and James in the Pragmatic school.

Two other important American Pragmatists were: the social behaviorist George Herbert Mead (1863–1931); and the logician, Clarence Irving Lewis (1883–1964), who developed a conceptualistic Pragmatism, emphasizing the view that there exist choices among theoretical systems for application to (or explanation of) specific experiential situations.

CHARLES SANDERS PEIRCE

Peirce, the founder of Pragmatism, introduced to this characteristically American system of philosophy the two other giants, namely, James who was an associate of Peirce's at Harvard University and Dewey who was a student at Johns Hopkins University where Peirce was then teaching. Only a few (about twenty-five) of Peirce's papers were published during his lifetime, and hundreds of others were purchased by Harvard University, which has published many of them as a multi-volume set. Although James and Dewey became the most influential exponents of Pragmatism, it was Peirce who contributed to it the most original thought, his originality extending far beyond the contribution of Pragmatism to the logic of classes and relations, to the theory of signs, and to the theory of probability, encompassing the entire field of scientific method and the logic of mathematics. As a forerunner of symbolic logic, Peirce attained a position of importance comparable to that of George Boole (1815–1864), Ernst Schroeder (1841–1902), and Gottlob Frege (1848–1925).

The Pragmatism of Peirce. Peirce, who was much more conservative in point of view than Dewey and very much more conservative than James, was concerned with metaphysical realities and discussed the ontologically real. To Dewey and James these ontological considerations were anathema. Nevertheless, Peirce was faithful to what he regarded as the central thesis of Pragmatism, namely, the theory "that the whole function of thought is to produce habits of action." In 1905, discussing the nature of Pragmatism, he stated that the rational meaning of a word "lies exclusively in its conceivable bearing upon the conduct of life." Objecting to distortions of his views, he coined the term *Pragmaticism* to identify his precise interpretation of Pragmatic philosophy. It should be noted that James and Dewey, while differing from Peirce about metaphysical and ontological problems, held the same belief that speculative thought cannot be divorced from action, that the function of speculative thought is the production of habits of action, and that the perceptible consequences of any theory constitute the test or explanation of its validity because such results fulfill the very purpose of speculative thought. In Peirce's interpretation, it is meaning in the concrete that reveals truth, which consists of practical experience with individual, concrete things. "Our idea of anything *is* our idea of its sensible effects," he insisted.

Peirce regarded Pragmatism as the application of the logical principle underlying the statement of Jesus: "By their fruits, ye shall know them." On the other hand, religious beliefs which are consequentially indifferent or sterile he rejected. He cited as an example the doctrine of transubstantiation, which assumes that the wine employed in the eucharistic mass is transformed metaphysically into the very blood of Christ; Peirce argued that, since the properties of the wine do not change in respect to their sensible and consequential effect, no ontological transformation could occur. He subjected all such doctrines and, in fact, all generalizations to the tests of clarity, distinctness, and practicality. A clear idea is recognized for what it is unmistakably without the possibility of confusing it with any other. A distinct idea "contains nothing which is not clear." Note the Cartesian nature of these first two criteria. The third criterion, which provides the highest level of clarification, enjoins us to seek the meaning of an idea in its effects or practical bearings, for these constitute the conceptual foundation or essence of a given object.

Doubt, Belief, and Action. According to Peirce, doubt, belief, and action are interrelated processes, each with its specific function. The function of doubt is to stimulate thought, and the purpose of thought is to arrive at belief. "Action of thought is excited by the irritation of doubt, and ceases when belief is attained; so that production of belief is the sole function of thought." When we arrive at belief, mental disturbances created by doubt disappear; furthermore, belief provides us with a rule of action or habit of action. Beliefs both influence future thinking and establish habits. Although habits are found in nature as well as in man, in nature they are called laws, whereas in man beliefs as well as behavior become habitual modes. A belief is "that upon which a man is prepared to act." Beliefs are more than laws of human nature; they are acquired habits of the mind as well as part of our constitutional make-up. Our fixed beliefs or habits of thinking come into existence owing to their practical value, and, not being limited to overt action, they guide logical thought processes. "Beliefs are really rules for action, and the whole function of thinking is but one step in the production of habits of action." Truth is "that character of a proposition which consists in this, that belief in the proposition would, with sufficient experience and reflection, lead us to such conduct as would tend to satisfy the desires we should then have." The irritation of doubt initiates mental activity, whereas doubt resolved means that we have attained our purpose or object of inquiry, i.e., the goal of our thinking which is true opinion pragmatically grounded in belief or habit of action.

The Fixation of Belief. Peirce noted four methods of fixing belief: the method of tenacity or dogmatism which ignores problems or difficulties and arrives at simple conclusions conducive only to mental tranquility; the method of authority whereby rulers dictate beliefs to a whole community thus intellectually enslaved by them; the *a priori* method of metaphysicians who convince others to accept logically arranged propositions without subjecting them to empirical investigation or scientific inquiry; and, finally, the scientific method, the preferred method for establishing pragmatically sound, objective beliefs which constitute practical values and true conclusions.

The Metaphysics of Peirce. Unlike other Pragmatists, Peirce believed in a metaphysics postulating ontologically real objects. In this sense he was a Realist, but his Realism was consistent with his Objective Idealism. He rejected Cartesian Dualism because mind and matter seemed to him to be a single substance. He was also opposed to Nominalism, the Scholastic theory which reduced universals to mere signs or names.

Peirce regarded the universe as having evolved from chaos steadily toward a goal as a consequence of three cosmological forces or principles: (1) tychism (or chance); (2) agapism (or evolutionary love); and (3) synechism (or the principle of continuity). It is tychism (chance) which accounts for the variety and diversification found in the universe as it evolves in accordance with agapism, the fundamental principle which causes all things in the world to be governed by laws. This concept combining chance with law was inspired by John Duns Scotus' doctrine of will. The third cosmological principle of synechism, "the doctrine that all that exists is continuous," accounts not only for continuity, but also for the tendency of things toward reasonableness. These three cosmological principles correspond respectively to three phenomenological categories which Peirce named the First, Second, and Third categories of Being. These three ontological categories are logical principles comparable to the Hegelian dialectic of triads. Peirce, who was profoundly influenced by Hegel's views, identified the origin of a thing with the First category, its end with the Second category, and their mediation or synthesis as the Third category.

WILLIAM JAMES

To William James, noted American philosopher who taught physiology, psychology, and then philosophy at Harvard University during the latter nineteenth and early twentieth centuries, must go most of the credit for the wide acceptance of Pragmatism in the United States. Peirce's writings had commanded but slight attention among philosophers, most of whom had adopted Neo-Kantian or Neo-Hegelian points of view. James' eloquent lectures at Harvard, Edinburgh, and Manchester Universities and his numerous significant published works contributed immensely to the establishment of Pragmatism as the characteristically most American system of philosophy.

Among his highly significant writings were: *Principles of Psychology* (1890); *The Will to Believe* (1897); *Human Immortality* (1898); *The Varieties of Religious Experience* (1902); *Pragmatism* (1907); *A Pluralistic Universe* (1909); and *Essays in Radical Empiricism* (1912).

James' View of the Pragmatic Method. Reminding us that the term *pragmatism* comes from the Greek *pragma,* meaning action, and consequently means practice or practical, James asserted that the Pragmatic method is a technique for resolving disputes which would otherwise remain unsettled—an inquiry as to the practical meanings of events or issues. "What difference would it make practically to any one if this notion rather than that notion were true?" Anything that is meaningful or real must have some influence on practice, on our experience, and everything that has a practical effect must be acknowledged to be meaningful and real. A theory which lacks consequential results is nonsense. Meaningful statements have concrete consequential outcomes. Meaninglessness is, then, synonymous with inconsequential.

Abstract truths are meaningless unless they make a difference in concrete facts. Metaphysical terms, such as *God, matter, absolute,* and the like must possess *cash-value,* practical worth. "You must bring out of each work its practical cash-value, set it at work within the stream of your experience." The theoretical has value only when it bears upon the practical. "Theories thus become instruments, not answers to enigmas, in which we can rest." Pragmatism is both Nominalistic in that it stresses the concrete particular over the abstract universal and anti-intellectualistic in its stand against Rationalism.

The Pragmatic Theory of Truth. Pragmatism is more than a method; it is a theory of truth as well. To be sure, truth is the agreement of our ideas with reality, but for the Pragmatist, it is much more than that. Truth must possess consequential characteristics or practical significance; truths are *plural,* consisting of many different types or varieties rather than an Absolute; truths are created in the same manner that health and wealth are created; and, finally, truth is a system of verification, a process whereby ideas become true, are made true, by events in experience.

The Pragmatic Criterion of Truth. According to James, the Pragmatic criterion of truth is based upon the workability of any theory or proposition. If the idea works when applied to the concrete facts of experience, then it is a true idea. What does not work cannot be true. True ideas have practical value, while false ones do not. Pragmatism's "only test of probable truth is what works best in the way of leading us, what fits every part of life best and combines with the collectivity of experience's demands, nothing being omitted." James applied the Pragmatic test even to theological ideas. Thus, whether God exists would depend upon the extent to which a belief in God affects our lives. Does the belief augment our strength, courage, and happiness? Does it improve our adjustment to life? If it does, then we have every right to accept it as true.

Tough-Minded and Tender-Minded Philosophers.   James believed that an individual's personality or temperament accounts for his philosophical attitude. Our philosophies are shaped by our temperaments because intellectually we seek a universe appropriate to our predispositions. Two fundamental intellectual temperaments are tender-mindedness and tough-mindedness. The tender-minded are rationalistic, intellectualistic, idealistic, optimistic, religious, free-willist, monistic, and dogmatical, whereas the tough-minded are empiricistic, sensationalistic, materialistic, pessimistic, irreligious, fatalistic, pluralistic, and skeptical.

James' Metaphysics.   James described his philosophical position as follows: "My philosophy is what I call radical empiricism, a pluralism, a 'tychism,' which represents order as being gradually won and always in the making. It is theistic, but not essentially so. It rejects all doctrines of the Absolute. It is finitist. . . ." At Harvard University, in his "Syllabus of Philosophy 3," he stated that his philosophy was consistent with Empiricism, Personalism, democracy, and freedom.

The thesis of James' Radical Empiricism is that "There is only one primal stuff or material in the world, a stuff of which everything is composed, and . . . we call that stuff 'pure experience.' " James' Empiricism differs from traditional British Empiricism in his insistence that we remain within concrete experience, his insistence that "conjunctive and disjunctive relations are, when experienced, equally real." The world of facts as we experience them comprises a mosaic or set of mosaics and some of these directly experienced mosaics of plural facts appear to be connected, while others are experienced as disjunctives. The unity of the universe as a neat set of interconnected relations in an Absolute is false, said James, because direct experience informs us of a discontinuity of facts in a mosaic design. Thus Radical Empiricism claims that data in our experience show the universe to be pluralistic, comprised of facts which form neither a perfect unity nor any absolutely perfect relationship to one another. James termed this Metaphysical Pluralism a "mosaic philosophy."

Nevertheless, he pointed out that there is some unity, relation, or causal connection in those things which we directly experience. Relationships are as real as anything else and as truly experienced. Here James disagreed with the British Empiricists who assert that we do not experience a connection between things, but only discontinuous possibilities (John Stuart Mill's view) or disjunctions (as in Berkeley's Nominalism and in Humeanism). James' Radical Empiricism was unbiased, reporting each experience without favor or disfavor, at its face value. This view of reality as pure experience came rather close to Panpsychism, which attributes to all reality a mental characteristic.

James accepted Peirce's hypothesis of tychism, which states that there is an aspect of chance in nature, a factor of novelty or indeterminism which is reflected, for example, in moral conduct as man makes free, ethical choices among alternative courses of action. We tend to unify the world. The universe evolves toward ultimate unification which is never fully achieved, but during the process our "multiverse" develops into a universe. "The world is . . . a pluralism of which the unity is not fully experienced as yet. . . . The universe continually grows in quantity by new experiences that graft themselves upon the older mass; but these very new experiences often help the mass to a more consolidated form." These ideas about freedom in nature and free will in man, which first occurred to James as a young student in Europe under the influence of the French philosopher Renouvier, were reinforced during his thorough study of Bergson's philosophy of Vitalism and became permanent facets of his Pragmatism.

Since the world is made of the stuff of pure experience, it follows that mind and matter are reducible to the same substance. For James, mind and matter are composed of the same entities, which are not simply mind or matter but neutral, sometimes appearing as mind, sometimes as matter. He adhered therefore to the doctrine of Neutral Monism, which reduced mind and matter to the same neutral entities, but since there are multiple entities, he also accepted the basis of Metaphysical Pluralism. He identified metaphysical reality as the stuff of pure experience, the *flux of life,* terming it "a stream of consciousness" and accepting it at its face value as real. Thus the functional psychology of James permeated his philosophy, shaping many of his views, not only in metaphysics but in his philosophy of religion as well.

James' Philosophy of Religion. James set forth the main theses of his philosophy of religion in three significant works: *The Will to Believe and Other Essays on Popular Philosophy* (1897); *Human Immortality: Two Supposed Objections to the Doctrine* (1898); and *The Varieties of Religious Experience: A Study in Human Nature* (1902).

The thesis of *The Will to Believe* states as justification of belief the argument that the believer has a greater chance than the doubter to discover truth and to gain other practical advantages. Furthermore, the one who disbelieves faces the added risk of losing any chance of discovering the truth. What James is essentially affirming is our *right to believe*. We have a right to believe in God even in the absence of absolute proof. Not only does probability favor God's existence, but the belief therein can enrich our lives and behavior with benefits which in the absence of belief would be lacking.

The thesis of *Human Immortality* states that the mind is not dependent for its existence upon the body and hence may survive the body into immortality. James could find no contradiction between the theory of physiological psychology that consciousness is a function of the brain and the doctrine of immortality of the soul. The interrelationship between mind and body seemed to be only a functional one whereby the brain is merely the mind's channel, canalizing, straining, or releasing impediments and permitting consciousness to flow through. James argued that the mind is not a product of the body, that the brain does not create but only transmits consciousness. The distinction between productive and transmissive functions of the brain is the essential point to be grasped. Immortality is possible because, although the mind utilizes the brain in its communication with the outside world, it has the power to continue to exist even when the veil of the "soul" (the body) has been removed through death. The soul is like light shining through colored glass (the brain), but when the glass disappears, the light (soul) remains and shines still brighter. James envisioned human consciousness as eventually entering the "mother-sea," as he was fond of expressing it.

In *The Varieties of Religious Experience* James held that experience, not theoretical philosophy or theology, should form the basis for the religious life. Despite certain absurd creeds, the life of religion (taken as a whole) is "mankind's most important function." Evidence for God's existence is to be found primarily in one's personal inner experiences. According to James, religious experience is unique, and it enables the individual to realize that the world he perceives is part of a spiritual universe which alone gives the sensory world value; that man's proper goal is to unite himself with that higher universe; that prayer or inner communion with the universal spirit ("God" or "law") is the means whereby spiritual energy flows in and produces effects, psychological or material, occurring in the phenomenal world; that religious faith imparts a new zest to life, taking the form either of lyrical enchantment or of appeal to earnestness and heroism; and that religion contributes some assurance of safety and peace, and teaches love in human relationships.

The concept of God which James approved, namely that of theistic finitism, placed a limitation on the divine powers because the presence of evil in the world seemed contrary to God's will; but God is known to be present in the world and, since his ideals are in harmony with ours, his values favorable to ours, we can cooperate with the Deity in realizing common values and purposes.

Although James' concept of a pluralistic universe implied a plurality of gods—polytheism rather than monotheism—James referred to this implication in jest only. He himself was a theist.

JOHN DEWEY

John Dewey began in philosophy as a Hegelian and Neo-Kantian, and although he eventually condemned the Absolutism of Hegel's Idealism, traces of Hegelian thinking never completely disappeared from his thought. During his teaching career at the universities of Minnesota, Michigan, and Chicago, he gave up most of his Hegelian views, accepted the Pragmatism expounded by Peirce and James, as well as ideas of the Evolutionary Naturalists Darwin, Spencer, and Huxley, and developed his own philosophy of Instrumentalism, Operationalism, Functionalism, and Experimentalism.

Dewey's Instrumentalism. Instrumentalism or Experimentalism—Dewey used both terms for his brand of Pragmatism—had its first comprehensive exposition in 1903 with the appearance of *Studies in Logical Theory*, a volume written "with the co-operation of Members and Fellows of the Department of Philosophy" at the University of Chicago and expressing its indebtedness to James in such a manner that it may be interpreted as being dedicated to him.

Dewey built his system of Instrumentalism on the foundations of Behavioristic psychology and a Pragmatic theory of knowledge. His views also reflected the theory of organic evolution and a faith in man's capacity to achieve moral progress and a more nearly ideal social environment, especially through improvements in education. He defined Instrumentalism as "an attempt to constitute a precise logical theory of concepts, of judgments and inferences in their various forms, by considering primarily how thought functions in the experimental determinations of future consequences." In *The Quest for Certainty* he wrote that "the essence of Pragmatic Instrumentalism is to conceive of both knowledge and practice as means of making goods—excellencies of all kinds—secure in experienced existence."

In other words, theories must have operational import; they must be capable of being put into action, yielding desirable or at least predictable consequences. The proof of an idea consists in its being subject to predictable results. "According to experimental inquiry, the validity of the object of thought depends upon the consequences of the operations which define the object of thought." Ideas which measure up to the foregoing criterion of truth possess "warranted assertibility," Dewey's preferred term for belief, knowledge, or proof. He restated his theory in *Logic: The Theory of Inquiry*, as follows: "The theory, in summary form, is that all logical forms (with their characteristic properties) arise within the operation of inquiry and are concerned with control of inquiry so that it may yield warranted assertions."

Dewey accepted Peirce's view that the object of *inquiry* is belief. Inquiry originates in doubt caused by an indeterminate, problematic situation. The problem, said Dewey, must be sensed and defined in order that a solution may be reached that will resolve the situation and settle one's disturbed state of mind. This end is accomplished by accepting observed, empirical facts as well as ideas which anticipate solutions. The first step consists of practical, experimental action to change the external environment and thus more successfully to fulfill human needs, this being the final outcome of inquiry.

These phases of experimental inquiry are presented in *How We Think* in five steps and in less sophisticated form. The specific procedures for solving problems are set forth as follows: (1) we observe a problem and think of its nature (main aspects); (2) we intellectualize the problem further to analyze the total difficulty or situation of which it is a part; (3) we make hypotheses (guiding ideas) which bear upon the problem and constitute possible cues to a solution; (4) we analyze our hypotheses in the light of past experience, choosing potentially feasible solutions; (5) we put these possible solutions into practice experimentally or inductively and ascertain the results in actual experience. These five steps comprise the process of reflective thinking, which always serves a useful purpose beneficial to man. All sciences, according to Dewey, must be humanized, must subserve human needs. He defined truth as a means of satisfying human needs and improving upon social conditions which create problems. Truth is useful, public, and objective; truth benefits society, not merely the individual. All Pragmatists agreed that practical consequences are the only valid test of truth, but it was Dewey who worked out these five step-by-step procedures, beginning with the initial awareness of a problem and ending with a satisfactory solution.

Dewey's Ethical Theory. The proper ethical goals, according to Dewey, are the fulfillment of human needs and desires, the continuous growth of human beings in moral sensitivity, and human progress in the practical realization of a better social world. "The good man is the man who no matter how morally unworthy he *has* been is moving to become better. . . . Growth itself is the only moral 'end.' " One speaks of moral good or moral objectives only when certain consequential results are being achieved. Absolute goods or evils do not exist; each situation is specific and calls for specific methods of inquiry. The greatest good is the elimination of the greatest evil or the fulfillment of man's greatest need. The choice between good and evil is not made on theoretical grounds but for the purpose of reducing or alleviating as much as possible the specific evils which plague man.

Dewey was neither an optimist nor a pessimist. Like James, he was a meliorist, believing that the world can be made better solely through man's initiative in bringing about desirable consequences. Neither happiness nor goods can be fully achieved to perfection, for they are but steps to higher levels of moral progress. Moreover, as further developed in *The Quest for Certainty*, Dewey's value theory distinguished between the Utilitarian goal of achieving whatever is actually desired and his own goal of progressing toward whatever is most desirable and satisfactory, worthy to be prized, cherished, and enjoyed. The satisfactory or the desirable courses of action must meet certain specifiable conditions which are subject to prediction, and as such should be based on judgments, estimates, or appraisals, which serve as guides to future action. "Judgments about values are judgments about the conditions and the results of experienced objects; judgments about that which should regulate the formation of our desires, affections and enjoyments." Value exists only where there is satisfaction. The fulfillment of specific conditions transforms satisfactions into values.

Moral laws are comparable to physical laws, for they serve as formulas, guiding us in eliciting certain responses under given conditions. Moral laws are not absolute rules which never permit exceptions. Since it is in the nature of man to act rather than merely to speculate or theorize, theory divorced from concrete action is empty, sterile, or vain. It is the function of intelligence to serve action, and action benefits man when it obeys the dictates of intelligence. Values must be regarded as goods of practical significance which result from intelligently directed activity.

Dewey stressed the principle that moral responsibility is social, that "all morality is social." Man cannot live in a society without assuming moral obligations. If one does not care for the moral regimentation of his own society, then he probably would escape it by entering some savage society, but even there moral strictures could not be avoided entirely, for he would find that he is merely exchanging one set of obligations for another. Only if man were alone in the world, would he not be obligated to be moral, but then the question would not arise.

Rights also are social, since a person cannot claim his rights without accepting the responsibility for them. To claim one's own rights to free speech places upon an individual the responsibility of respecting the right of others to free speech. Immoral behavior is detrimental to the entire society, and it is for this reason that dangerous transgressors are removed from society.

Dewey's Philosophy of Religion. Dewey's point of view on religion, referred to as Religious Humanism, identified God with man's highest social experiences and is comparable to the Humanism of Comte and Feuerbach. As a Pragmatist, Dewey defined God as the "*active* relation between ideal and actual." He could not accept the term as referring to a particular Being, a pure Being in the intellectual sense, but preferred a definition which "denotes the unity of all ideal ends arousing us to desire and actions." Such a

God summons us to intelligent action which calls for deliberate choice, purposive behavior that is selective. Such a God also lends unity to our values. "The word 'God' means the ideal ends that at a given time and place one acknowledges as having authority over his volition and emotion, the values to which one is supremely devoted, as far as these ends, through imagination, take on unity."

In *The Quest for Certainty* Dewey reminded us that we cannot achieve absolute certainty or perfection in our conduct or belief and therefore must rest content with absolute commitment, faith, which helps us to face the future resolutely, reconstructing our environment in order to attain more satisfactory adjustments. But all such reconstruction is only temporary, never final, and must continually be revised or modified. Nevertheless, we must seek a practical faith in ideal ends, a *common faith* free from the limitation of sect, class, or race, a faith that all mankind may embrace, consisting of a heritage of values which we most prize in civilization. Ours is the responsibility of accepting the precious heritage of values (accumulated by the "continuous human community" at great cost in effort and suffering) and to expand, conserve, transmit, and rectify these values bequeathed to us.

Dewey's Philosophy of Education. Dewey's views on education grew out of his work at the laboratory school for children at the University of Chicago, where in 1896 he tried to organize the school as a miniature community with first-hand experiences that would enable pupils to do practical things co-operatively and thereby learn the attitudes and skills of good citizenship.

Later, in his *Democracy and Education* (1916), Dewey elaborated upon his theory that the school should reflect the community and be patterned after it so that when children graduate from school they will be properly adjusted to assume their places in society. Further, he interpreted democracy as a high ideal or goal to be more and more perfectly attained through educational experiences which continuously reconstruct and reorganize human life and society. He insisted that the problems of philosophy are rooted in social conditions, that social reform is urgently required, that philosophy has a social responsibility to influence the intelligent management of human affairs. No philosophy can be fixed, finished, or absolute. All ideas must be tested in the laboratory of educational experience where they can be challenged, their consequences evaluated, and where they can be continuously modified or reconstructed.

F. C. S. SCHILLER

One of the leading exponents of Pragmatism in Europe was F. C. S. Schiller, an enthusiastic disciple of Peirce and James. Schiller's views which emphasized the humanistic elements of their philosophy, became known as Humanism, representing an extreme form of Pragmatism based upon the concept of the Greek Sophists that man is the measure of all things. According to Schiller, man is incapable of attaining reality, but must remain content with his subjective opinions. The external world of reality is dependent upon human experience; further, since all beliefs must possess practical value, speculative ideas or interests must be subordinated to practical affairs. Truth is a human product, and its test is its consequences judged from the standpoint of human interest and welfare. All truth must have a bearing on human interest to be meaningful; it must have consequences for man and his life's purposes. Truth must have practical value for man as well as proving to be of some benefit to him.

In his *Studies in Humanism* (1907) Schiller enumerated seven principles of Pragmatism: (1) All truths possess logical values. (2) The truth of any proposition depends upon its application. (3) The meaning of any rule lies in its application. (4) All meaning depends on purpose. (5) All mental life is purposive. (6) Man must never ignore the fact that every act of knowing is purposive. (7) The principles of psychology must be applied to explain how human purposes work in achieving knowledge and an understanding of reality.

For Schiller, truth is not universal but individual, dependent upon the specific experiences of individual men. Each person, with his unique experiences, should arrive at a philosophy which is distinctive from that of all other persons. Truth is a product of human habit, a fabrication or construction. "Truth is human truth." Finally, in addition to ready-made universally accepted truths, varying degrees of other truths exist, and truth is always in the process of being made.

Chapter 16

Idealism and Personalism

Idealism, as a school of philosophy, incorporates a wide variety of philosophical views, but its diverse adherents agree on the fundamental hypothesis that the universe is the embodiment of mind, that reality is of the nature of mind—a spiritual or psychic quality. Consequently, the Idealist regards ultimate reality as an entity transcending phenomena; consciousness (mind or reason) as the fundamental nature of reality; and all knowable things as mental states or mental entities.

TYPES OF IDEALISM

A distinction should be drawn between Metaphysical and Epistemological Idealism. The system which emphasizes the analysis of the entire universe as a psychic reality is Metaphysical Idealism, which may be subdivided into philosophies (e.g., of Plato, Aristotle, and St. Augustine) postulating an ideal element permeating all things, and philosophies (e.g., of contemporary Personalist Idealists) depicting ultimate reality as consisting of consciousness, mind, or personality. The system which emphasizes the identification of reality with the "mentally knowable" data, the perceptible truths— or, alternatively, denies that any non-spiritual entities could ever be known—is Epistemological Idealism, accepted by Descartes, Locke, Berkeley, and Hume. Descartes and Locke adhered to a Metaphysical Dualism which formed the basis for a subsequent philosophy of Realism. Berkeley favored a form of Metaphysical Idealism with reality dependent upon a relationship with the individual's mind or the divine mind, and hence became known as a Subjective Idealist. Hume, denying metaphysical reality as an independent entity, adopted the extreme form of Skepticism (or Nihilism) known as Phenomenalism.

The central theses of Idealism, the beginnings of which may be traced as far back as Greek philosophy antedating Plato, are mainly rooted in the philosophical systems of Plato, Berkeley, Kant, and Hegel. Platonic Idealism asserted that ultimate reality consists of ideal constructs which are real; Berkeleyan Idealism contributed the hypothesis that only spirits (souls) and their experiences are real (that to be is to be experienced); and German Idealism developed the creative ideas of the Kantians as Transcendental Idealism and those of the Hegelians as Absolute Idealism. A modern form of Kantian Idealism, namely, American Transcendental Idealism, is exemplified by the philosophy of Ralph Waldo Emerson (1803–1882).

The principal recent and contemporary schools of Idealism and their best-known exponents have been the following: *in America,* the Personalism of Borden Parker Bowne (1847–1910), the Finalistic Personalism of George Holmes Howison (1834–1916), the Speculative (or Objective) Idealism of James Edwin Creighton (1861–1924), the Dynamic Idealism of George Sylvester Morris (1840–1889), and the Absolute Idealism of Josiah Royce (1855–1916); *in Great Britain,* the Personal Idealism of William Ritchie Sorley (1855–1935), and Hastings Rashdall (1858–1924), the Atheistic Personalism of John McTaggart Ellis McTaggart (1866–1925), the Neo-Kantian Idealism of Thomas Hill Green (1836–1882), and the Absolute (Neo-Hegelian) Idealism of Francis Herbert Bradley (1864–1924); *in France,* the Personalism of Charles Bernard Renouvier (1815–1903) and Emmanuel Mounier (1905–1950), and the Synthetic Idealism of Leon Brunschvicg (1869–1944); *in Italy,* the Neo-Hegelian Idealism of Benedetto Croce (1866–1952) and the Neo-Idealism of Giovanni Gentile (1875–1944); *in Germany,* the Pantheistic Personalism of William Stern (1871–1938) and the Neo-Kantian Idealism of Ernst Cassirer (1874–1945); *in Russia,* the Personalism of Nikolai Aleksandrovich Berdyaev (1874–1948) and the Neo-Idealism of Leo Isakovich Shestov (Schwarzman) (1866–1938); and *in Spain,* the Personalism of Miguel de Unamuno (1864–1936) and the Neo-Kantianism of José Ortega y Gasset (1883–1955).

The following discussion will review briefly the main concepts of contemporary Idealism as represented in the various schools of Personalism, in Absolute Idealism, and in Neo-Idealism.

PERSONALISM

In the United States the philosophy of Personalism has achieved pre-eminence within the Idealistic movement. Idealism in modern philosophy was developed chiefly by German philosophers and thereafter spread throughout western Europe and America. The Personalist movement is essentially American with some notable British adherents. It originated in the works of George Holmes Howison and Borden Parker Bowne. Howison, a member of the St. Louis Philosophical Society, taught at the Massachusetts Institute of Technology, and later at the University of California where he founded the Philosophical Union. The St. Louis Philosophical Society, organized in 1866 for the study of speculative philosophy, favored the views of the Hegelian Absolute Idealists. Another influential member of the society, William Torrey Harris (1835–1909), also taught philosophy at the Massachusetts Institute of Technology (from 1872 to 1878). Harris was one of the leading philosophers identified with the Concord School of Philosophy, another being Amos Bronson Alcott (1799–1888) who is credited with having coined the term *Personalism* in 1863. Alcott defined Personalism as "the doctrine that the ultimate reality of the world is a Divine Person who sustains the universe by a continuous act of creative will." Personalism enjoyed its greatest development during the years of Borden Parker Bowne, and his students Brightman and Knudson, at Boston University. The movement spread rapidly to other universities in the United States. The chief American journal for the Personalists, *The Personalist,* was first published in 1918 at the University of Southern California under the editorship of Ralph Tyler Flewelling (1871–1960). From the United States, the movement spread to South America where it similarly attained high prestige.

Varieties of Personalism. Although Personalistic ideas can be traced as far back as Anaxagoras, Plato, and Augustine, the modern development of Personalism is rooted in the theories of Berkeley and Leibniz, especially the Berkeleyan hypothesis that ultimate reality consists of spiritual forces creating ideas and perceptions and the Leibnizean concept of reality as an active principle (the doctrine of monads). Schleiermacher employed the term Personalism as early as 1799 in his *Reden;* in 1868 Walt Whitman's essay, *Personalism,* appeared. Several works helped to establish Personalism as a term and movement: Renouvier's *Personalism* in 1903, Bowne's *Personalism* in 1908, and Knudson's *Philosophy of Personalism* in 1927. It was only natural for differing interpretations and subdivisions of the movement to appear, among which each of the following has attracted adherents:

(1) *Typical Theistic Personalism* constitutes the mainstream of

Personalist philosophy. The great majority of noted Personalists have been theists, including philosophers such as Bowne, Rashdall, Sorley, Knudson, Brightman, Flewelling, Werkmeister, and Bertocci.

(2) *Atheistic Personalism* has attracted a few Personalists. Its chief protagonist was John M. E. McTaggart, the Cambridge University philosopher who denied the existence of God while affirming the immortality of persons. Some Personalists have regarded Jean-Paul Sartre as belonging to this group.

(3) *Pantheistic Personalism* was ably represented by William Stern (of the University of Hamburg), who called his system Critical Personalism, to distinguish it from Personalism of the theistic or dualistic type. Stern's view of the universe was monistic. His *Person and Thing* (1906, revised in 1918 and 1924) used the terms *person* and *thing* (replacing the Aristotelian terms *form* and *matter*) to denote two phases of a unified psychophysical reality.

(4) *Absolute Personalism* may be interpreted as a type of Absolute Idealism in which the Absolute is thought of as spiritual, as Personalist, in nature. (Some Neo-Hegelians accept this point of view.) Included in this group are the Personalistic Singularists, who regard individual persons as mere aspects of the one Absolute personality; thus Josiah Royce believed that individuals are part of a unified spiritual World Soul, a beloved community, a social mind.

(5) *Realistic Personalism* accepts the theory that personality is the highest type of being, the only free and creative form of being, but insists that unconscious being or matter also exists, a point of view expounded by Douglas Clyde Macintosh (1877–1948), James Bissett Pratt (1875–1944), and Thomistic Personalists, such as Jacques Maritain. (1882–   ).

(6) *Relativistic Personalism*, as developed in the work of Charles B. Renouvier (1815–1903), emphasized the ultimate reality of personal experience, the finite nature of God, and the facts of human freedom and immortality. (Renouvier's system has also been referred to as *Neocritical Personalism.*)

(8) *Panpsychistic Personalism*, a Leibnizian mode of Personalism, was developed in the works of James Ward (1843–1925) and Walter T. Stace (1886–   ). Immediate experience is trusted as a cue to or reflection of the psychic nature of reality.

(9) *Anthropomorphic Personalism* emphasized the hypothesis of Henri Bois (*b.* 1862) that God possesses the same personal characteristics (such as emotions, passions, and will) as human beings.

Some aspects of the contemporary philosophies of Phenomenology (as expounded by Max Scheler) and of Existentialism (e.g., in the works of Jean-Paul Sartre) may justify the classification of these philosophies as basically Personalist systems.

Lotzean Foundations of Personalism. In his *Metaphysics: A Study of First Principles* (1882) Bowne commented that "Leibniz furnishes the starting point, Herbart supplies the method, and the conclusions reached are essentially those of Lotze." Bowne's Personalist philosophy was fundamentally Lotzean, and Lotze (1817–1881) himself was a disciple of Leibniz and Spinoza, attempting to synthesize the Monodology of the former with the Pantheism of the latter and thus to reconcile Pluralism with Monism, Mechanism with Teleology, and Realism with Idealism. Lotze called his system Teleological Idealism. He held that the natural world can be explained in terms of physico-chemical laws, but also that man's religio-ethical life requires mind more than a mechanistic universe. Man reacts to external stimuli so that the world existing in space and time is a function of the individual's own consciousness. Consequently reality is idealistic in nature, undergoes change yet retains its identity, and is comparable to the human personality which unifies diverse phenomena as a mental experience. Reality is spiritual and good; the Absolute is divine, an absolutely good personality. Lotze accepted immortality on faith based on the ideas that the soul rules the body and that a person will receive his just deserts. He contributed to Personalism the concept of reality as concrete, spiritual, and individual, the theory that reality goes beyond the realm of thought (true experience includes more than conceptual thinking), and the notion of the self as a presupposition of all reasoning.

Basic Concepts of Leading Personalists. The main principles of contemporary Personalism may be discovered in the works of the American philosophers Bowne, Knudson, and Brightman, and the British philosophers Rashdall, Sorley, and McTaggart.

BORDEN PARKER BOWNE. Bowne, the founder of the Personalist movement, emphasized the conception of human personality as the key to reality, stating that the ontologically real is personality, the entity through which all things must be viewed. Personalism is thus a form of Idealism: for any object to exist it must be a person (the self) or the act of a person, or the experience of a person. Bowne applied Personalism to ethics, concluding that the universe is friendly to moral value, that a good God exists, that

nonpersonal values are inconceivable. He applied Personalism to
metaphysics, insisting on the personal nature of the cosmos (the
World-Ground or personal God revealed by the Universe). He
applied Personalism to epistemology, asserting that knowledge can
be found only in (and must be mediated through) persons, that
God, as the World-Ground is the source of all knowledge. Finally,
he applied Personalism to logic, stating that practical moral consequences of actions are more significant than mere logical forms.
He rejected what he called the fallacy of the universal, the error of
imputing substantial reality to general terms or universals. According to his doctrine of Transcendental Empiricism, the sole reality
that exists consists of the conscious experience of the self, the ideas
which belong to the self. Only the assumption of the uniqueness
of personality can explain or reconcile contradictions and dilemmas
in the world: unity in diversity, permanence in change, causal pre-
determination and free potentiality of events, subjective ideas and
objective things, mechanistic and purposive actions, identity of
new with old, and true creativity. Personal freedom is basic, for
without freedom truth could not be distinguished from error. Freedom is an indispensable constituent of both knowledge and reality.

ALBERT CORNELIUS KNUDSON (1873–1953). Knudson defined
Personalism as a form of Idealism which recognizes equally "both
the pluralistic and monistic aspects of experience and which finds
in the conscious entity, identity, and free activity of personality
the key to the nature of reality and the solution of the ultimate
problems of philosophy." In his *The Philosophy of Personalism*,
he discussed six metaphysical principles of Personalism as follows:
(1) Reality is concrete and universal. (2) The world is a unified
entity. (3) Reality is an active force. (4) The universal force,
power, or cause is personal, spiritual, and volitional—an act of
will. (5) Matter is a phenomenal manifestation of the spirit or
soul, the product of the divine energy. (6) Personality is the key
to and essence of reality. Finally, Knudson cited four epistemological principles of Personalism, as follows: (1) Any subjective
thought must be considered distinct and separate from the object
of thought—Epistemological Dualism. (2) The self is an active,
creatively thinking personality (much more than Locke's passive
tabula rasa). (3) All reality (including intelligence) is an expression of thought, explicable in terms of intelligence. Reality is
knowable, intelligible. (4) Faith and moral purpose take prece-

dence over intellectual or logical reasoning; faith validates knowledge and, to quote Bowne, "life is deeper than logic."

EDGAR SHEFFIELD BRIGHTMAN (1884–1953). Brightman applied the main ideas of Personalism to psychology (postulating a self or Gestalt), to logic (defending its synoptic method and its acceptance of the total personality as a criterion of truth), to epistemology (asserting that knowledge depends on mental activity and that the idea must be distinguished from its object), and to metaphysics (insisting that the universe is a society of persons). He defined the concept of a personality as "a complex unity of consciousness, which identifies itself with its past self in memory," free to control itself, construct and achieve moral purposes, "private yet communicating, and potentially rational." Brightman rejected Platonic forms, norms, or extrapersonal values, agreeing with T. H. Green that values exist only in and for persons. Only persons are the reservoirs of value, so to speak, and they impute value to objects. Consequently, Kant was right in stating that persons have infinite intrinsic value as ends in themselves. Without persons, objects are devoid of value.

From what has been said, it is not to be inferred that values lack objectivity; on the contrary, Personalists believe that values are objective, although Brightman distinguished between values and norms. Values, he contended, are subjective evaluations (what a person actually likes, esteems, desires, approves, or enjoys), while norms constitute the objective standard of values, that is, values as they exist in the mind of God. Accordingly, norms are what persons ought to value, since they are truly desirable; norms are what a coherently reasoning mind would desire and approve.

Note that although, for the Personalist, truth is to be found in personal experience taken as a whole, an analysis of all the diverse events in experience is necessary for understanding of the whole. Consequently, Personalists accept the analytic-synoptic method of interpreting reality. Eventually, "the arrow of intelligibility," as Brightman termed it, must fly from the analysis of parts to the coherence of the total personality. Thus, *empirical coherence* is the criterion of truth. The immediate, first-person experience is the starting point of all knowledge. When one has rendered a coherent account of all the facts in first-person experiences, then he has achieved the goal of knowledge. Personalists are Epistemological Dualists, who believe that the knower and his ideas are distinct from the object of his knowledge. Brightman differentiated the *situation-experienced* from the *situation-believed-in*. Personalists assert the privacy of human consciousness, that is, the privacy of the situation-experienced (first-person experience). The situation-believed-in, however, is public, shared knowledge of free persons endowed with reason and faith.

HASTINGS RASHDALL (1858–1924). Rashdall was one of the leading British exponents of Personal Idealism, taking as his starting point Berkeley's assertion that matter cannot exist without mind and asserting the Personalist conclusion that minds exist only in persons who are capable of knowing and willing. In addition to finite minds of humans, Rashdall held that the infinite mind of God is the objective ground of all things which exist in the external universe. Each mind is an individual entity possessing independent consciousness in its private realm which cannot be entered by any other consciousness. Each person is in his own right a reality which excludes all other persons as well as the mind of God. The divine mind cannot absorb individual minds or persons, said Rashdall, rejecting the pantheistic contention of the Absolute Idealists. Personality is inviolate and cannot be penetrated even by God, the supreme personal reality. Moreover, said Rashdall, God is not the sole Absolute, for Absolute Reality consists of individual persons in addition to God; therefore reality comprises a community of personal spirits.

In his *The Theory of Good and Evil* Rashdall concluded that God is limited in power because of the presence of surd (genuine) evil in the world. Evil is not an illusion but a reality which discourages optimistic views about the future of mankind. Nevertheless, Rashdall accepted the idea of immortality, the existence of a personal God, and the limitations of human intelligence as valid postulates based upon moral values and principles of ethics. Individuals, he said, create moral standards, but the fundamental moral values must be attributed to their divine origin.

WILLIAM RITCHIE SORLEY (1855–1935). Sorley, another eminent British Personalist, accepted the view of Lotze that moral values cannot be explained merely by ascertaining their origin. He rejected the notion of an evolutionary process in moral standards whereby the higher of mankind developed from the inferior morals of lower animals; on the contrary, the lower species of animals must be understood in the light of the higher.

Sorley divided the universe into two realms: that of facts (the natural realm containing all existing objects) and that of value (the axiological realm). Both realms possess objective reality as well as being experienced subjectively. The natural realm of things is, however, subordinate to the axiological realm of moral values. Further, moral values are superior realities which each person can choose to accept or reject, thus reflecting man's free will, a quality of freedom that is an indispensable part of his goodness. Values are essentially personal because their existence is always within a personality: "Intrinsic values always require persons as their bearers; nothing is ultimately of worth for its own sake except persons or some quality or state of a person." Without free choice man could not become a moral being. Moreover, man's power to act contrary to the moral law indicates that God has not arranged for a perfect universe but has placed a limitation upon his own omnipotence. Nevertheless, God has created a universe that is friendly to values and works out its purposes in the light of them. Nature keeps striving to perfect itself so that the world will become a "fit medium for the fashioning and training of moral beings." Sorley accepted two important postulates: the freedom of man and the purposeful nature of the universe.

Since the two orders of the universe (moral and natural) find their unity in the personality of man, it follows that their objective union in the universe must likewise be found in a personality, namely, the personality of God as the supreme unity. Consequently, God must be considered a Personality constituting the only coherent means of explaining how the world of natural facts unites with the world of moral values. Sorley maintained that belief in a personal God, theism, is a necessary postulate. God is the great unifying Personality, serving both as the creator of all objects in nature and as the source and essence of value. (See the development of this point of view in his classic *Moral Values and the Idea of God.*)

JOHN M. E. McTAGGART (1866–1925). McTaggart propounded a significant atheistic form of Personal Idealism in his *Some Dogmas of Religion* (1906), *Human Immortality and Pre-Existence* (1915), *The Nature of Existence* (vol. I, 1921; vol. II, 1927, posthumously published under the editorship of C. D. Broad), and "An Ontological Idealism" in *Contemporary British Philosophy* (1924, J. H. Muirhead, ed.). Although McTaggart, like the other Personalists (or Personal Idealists), adhered to a Metaphysical Pluralism which portrayed ultimate reality as a composite of many ontologically real persons, he rejected the belief in a supreme person (God), positing instead an Absolute consisting of a system of selves, that is to say, a unity made up of persons but not itself possessing personality. The Absolute is related to its parts in the same way that a college is related to its members. Both the college and its members are spiritual entities but only the individual members may properly be considered persons, for the organization as a whole merely brings them together as a single unit. Accordingly, for McTaggart, reality is essentially spiritual in nature, consisting of spiritual selves or persons. Selves are of highest metaphysical significance, as active primary percipients in the Berkeleyan sense, whereas impersonal or secondary entities are only the insensible objects of a percipient Being or self.

McTaggart held that, although selves or persons are the only genuinely real entities (independent spiritual substances existing in their own right as *sui generis*), they are finite. Each self, being truly real in its own right, cannot be absorbed into any other self, nor into the Absolute self. Furthermore, selves or persons, as ultimate reality, cannot change, be created, or be destroyed. Their existence is timeless, continuing throughout eternity, without beginning and without end. Under these conditions it is unnecessary to postulate the existence of God as creator. In fact, if a God existed, then both God and all other persons would be equally immortal. For McTaggart the highest level of existence, of reality, is personal; the Absolute, which consists of impersonal entities (objects in nature as perceived by individuals) is inferior to persons, and it would be therefore inappropriate to identify God with such an inferior impersonal substance.

Neither consciousness nor memory is a necessary condition for personality. A person may lose his consciousness without losing his personal Being, and the same holds true for memory. To prove this point, a person need only consider the fact that his present life is of definite value to him despite his inability to recall any previous life preceding this one on earth or even for that matter many experiences of his childhood. The possibility remains that we may have had a life (or many lives) before birth and will probably have one or many future lives.

If we admit the existence of evil in the world, it must follow that an assumed God could not be both absolutely good and omnipotent. If God were all-powerful, he would abolish every vestige of evil. Accordingly, if we assume that God exists, then he must be either limited in power or morally imperfect. Why, then, make the theist's entirely unnecessary assumption that God exists?

McTaggart did not consider his atheistic philosophy irreligious. Rejecting the idea of a personal, all-powerful God, he believed instead in autonomous persons, entities of the highest reality and worth, united by the bond of love, life's most important relationship. It was his view that love, as the greatest good and the highest value, emerges from the self's ultimate nature. Love, which is an indication that the world has attained its highest stage—that of selfhood or personality—is decisive proof that the world is essentially good rather than bad. When love attains its final stage and becomes an integral part of absolute reality (rather than a transitory occurrence), then through its passionate power, it will dominate and permeate the entire universe. Such a perfect love in absolute reality will find every self loving every other self which it encounters. Perfect love unites two selves into one so that each belongs to the other. Perfect love is autonomous, free from external causes or outside determination. The stage of perfect love, that of absolute reality, will find good triumphing over evil, truth over error, and joy over pain, with an absolute minimum of evil. Thus, we find the Personal Idealism of McTaggart culminating in atheistic mysticism.

ABSOLUTE IDEALISM

Leading exponents of Absolute Idealism—the view of reality as the embodiment of mind—have included British, American, and Italian philosophers. Francis Herbert Bradley (1864–1924) was England's foremost adherent to Absolute Idealism. His contributions were preceded by significant Idealistic writings of James Hutchinson Stirling (1820–1909), Thomas Hill Green (1836–1882), Edward Caird (1835–1908), John Caird (1820–1898), William Wallace (1844–1897), Bernard Bosanquet (1848–1923), Richard Burdon Haldane (1856–1928), John Henry Muirhead (1855–1940), and John Watson (1847–1939). The works of Green and Bradley were especially influential in giving new impetus to British philosophy. Josiah Royce was most representative of American Absolute Idealists. Benedetto Croce (1886–1952) and Giovanni Gentile (1875–1944) were prominent Italian contributors.

Thomas Hill Green. Green pioneered in establishing Idealism, based upon German foundations, as a dominant philosophy in British circles. Green Hegelianized Kantian thought. The essence of his Idealism is to be found in the doctrine of relations which claims that the reality of any object does not depend upon isolated facts about the object as such, but exclusively upon its relations to other objects.

GREEN'S METAPHYSICS. Green believed that relations constitute reality, that the absence or elimination of its relations to other objects would reduce any object to practically nothing. Reality consists of the relations which connect or unite objects. It is that activity of mind which, as the uniting principle, creates relations. Thus, in this respect, Green is a Kantian, claiming that not only relations but the laws of nature as well are produced by the rational activity of the human understanding.

GREEN'S ETHICAL THEORY. In ethics Green advocated the goal of self-realization for all faculties of the soul. Self-realization is the greatest good and the only result capable of satisfying an individual. Moral good, virtue, fructifies into lasting self-satisfaction. Complete realization is never simply a matter of isolated experience for any individual, but involves his role in society. Since man is fundamentally a social being, self-realization (morality) always occurs in and for persons. Reality itself, including both God and man, is personal. The universe is a process or activity designed to achieve the self-realization of the divine principle, unfolding in man and nature. Thus perfect self-realization would encompass all powers of the individual person, of society, and even of the divine.

Green defined personality in terms of self-consciousness, as "the quality in a subject of being consciously an object to itself." It is personality or self-consciousness which relates man to God and to other persons. Man owes his freedom to self-consciousness, a fact which is inexplicable by the laws of physical nature. "In all willing a self-conscious subject seeks to satisfy itself." Moral good is therefore satisfying to a person; it is a state of mind in which he can rest content.

Francis Herbert Bradley. As the best-known and most influential of the British Absolute Idealists in recent times, Bradley constructed a philosophy based primarily on Hegelianism with some concepts patterned after the views of Lotze, Schelling, Herbart, Spinoza, and Schopenhauer—a philosophy which has gone far to shape British philosophical thinking today. His principal works (*Ethical Studies, Appearance and Reality, The Principles of Logic,* and *Essays on Truth and Reality*) reflect his fondness for paradox and contradiction. Philosophy for him was a means of obtaining intellectual satisfaction through discovery of ultimate truth, and the discovery of ultimate truth provided intellectual satisfaction.

BRADLEY'S METAPHYSICS. Bradley regarded man as a metaphysical animal who cannot help but philosophize as he tries to reconcile the contradictions in the appearances of things. In *Appearance and Reality* (1897) he defined metaphysics as "the finding of bad reasons for what we believe on instinct" and insisted that the universe must be viewed as a whole, not in its parts: "About the Unity of Science I have set down that 'Whatever you know it is all one,' and of Introspection that 'The one self-knowledge worth having is to know one's mind.' "

A dual task confronts metaphysics: that of distinguishing genuine reality from mere appearance, and that of understanding the universe as a whole rather than as segments or fragments. Bradley defined reality as the Absolute, that is, as complete truth in the sense of a unity or wholeness, an all-comprehensiveness or harmony which is free from contradiction. Reality is oneness (Metaphysical Monism) in which all appearances come together and in so doing lose their distinctiveness. Absolute reality, being a unitary whole, integrates all appearances into a unity of the whole. "Everything is experience, and experience is one." The self is the sum of its experiences (comparable to Hume's theory). It is in the experience of feeling that variegated parts are experienced as unified parts of the whole. "The real, to be real, must be felt."

Appearance, on the other hand, must be understood negatively or in contradictory terms, for it involves a discrepancy between thought and existence, a process of thinking replete with contradictions. Such contradictions arise because of inability to grasp the world as a whole, for in immediate appearances we deal only with a part abstracted from the whole, with the relative (or relational) instead of the Absolute, or with multiplicity instead of unity. Appearance is fragmentary, relational, changing, meaningless, and valueless. Error, evil, and sin exist in appearance, whereas in the Absolute, that is, in reality we find our satisfaction.

Thus reality must be understood by combining appearances (in fragmented immediate experience) with awareness of the whole reality in our experience—immediate relational experiences being inadequate without reference to unified ultimate reality. Both aspects (feeling and thought) are fused as interdependent processes. Although reality is, in the last analysis, spiritual, it is not to be understood in terms of Personalism, of the self or of a theistic personality, for personality is relegated to the realm of appearance. Nor does Bradley identify the Absolute with merely relational thought, but rather with sentient experience as a single, unified, all-comprehending system. All experiences and events belong to the Absolute as a system of unbroken unified reality.

BRADLEY'S ETHICS. Bradley propounded a self-realization ethic comparable to that of his co-Idealist, Thomas Hill Green. The ethical goal is fulfillment of the self, the higher or universal self. " 'Realize yourself as an infinite whole' means, 'Realize yourself as the self-conscious member of an infinite whole, by realizing that whole in yourself.' "

Bradley regarded the question "Why should I be moral?" as an inquiry about the value of virtue. Rejecting the Kantian idea of "duty for duty's sake," he defined moral action as an end in itself, that end being fulfillment of the true self as an infinite whole. One must know his station in life and its duties in order that he may identify his own will with the universal will and achieve an ideal self with consequent self-realization, fulfillment, surcease of striving, and the experience of personal satisfaction.

Josiah Royce (1855–1916). American Absolute Idealists have included a number of philosophers serving on the faculties of Harvard, Yale, and Cornell universities, such as, at Cornell, Jacob Gould Schurman, James Edwin Creighton, Frank Thilly, and G. Watts Cunningham; at Yale, George Trumbull Ladd and Brand Blanshard (perhaps the most influential Idealist on the contemporary scene); and at Harvard, Josiah Royce (America's foremost exponent of Absolute Idealism) and William Ernest Hocking. The contributions of Royce were most significant, and his central ideas may be accepted as most nearly representative of the school of American Absolute Idealists.

Royce differed from Bradley and Bosanquet in his fundamental concepts that Absolute Reality is a Self (a Personalist view), that logical reasoning proves the existence of an Absolute Mind, and that all finite individuals are real persons only because we comprise a "Beloved Community" (a pantheistic view of God as a society of persons).

ROYCE'S METAPHYSICAL IDEALISM. Royce's basic Idealistic thesis posited a real world "of outer and ideal truth, a world of mind." The Absolute is an all-embracing and overruling spiritual Being. "All reality must be present to the Unity of the Infinite Thought." Royce stated his interpretation of truth as follows: "The world

is in and for a thought, all-embracing, all-knowing, universal, for
which are all relations and all truth, a thought that estimates perfectly our imperfect and halting thoughts, a thought in which and
for which are we all." Thus for Royce, true relations in thinking
do not dissect or cut things apart but bring them together, integrating them into a synthesis of an ideal Absolute Reality or Mind.

Royce's principal concept of Absolute Reality is based on the
possibility of error; unless there were Absolute Truth, there could
be no error. The very denial of truth constitutes an admission that
truth exists—at least the "truth" that no truth exists. Consequently,
every effort of the Skeptics or relativists to refute absolute truth
must terminate in self-contradiction. Anyone who attempts to deny
Royce's doctrine of Absolute Truth must contradict himself by
simultaneously affirming such a Truth and, having become an adherent of the doctrine, he cannot logically refute it. In order to
refute Royce, it is necessary to agree with him. That being the
case, why make the attempt?

What, then, is error contrasted with Absolute Truth? Without
truth there cannot be error. For Royce error is an incomplete
thought, which to an omniscient mind or higher thought would
appear out of place, that is, incongruous and incoherent. The higher
inclusive thought of an all-embracing mind is a necessary postulate
in order to identify error as such, that is, as a fragmentary, incomplete, incoherent statement. Without an Absolute Mind, truth
and falsehood could not possibly exist. The truth or falsity of an
idea depends upon its relationship to other ideas, but ultimately
it depends upon a complete unity of an infinite mind. If any thought
may or may not be in error, it is right or wrong only by reference to an infinite all-inclusive mind which can make the correct
judgment. "Unless the thought and its object are parts of one
large thought, I can't even . . . be in error about it, can't even
doubt its existence." In the same manner that error necessarily
implies the existence of Absolute Truth, evil implies the existence
of absolute good.

The sum of the matter is simply that since error exists, there
must be truth from which it errs; and since there is truth, there
must be a mind which possesses conscious knowledge of it. However, to comprehend Absolute Truth requires an Absolute or Omniscient Mind which stands ready to serve as the corrective of any
and all errors. Therefore, the very fact of error implies the existence of God, the universal thought or Absolute Mind.

The fact that the world is made of the same stuff as ideas does not mean that the world is unreal, but only that the world is a universal mind which extends infinitely beyond the individual's private consciousness. Experience informs us as to the facts of the world. We can be certain that the world is intelligent, rational, orderly, and essentially comprehensible; that is to say, no unsolvable problems exist, for the solutions to problems must be known to an Absolute Mind, i.e., to the Supreme Self, an infinite self which transcends our consciousness, yet includes each of us. The Supreme Self is of the nature of personality and far more conscious than individuals. Consciousness is knowledge aware of itself; in other words, it is self-reflecting knowledge. Finite problems are solved in the light of the eternal insight of the Supreme Self. Every thought of a person is the embodiment of the Supreme Self, the divine Logos. As persons, we comprise the Great Community, our larger self or the Beloved Community of God.

Thus we see that Royce's Metaphysical Idealism has two aspects: Idealistic analysis and the doctrine of the Absolute Self. Idealistic analysis shows that the outside world of stubborn reality is a world of ideas, that genuine facts are ideal facts. Truth is ideal; sound waves are ideal; atoms are ideal; symphonies are ideal. Behind all things stands the thought of a World Spirit. Matter is explicable, according to the definition of John Stuart Mill, as "permanent possibilities of sensation." There is nothing which we can say, think, or experience about the world around us which is not expressed in terms of mind. The more we know our world, the more of a mind is necessary to comprehend it; the closer we approach the truth of things, the more ideas we acquire respecting it.

The world is essentially mental or spiritual. Since truth is defined as the agreement of our ideas with reality, the only thing which can truly agree with an idea is another idea. It is only because our minds conform to the mind of the world that we can understand it. Reality, being of the nature of mind, can and does resemble our own minds which are also mental. Since only ideas are knowable, then that which is absolutely unknowable cannot possibly exist. To assert that the unknowable (not the unknown) can exist is to speak of nonsense and contradictions, such as the concept of round squares. If the outer world is real, then it is knowable, and if knowable, then its essence is of the nature of mind.

Hence, the real world is either a mind or a group of minds. The other minds which exist in this universe are in essence the same as your own. "The whole world of ideas is essentially one world, and so it is essentially the world of one self and That art Thou." Our real self is the larger self, complete consciousness where truth is found. Our larger self is the deeper personality, our real self. Truth is present to the larger self, for reality is identical with it. This deeper or larger self "is the self that knows in unity all truth."

ROYCE'S ETHICS AND PHILOSOPHY OF RELIGION. Royce's basic hypothesis in his ethics and philosophy of religion is that of loyalty, the foundation both of morality and of religion. A religious brotherhood consists of those who live loyally together. "All the loyal, whether they individually know the fact or not, are, and in all times have been, one genuine and religious brotherhood." The invisible church is composed of those who seek salvation through loyalty. Loyalty, service, devotion, suffering, accomplishment, tradition, example, teaching, and the triumph of those faithful in the invisible church are the crowning sources of religious insight.

In addition to the religion of loyalty, Royce developed an ethical system based on the same ideal of loyalty, which he defined as the supreme good, "the willing and practical and thoroughgoing devotion of a person to a cause." It is the embodiment of all virtues in one. Specific virtues are forms of loyalty. The quality of loyalty has intrinsic value. Whatever increases the spirit of loyalty within a person is good, and whatever diminishes it is evil. Although an enlightened and worthy cause in which to invest one's loyalty is desirable, it is not the cause, *per se*, which is important but the quality of loyalty dwelling within the personality. We may attack a person's ill-chosen cause in which he has placed his loyalty, but to destroy his loyal spirit would be disloyal to the ideal of loyalty, hence morally wrong. One must never be disloyal to the sense of loyalty. When our loyalties conflict, it is still imperative for us to be loyal to loyalty, i.e., to remain loyal to the spirit of loyalty so as never to abate the inner feeling of loyalty as such.

ITALIAN NEO-IDEALISTS

Italy's leading philosophers in recent years were the Neo-Idealists Benedetto Croce (1866–1952) and Giovanni Gentile (1875–1944), who carried on the tradition of the Neapolitan Hegelian movement of the nineteenth century. They accepted the Hegelian concepts that reality is thought (a progressive development which is both active and creative) and that philosophy is history (reality is identified with historical processes as it undergoes its evolutionary course creatively and with freedom). They rejected British Absolute Idealism because of the subordinate role which the British assigned to the progressive historical attainments of the human spirit. The Italian Neo-Idealists repudiated the Hegelian Absolute but accepted the Hegelian philosophy of the spirit, the philosophy of history.

Benedetto Croce. Croce identified reality with self-creating mind; a self-creative mind alone exists. Spirit or mind as the basic reality expresses itself in thought and experience, but this reality is not that of an impersonal Absolute; it is human experience, with human characteristics which restrict it to the temporal and to the immediate present, with past and future merely subserving the present. Hence, nothing exists but mind.

Mind has both a theoretical and a practical aspect. The mind's theoretical activity includes the creative expression of art and the conceptual expression of logic. Its practical aspect, which involves the will, includes social action (economic and moral) and the interpretation of history. These four aspects of reality (represented by art, logic, social activity, and the evaluation of the past) are phases in which spirit or mind manifests itself; they constitute four modes of appearance of spirit or mind.

Art, as the first activity of the universal creative mind, is at the beginning of all theoretical experience. Each person's inner intuition expresses itself in aesthetic appreciation. We are all artists, for artistic beauty is not found in the physical object, but in artistic self-expression.

Conceptual thinking, as the second activity of mind, is logical, in contrast to the intuitive experiences of art. The logical activity organizes the intuitively gathered data into categories of quality, evolution, shape, and beauty. Each of these categories or pure concepts is characterized by universality, expressiveness, and concreteness. The categories are present in every human experience, for without them reality would be inaccessible. Note that the universal must also be concrete and expressive as well.

Economic and ethical activity of mind is the third mode of expression, a practical carrying out of theoretical knowledge. Economic activity is motivated by egoism, whereas ethical activity is motivated by altruism.

The fourth activity of mind is represented in the evaluation of history, not as a passive record of the dead past, but as an active present creation. Being an act of thinking, history is identical with philosophy. Inasmuch as history is the culmination of mind or spirit (whose initial activity was artistic expression, moving toward conceptual expression, and later to practical expression in economics and ethics, eventuating in history), it is the highest expression of philosophy, the other phases being lower modes of the manifestation of spirit or mind. History is not a mere description of the past, but an evaluation of it, with each generation rendering its own value judgments of it. The interpretation of history creates history by constructing the mind's self-creative value judgment of events. Since the philosophical interpretation (value judgment) of the present generation will one day be history, philosophy and history must be considered identical.

Giovanni Gentile. Gentile's philosophical system is referred to as Actual Idealism, deriving its name from the fundamental thesis of this philosopher that the act of thinking is the only reality. Everything which exists is present in the act of thinking. The mind is pure act. Logic, metaphysics, and political philosophy are the dialectical expression of reality (the act of thinking), that is, the actualization of idea.

Reality is cosmic mind; the mind's creativity produces its own objects. The mind's highest form of experience is self-consciousness, the synthesis of subject and object, of plurality in unity, and of knower and known. In individual self-consciousness, universal experience is unified; in it subjective artistic creativity finds its objective expression in religion. Self-conscious experience finds its complete expression, not in art or religion, which are but partial or abstract expressions, but in philosophy. Philosophy is more than self-consciousness, or simply knowledge of reality in its greatest manifestation; it is reality *per se*.

Inasmuch as reality is self-consciousness, philosophical activity itself creates reality. All reality exists by virtue of the philosopher's thinking process which constitutes his self-consciousness. Philosophical speculation is more than the theoretical understanding of reality; it is the creation of it. Like Croce, Gentile identified philosophy with history, with the result that the dialectical expression of reality as the self-conscious expression of the human mind embraces all the artistic, historical, and philosophical aspects of human activity.

Chapter 17

Neorealism and Critical Realism

Neorealism, or the New Realism as it is sometimes called, developed largely as a reaction against Berkeleyan Idealism. This fact is true both of British and of American versions of Neorealism. Although Neorealists differ from one another on a number of points, all of them accept the thesis that real objects exist and that their existence is not dependent upon any mind which happens to be conscious of them. All of them reject Berkeley's contention that "to be is to be perceived."

Among American philosophers, two important groups have been the Neorealists and the Critical Realists, a chief distinction between the two being the rejection by the Critical Realists of the Epistemological Monism of the Neorealists. A group of highly influential British and American Neorealists has generally emphasized a monistic view in epistemology.

American Neorealists. This group of Neorealists included Ralph Barton Perry (1876–1957), Edwin B. Holt (1873–1946), William Pepperell Montague (1873–1953), Walter B. Pitkin (1878–1953), Edward Gleason Spaulding (1873–1940), and Walter T. Marvin (1872–1944). On July 21, 1910, these philosophers published in the *Journal of Philosophy* a statement of their point of view as "The Program and First Platform of Six Realists," an analysis later expanded into the volume, *The New Realism: Coöperative Studies in Philosophy.* The main tenets of the group may be summarized as indicating adherence to Naïve Realism and Epistemological Monism; doctrine of external relations, Metaphysical Pluralism (separating metaphysics from epistemology), and Platonic Realism (the subsistence of essences or universals); the method of analysis; and the doctrines of Neutral Monism (or neutral entities) and scientific method as the only valid path to knowledge. (The American Neorealists attacked all forms of Subjective Idealism and Epistemological Dualism; solipsism; Idealistic concepts about the ego-centric predicament; Hegelian Absolutism; and the doctrines of internal relations and Metaphysical Monism.)

Naïve Realism and Epistemological Monism. The American school of Neorealism, emphasizing the concepts of Epistemological Monism (based on the theory that the knowing process and the thing known are one and the same) adhered to the arguments of the Naïve Realists, that is to say, of Thomas Reid and the other Scottish philosophers who had attacked the position of the British Empiricists or Representative Realists. The early British Empiricists (including Locke, Berkeley, and Hume) had developed a representative theory of knowledge which stated that we never obtain objects directly in experience but only as copies or images comprising mental states. This so-called "picture theory" of knowledge (which treats perceptions as representations of reality) was replaced by Reid and the Neorealists with the central doctrine of Presentative Realism that objects of reality are presented to consciousness directly, not through an intermediate process as second-hand copies. Instead of merely constructing or receiving a mental copy of any object, we come into direct contact with the real object itself. The Epistemological Monism (or Presentative Realism) of the Neorealists impelled them to accept Naïve Realism, the belief that real things, because they present themselves to us directly, are precisely as they appear to us in consciousness. No distinction is to be drawn between what a thing seems to be and what it is in reality, since nothing intervenes between the knower and the object of his knowledge (the external world of reality).

But if real objects are precisely identical with our perceptions of them, how could there be any possibility of perceptual error? The Neorealists, though unable to solve this problem completely, employed the representational theory of Berkeley and Hume as leading to solipsism, and it should be noted that Berkeley did in fact claim that, although we cannot perceive souls (ideal realities), we do build a notion about them, while Hume took refuge in explanations of the soul as a "bundle of perceptions."

The Ego-Centric Predicament of Idealism. Berkeleyan Idealism and the theory of Epistemological Dualism (the picture theory of knowledge) created what Perry termed the *ego-centric predicament*, referring to the impossibility of "conceiving known things to exist independently of my knowing them." This problem should not be confused with the *psychocentric predicament* which refers to the "difficulty of conceiving objects apart from any consciousness." The ego-centric predicament implies the "impossibility of finding anything that is not known." The Idealist claims that all knowledge is mental state (in the form of thought, theory, reasoning, idea, conceptual fact, etc.) and therefore depends upon the presence of the knower. The question is, Can things exist without being known by anyone? The Neorealists reply that things "are in no sense conditioned by their being known . . . things known may continue to exist unaltered when they are not known." They attempt to separate metaphysics from epistemology by proving that the nature of real things is not to be found simply in the nature of knowledge. Thus the emancipation of metaphysics from epistemology is seen as the "most notable feature" of Neorealism.

Metaphysical Pluralism. Neorealists have an aversion for mystical views, particularly the implications of Monistic Absolutism —not only that reality is a single entity (Monism) but also that the essence of reality is a sum of relations (the doctrine of internal relations). Rejecting the idea that all relations are internal, they assume the existence of a variety of real objects possessing external relations to one another (Metaphysical Pluralism). Real objects exist independently of our mental processes or knowledge, including ordinary things in perception, universals in the Platonic sense, and even mathematical and logical principles. Each of these has an ontological status in reality irrespective of its being known or unknown to us. Existential Realism states that specific things—facts in our experience—exist, while Subsistential Realism asserts that universals (or essences of objects) subsist. Knowledge is acquired through the method of analysis (defined by Holt as a "careful, systematic, and exhaustive examination of any topic of discourse," requiring clear and accurate definitions of terms) which uses the "unequivocal and conventional reference of words." Using this method of analysis, the Neorealists developed the concept of neutral entities and the relational theory of mind. They concluded that mind is neither mental nor physical, but exists as a relation among neutral entities which may appear at times to be mental and at other times physical. The concept of neutral entities became the basis for the doctrine of Neutral Monism (adhered to by Bertrand Russell and the other British Neorealists). This doctrine was discussed as early as 1904 by William James in his essay "Does Consciousness Exist?" Although the point of view is called Monism, it is Monist in the sense that it admits only one kind of reality, but it is metaphysically

Pluralist in assuming the existence of a great multiplicity of neutral entities. It was William James who wrote that "Thoughts in the concrete are made of the same stuff as things are."

American Critical Realists. This group of American philosophers, rejecting the Epistemological Monism (the representative theory of knowledge) espoused by the Neorealists, set forth a different thesis of their own in *Essays in Critical Realism: A Cooperative Study of the Problem of Knowledge* (1920). The Critical Realists have included George Santayana (1863–1952), Durant Drake (1878–1933), Arthur O. Lovejoy (1873–1962), James Bissett Pratt (1875–1944), Arthur Kenyon Rogers (1868–1936), Charles Augustus Strong (1862–1940), and Roy Wood Sellars (1880–   ). (Sellars, an Evolutionary Naturalist, eventually developed his own philosophy of Physical Realism.)

Epistemological Dualism. A major concept of Critical Realism, in opposition to Neorealism, is that of Epistemological Dualism, the representative theory (accepted by Locke and Descartes) that the knower and the thing known are two distinct, separate entities, namely, material objects and ideas or mental states. According to this dualistic concept, ideas are *immediately* known to the individual as objects directly presented to his consciousness, whereas material objects are mediately known to him—that is, they require an intermediary and become known by inference or through the vehicle of ideas. Material objects differ fundamentally from ideas, being real and distinct entities quite independent of the images, perceptions, or reasoning by which they may become known to the individual.

Although the Critical Realists found common ground in epistemology, they failed to obtain a consensus in metaphysics. Thus, Rogers was an Idealist who eventually defected in favor of Naturalism and Skepticism. Strong, Santayana, Drake, and Sellars adhered to Naturalism, but Sellars preferred a sharply evolutionary point of view, while Strong and Drake leaned toward Panpsychism. Lovejoy and Pratt were Metaphysical Dualists as well as Epistemological Dualists, hence referred to as Psycho-physical Dualists. Lovejoy was an outspoken opponent of Behaviorism and Objective Relativism. Pratt was sympathetic to Metaphysical Spiritualism, Idealism, and Theism. Among this group the most influential was Santayana, who accepted Naturalism in conjunction with Metaphysical Materialism, Platonic Realism, and atheism.

George Santayana. Santayana agreed fully with his fellow Critical Realists on Epistemological Dualism, but in metaphysics developed his own unique viewpoint, drawing heavily upon the works of the ancient Greek philosophers.

The principal ideas forming the basis of his system of philosophy may be described as a composite of Naturalism; Materialism; Behaviorism; Realism; belief in animal faith, instinct, and intuition; Skepticism; Epistemological Dualism; the doctrine of essence; Epiphenomenalism; and atheism.

Santayana's Skepticism was more extreme than that of Descartes, for Santayana asserted that nothing can be known with absolute certainty, not even the soul or the Cartesian *Cogito*. Since scientific evidence provides no certainty of truth, man must ultimately resort to *animal faith* in all matters. No system, including science, can be trusted to disclose the truth; hence animal faith becomes our only recourse. It is in this way that we arrive at our belief in matter as the only ultimate existing object, the ground for all spiritual entities, these being merely epiphenomena, by-products, of matter. The soul (or spirit) of man is an offshoot of matter, and dependent upon it for existence; therefore, Santayana accepted a Behavioristic view of matter as a mechanical substance reflected in our sensory experience and ideas, thus known only indirectly to us—the view of Epistemological Dualism.

Santayana referred to Essences, not as existing entities in the sense that matter exists, but rather as subsisting entities comparable to Platonic Ideals. The Essences (qualities, universals, forms of Being) are known to us through pure intuition. Truth is a quality or a segment of that part of Essence which comes into relationship with existing things, but the Essences themselves are nonexistent forms of Being which are infinite, eternal, and universal. Santayana made a crucial distinction between existence and Being; material things possess existence and are sensed by us, but Essences possess Being (not existence) and are known to us only through intuition. Whereas material objects occupy time and place, Essences possess Being by virtue of their nature as universals governed by the principle of identity—characteristics familiar to us in pure mathematics. Furthermore, the realm of our spirit or soul, of sensations, passions, and ideas (wherein we fulfill our highest aspirations in art, morality, religion, science, and philosophy) is inferior to the realms of matter and Being.

British Neorealists. The beginnings of a concerted Neorealist reaction against modern Idealism may be traced to the works of the British philosopher George Edward Moore (1873–1958), especially his essay "The Refutation of Idealism," published in *Mind* (1903). The revolt was joined by other leading British thinkers, such as C. Lloyd Morgan (1852–1936), Samuel Alexander (1859–1938), Alfred North Whitehead (1861–1947), T. Percy Nunn (1870–1944), Bertrand Russell (1873–   ), Charlie Dunbar Broad (1887–   ), John Laird (1887–1945), C. E. M. Joad (1891–1953), Henry Habberley Price (1899–   ), and Alfred Cyril Ewing (1899–   ). Moore, Russell, and Whitehead may be regarded as the most influential contributors to the British Neorealist movement.

George Edward Moore. Moore's "The Refutation of Idealism" made a sharp distinction between consciousness (or idea) and the thing perceived as the object of consciousness. Our sense experience of blue is not identical with the blue object we see. It is true that consciousness accompanies all sensations, but the Berkeleyan formula "To be is to be perceived" cannot be correct, for if it were, we would not be able to distinguish among colors as we do. If our perceptions were the only things in existence, what would prevent us from seeing blue as red or yellow or brown? We are compelled to see a blue object as blue because its color and our perception or consciousness of it are two separate things. The blue color in an object can exist independently of our sensation of blue, although the color and our sensation form an "organic unity" which can be severed only by means of an "illegitimate abstraction." We should not confuse the existence of an object with our perception of it, just as we must not mix up the blue color of a sweet, blue object with its taste. Sweet blue things that exist may be perceived by us, but the fact that they are at times not perceived by us does not mean that they do not exist. It is only common sense to say that we sense the color blue and also that at the same time the blue object itself exists in space.

Moore asserted, as an Epistemological Monist, that the object known cannot be separated from the knowing process, that the act of knowing any object consists of an immediate contact with it. To know anything means to apprehend the real thing itself. Moore rejected the representative or picture theory of knowledge and held that sensibles or sense-data are not mere mental images in consciousness, that they are objective things in the real world entering immediately into the mind which shines through them. Since perception is immediate, we apprehend real objects without the medium or vehicle of mental images. Although we do not immediately apprehend the Kantian things-in-themselves directly, we do have an immediate apprehension of sensibles or sensa from which we can make perceptual judgments about the things themselves and thus obtain knowledge which was not given in our perceptions. Thus, through the immediate experience we discover facts about the reality not yet experienced.

Moore applied his Realism to ethics. As an Ethical Realist, he advocated the view that good is a real object which is simple and ultimate and therefore cannot be defined, and that, furthermore, good actions are organic unities which are not subject to analysis. The attempt to analyze a good act and separate its component parts could never arrive at a part that is purely good as such, for good is an integral part of the whole which can be found only in the presence of the whole. Dissection of the whole would result in the loss of whatever good is present.

Bertrand Russell. The Realistic theses of Bertrand Russell reflect some of the comparable ideas of Moore and Whitehead, and particularly the Neutral Monism elaborated in the works of William James and Ralph Barton Perry. Russell contributed significant Realistic emphases to mathematical logic, his *magnum opus* being *Principia Mathematica*, three volumes (1910–1913) completed in collaboration with Alfred North Whitehead. The primary aim of their work was to verify the statements that all pure mathematics utilizes concepts definable in logical terms only and that pure mathematics follows from purely logical premises, conclusions regarded by Russell as antithetical to Kantian doctrines. Although he applied Skepticism to concepts of free will, immortality, and God, he was never able (despite his steadfast bent toward Empiricism) to believe that mathematical principles (such as $2 + 2 = 4$) were merely inductive generalizations stemming from experience. As a Realist he believed that the external world really does exist, and that its existence does not depend upon our continuously perceiving it. (Mathematical principles and other universals subsist forever.) As a Skeptic, he held that the existence of a real world beyond sense data cannot be proved. Unlike Moore, he accepted Berkeley's theory that the existence of sense-data depends upon their being perceived. Russell attempted to cope with the problem arising from the "crude data of sense," which conflict with the "space, time, and matter of mathematical physics," that is, the difference between things as they appear to the senses and things as understood from the standpoint of the physical sciences, such as nuclear physics. Thus a typewriter as it appears to us is quite different from the atomic description of it by physicists. Our knowledge of *sense-data* is immediate *knowledge by acquaintance,* but our derived knowledge of *things* is *knowledge by description.* Our knowledge of truths (universals, principles of logic and mathematics) is *intuitive knowledge (a priori* knowledge) ; such truths are self-evident. Since knowledge by acquaintance is direct or immediate (Epistemological Monism), there is no possibility of error, but knowledge of truth is subject to the possibility of error since different people may arrive at opposite conclusions. Russell accepted the *correspondence theory of truth*—that a belief is true if it agrees with the fact with which it is supposed to correspond. Although he rejected the coherence theory of truth, he accepted coherence as a *criterion of truth.*

With the publication of his *The Analysis of Mind* in 1921, Russell turned to the doctrine of Neutral Monism that minds and sensations are neutral entities. This view of both material and mental objects as neutral was consistent with the Behavioristic psychology which regarded the mind and its known object as a single entity. More recently, however, Russell reverted to his earlier belief in Epistemological Dualism and the representative theory of knowledge. In his "My Present View of the World" in *My Philosophical Development* (1959) he concluded that the mind plays no part in the continuing processes of stellar evolution, noting that the only evidence for the existence of mental phenomena is a mere fragment of space-time, which is not a substance, but a system of relations. He asserted that matter must be interpreted as consisting of nothing but a series of events, with energy replacing force as the real motive power; that cause-effect relationships have little effect on the genuine events comprising reality; and that reality consists of logical structures whose intrinsic character is unknown. The world of the physicist, of events, is an inferred world, not one which is directly known through sense experiences which provide us with data about the perceived world (*sensa*) we do not infer but sense. Russell thus upheld Epistemological Dualism, commenting in regard to the ego-centric predicament "that we *can* witness or observe what goes on in our heads," and that "we cannot witness or observe anything else at all."

In ethical theory, he rejected the Ethical Realism advocated by Moore and adhered instead to an Ethical Naturalism, or the Emotive Theory of Ethics. Although at first he admitted that ethical propositions may be known intuitively as self-evident truth (though not so surely as principles of logic), he later dismissed ethics as a set of emotional attitudes which cannot be regarded as true or false. He preferred the point of view of Scientism, the doctrine that all valid knowledge is attained through use of the scientific method and that whatever cannot be known scientifically cannot be known at all. Since moral right and wrong are not subject to scientific tests, moral judgments cannot be proved. Consequently, values lie outside the domain of knowledge; they represent merely the venting of our emotions. The point of view is that of Ethical Subjectivism. Good as an ethical phenomenon is reducible to desire, and social good refers to the collective desires common to a given group. Individuals who attribute universality to good are only attempting in this way to universalize their personal desires.

Alfred North Whitehead. The significant works of Whitehead were his contributions to mathematics—the celebrated *Principia Mathematica* (1910–1913) mentioned above; writings in the fields of physics and natural science, such as *The Concept of Nature* (1920) and *The Principle of Relativity* (1922); and finally, major philosophical works, such as *Process and Reality*. It was during his third period, the one of metaphysical philosophy, beginning with his appointment at Harvard, that he produced several works of enduring value in philosophy which brought him fame in the philosophical world: *Process and Reality* (his Gifford Lectures of 1927–28); *Science and the Modern World* (1925); and *Adventures of Ideas* (1933). His philosophical views have reflected diverse influences: Neorealism, Platonism, Aristotelianism, Panpsychism, and the works of Leibniz, Spinoza, Kant, and Samuel Alexander.

Whitehead's organismic philosophy posited a universe systematically and coherently ordered and containing within the organic whole ultimately real objects, the actual entities or actual occasions which evidence the fact that the universe is in constant process. Reality consists of a multiplicity of objects. Hence Whitehead's may be described as Process Philosophy and Metaphysical Pluralism. The universe, always in process, is not mechanically driven or controlled but develops freely in time, which represents real duration without a beginning or an end. The entities comprising the universe are units of Being in a state of Becoming in order to fulfill their potentialities. Abstract ideas must not be confused with these concrete realities or events which have a life history and a pattern. Whitehead attributed the origins of the entities or events to *creativity*, an ultimate ontological principle constituting the basic nature of God (possibly as the primordial nontemporal chance result of creativity). But God has a dipolar nature: (1) a primordial nature which is eternal, conceptual, infinite, free, complete (though incomplete if we disregard God's other nature—the actual entities), unconscious (devoid of feeling), and including all universals as eternal objects; (2) a consequent nature which is one of feeling (consciousness), and is identical with predetermined, incomplete, everlasting goodness. Through creativity, which is the principle of novelty, God brings into actual existence novel entities as actual occasions, or events.

Actual occasions are not alike, yet they are unified as an organized set of the multiplicity of things. Whitehead used the term *concresence* for the process whereby this world of many things acquires integration or unity, or whereby an entity becomes an actuality. He applied the term *actuality* to the process whereby an actual entity enters the concrete world, thus becoming an actual occasion. His ontological principle (the principle of efficient and final causation) implies that actual entities are reasons; hence the search for reasons is the same as the search for actual entities, with the latter providing the explanations for the present state of things. Locke's concept of force or power is here interpreted as a principle, namely, the law of causation.

Prehension is Whitehead's term for a set or category of relationships among actualities or realities comprising the universe. This dominant category of relationships is superior to and more important than qualitative distinctions between the actual entities or realities. Prehension depends upon three factors: (1) the prehending individual or subject; (2) the prehended data, or facts revealed; and (3) the "subjective form" or the way in which the individuals or subjects prehend the data. Subjects are the occasions or events; their objects are the data; and prehension provides the relationship between them. Prehension is an "incognitive apprehension"; it involves more than mere perception but lacks the cognitive element of apprehension. It is in a sense comparable to Alexander's compresence or togetherness, and plays a role similar to that of Leibniz' monad, which mirrors the universe or provides us with *petites perceptions* (small perceptions of an unconscious nature).

Both God (as consciousness and eternal goodness) and man consist of these actual entities or occasions. (The actual entities may be regarded as identical with substance, as final facts beyond which nothing exists; Whitehead referred to them as "drops of experience.") Persons as temporal events (since there is no permanent unchanging substance) are related to other persons in a society, all being motivated by subjective aims, that is, by purposes or values. Ethical value is defined on the basis of its contribution to the fulfillment of potentialities or to co-ordination of actualities in the universe as a whole. According to Whitehead, the conceptual feelings issuing from God's primordial nature, that is to say, God's purposes, are realized through the expression of his role as goodness and conscious activity. God, as the savior of the world, exercises scrupulous care to make certain that every worthwhile value will be saved in agreement with his vision of truth, beauty, and goodness. God strives to enrich both himself and the world, being the guarantor of value as well as the world's principle of order and harmony. He maintains a vigilant warfare against the evils which he seeks to eradicate from the world. Evil is not the result of God's will, but, on the contrary, exists despite his purpose to abolish it. Mankind will join in this increasingly successful, though still imperfect, process of gaining complete victory over evil.

Chapter 18

Logical Positivism

Moritz Schlick (1882–1936), philosopher and scientist at the University of Vienna has been credited with the founding of Logical Positivism as a philosophical movement active during the period between the two World Wars. In 1924 he brought together a group of philosophers who within a few years thereafter became known as the Vienna Circle. In addition to Logical Positivism, other names have been applied to the views of the Vienna Circle, such as Scientific Empiricism, Neopositivism, and Logical Empiricism. Logical Positivists counted among their adherents the members of the Berlin Society for Scientific Philosophy, philosophers of the Warsaw School, Operationalists, and even some members of the Cambridge School for Analytic Philosophy. Leading figures in the Vienna Circle were Schlick, Friedrich Waismann, Otto Neurath, Rudolf Carnap, Herbert Feigl, Victor Kraft, Edgar Zilsel, Felix Kaufmann, Hans Hahn, Kurt Gödel, Karl Menger, and B. von Juhos. The majority were scientists and mathematicians uninterested in metaphysical problems as such. Logical Positivists in Germany included Hans Reichenbach, Friedrich Kraus, E. Dubislav, A. Herzberg, A. von Parseval, and K. Grelling. Alfred Jules Ayer was the foremost British representative of this point of view. Alfred Tarski of the Warsaw School of Logicians contributed a Semantic theory of truth to the philosophy of Logical Positivism.

With the rise of Hitler, many in the Vienna group joined the faculties of British or American universities.

The philosophical ideas of the movement have persisted, and its present-day influence is reflected in familiar slogans of the Logical Positivists, such as "Philosophy is a logical syntax," and "The meaning of a proposition is the method of its verification."

The Influence of Ludwig Wittgenstein. Although the Viennese Wittgenstein (1889–1951) was not a member of the Vienna Circle, his celebrated work, *Tractatus Logico-Philosophicus* (1921), became one of the foundation treatises of Logical Positivism. On the other hand, some of his ideas were repugnant to the Neopositivists.

Wittgenstein's *Tractatus* set forth a number of ideas accepted by the Logical Positivists, including the verification principle, a key tenet of that philosophy. He stated the principle as follows: "To understand a proposition means to know what is the case if it is true." In other words, the meaning of a proposition coincides with its truth-conditions, without which the proposition would be meaningless. Anyone who wishes to understand a proposition must first know the conditions under which it is true, that is, what information is required by way of evidence of its truth. For the Logical Positivist, the meaning of the proposition cannot even be known unless it is possible to state the conditions under which the proposition can be verified. Sense observation, or information ultimately derived by means of sense observation, is necessary for verification. The *Tractatus* also contributed to Logical Positivism a new definition of philosophy as a mental activity which seeks to analyze or clarify the meanings of scientific propositions. Philosophy, then, does not possess a factual content, nor is it a theory or set of theories; it is an active attempt to clarify thought. Schlick, although he regarded science as a pursuit of truth, agreed with Wittgenstein that philosophy must be defined as "the pursuit of meaning." Finally, according to Wittgenstein, the propositions of logic and mathematics are tautologies, that is, uninformative assertions which state nothing factual about the world; consequently, they are empirically void, empty, providing mere identities of subject and predicate. Propositions of logic and mathematics can be demonstrated, but they cannot be verified through use of the experiential data required by the verification principle. They may be said to be valid or invalid, but not true or false like empirical propositions. Since propositions pertaining to metaphysical realities are neither tautological nor empirical, it is impossible either to demonstrate their validity or to verify their truth. The Logical Positivist takes the next step, asserting that metaphysical statements are therefore meaningless, but Wittgenstein left the matter open by claiming that a metaphysical or mystical idea, even though not expressed in words, can be felt or appreciated "without knowing whether it is true." The Logical Positivists disagree with Wittgenstein's view concerning mystical or metaphysical propositions. Whereas they insist that a metaphysical proposition has no meaning whatever because it is without truth-conditions, Wittgenstein left the matter an open issue, stating merely that "what we cannot speak about we must consign to silence."

Alfred Jules Ayer. The principal views of British Neopositivism concerning metaphysics were summarized in Ayer's *The Revolution in Philosophy* (1956). According to the verification principle, empirical evidence (observation) is necessary in order to determine the meaning of a statement or proposition. Consequently, the nature of ultimate reality is not a legitimate topic for philosophical consideration; and assertions about God, souls, immortality, moral values, aesthetic values, and universal substances (matter or spirit) cannot be accepted as valid or invalid, true or false. It is interesting to note that the verification principle of the Logical Positivists (inasmuch as it is a principle instead of an observable fact of experience) is not itself verifiable and hence confronts the adherents of this school with an embarrassing self-contradiction. Neopositivists attempt to solve this predicament by claiming that the verification principle can be used as a meaningful criterion of truth and as an arbitrarily accepted guide to the conditions required for adherence to specific philosophical conclusions. Value judgments are not permissible, for they fall outside the province of knowledge. Science is the only legitimate form of knowledge, and what cannot be known scientifically (through sense observation) cannot be known at all. According to Ayer, the philosopher's task "is to act as a sort of intellectual policeman, seeing that nobody trespasses into metaphysics."

Since there is no verifiable evidence for or against any given value judgment, we cannot judge one act morally right and another morally wrong. Morality is not subject to sense observation; therefore it is unverifiable and must be eliminated from the province of knowledge. We can observe an act of murder but not the immorality attributed to the act. What, then, do we mean when we say that killing is wrong? In *Language, Truth and Logic* (1936, 1946) Ayer claimed that we are only giving vent to our feelings and nothing more, although at a later date he moderated this extreme point of view which he admitted to be an oversimplification, stating that "moral attitudes consist in certain patterns of behaviour, and . . . the expression of a moral judgement is an element in the pattern. The moral judgement expresses the attitude in the sense that it contributes to defining it." He defended his ethical theory, not as a code of morals to be put into practice, but as a means of explaining the entire gamut of ethical theory (what he called a *metaethics*), suggesting that he had transcended morality *per se*. Denying that he had impugned moral or aesthetic values, he said that he had merely claimed that normative statements which obligate us to live up to certain moral principles cannot possibly be derived from descriptive statements of fact. "You cannot deduce 'ought' from 'is.' Laying down a standard is not reporting a fact," he wrote, adding that a moral standard need not be adversely affected by the lack of its verification.

Ayer's Skepticism applied to aesthetics and religion as well as to metaphysics and ethics. Like ethical judgments, aesthetic and religious statements of value are emotive—not factual descriptions required for validity but only pseudoconcepts and expressions of feeling, and therefore neither acceptable as true nor unacceptable as false.

Moritz Schlick. Schlick, in *Problems of Ethics* (1939), defined morality as a means of achieving happiness resulting from altruistic desire. Avoiding Ayer's extreme Skepticism in ethics, he attempted to synthesize Kantianism and Utilitarianism and Hedonism. He argued that moral obligations can be explained in descriptive terms of desire and kindness. He rejected Hobbesian egoism, preferring the Schopenhauerian philosophy of sympathy. Morality is a question of "How must I live to be happy?" Consequently, desires replace obligations, but they are social and altruistic desires, those leading to happiness. Kindness, happiness, and altruistic dispositions always coincide; in order to be moral and happy, we must cultivate our altruistic impulses. Schlick's theory of moral values (Ethical Naturalism) represents a much more moderate point of view than that of Ayer, his philosophical compatriot.

Schlick agreed with the arguments in Wittgenstein's *Tractatus* concerning the verifiability principle; philosophy as an activity; the activity of philosophy as a search for meaning and analysis (the clarification of propositions); and logical and mathematical propositions as tautologies (identities). He rejected all metaphysical propositions, owing to the lack of any supporting evidence from sense experience or observation. Philosophy, as the mental activity of searching for meanings, should not be confused with science as the pursuit of verifiable truth.

Schlick defined a proposition as "a series of sounds or other symbols (a 'sentence') together with the logical rules belonging to them." The logical rules, which constitute the meanings of propositions, are based upon deictic (ostensive) definitions, that is, upon definitions arrived at by pointing directly to the object of each word. According to Schlick, propositions are meaningless only if they are *unverifiable in principle*, and are not necessarily to be considered unverifiable merely because present circumstances prevent verifica-

tion. The Classical Positivists rejected as meaningless many propositions (for example, some in stellar chemistry) which today are
verifiable by modern scientific techniques.

Since Schlick believed meaning to be dependent upon verifiability,
and verification dependent upon sense experience, how could any
individual prove the existence of minds other than his own? All
experiences are private; hence no one except the single individual
accepting a proposition could verify it. He alone could know the
meaning of a proposition, and it would be meaningless to assert that
someone else knows the meaning of the particular proposition in
question. Precisely what, then, is the scientific knowledge which we
have in common? Schlick concluded that knowledge must consist of
structural relations which we all have in common as a consequence
of our private experiences. Although I cannot convey my private
experiences to you, I can communicate their structure to you. I
cannot give you my experience of "green" color, but I can inform
you that the green rays possess a wave length of 550 millimicrons.
My experience of green color must differ from yours, but we share
the information about its formal structure or pattern. Thus all of
science as the structure of human experience becomes public knowledge. Realizing, however, that scientific propositions should have
some experiential content, instead of being described as mere forms
or patterns, Schlick asserted that each of us fills in his own content
by sense observation. But the content or facts based upon the individual's personal experience could not be communicated to others
with quite different experience. Strictly speaking, the communicable
facts in scientific propositions (as distinguished from the mere forms
or patterns) would have to be repudiated as metaphysical or inexpressible realities, neither true nor false, by Logical Positivists.

Otto Neurath.   Neurath (1882–1945) rejected Schlick's method-
ological solipsism and protocol statements (first-hand initial reports
of direct sense observations), and he attacked Schlick's idea of "inexpressible reality" on the ground that statements can be compared
only with other statements. Protocol statements are like any other
factual statements and must be subject to common observation and
verification by all minds, not simply to one's private experience. In
other words, protocol statements refer directly to physical events
themselves which are common to all men alike. If this conclusion
were true, then an individual's experiences could be nothing more
than the physical states of his body or the acts comprising his behavior (as maintained in Behavioristic psychology). To avoid the

dilemma involved in Schlick's metaphysical "reality," Neurath contended that sense experience is a biological process, that is, a physical, not a mental, state, thus reducing all mental activity to physically observable facts. Statements about mental experiences are therefore exactly the same as statements about physical events, and the language of physics (including descriptions of all physical events) constitutes a universal language by means of which we are able to express every empirical fact or experience. Neurath believed that this doctrine and philosophy of Physicalism would bring about the "unity of science," for the diverse sciences must all be fundamentally the same as physics and speak the same language as physics. It is now clear that Neurath's doctrine of Physicalism is nothing more than Materialism in modern garb.

From Schlick's point of view, protocol statements represent our immediate contact with the facts of experience; consequently only these statements are directly verifiable, and all other propositions are verified by being related to the protocol statements. But the Physicalists, such as Neurath, denying that protocol statements are records of our contacts with immediate experience, contended that, being like other statements, they had to be verified in the same manner, that is, by a coherent interrelationship of one with another in a unified system. From protocol statements we can build up a network of sentences. With the system of sentences at our disposal, we can determine whether new sentences are true or false by ascertaining their coherence or agreement as parts of the system as a whole. Thus, like his opponents, the Absolute Idealists, Neurath resorted to the coherence theory of truth! Rejecting the correspondence theory that an idea is true if it corresponds with its real object, he depended upon the criterion of coherence: ideas are true if they consist of logical, integrated, consistent, interrelated statements. But the coherence theory could not solve the problem of choosing between two internally consistent systems of ideas or facts. If the ideas which happen to be accepted by present-day scientists are preferred, then the criterion of truth has shifted from coherence to scientific consensus. Moreover, subsequent facts of experience may induce future scientists to reject the present system of ideas as untrue and accept the rejected system as the true one.

Rudolf Carnap. Although adhering to Neurath's theories of Physicalism, nevertheless Carnap (1891–   ) used the protocol statements (referring to immediate facts of experience) as foundation sentences requiring no justification but accepted as if they were metaphysical truths such as those which Neurath rejected. Carnap was confronted with the same problem that disturbed Schlick. If protocol sentences record the privacy of sense experience, how can they be regarded as foundation sentences (intersubjective statements of science which are publicly verifiable)? Carnap tried to resolve the issue by viewing science as a unity in which all empirical statements are expressed in but a single language, a unity in which all facts are of a single kind and become known by the same method. The language of physics must be applied to all the "natural and psychological sciences." Protocol statements are records of direct experience, but experience is merely a state of the human body. Carnap, like Neurath, resorted to the point of view of Behaviorism in order to support his basic premise that psychology is merely physics. Whereas Neurath, however, contended that protocol statements are within the language of science (possess a fixed format), Carnap regarded them as "direct records of experience," truths outside the language of science and requiring translation into statements upon which scientific propositions can be based.

If philosophical propositions are to be accepted as scientific and valid, said Carnap, they must obey the logic of science which is "nothing other than the logical syntax of the language of science." In other words, philosophy is to be replaced by the logic of science, and the logic of science is nothing more than the syntax of the language of science. "All problems of the current logic of science, as soon as they are exactly formulated, are seen to be syntactical problems." His *The Logical Syntax of Language* (1937) held that all philosophical statements (and possibly all statements) are syntactical, and that these statements have created difficulty because of their being expressed in a material mode. To give validity to the words in a statement, one must translate it from the material to the formal mode. Thus, the statement (in the material mode), "A rose is a thing," may at first seem to be factual, structurally similar to "A rose has thorns," whereas it is only a syntactical statement (one in the formal mode) that "Rose is a thing-word" (a substantive or noun). Syntactical statements (probably including all philosophical ones) are those dealing with the form or order of the symbols rather than the meanings of the statements.

According to Bertrand Russell, Wittgenstein believed it impossible to talk about a language in that language itself, but Carnap argued that a language could formulate a structure of its own for this purpose and in *The Logical Syntax of Language* he set forth a technique for constructing sentences about sentences. Taking an extreme position, he condemned as metaphysical all propositions referring to *meaning* which go beyond the mere reporting of the linguistic relationships among statements. In his *Introduction to Semantics* (1942), he argued that a *metalanguage* (a language about a language) is necessary in the study of any particular language. Semantics, as a system of semantical rules constructed upon the basis of a metalanguage, is necessary in order to determine the truth-conditions of sentences in any given language. Semantic rules determine the logical truth of sentences.

Alfred Tarski. According to Tarski (1902–   ) truth is predicated on sentences as a metalanguage (a language which makes symbolic assertions about another language). Truth is applicable only to sentences, and it is basically a semantic problem, for "it deals with certain relations between expressions of a language and the objects 'referred to' by those expressions." The problem of truth is akin to the establishment of foundations of theoretical semantics. The semantic definition of truth is: "All equivalences of the form (T) can be asserted, and we shall call a definition of truth 'adequate' if all these equivalences follow from it." For example, we may predicate true (T) to the sentence "Snow is white," if and only if snow is white—that is, a material adequacy must exist between the sentence and the fact, an equivalence between the sentence and the existing state of affairs. The reader will recognize Tarski's semantic theory of truth as a form or offshoot of the correspondence theory of truth.

Chapter 19

Analytic Philosophy

A revolutionary school of twentieth-century philosophy, rejecting traditional points of view, is that of Analytic Philosophy, often referred to under other names, such as Analysis, Linguistic Analysis, Logical Analysis, Philosophical Analysis, Ordinary Language Philosophy, Cambridge School of Analysis, and Oxford Philosophy. Its adherents contend that the entire business of philosophy is that of analysis. As such, philosophy is devoid of content in the sense that it does not add to the scope of scientific knowledge, but instead consists of linguistic activity designed to eliminate problems and perplexities arising from intellectual confusion or misunderstanding and thus to clarify the knowledge which we already possess. It is no longer to be the task of philosophy to search for ultimate or metaphysical truth; the metaphysical quest which originated with Descartes is to be replaced by the radically different task of philosophical analysis undertaken by Analytic Philosophy as a nonmetaphysical school of thought. During the past several decades the new point of view has dominated the British philosophical scene and has had considerable influence in the United States as well.

Analytic Philosophy may be traced to its beginnings in the "ordinary language" philosophy of George Edward Moore and the "ideal language" philosophy of Bertrand Russell, but its chief initial impetus seems to have come from the "picture language" and "language games" philosophy of Wittgenstein. The next stage of development may be attributed to the Cantabrigian philosopher John Wisdom (Wittgenstein's successor at Cambridge University), who gave Analytic Philosophy a new turn as a form of "therapeutic analysis." The most recent development (after World War II) shifted the dominant role from the Cambridge adherents of "therapeutic analysis" to the Oxford University group advocating the Ordinary Language Philosophy. The principal spokesmen for this philosophy have been Gilbert Ryle and John Austin. (Other notable adherents have been Stephen E. Toulmin, H. L. A. Hart, R. M. Hare,

P. Nowell-Smith, Peter F. Strawson, and J. O. Urmson. Frank P. Ramsey of Cambridge University also made significant contributions to the Linguistic movement.)

Analytic Philosophy represents a reaction against the Idealists' synthesis and concept of Absolute Reality originating with Hegel. In England, the reaction was directed against Francis Herbert Bradley (1846–1924), the distinguished Hegelian Idealist at Oxford who argued that the facts of common sense are not what they appear to be, but are only appearances. Bradley, for example, put forth the argument (supported by his co-Idealist McTaggart) that time is unreal. He maintained the Hegelian position that reality is metaphysical (spiritual) and must be viewed as a synthesis, as "the universe-as-a-whole." This fundamental theory and its implication that reality consists of internal relations came under heavy attack by the Analytic School.

CAMBRIDGE PHILOSOPHY

The leading exponents of the Cambridge group of Analytic Philosophers were Moore, Russell, Wittgenstein, and Wisdom.

G. E. Moore. Although Moore has been regarded as the founder of Linguistic Analysis, his views are in many respects different from those of the majority of adherents to Analytic Philosophy. He justified the view of philosophy as analysis of the language used in philosophical propositions, but he refused to limit philosophy to this one kind of thinking: "in fact, analysis is by no means the only thing I have tried to do." His method of posing questions or problems to be analyzed, instead of postulating answers or solutions to problems, became popular in England. The British philosophers welcomed his view that most difficulties in philosophy are caused by "the attempt to answer questions without first discovering what question it is which you desire to answer." He distinguished between meaning and analysis, also between the ordinary use of language by the average man and its extraordinary use by philosophers. In the common-sense use of language the terms of which have but a single literal meaning and are readily understood as such by anyone comprehending the language, it is the philosopher's responsibility to make a correct analysis of them rather than to determine whether or not they are true. The word "time" conveys one definite meaning in everyday communication, but philosophers use it in an altogether different sense, creating strange paradoxes. When Bradley asserted that time is unreal, he did not mean to deny that day occurs before night, but he had in mind a meaning peculiar to his own philosophy. He ascribed to "time" and "unreal" a special meaning—and such use of technical terminology was condemned by Moore, who was interested not only in common-sense "truths," but perhaps even more in defending the use of ordinary language to express philosophical ideas. Common-sense propositions, such as the assertion, "there exists a living body, which is *my* body," are wholly true and known to be true by everyone. Philosophical debates can never disprove the truth of such common-sense propositions. Moore held that philosophical statements violating ordinary language are false.

Thus, it is not the task of philosophy to prove the truth of common-sense statements of ordinary language; instead the task is to analyze and clarify them. It is absurd to say, as Berkeley did, that matter does not exist, for such a contention is immediately repudiated by common sense, which at the same time refutes the Behaviorists' doctrine that minds do not exist. What is needed is the analysis of the language used in common-sense statements as a means of clarifying the ideas being expressed. Moore explained that his purpose was to analyze the concepts themselves, not merely the sentences as language elements: "I was always using 'proposition' in such a sense that no verbal expression . . . can be a 'proposition' . . ." Thus Moore inadvertently created a new departure in philosophy: the search for truth and discovery was displaced by the search for meaning and clarification, and the evaluation of facts was replaced by the examination of language. Philosophy is in this sense to be a linguistic endeavor.

Bertrand Russell. Russell's name is often linked with that of Moore in the attack upon Bradley's Neo-Hegeliansim and in the founding of the Analytic Movement in philosophy. He formulated the doctrine of Logical Atomism, the theory that the world consists of a number of simple facts, each independent of all the others yet related externally to the others. In contrast to Hegel's synthetic system, his monistic Absolute, Russell developed an atomistic logic based on the concept of a pluralistic universe, that is, on "the common-sense belief that there are many separate things." Comparable to the atoms of physics, which is the ultimate element of things, Russell's logical atoms constitute "a sort of last residue in analysis."

Logical atoms consist of two fundamental types or constitutents of facts: those of sense-data and those of universals. An example of sense-data is the fact that "this snowball is white," and an example of the universals is the fact that "all men are mortal." Universals must be included. To limit the world to particular facts would be logically self-defeating because the very assertion that "atomic facts are the only facts that exist" would itself become a generalization or universal. Not facts, but propositions are true or false; propositions are symbols, not facts. Propositions are divided into two classes: atomic and molecular. To ascertain the truth of an atomic proposition, one need only go to the fact which the particular proposition states. In the case of molecular propositions, however, it is necessary to refer to those atomic propositions with which the molecular ones are constructed. The molecular propositions are "truth functions" of the atomic propositions.

The *Principia Mathematica* (1910–1913), that monumental work by Russell and Whitehead, set the stage for Logical Atomism and Analytic Philosophy. The *Principia* provided the requirements for a logically perfect language needing only a vocabulary. "It aims at being that sort of language that, if you add a vocabulary, would be a logically perfect language." Every truth is analyzable into a statement or a set of statements. A truth reduced to a single statement is stating a particular fact; a truth analyzed into a set of statements consists of the relationship which maintains between particular facts. The former is an atomic proposition, the latter a molecular one. All that remains is for our experience to provide the data which will fit into the linguistic forms. Error arises when the forms are improperly supplied by facts which are not atomic, that is, which are not genuinely simple particulars or single characters. Russell hoped to found an ideal language which is logically perfect, grounded in his thesis that atomic facts are the only real ones and that language consists of atomic and molecular propositions only. The ultimate "residue of analysis" leads to logical atoms, either linguistic or factual; they characterize both language and the world.

Russell credited Wittgenstein with originating Logical Atomism, but the doctrine was implicit in the *Principia;* furthermore, it was Russell who developed it as the foundation concept of a pluralistic Analytic Philosophy.

Ludwig Wittgenstein. Wittgenstein's great influence upon British philosophy during the first half of the twentieth century may be divided into two stages: the earlier period of his revolutionary *Tractatus Logico-Philosophicus* (1921), containing basic concepts of Analytic Philosophy; and the later period of the nineteen thirties at Cambridge University when he broke away from his previous thinking and expounded an extraordinary language-games theory which repudiated and replaced the picture theory set forth in the *Tractatus*. His later views, reflecting the influences of Saint Augustine, Schopenhauer, Gottlob Frege, and Bertrand Russell, were posthumously published in *Philosophical Investigations* (1953), *Remarks on the Foundations of Mathematics* (1956), and lecture notes, i.e., the *Blue Book* and the *Brown Book* subtitled *Preliminary Studies for the Philosophical Investigations* (1958).

In the *Tractatus* Wittgenstein had claimed that atomic propositions (interpreted by Russell as the components or truth-functions of compound propositions) depend for their validity upon the reliability with which they accurately picture atomic facts. "A proposition is a picture of reality.)... A picture is a model of reality. ... A picture is a fact. ... The world is the totality of facts. ... The totality of true thoughts is a picture of the world." Thus, language is a picture of reality. Propositions or statements of ideas provide merely the form, telling us not "*what* things are, but only *how* they are," and the names of things are only indivisible primitive signs and symbols. The *Tractatus* held that most philosophical propositions should not be considered false but merely devoid of sensory facts, of sense content, and therefore nonsensical, whereas a genuine proposition presents sense content, "shows how things stand if it is true." Propositions must describe reality completely by means of "logical scaffolding," exhibiting the logical form of reality; and whatever cannot be shown, cannot be said either. "To understand a proposition means to know what is the case if it is true," but it can be understood without knowing its truth. Its truth or falsity depends upon its being a genuine picture of reality. Philosophy, as a critique of language, is an activity which seeks the "logical clarification of thoughts," the elucidation or clarification of propositions. By determining the kinds of thinking that are possible, it also demarcates the limits of natural science. Thus, ethical propositions and any statements about God and immortality are mystical and inexpressible in words.

The strictly correct philosophical method requires that we limit ourselves to the propositions of natural science only, because they alone have meaning expressible by signs and propositions. Wittgenstein, noting that his own propositions stated in the *Tractatus* are "nonsensical" (devoid of sense content), held that a person must transcend them in order to view the world correctly. He acknowledged the difficulty that his "verification principle," accepted by the Logical Positivists, is a pseudoproposition, for it cannot be verified by application of any other criterion and is therefore self-refuting. Moreover, the individual is limited to his own sense experiences ("The world is my world. . . . The limits of language mean the limits of my world. . . . I am my world."), so how can he refer to himself as part of an existing (not experienced) external world? Since one has no sense impressions of the self, statements about the Ego are meaningless pseudopropositions—a view described as "solipsism without a subject."

Wittgenstein's later language-game theory, based on Saint Augustine's suggestion of a "naming game," contradicted his earlier view that there is only one language and that it consists of terms which portray reality. He now emphasized that the way in which a word is used, not its meaning as a name for some object, gives language and statements their validity. When we ask, for example, "What is the meaning of *good?*" we must inquire as to how we learned the meaning of the word, what its functions have been, and strive to clarify its use, not as a picture of reality, but as a tool for describing, reporting, and asserting facts or ideas. If we analyze the uses or functions of language, philosophical problems will disappear. The philosopher must only describe the actual uses of language, never interfering with it, in order to achieve complete clarification. Wittgenstein's revolutionary theory was taken up by the Cambridge group of linguistic analysts who proposed the new slogan, "Don't ask for the meaning, ask for the use."

John Wisdom. As Wittgenstein's successor at Cambridge University, Wisdom accepted the new theory that philosophy is essentially therapeutic activity designed to clarify the uses of language. He agreed with Wittgenstein that philosophers present us with old facts in a new light, but do not discover new facts. Wisdom emphasized Therapeutic Positivism, asserting that metaphysical statements should not be abruptly discarded as "nonsense," for metaphysics possesses a positive value. Metaphysical statements are both false (meaningless) and illuminating. They are meaningless or absurd when they use ordinary words to mean something quite different from their normal meanings and in this way create philosophical difficulties and paradoxes. The verification of philosophical statements requires a logic and analysis different from those used in the verification of statements about physical objects (e.g., chairs, tables) or scientific facts. The value of philosophers' paradoxical assertions, said Wisdom, "depends upon their paradoxicalness. . . . Philosophers should be continually trying to say what cannot be said." Wisdom maintained that analysis is not identical with Analytic Philosophy, but only an approach in that direction.

OXFORD PHILOSOPHY

At Oxford University during the period after World War II a group of Analytic Philosophers succeeded in replacing Idealism with the Ordinary Language Philosophy, as the dominant point of view. According to P. L. Heath, incorrect use of ordinary English is responsible for philosophical problems, and these can be solved only by "pointing out the normal usage of the words employed and the normal grammatical form of the sentences in which they appear. Ordinary language is correct language." The Oxford group concerned itself not so much with the activity of philosophers attempting to get rid of paradoxes, but rather with the "elucidation of concepts" and the "logic of expressions." For them ordinary language, used in its customary manner, will clarify philosophical problems and reduce many of them to linguistic issues.

Critics have charged that the Oxford philosophers consider ordinary language a panacea for all philosophical activity, that they attempt to convert all philosophical problems into linguistic ones, that they mistakenly regard metaphysics and epistemology throughout the history of philosophy as merely the abuse of ordinary language, and that their fundamental aim is simply to restrict philosophical thought and communication to ordinary language. As previously noted, the two principal exponents of the Oxford philosophy have been Gilbert Ryle and John L. Austin.

Gilbert Ryle. In his *The Concept of the Mind* (1949) Ryle rejected Cartesian metaphysics, particularly its Dualism of mind and matter, as a *category mistake* which created false issues and philosophical dilemmas—for example, by confusing the logic of discourse pertaining to minds with the logic of discourse pertaining to physical bodies. He contended that philosophers should analyze and clarify ideas by careful use of the logic ordinarily applied to relevant verbal expressions. In referring to the human mind, for instance, they should not talk about it as if it were a repository like a physical body or receptacle but rather as a term involving a "person's abilities, liabilities, and inclinations to do and undergo certain sorts of things, and of the doing and undergoing of these things in the ordinary world." It has been said that his conclusion regarding the nature of the mind turns out to be the Behavioristic assertion that mind is the function of bodily activity. Nevertheless, he claimed to have exposed Dualism as a myth, as the "dogma of the Ghost in the Machine," and to have demonstrated that the persistent dilemmas which confront man (such as the paradoxes of freedom and determinism or of motion and rest) are pseudoconflicts and not genuine. If logical argument defends the concept of fatalism by citing definite causes of behavior, common sense rejects it by informing us that we can control our own lives. Ryle attempted to dispose of such antithetical positions by showing that they are false dilemmas, that they are erroneous disjunctions and not genuine either/or choices. Both of two seemingly contradictory statements may be true, and the conflict may be only an apparent one because each theory pertains to "a different line of business," a different interest, and it is unnecessary for them to be reconciled. Each theory pertains to a different category. According to Ryle, philosophers often imagine disagreements which do not exist and talk "at cross-purposes with one another . . . hinging their arguments upon concepts of different categories, though they suppose themselves to be hinging them upon different concepts of the same category, or vice versa."

John L. Austin. The principal contributions of John Langshaw Austin (1911–1960) to Oxford philosophy were the doctrines set forth in his *Philosophical Papers* (1961), comprising three unpublished papers plus most of his papers published from 1939 to 1958, and his *Sense and Sensibilia* (1962), a volume of lecture notes constituting a critique of three works: Ayer's *The Foundations of Empirical Knowledge* (1940), H. H. Price's *Perception* (1932), and G. J. Warnock's *Berkeley* (1953).

Austin was primarily concerned with the philosophical problem (persisting ever since the time of Heraclitus) of determining whether sense (or ideas) and sensibilia (or sense-data) are different real entities or merely expressions which give the illusion of two different realities. He concluded that philosophers who disagree with one another about this problem may actually be in agreement as to basic assumptions without being aware of it. He restated one point of view in philosophy as follows: "We never . . . perceive (or 'sense'), or anyhow we never *directly* perceive or sense, material objects (or material things), but only sense-data (or our own ideas, impressions, sensa, sense perceptions, percepts, etc.)" [1] and he attributed this Scholastic (or typically philosophical) dilemma to preoccupation with a few oversimplified terms, poorly understood, and to an obsession with a few imperfectly understood facts. It was his view that "ordinary words are much subtler in their uses, and mark many more distinctions, than philosophers have realized." The question as to whether we perceive material objects or merely sense-data is a spurious antithesis, a consequence of "taking in each other's washing." "There is no *one* kind of thing that we 'perceive' but many different kinds." Pens are like and unlike rainbows, after-images, moving-pictures, mirages, dreams, etc. It is the responsibility of science, not philosophy, to determine how many kinds or classes of things exist.

Austin advised us to get rid of "such illusions as the 'argument from illusion,'" designed to prove that what a person directly perceives consists always of sense-data which must be differentiated from the objects producing the sense-data. The argument from illusion was accepted by Berkeley, Schopenhauer, and other philosophers. Austin tried to refute the argument by exposing its dependence upon "a mass of seductive (mainly verbal) fallacies" and concealed or unconscious motives. He succeeded in eliminating some, but not all, kinds of philosophical dilemmas, and helped to clarify the meanings of terms such as "reality," "seems," and "looks"—terms which, "besides being philosophically very slippery, are in their own right interesting." The elimination of linguistic shortcomings or errors is in itself a contribution to philosophy.

---

[1] J. L. Austin, *Sense and Sensibilia* (New York: Oxford University Press, 1962), p. 2.

Chapter 20

Neo-Scholasticism and Neo-Thomism

Neo-Scholasticism consists of a group of philosophies based upon medieval Scholasticism and widely accepted among Catholic philosophers. The dominant Neo-Scholastic philosophy of contemporary times, Neo-Thomism, represents a modification and adaptation of Thomism, the system set forth in the works of Thomas Aquinas who attempted to harmonize Aristotelian philosophy with the concepts of Christian theology. Most of the contemporary Neo-Thomists are Catholic philosophers. In the Roman Catholic world, Thomistic philosophy enjoys a privileged status among philosophies inasmuch as it was recommended to Roman Catholics by papal encyclicals in 1879 and 1891. Nevertheless, a number of Roman Catholic philosophers have preferred other Neo-Scholastic systems to Neo-Thomism; in fact, owing to recent drastic changes on the Catholic scene, some Roman Catholic philosophers have ventured even beyond the limits of Scholasticism, including, for example, Maurice Blondel (1861–1949) and Teilhard de Chardin (1881–1955).

Neo-Scholastic philosophies include Augustianism (Intuitionists, Actualists, Willists); Scotism (favored among the Franciscans); Suarezianism (based on the moderate Thomism of the Spanish Jesuit, Francisco Suarez (1548–1617); and Thomism. As the dominant philosophy, Thomism has been ably represented by Jacques Maritain, Etienne Gilson, and many other eminent philosophers. In addition, there are two special groups of Thomistic philosophers: the Synthetic group, who combine Thomism with other types of Neo-Scholastic doctrines; and the Molinists, who adhere to the views of the Spanish Jesuit Luis de Molina (1535–1600).

Thomism, endorsed by leading Roman Catholic philosophers in Europe and North and South America, constitutes one of the largest philosophical schools in the world, rivalled only by Communist groups (adhering to Dialectical Materialism) in its appeal to vast numbers of people. Its chief center in recent years has been the *Institut Superieur de Philosophie* (founded by Cardinal Désiré

Mercier) at the University of Louvain. Other important centers include the *Institut Catholique* in Paris, where Jacques Maritain, the foremost living Neo-Thomist, was Professor of Philosophy; *Cattolica Università del Sacro Cuore* (founded by Agostino Gemelli) in Milan, Italy; the *Albertinum* in Fribourg, Switzerland; *Instituto Luis Vives de Filosofía* of the "Consejo Superior de Investigaciónes Científicas" in Madrid, Spain; a center at the *University of Notre Dame* in the United States; the *Pontifical Institute of Mediaeval Studies* (directed by Etienne Gilson) in Toronto, Canada; and the *Angelicum* and the *Gregorian University,* in Rome. Most of the Thomist centers mentioned are administered by Jesuit or Dominican Orders.

THE TWENTY-FOUR THESES OF THOMISM

The Sacred Congregation of Studies has issued "The Twenty-four Fundamental Theses of Official Catholic Philosophy" which were translated by P. Lumbreras and published in the *Homiletic and Pastoral Review* (1923). Of these twenty-four theses, the first seven deal with ontology, the next five with cosmology, the next nine with psychology, and the remaining three with the philosophy of religion. The theses were stated in the *Homiletic and Pastoral Review* as follows:

1. Potency and Act so divide being that whatsoever exists either is Pure Act, or is necessarily composed of Potency and Act, as to its primordial and intrinsic principles.

2. Act, because it is perfection, is not limited except by Potency, which is capacity for perfection. Therefore, in the order in which the Act is pure, it is unlimited and unique; but in that in which it is finite and manifold, it comes into a true composition with Potency.

3. Wherefore, in the exclusive domain of existence itself God alone subsists, He alone is the most simple. Everything else, which participates in existence, has a nature whereby existence is restricted, and is composed of essence and existence as of two really distinct principles.

4. Being, which derives its name from existence, is not predicated univocally of God and creatures; nor yet merely equivocally, but analogically, by the analogy both of attribution and of proportionality.

5. There is, moreover, in every creature a real composition of subsisting subject with forms secondarily added—that is, accidents; but such a composition could not be understood unless the existence were received into a distinct essence.

6. Besides the absolute accidents there is also a relative accident, or "toward something." For although "toward something" does not mean, by its own nature, anything inhering in something, frequently, however, it has a cause in things, and, therefore, a real entity distinct from the subject.

7. The spiritual creature is as to its essence altogether simple. Yet there remains a twofold composition in it: that, namely, of essence with existence and that of substance with accidents.

8. The corporeal creature, on the contrary, is in its very essence composed of Potency and Act. Such a Potency and Act of the essential order are designated by the names of matter and form.

9. Neither of those parts has existence, properly speaking; produced or destroyed; nor is placed in a Category except by way of reduction, as a substantial principle.

10. Although extension into integral parts follows corporeal nature, it is not, however, the same for a body to be a substance and to be extended. For substance of itself is indivisible; not certainly after the manner of a point, but after the manner of that which is outside the order of dimension. On the other hand, Quantity, which makes substance to be extended, really differs from substance, and is a veritable accident.

11. Matter as subjected to quantity is the principle of individuation or numerical distinction—impossible among pure spirits—whereby individuals of the same species are distinct from each other.

12. It is also Quantity that makes a body to be circumscriptively in one place and to be incapable, by any means, of such a presence in any other place.

13. Bodies are divided into two classes: some are living, others without life. In living bodies, in order to have intrinsically a moving part and moved part in the same subject, the substantial form, called the soul, requires an organic disposition, or heterogeneous parts.

14. Souls of the vegetative and sensitive order, properly speaking, do not subsist and are not produced, but merely exist and are produced as a principle whereby the living thing exists and lives. Since they depend entirely on matter, at the dissolution of the compound, they are indirectly destroyed.

15. On the contrary, the human soul subsists by itself, and is created by God when it can be infused into a sufficiently disposed subject, and is incorruptible and immortal by nature.

16. This same rational soul is so united to the body as to be its single substantial form. By it man is man, and animal, and living, and body, and substance, and being. Soul, therefore, gives man every essential degree of perfection. It communicates to the body, furthermore, the act of existence whereby itself exists.

17. Faculties of a twofold order, organic and inorganic, naturally spring from the human soul. The subject of the organic, to which sense belongs, is the compound. The subject of the inorganic is the soul alone. The intellect, then, is a faculty intrinsically independent of any organ.

18. Intellectuality necessarily follows immateriality, and in such a manner that the degree of intellectuality is in proportion to the remoteness from matter. The adequate object of intellection is being as such; but the proper object of the human intellect, in the present state of union, is restricted to the essences abstracted from material conditions.

19. We, therefore, receive our knowledge from sensible things. But since no sensible thing is actually intelligible, besides the intellect which is properly

intelligent we must admit in the soul an active power which abstracts the intelligible forms from the phantasms.

20. Through these species we directly know the universal; the singular we know by the senses, and also by the intellect through a conversion to the phantasms; we rise by analogy to the knowledge of the spiritual.

21. The will follows, does not precede, the intellect; it necessarily desires that which is offered to it as a good which entirely satisfies the appetite; it freely chooses among several good things that are proposed as desirable by the wavering judgment. Election, then, follows the last practical judgment; still, it is the will which determines it to be the last.

22. That God exists we do not know by immediate intuition, nor do we demonstrate it *a priori*, but certainly *a posteriori*, that is, by things which are made, arguing from effect to cause. Namely, from things, which are in movement and cannot be the adequate principle of their motion, to the first mover immovable; from the procession of worldly things from causes, which are subordinated to each other, to the first uncaused cause; from corruptible things, which are indifferent alike to being and non-being, to the absolutely necessary being; from things, which, according to their limited perfection of existence, life, intelligence, are more or less perfect in their being, their life, their intelligence, to Him who is intelligent, living, and being in the highest degree; finally, from the order, which exists in the universe, to the existence of a separate intelligence which ordained, disposed, and directs things to their end.

23. The Divine Essence is well proposed to us as constituted in its metaphysical concept by its identity with the exercised actuality of its existence, or, in other terms, as the very subsisting being; and by the same token it exhibits to us the reason of its infinity in perfection.

24. By the very purity of His being God is, therefore, distinguished from all finite beings. Hence, in the first place, it is inferred that the world could not have proceeded from God except through creation; secondly, that the creative power, which directly affects beings as being, cannot be communicated, even miraculously, to any finite nature; and, finally, that no created agent exercises any influence on the being of any effect except through a motion received from the first cause.

JACQUES MARITAIN

The French philosopher Jacques Maritain (1882–   ), the most distinguished of modern Thomists, developed a comprehensive philosophy which (not withstanding its indebtedness to Bergsonism, Existentialism, and Personalism) he has himself described as strictly Thomist, or Paleo-Thomist—as a correct interpretation of the precise unaltered doctrines of Aquinas.

Maritain's Metaphysical Doctrines. As a Thomistic Existentialist, he agreed with the exponents of Atheistic Existentialism about the primacy of existence, but disagreed with their rejection of essence (or nature); in fact, he interpreted the philosophy of Aquinas to justify the conclusion that mere existence without essence, that is, the act of existing without rational, intelligible natural Being (of which man becomes aware through his senses and intellect) would be impossible. The Atheistic Existentialism of Heidegger and Sartre leaves the world orderless, unintelligible, impelling its adherents to devise novel arguments in an effort to make atheism livable. No such difficulty confronts Thomistic metaphysics, which defines truth in the traditional Scholastic sense as "the adequation of the immanence in act of our thought with that which exists outside our thought." Our sense activity occurs on an immediate level of experience without conscious awareness of itself, but we acquire true knowledge of reality through intuition, and our intellect interprets that reality as Being or nature. Our intellect converts existing things into immaterial (spiritual) entities by abstracting from them the intelligibles, the objects of thought. Thus Being is known intuitively. *Pure act* makes ultimate reality intelligible. God, as pure act, through his self-awareness makes human nature possible. The divine intellect perceiving its own essence creates the idea of man realized in the existence and nature of mankind.

Thomists distinguish between actual Being and potential Being, between act and potency. The act *is* (exists in actuality), while a potential thing or quality represents only the possibility of existing. A child, who is a potential musical genius, is only potentially a musician, possessing the *power* to become one. Everything possesses act and potency except God who is pure act. Actual Being and potential Being are comparable to existence and essence, respectively. All Beings with the exception of God consist of existence and essence. Existence is the actualizing of essence. In every concrete Being, existence and essence are inseparable. The doctrine that there is a transitional state in which objects advance from potency to act—the Thomistic theory of *Becoming*—assumes that there is a real substance in the process of becoming what was previously only a possibility, thus moving from potency to actuality.

The essence of an entity is its intelligible nature apprehended within the realm of one's ideas; it is attained by simple apprehension or the intellect's first operation. By making a judgment we conceptualize the existence of an object; our intellect forms the idea of Being. "At the instant when the finger points to that which the eye sees, at the instant when sense perceives, in its blind fashion, without intellection or mental word, that *this exists;* at that instant the intellect says (in a judgment), *this being is* or *exists* and at the same time (in a concept), *being.*" Existence cannot be separated from essence. Being is not to be regarded as a universal concept, for "being is that which exists or is able to exist, that which exercises or is able to exercise existence." To exist is to act. The essence (nature) of any object is its power to exist and to be known, not the act of existing; the act itself is primary, more fundamental than the power or mere potentiality.

Maritain's View of Thomistic Ethics. Maritain referred to Thomism as Existentialist Intellectualism. God exists as pure act and in so existing creates intelligence and love. Man reaches the summit of wisdom when he becomes capable of loving God lovingly, for this is human perfection. Ethical conduct consists of activity directed toward a good end which man naturally tends to seek, and the goal of man's striving is to love God who is all good and devoid of evil. Ethical life therefore requires prudent direction of one's moral acts in obedience to conscience (or reason) so as to achieve that perfect love of God which gives significance to one's experience of being a living self and spiritual personality.

Maritain emphasized a Realistic aspect of Thomism in the sense that all-knowing God knows reality as it exists and also as it has the potentiality to become, including the nature of man; thus the all-knowing, pure God possesses only good, being devoid of evil, but knows the potential evil in the mind of man, even though the idea of evil is otherwise completely absent in the divine intellect.

Maritain's Personalism. In *The Person and the Common Good* Maritain set forth a doctrine of Personalism based on Thomistic philosophy. The main emphasis is upon the human being as nature's most perfect creation, possessing a material aspect of individuality and a spiritual aspect of personality. Man is both carnal and spiritual, a Being endowed with co-principles of matter and soul, which however constitute one substance. The flesh is animated by spirit. By virtue of the spiritual soul, our Being subsists. The soul is a creative unity, independent and free. "Personality is subsistence of the spiritual soul communicated to the human composite."

The personality of God is a superexistence of intellection and love. Man's highest attitude is his resemblance to God in whose image he was created. His spiritual soul has the capacity of knowing and loving God, thus participating in the life of God. Although man's individuality and personality are not separate metaphysical aspects of his Being, it is by means of his spiritual personality that he knows and loves God, that he is a moral person; conversely, it is by means of his material individuality (when it is given ascendency) that evil arises. But the corporeal individual is not in itself evil. On the contrary, when it is properly related to the personality, it is good.

This view of the nature of man is consistent with the Thomistic doctrine of *hylomorphism* (postulating a Dualism of matter and form) which identifies Thomists as Moderate Realists. Not only do all contingent Beings (these include everything except God) possess matter and form (spirit) or potency and actuality, but also there is a hierarchy of Beings based upon the extent of the actuality attained, that is, upon the perfection which each Being achieves. At the lowest level is matter devoid of any power to reach toward spiritual activity; such primary matter is like nothingness or non-Being. A superior Being is one which purposefully reaches toward higher degrees of form or spirit; consequently, a spiritual personality is a superior form of Being to vegetative or animal forms. Man is on a high level of Being as shown by his ability to will freely and to choose whatever goal his intellect identifies as his proper function.

Thomistic Epistemology. A similar hierarchy is applied to levels of knowledge. In his *The Degrees of Knowledge* Maritain discussed a hierarchy of types of knowledge, concluding that man should seek metaphysical truth, that metaphysics is the archetype of philosophy, and that knowledge is correct only if it discloses metaphysical realities or essences. Reason as a means of gaining knowledge is supplemented by superrational (mystical) knowledge, just as the natural order has its complement in the supernatural order. To gain knowledge about supernatural realities, Christian wisdom, a composite of theological and mystical wisdom is required. Maritain pointed out that we derive knowledge intuitively from the intellect, discursively from reason. The practical side of the intellect, represented by the will, is a reaction to spiritual realities, but the speculative aspect of the intellect is a superior means of attaining knowledge.

Maritain's Humanism. In his *True Humanism* Maritain distinguished between Anthropocentric Humanism and his own doctrines of Theocentric Humanism or Integral Humanism. Anthropocentric

Humanism secularizes by deifying man without admitting the necessity of including God. In its advocacy of human rights and powers, it portrays evil as an imperfect stage which will be overcome in the evolutionary process. Its social consequences have included the loss of individual personality, paving the way for the collectivism of Marxism and Nazism. In Anthropocentric Humanism, God becomes a *Volksgeist*, a political body, an idol.

Theocentric Humanism (or Integral Humanism) states that man is united with God by means of a process wherein a new Christian order integrates the human with the divine. Man is viewed as a body which he has acquired through evolution, and a soul, which is a creation of God. Man's dignity comes from his having been created in the image of God; human rights have also been derived from the Deity. Natural laws imbedded in the nature of man follow from eternal law existing in the nature of God. By using practical reason, man knows and implements such laws. He is naturally inclined toward moral law (natural law) through connaturality or congeniality.

The history of civilization is invigorated through reason and love; both man and God participate in love which vitalizes friendships and raises unequals to the status of equals. Man's sacrificial activity is unimpeded by the fear of death, since he knows that death is not his end. Everything is directed toward God, man's final end and stage of perfection. History acquires significance and direction as it advances toward a supreme ideal, the State of brotherly love in which justice and friendship prevail with ever increasing perfection.

ETIENNE GILSON

As an interpreter of Thomistic philosophy, Gilson (1884–   ) devoted himself to explaining the interrelationships between Christianity and Greek philosophy, and to constructing in this way a Christian world view (*Weltanschauung*).

He declared that the spirit of medieval Christian philosophy was consistent with Greek secular thought, and that the revealed truths of the Christian Bible agree with Greek rational philosophy. Since God is identified with Being and efficiency, whatever exists owes its existence to the creative action of a free, perfect, Supreme Being. Christian revelation is "an indispensable auxiliary to reason." From Gilson's point of view, faith seeks the truths or evidence beyond reach of intellect alone. Thus the difference between medieval Christian thought and Greek philosophy arises from the special contribution of revelation. The medieval philosophers equated Being with God, identifying both as the same ultimate reality, whereas the Greeks regarded Being as identical with intelligibility and perfection. According to Thomistic philosophy, sense reality is not true reality, for only in God are essence and existence identical. Gilson stated that if Aristotle and the other Greek philosophers had realized this fact, they would have understood God to be the Creator who created the world out of nothing (*ex nihilo*) and fashioned man in the divine image, in the image of Being. God's self-sufficiency and perfection are implicit in the fact of his existence.

The Moral Universe. An uncritical interpretation of Christian philosophy may at first seem pessimistic, owing to the doctrine of man's fallen nature, Jesus' renunciation of wordly goods, St. Paul's condemnation of the flesh, and the like; but on careful examination, Christian philosophy is seen to be optimistic, for, instead of denying the existence of evil, it sets out to regulate, combat, and destroy evil because the universe is at bottom not evil but good, and it is ultimately Being, God, and goodness. God is the supreme good and glory of every created thing. All action leads to God; the act of contemplating God, the supreme good, is man's greatest blessing. The Christian universe is good in itself, but owing to its incomplete development, it is necessary to effect this good through the realization of its true Being. God's providence governs man, and it becomes man's ethical duty to live according to God's will.

Human Nature and Ethical Conduct. Man is a complex (but single) substance composed of soul and body, but his substantiality is identified with only one of his two constitutive principles, namely, that of the soul. As pure activity (act), the human soul is an ultimate substance, capable of development without the body, and of continuing after the dissolution of the body by withdrawing from the body. The soul, as a simple substance, is indestructible, yet it develops its actuality in its fullness via the body. On the other hand, the body lacks both actuality and subsistence, except that which it receives from its form, namely, the soul. Thus, souls are immortal substances, capable of subsistence without a material body or sense organs, but souls develop their activity with the co-operation of a material body and its sense organs. Man is a unified composite whose soul gives substance to his body in which the soul subsists.

Gilson referred to Christian Socratism as the correct method of combining knowledge about God with knowledge about the self. Through use of his reason, man can discover the proper goals of his life activities and advance toward the fulfillment of his nature. The supreme objective is to come face to face with God, to achieve goodness and happiness during eternal life in the society of God. Gilson defined the work of the intellect as the search for truth, thus being faithful to one's own essence by uniting the intellect with the divine Being. Love, too, has God as its object, and even love of the self is the same as love of God since man was created in the image of God. The more man fulfills himself (his essence), the more godlike he becomes, for he perfects his Being, perfects himself as God's image, and achieves the happiness and beatitude he seeks. Man is endowed with an indestructible free will which has the power to choose among alternative purposes. This freedom of choice constitutes Christian liberty, but Gilson pointed out that despite its autonomy, the will is subject to moral law, to the law of God, an infallible guide which must be followed but which actually enhances the freedom of the person instead of destroying it.

Elements of Christian Philosophy. Noting the diversity of ideas among Scholastic philosophers, Gilson nevertheless tried to set forth basic Thomistic doctrines which would harmonize and unify Christian philosophy and faith. He accepted Aquinas' arguments for the existence of God, identifying God with Being, perfection, pure thought, and infinite goodness. All substances were created by God out of nothing. As a soul, man constitutes an intellective principle, reasons, and is immortal, the highest earthly creation in the hierarchy which God has established, ranging from the lowest level of physical objects to the higher level of the vegetative kingdom and to the still higher level of the animal kingdom. The lower class of things must always be subordinate to the higher classes. This principle should be applied in human society in which the followers or inferiors must obey their leaders or superiors, with a single sovereign ruling over all other persons. Of the three main types of constitutions (monarchy, aristocracy, and democracy), the best is rule by a monarch, assisted by his able aristocrats, with the democratic election of rulers.

In *The Unity of Philosophical Experience* (1937), Gilson analyzed the relationship between the history of philosophy and the nature of philosophical knowledge. He referred to the historical attempts to gain unified, integrated philosophical knowledge (by applying a systematic approach to problems) as providing a philosophical experience, concluding that "there is a centuries-long experience of what philosophical knowledge is" and that "such an experience exhibits a remarkable unity." Finally, he set forth conclusions based upon his analysis of the history of philosophy, as follows: (1) "Philosophy always buries its undertakers"—that is, a philosophy outlives its philosopher and is often resurrected. (2) "By his very nature, man is a metaphysical animal"—that is, man is a philosophical or rational Being. (3) "Metaphysics is the knowledge gathered by a naturally transcendent reason in its search for the first principles, or first causes, of what is given in sensible experience." (4) "As metaphysics aims at transcending all particular knowledge, no particular science is competent either to solve metaphysical problems, or to refute their metaphysical solutions." (5) "The failures of the metaphysicians flow from their unguarded use of a principle of unity present in the human mind." (6) "Since Being is the first principle of all human knowledge, it is *a fortiori* the first principle of metaphysics." (This conclusion follows from the assumption that human thought always concerns Being, for it is inconceivable to think about absolute nothingness.) (7) "All failures of metaphysics should be traced to the fact that the first principle of human knowledge has been either overlooked or misused by the metaphysicians."

Thus we see that Gilson's interpretations of ancient Greek philosophy and the doctrines of Aquinas resulted in a comprehensive philosophy of Being based on rational, scientific principles supplemented and modified or corrected by Christian faith in the divine laws governing the universe.

Chapter 21

Phenomenology

The Phenomenological movement, like so many other contemporary schools of philosophy, is in a state of transition, with its influence reaching out in a number of directions. Its doctrines have had an impact upon the Neorealism of Moore and his followers and upon the Existentialist views of Heidegger, Sartre, and Merleau-Ponty. (Heidegger's classic *Being and Time* was published in the 1927 *Yearbook for Phenomenology and Philosophical Research.*) The beginnings of the movement may be traced to the works of Franz Brentano (1838–1917) and Carl Stumpf (1848–1936), but its major development must be credited to Edmund Husserl (1859–1938), who, with Moritz Geiger (1880–1937), Alexander Pfänder (1870–1941), Adolf Reinach (1883–1917), and Max Scheler (1874–1928) formulated the platform of Phenomenological principles published in 1913 under the title, *Yearbook for Philosophy and Phenomenological Research.* As early as 1905 Husserl's ideas attracted wide attention in German philosophical circles, and his point of view was accepted by noted philosophers, including Theodor Lipps (1851–1914) of the University of Munich. The movement spread abroad through the contributions of Husserl's students (at the University of Göttingen), many of whom came to the United States during the Nazi period.

Phenomenology has been applied to numerous disciplines. Lipps applied it to aesthetics; Max Scheler to anthropology, axiology, and the philosophy of religion; Nicolai Hartmann (1882–1951) to ethics; Rudolf Otto (1869–1937) to the philosophy of religion; Karl Mannheim (1893–1947) to sociology; Ludwig Binswanger (1881–1966) to psychology and psychiatry; Viktor E. Frankl (1905–   ) to psychiatry and psychotherapy; and Carl Rogers (1902–   ), to the psychology of personality. So far as the central doctrines of Phenomenology are concerned, the most significant contributions were those of Brentano, Husserl, Scheler, Hartmann, and Merleau-Ponty.

FRANZ BRENTANO

Although Brentano, strictly speaking, could not be regarded as a Phenomenologist, nevertheless his *Psychology from an Empirical Standpoint* (1874) and the influence he exerted upon his student Husserl set the stage for this contemporary movement. His emphasis on inner perception as a source of intuitive, infallible self-knowledge preceded Husserl's concept of Phenomenology as the intuitive study of essences through descriptive analysis of inner experience. Brentano's main purpose was to determine the precise contents of the consciousness of an object without attempting to describe the external object itself.

Inner Perception. Brentano was an Empiricist who believed that all philosophical conclusions must be derived from human experience, but he rejected introspection as an unreliable cue to reality and he advocated instead the analysis of immediate conscious experience, which he called inner perception or *ideal intuition*. Such experience, he said, is self-evident, infallible, becoming known to us at once in the form of emotions, desires, ideas, judgments, and the like. However, noting that all immediate experiences have a direction as well as a content, he formulated the concept of intentionality, a term familiar to Scholastic philosophers but to which he gave a new connotation and attributed decisive importance as the basic psychological phenomenon. The medieval Scholastics had thought of *intentional* as referring to the mental counterpart of an object, its *inexistence*. Brentano meant by intention the fact that the contents of conscious experience are directed toward objects which are immanent in consciousness. All psychical phenomena refer to objects; thus, an idea refers to the object which it represents, a desire refers to the object desired, and a judgment refers to a proposition which is acknowledged. But for Brentano intentional inexistence pertains only to psychical phenomena; it is completely absent in the physical realm. (Intentionality became a most important concept in Husserl's Phenomenology and, in a somewhat different interpretation and application, in Sartre's Existentialism.) He saw in all intentionality some reference to an object; that is to say, every psychic phenomenon in consciousness is an act which refers to an object beyond its own consciousness, but the object remains immanent in consciousness, for it is not merely a target at which intentional awareness aims. He explained that there can be no consciousness of hearing without some object that is being heard, no consciousness of believing without something which is believed, no act of hoping without that for which one possesses hope, no act of striving without that for which one strives, no joyousness (as a mental experience) without some object about which one can be joyous. The psychical phenomenon or act is the secondary object; the phenomenon to which it refers, that which appears as if it were external to consciousness, is the primary object.

Types of Psychical Acts. There are three types of psychical acts or psychological phenomena: (1) *ideas*, which are the images in sense experiences; (2) *judgments;* and (3) *emotive acts,* i.e., desires and feelings. Each of these psychological acts refers to its respective object and displays characteristics ascribed to the object to which it refers. We must admit that all objects have a reality in themselves, but what they seem to be as they appear in diverse forms will depend upon the intentional reference, that is, upon the kind of psychological act as one of representation, judgment, or feeling.

Thus, Brentano's descriptive psychology dealt with the contents of psychical consciousness and made no effort to analyze the intentional referent objects as real things to which the psychical acts correspond or refer. In this way he contributed a new approach taken up by the Phenomenological movement. Upon this foundation was built a Phenomenological theory of ethics in which value reference is a self-evident fact of experience and moral values are as real as any other objects of intentionality. Upon this foundation was also built the Phenomenological theory of essential structures based upon an analysis of subjective processes.

EDMUND HUSSERL

Husserl's Phenomenological ideas owed much to the works of Brentano, Stumpf, Descartes, and Kant, as well as reflecting to a lesser extent the influence of Plato, St. Augustine, Leibniz, Hume, Hegel, Mill, James, and Royce. He thought of Phenomenology as a descriptive analysis of subjective processes or as the intuitive study of essences. It was to be the task of philosophy to describe the data of consciousness without bias or prejudice, ignoring all metaphysical and scientific theories so that an accurate description and analysis of the phenomena within consciousness could be intuitively experienced and reported. Philosophy must begin with phenomena; thus the battle cry of Husserlians is: "To the things themselves." Phenomena are the manifestations or the ways in which objects present themselves through their appearances.

Phenomenological Method. Three techniques are necessary for the analysis of subjective processes that lead to the goal of Phenomenological inquiry, namely, the finding of essences. The first is Phenomenological reduction; the second is eidetic reduction or abstraction; and the third is an analysis of the "correlation between the phenomenon of cognition and the object of cognition."

By Phenomenological reduction Husserl meant the exclusion from consideration of everything which is transcendent, such as Kant's things-in-themselves, and anything else which is derived through scientific or logical inference. Only what is immediately and immanently presented to consciousness is to be considered. The rest must be *bracketed* out (a term he borrowed from mathematics) and any judgment concerning it must be held in suspension. From the ancient Greek philosophers, the Skeptics, he borrowed the term *epoché* to signify the suspension of judgment. Like Descartes he sought only the knowledge which would be absolutely certain. Phenomenological reduction, then, restricts our attention to the absolute data of pure consciousness, that is, to the pure phenomena of consciousness. Everything must be reduced to this given content of consciousness as pure phenomena. The given content is the "principle of principles" whereby the object of intuition, "authentic reality," is presented to us. Of this given content, we can be certain, for it is the only indubitable and authentic datum; as such it is apodictic, i.e., self-evident and absolutely certain. The indubitable given content of consciousness stands prior to all scientific interpretation, philosophical interpretation, and theorizing. This process of analyzing all pure phenomena, excluding transcendent or trans-phenomenal matter, is termed the Phenomenological reduction proper. The process excludes everything which Kant spoke of as transcending the bounds of experience, namely, things-in-themselves, noumenal objects, as well as the cause-and-effect relationships of science which, as Hume pointed out, are not within the scope of impressions. Also excluded are scientific explanations of conscious phenomena. By excluding transcendent objects we concentrate our attention on essences, which we know at once through the act of *seeing*. By means of *a priori* intuition, we become directly aware of the objects we look at as they appear in our consciousness, but we cannot know transcendent objects directly as part of our consciousness. We see a green object, for example, and green color is immanent in our consciousness, but when we postulate the transcendent color, it is not immediately sensed but merely described scientifically as consisting of light waves measuring 550 millimicrons in length. In Phenomenological reduction, the color actually experienced is reduced to pure phenomena of consciousness, while the color described scientifically is bracketed out or held in suspension (*epoché*). The color we experience directly constitutes pure evidence; it is known with absolute certainty.

These objects appearing in our consciousness and known with complete certainty also have a universal aspect which becomes known to us through the technique of eidetic reduction, a method of abstracting essences, the Ideas underlying the pure phenomena of consciousness. (Husserl borrowed the term *eidetic* from Plato, who used the Greek *eidos* to denote his Ideals.) The essence we seek to abstract by means of eidetic reduction is the intelligible structure of the phenomena found in consciousness. Husserl defined Phenomenology as the doctrine of essences or the study of these essential structures of the phenomena found in consciousness. In eidetic reduction, we apply *Logos* to phenomena and thus utilize Phenomenology, instead of Phenomenalism. *Logos* (or the Platonic changeless forms) must be applied to phenomena to give them stability, a base, and thus rescue them from a state of constant change and unreality.

Essence is unlike pure phenomenon by virtue of its universality; that is, it is an experience which is shared by all persons alike. Pure phenomenon possesses a subjectivity to the particular Ego which experiences it, but essence possesses an intersubjectivity, a characteristic shared by all persons. The experience of sound as pure phenomenon is in the private subjective state of the person experiencing it, but the essence of sound, its universal characteristics (comparable to mathematical principles), is common to all persons (intersubjectivity). Husserl was opposed to psychologism, the theory that mathematical and logical laws are derived from psychology.

Phenomena are things themselves exhibited or represented in consciousness, but it must not be assumed that things send their "representatives into consciousness." Although things are given as if separated from appearance, they are essentially inseparable. We must discern a distinction between the *phenomenon* and the *object* of cognition, or between *appearance* and *that which appears*, or the "givenness of the appearing and the givenness of the object." This third level of orientation calls for a detailed analysis, a comparison between the object as presented in consciousness and the object of knowledge—for example, between the phenomenon of sound perception and the constitutive or intelligible essence of sound.

The Triad: Ego, Cogito, Cogitata. Through Phenomenological suspension (the *epoché*) everything in the world is reduced to pure phenomenon, that is, everything which can be so reduced. The Phenomenological residue which remains after Phenomenological reduction is the realm of pure consciousness which is absolutely certain and apodictic; i.e., it cannot be doubted or held in suspension (*epoché*). Husserl (following the Cartesian *Cogito*) characterizes this residual world as a three-fold structure resulting from the triadic formula: Ego, cogito, cogitata. From it, we derive the Phenomenological residue: (1) the Phenomenological Ego, (2) the cogitations, and (3) the cogitata.

The Phenomenological Ego. The Phenomenological Ego is not to be confused with the transcendental Ego; the former is the psychological or empirical Ego which is found in the individual's passing stream of consciousness, whereas the latter is the observer which is found behind this stream of consciousness. The Phenomenological Ego is not a substance as Descartes supposed, but an activity, a *monad*, as Leibniz taught. It is a philosophizing Ego, a "pure Ego with its cogitationes." As such, it is apodictic and ubiquitous. As far as the world is concerned, it is nothing but what the Ego is aware of and what appears in its cogitations. "The whole meaning and reality of the world rests exclusively on such cogitationes." I, as an Ego, am not another item in the world, but am the stream of consciousness in which the world acquires meaning and reality.

Husserl called the pure Ego and pure subjectivity "the wonder of wonders," considering it a mystery that the world should contain a Being which is aware of its own existence. The Phenomenological Ego becomes the fundamental fact of the universe in which all truth is found. The motto of the Socratic Delphic oracle, "Know thyself!" acquires new import, as does the injunction of St. Augustine: "Do not wish to go out; go back into yourself. Truth dwells in the inner man."

Cogitations (or Noesis). The Ego's cogitations comprise all of its acts, including doubting, understanding, affirming, denying, willing, refusing, imagining, feeling, judging, valuing, and all of the intentional acts comparable to the intentionality of Brentano. The Ego exists in its cogitations. Cogitating is the *act* of the Ego, an act which Husserl in his later writings termed *noesis*.

The Cogitata (or Noema). The act of cogitation must refer to that which is thought. The referents of cogitations, that is, their intentional objects, are termed cogitata, or noema. (The Greek word *noema* means "that which is perceived.") According to Husserl's theory of intentionality which he to a great degree appropriated from Brentano, every cogitation has its cogitata, every noesis its noema. Every thought has that which is thought about, every perception has that which is imagined, etc.—every intention has its referent object. It does not matter whether or not the noema is idea, for its truth rests upon its being a correlate of one's own intentionality.

Transcendental Phenomenological Idealism. In all perceptions, feelings, and thoughts, we find an Ego, an unobserved observer residing in them or a transcendental subjectivity, that is, a transcendental Ego, which is unaffected by transcendental reduction. The philosophizing Ego, while it suspends all beliefs about the world's reality because everything in it is subject to Cartesian doubt, in the very process of *epoché* finds itself the only "apodictically certain being." Truth dwells within. The world may be transcendent (beyond the bounds of experience), but Ego is transcendental (always present in experience). The individual, as a transcendental Ego, apprehends himself as an Ego. The pure or transcendental Ego is prior to the world and constitutes the sole object capable of judgment. The *Ego cogito* apodictically precedes the world's existence (cogitata) as far as any given individual is concerned. Through transcendental reduction, a Phenomenological Ego can become an observer of itself, aware of itself, self-conscious.

"Everything which is and has reality for me, that is, for man, exists only in my own consciousness." Every conceivable entity that has any meaning, and every Being, must fall within the realm of transcendental subjectivity. To know the world, we must gain knowledge of it through the Ego, through self-disclosure, that is, through "Ego-logical science." Reality is disclosed through the transcendental Ego, within the realm of its consciousness.

Husserl is not a solipsist; on the contrary, his doctrine of *intersubjectivity* assumes the existence of other people. The role of *empathy* and the fact that essences (the intelligible structures of phenomenal objects) are common to all persons compelled him to accept the belief in alter Egos, the conclusion that other Egos like his own exist, a view which identifies him in a sense with the doctrines of the "community of selves" set forth in the Idealism of Josiah Royce. Husserl referred to this concept as the "intersubjective transcendental community." It is through intersubjectivity that we attain objectivity concerning the external world. "I experience the world not as my own private world, but as an intersubjective world." Through this transcendental intersubjective world consisting of a community of monads, we can realize a universal philosophy by way of universal self-knowledge.

The Lebenswelt (Life-World). The Husserlian concept of *Lebenswelt*, which was little known or discussed during the lifetime of Husserl, became widely known through the emphasis given to it in the writings of Maurice Merleau-Ponty (1907–1961). The *Lebenswelt* is that world which encompasses our immediate experience, the world which makes up the entire complex of our conscious life. The *Lebenswelt* or life-world is inaccessible to us when we try to reach it through a scientific interpretation of it or through a mere reaction or natural attitude toward it. To reach the life-world we must utilize a special kind of reduction—Phenomenological reduction—which holds scientific interpretation suspended and thus allows us to view directly the *Lebenswelt* and see its structural reality.

MAX SCHELER

The Phenomenologist Max Scheler, second only to Husserl in importance, was mainly responsible for the rapid spread of Phenomenological doctrines in French and Spanish philosophical circles. His work may be divided into three stages: (1) a pro-Kantian period, reflecting also the influence of Rudolf Eucken, his teacher; (2) a period emphasizing ethical, theistic, Christian writings; and (3) a transition period (ended by death at the age of fifty-four years) of pantheistic views with a leaning toward a philosophy of Evolutionary Naturalism not unlike Bergson's position. Scheler's most significant work, *Formalism in Ethics and the Nonformal Ethic of Value,* was published during the second period, in the *Yearbook for Philosophy and Phenomenological Research* (1915).

Scheler's Phenomenology. Husserl had a profound influence on the philosophy of Scheler, but Scheler regarded Phenomenology as a way of viewing things rather than as a method or as mental *act* as Husserl understood it. Scheler's was "a picture book Phenomenology." For him the Phenomenological attitude meant an experience of entering into an immediate relationship with objects, the things in experience. The Phenomenological experience is concerned with pure or Phenomenological facts (i.e., the contents of immediate experience that are given in pure intuition) which must be distinguished from natural facts and from scientific data. Phenomenological facts present themselves through immediate intuition and are not dependent upon our beliefs. The given contents of immediate experience constituting Phenomenological facts present us with the *whatness* of things.

With Phenomenological facts there is no possibility of illusion, for the intuitively given content and its symbolic representations coincide with one another. There is a de-symbolizing quality about Phenomenological experience, a return from the conceptual symbols of science to the intuitively known experience itself. The danger of symbols is that they disguise phenomena.

Since pure facts are given immediately in experience, they are known intuitively *a priori*, hence are independent of scientific knowledge, whether it be inductive or causal knowledge. *A priori* knowledge is untutored experience, the given contents of immediate experience in its qualitative fullness.

An intuitive Phenomenological experience is one which is "lived through," that is, one which penetrates the given *whatness* or essence of things. Scheler held in suspended judgment any conclusion as to the existence of things. He made no distinction between eidetic reduction and Phenomenological reduction, i.e., between the particular and its universal. Eidetic reduction proceeds from the particular to its universal essence, while Phenomenological reduction proceeds from existence to simple phenomenal *whatness*. Scheler's Phenomenology of essences (Phenomenological reduction) is an *a priori* insight into the essence (the whatness) of things as they are intuitively given in immediate experience.

Three Types of Knowledge. Scheler distinguished among three types of knowledge, each with its special objective. The first is knowledge of control and achievement, the second is knowledge of essence or culture, and the third is knowledge of metaphysical reality or salvation. The first is of service in giving us power over nature, society, and history; it is the knowledge which we gain through the experimental and specialized sciences. The second relates to philosophical knowledge, to the essences of which Husserl speaks. Its concern is ontological in that it gives us the whatness or the essence of things, supplying us with the answers to such questions as: What is the world? What is the essence of a plant? The third, the most important, deals with problems of philosophical anthropology: What is man? What is man's place in the universe? What is his relationship to God? In his *On the Eternal in Man* (1921) Scheler defined philosophy from the Phenomenological standpoint, as follows: "In essence philosophy is strictly self-evident insight, which cannot be either augmented or nullified by induction and which has *a priori* validity for contingent existents: insight into all such essences and essential interrelations of beings as are accessible to us from available instances, in the order and hierarchy as they stand in relation to the absolute entity and its essence."

Scheler's Ethical System and Value Theory.   Like Husserl, Scheler was influenced by the ideas of Brentano, particularly in developing the concept of ethical sanction which affirmed man's ability to discern good and evil by immediate apprehension. Man's *a priori* ability to gain insight intuitively into the structure of moral values is a remarkable human power beyond the scope of his reason. Accepting Pascal's dictum that "the heart has its reason that the mind does not know of," Scheler concluded that there is an "order of the heart" or "logic of the heart" comparable to that of the intellect. The values known *a priori* (intuitively) are genuine objective entities possessing a pure whatness (essence or content) of their own. The objective reality of values corresponds to the intentionality of them in human consciousness. In this sense, Scheler is a value realist. In contrast to the Kantian view of moral values as rational, formal standards, he believed such values possess a material content which becomes immediately known to the individual through a process of emotional intuition.

According to Scheler, there is a value relativism, or more accurately, a value perspectivism. Although values vary in different societies, and even within the same society at different times, they are nevertheless eternal, immutable, and absolute. Their variations merely indicate views of the same absolute value. It is as if each of us were peering through a different window at the same value, consequently obtaining a different perspective in relation to it.

The Hierarchy of Values.   Differences of worth among values are discernible by means of a value preferential sentiment. A person can distinguish differences both in degree and in mode (quality). The quantitative differences may be measured as to their respective worth on the basis of the following five criteria: (1) duration of value; (2) extentionality and divisibility of value (the extent to which a value can be distributed among a number of persons without its having to be divided into segments); (3) foundation values (the degree to which one value is relatively independent of others); (4) depth of satisfaction of value (the worth of a value increases in proportion to its ability to satisfy a person); and (5) the relative independence of a value in respect to the subject who is experiencing it.

The qualitative differences (the value-modalities) permit a hierarchical arrangement of values as follows (in order of their importance): (1) sensuous values, or those which a person experiences as pleasant or unpleasant; (2) vital values, those which enhance one's physical well-being; (3) spiritual values, those which encompass culture, aesthetics, philosophy, science, morality, and the like; (4) religious values, or sacred and holy values which are objects of reverence and worship.

Scheler also distinguished between two types of value carriers. A value carrier is a person or thing that serves as the bearer of a certain value. Since only persons bear moral values, these are values of persons, and they are more important than any values of things.

Scheler referred to personal models or value persons that represent or embody values and function as models after which we may pattern our own lives. These personal models may be arranged in a hierarchy in order of their importance, as follows: (1) the sensuous artist; (2) the pioneering spirit; (3) the hero; (4) the genius; and (5) the saint.

Ressentiment, Sympathy, and Love. Scheler evaluated the moral worth of *ressentiment,* sympathy, and love. In *Ressentiment* (1912, 1915) he attempted to defend Christian morality against the Nietzschean charge that it is a slave morality emanating from repressed resentment or hostility.

Ressentiment (French for resentment) is used as a technical term in Scheler's vocabulary (and Nietzsche's also); it refers to the repressed feelings of vengeance directed toward one's superiors or victors against whom one feels impotent. Christian love, said Scheler, is not *ressentiment* or a sign of weakness as Nietzsche asserted, but is actually an indication of strength.

Sympathy (the term which for Schopenhauer meant a worthy relationship but for Nietzsche an unworthy value to be condemned) was interpreted by Scheler as consideration for the feelings of another person, a concern with his emotional state, and not as a subjective feeling of one's own. Scheler defined love as the more basic ethical phenomenon—"that movement wherein every concrete individual object that possesses value achieves the highest value compatible with its nature and ideal vocation: or wherein it attains the ideal state of value intrinsic to its nature." Love is not passive, but an act which draws us toward the loved object and leads us to higher values. Love is the real basis of genuine sympathy, not vice versa. Love is theistic, acosmic, and personal, directed solely toward persons, and it is modeled upon man's love of God, the supreme object of love and the greatest good.

Philosophical Anthropology. By philosophical anthropology Scheler meant philosophy as it applies to man, to his place in the world and in society. During the middle period of his philosophical work, he conceived of man's proper function in the cosmos as one of modeling himself after God in terms of spiritual and religious values, emphasizing love and Personalism. Later he turned away from theistic to pantheistic views in the direction of Darwinism, Bergsonism, and Freudianism. In *Man's Place in Nature* (1928) he portrayed spiritual man as merely a sublimated animal organism (as Freud had done) whose lower or baser nature supplies the energy for his higher or spiritual nature. God is in the process of becoming; man, in co-operation with God, brings the deity into existence and perfection. Like Nietzsche before him, Scheler came to believe that since "God is dead," man must strive for "self-deification." With Bergson, he agreed that the universe is "a machine for the making of gods," and that this is man's primary task.

NICOLAI HARTMANN

The Neo-Kantian philosopher Nicolai Hartmann as early as 1921 formulated a Phenomenological value system which gave decided impetus to the Phenomenological movement. His views were elaborated in his three-volume work *Ethics* (1926), reflecting the influence of Plato, Aristotle, Aquinas, Kant (and the Neo-Kantian Cohen), and integrating three ethical systems: the ethical Intuitionism of Kant, the ethics of Aristotle, and the Phenomenological value system.

Intuitive Morality. Hartmann agreed with Scheler about the Phenomenological method, the Absolutist nature of values, and the theory that value essences are nonrational, known to us intuitively, not through reasoning. But he rejected the Personalist concepts of Scheler, particularly the theory of collective persons. He preferred Aristotle's conclusion that only individuals (not groups or aggregates of individuals) are persons. He also rejected Scheler's idea that God represents the purpose or end of man's moral striving. He believed moral freedom to be absolute, not determined by God, subject only to moral law.

Adhering to the theory that values are objective realities existing, like Plato's Ideals, in a realm of eternal essences, Hartmann attributed man's knowledge of values to an emotional, *a priori*, intuitive apprehension. Man comes into direct contact with the value sphere by means of his Pascalian "order of the heart," a sphere from which his rational powers are excluded. Only persons are capable of moral insight.

A Hierarchy of Values. The moral realm consists of an integrated system of values, even though that system appears fragmentary and incomplete to us because of our limited knowledge. The relative standing of a moral value on an axiological scale depends upon its relationship to the will. On such a scale, love is primal, standing at the apex. Values form a hierarchy based on their content, force, and height. They obey the "law of inverse variation of strength and height," which states that disobedience to a relatively lower value, such as respect for human life, may be much more serious (as in the case of murder) than disobedience to a higher value, such as love for other persons—e.g., murder is perhaps the most heinous deed known to man, whereas to withhold love is not considered the most serious offense.

Hartmann identified four basic types of moral values: (1) the *good* represents an indefinable and partially irrational value; (2) the *noble* is a knightly virtue, the antithesis of what is average or common; (3) *richness of experience* reflects the search for a full life; and (4) *purity* means sincerity of heart.

MAURICE MERLEAU-PONTY

Maurice Merleau-Ponty patterned his system of philosophy largely after Husserlian Phenomenology, but with Existentialist emphases and interpretations. In fact, he could probably be more accurately classified as an Existentialist, despite his distinctive contributions to Phenomenology. For some time he was a close associate of the Existentialist Jean-Paul Sartre, but later became a severe critic of Sartre's point of view. Central to his system of Phenomenological

Positivism is the theory of the primacy of perception, elaborated in his best-known work, *Phenomenology of Perception* (1945).

Return to Immediate Experience. He rejected traditional Realism and Idealism, as well as the metaphysical and epistemological ideas of Naturalism and Positivism. He described Phenomenology as the study of essences, stating that "all problems amount to finding definitions of essences: the essence of perception, or the essence of consciousness . . ." It was his view that *facticity* must be the starting point for the understanding of man and the cosmos. "We must return to the *Lebenswelt,* the world which we meet in the lived-in experience, our immediate experience of the world." We must make a distinction between self-evident perception and merely adequate thought or apodictic self-evidence. "The world is not what I think, but what I live through. I am open to the world, I have no doubt that I am in communication with it, but I do not possess it; it is inexhaustible." It is the facticity in the world that causes it to be the world, "just as the facticity of the *Cogito* is not an imperfection in itself, but rather what assures me of my existence. The eidetic method is the method of a Phenomenological Positivism which bases the possible on the real."

In opposition to Sartre's "we are condemned to freedom," Merleau-Ponty contends that, in consequence of our being in the world, "we are condemned to meaning," and we are always condemned to express something. All of our actions and thoughts have or acquire historical consequences. "History is other people" contrasts with Sartre's assertion that "hell is other people."

Higher Realms of Experience. Phenomenology is a disclosure of the world, and "philosophy is not the reflection of a preexisting truth, but, like art, the act of bringing truth into being." Primary reality is perceived *Lebenswelt* (life-world). We have direct access to Being and truth through perceptual consciousness, which provides us with the bases of higher-level structures of the *intellectual consciousness,* but higher-order experiences are not reducible to perceptual consciousness. Furthermore, perceptual consciousness embraces not only mere sense-data or qualia, but also the immediate experiences of an intersubjective or social *Lebenswelt.* It involves history, other people, and culture, as well as the world in which we ourselves act. Man's *Lebenswelt* includes many realms of experience, such as the ideal, the imaginary, the cultural, and the historical, as well as the world of perception. Each realm is distinct with a peculiar meaning and value structure of its own.

From the Phenomenology of perception we arrive at other levels of experience, such as the Phenomenology of intersubjective truth and that of moral, religious, and aesthetic experience. Since each realm of experience possesses a quality peculiar to itself, it cannot be reducible to perception, *per se,* because there are "several ways for consciousness to be consciousness." Yet, everything is found in perceptual consciousness, for in it we live and move and have our being. This conclusion does not, however, mean Idealism, because "all consciousness is consciousness of something." In other words, the Phenomenological doctrine of *intentionality* is applicable and valid.

The Primacy of Perception. In the *Primacy of Perception* (1964), Merleau-Ponty explained the primacy of perception as meaning that our experience of perception comes from our being present "at the moment when things, truths, and values are constituted for us; that perception is a nascent *Logos;* that it teaches us, outside all dogmatism, the true conditions of objectivity itself; that it summons us to the tasks of knowledge and action. It is not a question of reducing human knowledge to sensation, but of assisting at the birth of this knowledge, to make it as sensible as the sensible, to recover the consciousness of rationality. This experience of rationality is lost when we take it for granted as self-evident, but is, on the contrary, rediscovered when it is made to appear against the background of non-human nature."

The primacy of perception is emphasized in Merleau-Ponty's argument that it is not sensations about the world which we perceive, but the world itself, that it is not the qualities of a person which we love, but the *real* person. John Wild, in *The Challenge of Existentialism* expressed this Phenomenological point of view as follows: "The first function of philosophy, therefore, is to study this primordial world of immediate experience, to describe its unique characteristics, to distinguish and classify the major kinds of data which appear, and to analyze the constitutive structure of this concrete experience." [1]

---

[1] John Wild, *The Challenge of Existentialism* (Bloomington, Indiana: Indiana University Press, 1955), p. 13.

Chapter 22

Existentialism

The transition from Phenomenology to Existentialism is readily made. In fact, many Phenomenologists have become adherents of Existentialism, and because of the close ideological relationships between the two philosophical systems, an understanding of one facilitates understanding the other. The fundamental difference between them depends upon whether the stress is placed upon *existence* or *essence*. The Phenomenologists accord priority to essence (whatness), whereas the Existentialists give precedence to existence (thatness). The Existentialist first takes into account the facts (and modes) of existence. From the freely chosen modes of existence, each person's essence (nature) results.

Existentialism, as a movement, grew out of the Phenomenological movement, but its basic philosophy can be traced back to the ideas of the Danish philosopher Søren Kierkegaard (1813–1855). For over a century, Kierkegaard's philosophy was largely unknown to English-speaking people owing to their lack of familiarity with the Danish language. In recent decades, however, the writings of this most influential philosopher, the acknowledged father of Existentialist philosophy, have been made available in English.

The great revival of Kierkegaard's Existentialism may be attributed primarily to Martin Heidegger (1889–   ), who transmitted much of it to his student, Jean-Paul Sartre (1905–   ). Jean Wahl (1888–   ), who coined the term Existentialism, is credited with having founded the French school of Existentialist philosophy. Among important contemporary adherents are the German thinker Karl Jaspers (1883–1969), the French-Algerian atheist Albert Camus (1913–1960), and the French Roman Catholic theist Gabriel Marcel (1889–   ). The religious interpretation of Kierkegaardian Existentialism attracted a group of theologians who prefer to be regarded as adherents of Neo-orthodoxy (assuming that they are willing to accept any label at all). These contemporary theologians, who revolted against the liberal group, have included the Swiss theologian Karl Barth (1886–1968), Paul Tillich (1886–1965), Rudolf Bultmann (1884–   ), who is known for his theory of "demythologizing," Heinrich Emil Brunner (1889–1966), George A. Buttrick (1892–   ), and Reinhold Niebuhr (1892–1971), as well as Martin Buber (1878–1965), a Jewish theologian with a decided Christian bent and well known for his philosophical work, *I and Thou* (1923).

Influential adherents of Existentialism have also included Nicolas Alexandrovich Berdyaev (1874–1948), the Russian Neo-Romanticist; Leo Isakovich Shestov (Schwarzman) (1866–1938), a Russian exponent of the philosophy of irrationalism; and José Ortega y Gasset (1883–1955) and Miguel de Unamuno (1864–1936), the two best-known of recent Spanish philosophers.

SØREN KIERKEGAARD

The essence of Kierkegaard's philosophy can be seen in his doctrine that there are three stages of life experience: (1) aesthetic, (2) ethical, and (3) religious. These represent three attitudes toward life, three philosophies of life. Some of us progress from one stage to the next, while others never go beyond the first stage. Kierkegaard sometimes fused the second and third stages, referring to them as the religio-ethical. The third stage is superior to the other two stages. All of them reflect man's attempt to win salvation, to gain satisfaction or life's greatest good, while it is still within reach. Kierkegaard discussed the three stages in a number of his writings, but he devoted a most famous work, *Either/Or*, to a detailed analysis of the first two stages.

Stage One: The Aesthetic Stage. In the first stage of life experience, the aesthetic stage, the individual may be either a Hedonist in search of pleasure or romance or an intellectual interested mainly in abstract philosophical speculation. Both types of aesthetic are alike in their inability to commit themselves to decisive action. Both remain uncommitted or, at best, only partially committed so far as action to achieve any definite ethical goals is concerned.

Typical of the abstract intellectual is the Hegelian Rationalist, who speculates or theorizes, formulates a philosophical system, but lives remote from the arena of real events, hiding in the ivory towers of his mind, his theoretical world of pure abstraction or universals, completely devoid of existence. The abstract intellectual merely observes the world in a detached and objective manner, never becoming involved. He treats the world as if history has ended, thinking about it abstractly, rather than concretely. Hegelianism, compared with Kierkegaardian philosophy, is like a thought without the thinker.

The Hedonist type of aesthetic person searches for immediate pleasures without regard for the future. Living only for the moment, he seeks his satisfactions in the erotic fulfillment of desire. He accepts romance and sensual gratification, but will not commit himself to conjugal love and marriage, for these represent responsibilities, duties, and involvements from which the Hedonist shrinks. He treats the woman he loves as though she were not an existing person and unique individual but merely an impersonal source of his pleasure without the burden of ethical commitment. He lives for the moment without concern for the future; consequently his life lacks integration and continuity.

Kierkegaard pointed out that the aesthetic mode of life remains futile, because the individual is caught in the clutches of boredom and is motivated by it. Boredom entered the world with the creation of man; and out of boredom the gods created man. With the increase in population, the world became bored *en masse*. The aesthete's way of life, concentrating either on pleasure or on intellectual activity, results in ennui. Boredom assumes two forms, namely, being bored with the activity in which one is presently engaged, and being bored with oneself. The second form of boredom, the more genuine type, is an indescribable emptiness which robs life of meaning. The emptiness of ennui is an enigmatic inexplicable spiritual ailment which brings man to the abyss of nothingness, entirely discontented with his existence. The aesthete attempts to conceal his tedium through diversions, engaging in pleasures which camouflage his melancholy moods. The deeper the flight into pleasure, the greater the severity of ennui and despair. Nero exemplified this technique of employing pleasure as a diversionary tactic. After fruitlessly hiring ministers of pleasure to devise momentary pleasures that would rescue him from the doldrums, he suffered extreme boredom and despair that drove him to the point of burning Rome. In Nero, we see the universal plight of mankind. To find authentic selfhood, we must confront the reality of choice; we must become consciously aware that life is an either/or decision. To exist means to make choices, to be committed to action, to enter into life's involvement, but the intellectual aesthete eludes existence by withdrawing into the realm of abstraction, and the Hedonist evades the either/or decision by becoming ethically unconcerned.

Thus, the aesthetic life terminates in despair, the sense of futility or hopelessness. The aesthete must abandon his way of life, i.e., the pursuit of salvation in something outside himself, whether it be sensual pleasure or abstract thought (philosophy). Genuine selfhood is not found in externals, but within, in passion, freedom, decision, and commitment, that is, in subjectivity. Despair, being a form of subjectivity, helps us to move toward authentic selfhood. In heeding or choosing despair, the self moves from indecision to decision, from dodging involvement to making a decisive commitment; the soul makes the leap from abstraction into existence, from the aesthetic stage to the ethical stage.

Stage Two: The Ethical Stage. The futility, meaninglessness, and despair of the aesthetic stage should impel the individual to progress to the ethical stage. This stage is one of decision and resolute commitment. In this act of choice, genuine selfhood or authenticity is found, for through decision and commitment the self is liberated from the immediacies of the aesthetic life (of pleasure and abstract thought which lack commitment) and is integrated as a unity.

Decision, the *conditio sine qua non* by which the self discovers its integrity and unity, is *awareness*. Authentic choices are made with inwardness, with passion, tension, and feeling. Kierkegaard asserts that a man facing death will always make the right choice. Anticipation of death makes a difference in how an individual lives. We must live as if each day is the last for us. Major import does not rest on what is in fact chosen, but on the manner in which the choice is made. The passion of inwardness is the criterion of the right choice, and it paves the way for a choice to be made. The inwardness of choice entails self-knowledge, self-commitment, the attainment of authenticity and selfhood. The Socratic injunction "know thyself" must be rendered "choose thyself." Through this inwardness in choosing the self, an authentic selfhood with integrated wholeness is found.

The integrated personality finds its nexus of unity in memory and hope, whereas the unhappy consciousness is alienated from past and future. Alienation from the past indicates a break in memory, and alienation from the future reflects hopelessness. Hope for the future is lost with the loss of memory, that is, with alienated consciousness. In the moment of decision, of commitment and involvement, the self, unifying the past with the future, establishes its integrity as an integrated whole.

Stage Three: The Religious Stage. We have noted that each stage is identified by the values to which a man aspires; the aesthetic stage is characterized by Hedonistic pursuits, the ethical by regard for duty, and the third by obedience and commitment to God. The chief distinguishing feature of the inwardness of the religious life is suffering and faith. Stages on life's way are stages in attaining selfhood; consequently, selfhood is an achievement rather than a given human nature. Since one must exist before he can achieve selfhood, existence is prior to humanity; or, as Sartre later expressed the idea, existence is prior to essence.

It is in religious life that commitment reaches a peak and the other two stages reach their culmination. Just as a despairing person advances from the aesthetic to the ethical stage, so now the alienated person progresses from the ethical to the religious stage. In the religious stage, the highest degree of intensification or subjectivity is found in the inwardness of suffering, comparable to that of Job.

In *The Sickness Unto Death*, Kierkegaard wrote that the opposite of faith is sin, and that despair is sin. "Sin is this: before God, or with the conception of God, to be in despair at not willing to be oneself, or in despair at willing to be oneself. Thus sin is potentiated weakness or potentiated defiance: sin is the potentiation of despair." Faith is shown by the self's act of relating itself to its own self, by willing to be itself (authenticity) and to stand transparently before God (integrity). Consciousness of self is the decisive criterion, for the more consciousness of self there is, the more there is of *will*, and the more there is of will, then the more there is of *self*. A man without a will is without a self.

Despair is the unwillingness to be oneself; Christian despair is "the sickness unto death," for the wish to die is the result of despair, despite the inability to be rid of the self in death (owing to the Christian doctrine of immortality). Detachment from the good is sin; despairing over sin constitutes only a further detachment from the good. It is by faith that sin and despair are conquered; i.e., "by relating itself to its own self and by willing to be itself, the self is grounded transparently in the Power which constituted it."

Ultimate salvation is attained in the religious sphere by the "Absolute Paradox," the appearance of the transcendent eternal

God in the temporal sphere of the world, whereby he makes salvation possible through Christ. Christ, the Absolute Paradox, reveals eternity in time, the eternal God in the temporal, and, while making man sin-conscious, summons him to faith which is the decisive commitment that conquers sin. Kierkegaard concluded his *Philosophical Fragments* with the moral: "We have here assumed a new organ: Faith; a new presupposition: the consciousness of Sin; a new decision: the Moment; and a new Teacher: God in Time."

Kierkegaard's Existentialism. Kierkegaardian philosophy is fundamentally in direct antithesis to Hegelianism. Whereas Hegel placed the emphasis on speculative thought, Kierkegaard placed it on existence. Hegel discerned truth in the rational system, Kierkegaard in paradox. The former sought the universal, the latter the individual or particular. The former saw in logic a mediation of antitheses or formulated an unbroken logic (Hegelian dialectic); the latter replaced it with the leap or logical gap (qualitative dialectic). Either/Or was the Kierkegaardian answer to the Hegelian synthesis or mediation. Hegel found truth in the Absolute and objectivity, while Kierkegaard found it in the relative and subjective. Hegel emphasized necessity, Kierkegaard freedom. Other Kierkegaardian concepts, which replaced Hegelian ones were: repetition for recollection, concealment for openness, possibility for actuality, indirect communication (Socratic maiuetic) for direct communication, transcendence of God for the immanence of God, and mediacy (or reflection) for immediacy.

For Kierkegaard, an Existential system is impossible, because a system implies finality, completion; existence is continuous, ever incomplete. When existence ends, then perhaps a system may be formulated. Thus Hegel, formulating his Absolute System while existence was continuing, was advocating a ludicrous proposal. Only God may have a system, for only in God's eyes is reality a system. For the existent individual, all is in the state of becoming, never in a finished state. "An existential system cannot be formulated . . . Existence itself is a system—for God; but it cannot be a system for any existing spirit. System and finality correspond to one another, but existence is precisely the opposite of finality." The writers of philosophical systems cannot extricate themselves from existence to write objectively about it; only God transcends existence.

Philosophical systems dissipate existence. The Hegelian Idea, typical of pantheistic systems, concludes the identity of subject and object, unifies thought with Being, while Existentialism separates them. This is the fundamental difference between Idealism and Existentialism. While the Hegelian is engaged in thinking, the existing subject of Existentialism is actively engaged in living; while one theorizes and contemplates, the other exists and acts. The irony of the Hegelian system is that it leaves us with a thought without a thinker, humanity without an existing individual, or a crowd without an individual. Pure humanity is an abstraction. The *objectivity* of the Hegelian system has lost the existing *subject*.

For Kierkegaard, truth is subjectivity, and the subjective truth is inwardness. Truth is not merely a statement of fact, an idea which corresponds to its object, or something which we possess; rather, truth is that on which the individual acts, a way of existence; he exists it and lives it. The individual is truth.

Truth is subjectivity; the highest expression of subjectivity is passion. To think Existentially is to think with inward passion. Objectivity accents *what* is said, but subjectivity accents *how* it is said. The inward *how* is passion; decision is found only in subjectivity. Subjectivity is the truth; truth is defined as "an objective uncertainty held fast in an appropriation-process of the most passionate inwardness." Uncertainty creates anxiety which is quieted by an exercise of faith. The preceding definition of truth also serves as a definition of faith. There is no faith without risk, choice, passion, and inwardness; nor is there truth without them. Uncertainty always accompanies subjectivity, calling for the leap of faith.

Objectively, truth is always a paradox, except for a transcendent God. For man, objective truth is always uncertain, and its uncertainty appears in the form of passionate inwardness—anxious uncertainty displaced by the passion of truth, i.e., by inwardness or faith. Whenever the existing individual confronts eternal objective truth, then it appears paradoxical. For the existing individual, *subjectivity is truth*, and it is also *reality*. Thought is abstracted from existence because existence cannot be thought (it must be lived) and because the particular cannot be thought (only the universal can). At this point the difference between God and man can be discerned. "God does not think He creates; God does not exist, He is eternal. Man thinks and exists, and existence separates thought and being."

Kierkegaard's chief philosophical works (in addition to *Either/*

Or) are: *Philosophical Fragments* (1844) and *Concluding Unscientific Postscript* (1846).

MARTIN HEIDEGGER

The German philosopher Martin Heidegger (1889–   ) relinquished his role as a leader of the Phenomenological movement to become the chief promoter of contemporary Existentialism of the Kierkegaardian type. His most distinguished student, Jean-Paul Sartre, became the leader of the French Existentialists. Heidegger's influence has been widespread. His classic *Being and Time* was published in 1927; other important works include *What is Metaphysics* (1929), *On the Essence of Truth* (1943, 1949), and *What is Philosophy* (1958). At one time, he was an assistant to Husserl at the University of Freiburg, where he later taught as Husserl's successor. He utilized the Phenomenological method in approaching the fundamental problems of the nature of Being, but since the problem of Being is an ontological consideration, he viewed philosophy as Phenomenological ontology based on the *hermeneutics* (the science which interprets or explains) of human existence. By means of the Phenomenological method, he attempted to go directly to the data of immediate experience, to the things themselves, or *that which manifests itself*, as the term *phenomenon* is defined.

Dasein. The idea of Being is an old one to a philosopher grounded in Scholasticism, as Heidegger was. But Heidegger was interested in the meaning of Being, its sense, or its purpose—i.e., what renders it intelligible. Furthermore, he was interested primarily in the *human* Being, for the nature of the human Being leads to other levels of Being or reality. Only *Dasein* (his term for the human Being) can be said to have or not to have meaning; hence *Being* is meaningful solely in terms of human existence.

Dasein (being-there), that is, the human Being or the human existent, Heidegger identified as: (1) concern (*Sorge*), (2) being-toward-death (*Sein zum Tode*), (3) existence (*Existenz*), and (4) moods (*Stimmungen*). The human Being's essence is in his existence, for numerous possibilities are open to him whereby he may choose different kinds of Being for himself. The possibilities of what he may become are the pivotal points by which the human Being is oriented. Heidegger was greatly interested in interpreting time in terms of temporality; consequently, in addition to the problem of Being (*Dasein*), time is of utmost importance. Accordingly, his interest was in the Being and temporality of *Dasein* (human existence).

Being-in-the-World. *Dasein* (the human Being) cannot be thought of as a thinking substance, nor can the world be considered an extended substance as Descartes had assumed, for either hypothesis would portray the world as if it were a container with man inside. Such a view is Phenomenologically false, because it pictures man and the world as objectively separate entities, whereas the world Phenomenologically or Existentially understood is a sphere of human concern, and man and the world must be understood as hyphenated concepts. Existentially speaking, without man there could be no world. Man and his world are one encompassing structural framework. Existentially, *Dasein's* Being is a state of *Being-in-the-world*.

Inauthenticity, Everydayness, Averageness, and Publicness. Two characteristics of *Dasein* are: (1) the priority of existence over essence; and (2) the fact that *Dasein* is *mine*, i.e., my existence, and must be treated as personal, identified with personal pronouns, as in the statements "I am" and "you are." Man's essence (reality) is his existence (*Dasein*). The possibility of what *Dasein* may become rests with his own choices; hence *Dasein* can choose himself and win himself by his own achievement. *Dasein* may be regarded also as authentic or as an entity characterized by averageness. *Dasein* is authentic when he is something of his own, and inauthentic when he is busy, excited, preoccupied. *Dasein's averageness* or *everydayness* makes him an undifferentiated self lacking individuality and personal decision. It is to be distinguished from the authentic self by being recognized as a *they-self*, that is, as the group self, the public self, or as part of the social existence into which the self is dispersed, falling into anonymity and depersonalization. Having fallen (*fallenness*) into inauthentic Being, such an individual is referred to by the impersonal pronoun *one*, or people. The anonymous individual is susceptible to *publicness*, the Existential character acquired by exchanging a personal self for a public one; the individual accepts and conforms to public opinion and socially established standards, thereby withdrawing from responsible independent decisions and commitments based upon his own personal choice.

Facticity. Heidegger postulated *Dasein's facticity*, the factuality of the fact of one's own *Dasein*, the fact that *Dasein* understands its own Being, i.e., is self-conscious. An implication of *facticity* is "that an entity 'within-the-world' has Being-in-the-world in such a way that it can understand itself as bound up in its 'destiny' with the Being of those entities which it encounters within its own world."

The human Being is caught in the situation of *facticity*, for he exists and *has* to be. He is *flung into the world*, and finds himself a fact within it, and subject to a concomitant mood of fear or dread.

Three structures which constitute the human Being (*Dasein*) are *Existentiality*, *facticity*, and *fallenness*. The fundamental structure of the human Being as a whole is *care* (*concern*).

Care as the Structural Nature of Dasein. Care (*Sorge*) is the promordial totality of the human Being, that is, his essential nature or structural whole. *Dasein's* Being reveals itself as concern or care, and its concomitants are will, wish, addiction, and urge. *Dasein* is disclosed in *anxiety* or *dread*, rather than fear. Fear has a definite object of which a person is afraid, such as a threatening fire or flood; but anxiety or dread is an indefinite nothing which is nowhere. It cannot be particularized or objectified; it is a *nothingness* into which the individual is suspended.

Reality is grounded in the phenomenon of care, and only as long as there is *Dasein* is there Being. Man, confronted by the world, is imbued with anxiety, and thus the threatening character of the world is disclosed, the fact that its very structure consists of anxiety. Nothingness (indefinite entity) is the source of anxiety.

The basic mood of man is *dread* (anxiety), and the fundamental structure of man is *care* (concern). The mood of anxiety or dread, which is caused by man's encountering the indeterminate and indefinable nothingness, is evidence of his *finitude*. The intentionality of thoughts or ideas is directed toward their objects, but the intentionality of anxiety is nothingness. Anxiety is an experience with no corresponding object in the external world. It reveals a world lacking any supporting structure.

Truth, Disclosedness, and the Unity of Human Existence. For Heidegger, truth is *unconcealment* or *revealment*, or the disclosedness (understanding) of *Dasein*, which is the disclosure of reality. The truth of *Dasein* is Being-true, understood as *Being-uncovered*. Truth is the uncovering of *Dasein*; "*Dasein is 'in the truth.'* " Truth is (exists) only as long as the human Being exists.

To *Dasein's* state of Being belong: (1) *disclosedness in general*, which reveals *Dasein's* structure as *care* or concern; (2) *thrownness*, the factical existence of *Dasein* flung into the world without his choice or doing; (3) *projection*, the potentiality for being an authentic self which is the truth of existence; and (4) *falling*, the human Being lost in the world, with *Dasein* becoming immersed in publicness, impersonal, inauthentic, disguised. The human Being is in a state of untruth because he is essentially falling. "Dasein's Being is care. It comprises in itself facticity (thrownness), existence (projection), and falling." The individual is something that has been thrown into existence, into the world out there, but the event was not of his own choosing.

Temporality, Finitude, and Man as a Being-toward-death. Anxiety, in addition to disclosing man as finitude, reveals his existence as transitory, as a *Being-toward-death*. In other words, his life is oriented from the standpoint of his consciousness of death, which is an indication of his temporality and finitude. The significance of care (concern) is found in *Dasein's* temporality; temporality is the ontological meaning of care. The consciousness of death makes a difference in the choices an individual makes during life. It tends to make him authentic and resolute, as Kierkegaard had once pointed out. Death is a singular experience in that each person must encounter his own, without any possibility of delegating it to another.

The voice of conscience is the person's interpretation of himself; as a *Being-guilty*, man's Existential guilt creates the feeling of indebtedness. Man, being summoned by his conscience to the numerous possibilities among which he may choose, experiences the frustrating awareness that whatever choice he makes leaves others behind. The realization of certain choices allows the unfulfilled choices to plague him with guilt. Guilt is an indelible quality of *Dasein;* human Beings always feel guilty.

Resoluteness, Time, and Historicality. Despite his dread, transitoriness, guilt, finitude, the nothingness of the world, and the reality of death, the individual must resolutely push onward toward authentic existence. Man's wish for a conscience arises from his anxious state of mind, his state of *Being-guilty.* "This reticent self-projection upon one's ownmost Being-guilty, in which one is ready for anxiety—we call *'resoluteness.'* " In resoluteness, the human is prepared for anxiety, and as he moves through time, he achieves authentic existence, that is, *Dasein's* authentic *Being-a-whole.*

Existentially, time (whether future or past) is real. *Dasein* is a *Being for the future,* oriented by the future, but the past is futural in the sense that it is not finished, because it holds future possibilities, things which bear repetition (originally Kierkegaard's concept). Heidegger speaks of *historicality,* that is, the temporality of the individual whereby he moves from the past into the future via the present where his decisions as to what he chooses to become are made.

JEAN-PAUL SARTRE

Among contemporary Existentialists, Heidegger and Sartre (1905–   ) have been the most influential, and both have owed a great deal in their thinking to Kierkegaard. But Kierkegaard was religious, writing from a definitely Christian orientation, whereas they have advocated a completely secularized version of Existentialism. Sartre has written from a confirmed atheistic position which he has attributed to Heidegger, although Heidegger has professed to be theistic. At any rate, Sartre has been deeply indebted both to Heidegger and to Husserlian Phenomenology. Sartre's philosophy also reflects the influence of Kant, Hegel, and Descartes.

Jean-Paul Sartre, the influential leader of the French Existentialists, wrote his magnum opus, *Being and Nothingness* (1943), as a prisoner of the Germans during World War II. He wrote several popular novels expressing his Existential philosophy. His philosophical works, in addition to his 1943 classic, included *Psychology and Imagination* (1936), *Transcendence of the Ego* (1937), *Outline of a Theory of the Emotions* (1939), *Psychology of Imagination* (1940), *Descartes* (1946), and *Existentialism Is Humanism* (1947). In all his writings he dealt with the fundamental problem of Dualism between subject and object, that is, between the subjective consciousness and objective Being, between the subjective experience of freedom and the experience of the objective *thing*. The title of his celebrated *Being and Nothingness* alluded to this basic problem of Dualism: *Being* refers to Sartre's version of the Kantian thing-in-itself or the Hegelian Absolute, while *Nothingness* refers to the structure of the individual subject which Sartre identifies as *freedom*.

Being-in-itself. To express the idea of objective Being, Sartre coined the term Being-in-itself (adapted from Kant's thing-in-itself). (To express the idea of the subjective individual, he coined the term Being-for-itself.) He agreed with Kant that we cannot exceed the limits of experience, hence must remain within Phenomenological limits of experience, but he rejected the Kantian thing-in-itself, claiming that only concrete phenomena have any ontological status, that only concrete phenomena are real.

On this question, he accepted Husserl's Phenomenological approach. Asserting, in opposition to Kant, that nothing exists beyond phenomena, he nevertheless contended that Being is more than its phenomenal appearances. Furthermore, although Being is greater than its phenomenal characteristics, Kant erred in assuming Dualism between phenomena and noumena, for the phenomena *are* their noumena, and appearance is reality.

Sartre rejected not only Kantian Idealism, but also Husserlian Idealism, scorning the transcendental Ego as a form of solipsism. He interpreted Husserl's intentionality as referring to an object beyond the individual's subjective consciousness.

While repudiating noumena and the thing-in-itself, Sartre ascribed a transphenomenal quality to Being. He pointed out that although Being consists of more than the phenomenal aspects found in man's consciousness, yet (at the same time) it composes the entirety of its phenomenal appearances. Man's view of phenomena does not exhaust all of its manifestations. Being (Being-in-itself) is nonconscious, contingent, inert, fixed, massive, opaque, uncreated, devoid of potency, lacking becoming, and without any reason for existing; furthermore, it is superfluous. This interpretation of Being is at the core of Sartre's view of the objective physical world of reality.

Nothingness, Freedom, and Being-for-itself. Being-for-itself refers to the subjective person or human consciousness, portrayed as possessing characteristics of incompleteness and potency, and an indeterminate structure. Man is without a nature because no God exists to design one for him. Man's essence is *nothingness,* that is, the absence of Being (a negative statement much like the Augustinian concept that evil is the privation of good); man as nothingness is the absence of Being. Nothingness may freely be interpreted as no thingness, a state of not Beingness, or of no Beingness. In man, there is a privation of Being; he lacks massiveness and viscosity. Being-for-itself manifests itself as nothingness. Nothingness enters the world through human existence. Nothingness is dependent upon Being for its very existence.

The structure of nothingness (human consciousness), Sartre declared, is freedom or free consciousness. Thus man's basic nature is essentially *freedom.* Freedom is the structure of consciousness. Man is more than free: his essence is freedom. He is condemned to be free, a fate from which he cannot escape; accordingly, he is responsible for all of his actions.

Atheism, Abandonment, Anxiety, and Bad Faith. Sartre's atheism rests heavily on the contention that man lacks any kind of definite nature, except that of freedom or nothingness. There is no definite human nature because there is no God to create one. Man's nature, such as it is, is only an indefinite state of freedom or nothingness, and whatever nature man has, he acquires through existence. By virtue of his freedom, he chooses himself, whatever personality or nature he desires. He makes himself whatever he chooses to be; he also creates his values. Man's nature consists of his past which he has freely chosen. He is an existence which chooses its essence. Man is never at an end until death; he is always in the making.

This idea is at the very heart of Sartre's Existentialism, providing the basis for his principle that existence precedes essence—i.e., that subjectivity is the starting point of all, that man cannot transcend his human subjectivity.

Inasmuch as man's essence is freedom, the thought that he changes himself and the world by means of his choices overwhelms him with responsibility which grips him in anguish or anxiety. Man feels tossed into the world (facticity) and completely *abandoned* (Heidegger's *thrownness*) by God. Since there is no God, man must face the world and choose for himself. "God is dead" (borrowed from Nietzsche); therefore we must rely upon ourselves alone. By virtue of his freedom, man can choose to be either a coward or a hero. Man's freedom places him beyond the mere personal making of himself; he is responsible for the making of a world of his own choosing. A man's choices involve other men, both by example and by commitment; thus man has social responsibilities. His choices involve all mankind (an ethical principle comparable to the Kantian categorical imperative). Man is always *engaged* or *involved;* his ethical life is always one of involvement and action.

Owing to his condition of freedom, nothingness, and anxiety, man is rendered susceptible to *bad faith*, a self-deception comparable to the Freudian subconscious mechanisms of defense, such as repression, projection, fixation, reaction-formation, and the like. Bad faith, engineered by the pre-reflective consciousness, must be replaced by choice and faith which are provided by the intuitive insight gained through *Existential psychoanalysis*. To exist in bad faith is to lose subjectivity, freedom, and responsibility for decision. Bad faith means treating oneself as an object, rather than as a person. In Existential psychoanalysis, a person is not adjusted to accept himself for the unsavory character that he is (a goal which reflects the bad faith of Freudian psychoanalysis), but he is expected to change by choosing for himself the person he ought to become.

Freudian psychoanalysis, wherein an individual is absolved from responsibility for self-deceit, is based on the concept of a "lie without a liar."

Thus, a person is responsible for all of his actions, and cannot excuse himself for any reason, such as blaming his environment or heredity. One cannot even blame his unconscious, for Sartre denied its existence, claiming that we must be conscious in order to know what to repress.

Man creates his values as well as determining what he himself is to be as a result of freedom and choices. The universe is a human universe, and man is his own lawmaker. The fate of the world rests on man's decisions. This optimistic tone is found in Sartre's *Existentialism Is Humanism,* but his *Being and Nothingness* offers fundamentally a philosophy of Pessimism, since in it he concludes that *man is a useless passion* vainly striving in a universe without purpose.

The Fundamental Project: Man's Futile Attempt to Become God. Man is nothing, and his nothingness consists of free consciousness. His free will is the result of his freedom, since he is abandoned by God (thrown into the world). He stands alone in the world entirely responsible for himself. Yet, the individual is not quite alone inasmuch as he is a Being-for-others, participating in social intercourse with others by means of his gaze as he looks deeply into another's eyes. He needs other persons for the sake of his own self-realization; in the others, his self is revealed to him; in the presence of the others, he is ashamed. Thus, the others are an aspect of himself. His gaze can turn another individual into a mere object, a thing instead of a person.

The fundamental project of mankind does not, as Freud thought, consist of libidinal cathexis (the libidinal urge whereby man achieves his object of desire), nor is it shaped by Heidegger's Being-toward-death as man's principal orientation in life. Man's fundamental project is determined by "the desire to be." He seeks thing-ness, rather than mere nothingness. He desires more than ephemeral consciousness, for he wants solidity, density, or viscosity. In other words, man seeks to be more than merely Being-for-itself (nothingness, freedom, consciousness); he also desires to be Being-in-itself. But the state of Being-in-itself-for-itself is identical with the state of Being of God, that is to say, with conscious absolute reality (the unity of object and subject). Accordingly, the fundamental project of man is determined by his desire to be God. The idea of

God, however, is contradictory (Sartre never was able to reconcile this Dualism of subject and object), for in reaching for this ideal, the self will lose the for-itself and its efforts will terminate in failure. "To be man means to reach toward being God. Or if you prefer, man fundamentally is the desire to be God. . . . Every human reality is a passion in that it projects losing itself so as to found being and by the same stroke to constitute the In-itself which escapes contingency by being its own foundation, the *Ens causa sui*, which religions call God." Thus, a man is useless passion because he is faced with the impossible project of becoming Absolute, that is, uniting his nothingness (conscious freedom) with that of Being-in-itself. According to Sartre's Metaphysical Dualism of subject and object, this is a self-contradictory situation. The Being-in-itself-for-itself, inasmuch as it is a self-contradiction on Sartre's premises, serves as an ontological argument for atheism.

Notwithstanding the pessimistic views in most of Sartre's writings, his Existentialism ends on a note of optimism, for his *Existentialism Is Humanism* concludes with the declaration that Existentialism does not plunge man into despair but is an optimistic doctrine of action, that man is his own lawmaker, a creator of values, living in a human universe of human subjectivity, and capable of self-fulfillment.

Index

Abandonment, 354–356
Abelard, P., 100–102
Abolition of private property, 247, 249
Absolute, 18, 185–186, 187, 188 *ff*.
Absolute Idealism, 187–201, 270
Absolute mind, 195
Absolute paradox, 347
Absolute Personalism, 272
Absolute reality, 195
Absolute truth, 49
Abstract, 189
Academic skeptics, 48–49
Academy, 20, 38, 50
Accident, 65
Accidental creation, 114–115
Achilles, 11–12
Actuality, 297
Adiaphora, 48
Aenesidemus, 48
Aesthetic Idealism, 186
Aesthetics, 78–80
Aesthetic salvation, 208–209
Aesthetic stage, 343–344
Agnosticism, 233
Agnostic Realism, 227–228
Albertus Magnus, 103
Alcidamas, 29
Alcott, A., 271
Alexander, S., 204, 235–240
Alexinus, 34
Algazel, 103
Altruism, 286
Analytic method, 130
Analytic Philosophy, 307–315
Anaxagoras, 13, 15
Anaximander, 1–3
Anaximenes, 1, 3
Anniceris, 43, 44
Anselm, 96–100
Anthropocentric Humanism, 323
Anthropomorphic Personalism, 273
Anthropomorphism, 5
Antimony, 174–175
Antipater, 38
Antisthenes, 34–36, 37
Antithesis, 22, 174
Anxiety, 354–356

Apeiron, 2, 12, 17
Appearance, 280–281
A priori insight, 335
Arabian philosophy, 103
Arcesilaus, 48
Arche, 6, 7
Archetypes, 57
Arete, 30
Aristippus, 41–43, 44, 45
Aristippus the Younger, 43
Aristocrat morality, 230
Aristotle, 32, 39, 50, 51, 62–80
Arius Didymus, 38
Art, 78–79, 286
Artisans, 59–60
Association of ideas, 217
Atheism, 354–355
Atheistic Personalism, 272
Atomic propositions, 310
Atomists, 11, 13–20
Augustine, A., 86, 88–92
Authenticity, 350
Authority, 88–89
Austin, J., 307, 314–315
Avenarius, R., 245
Averageness, 350
Averroes, 103
Avicenna, 103
Ayer, A., 299, 301–302, 314

Bacon, F., 217–218
Bacon, R., 104
Bad faith, 354–356
Baden school, 213
Barth, K., 343
Basedow, 168
Bauch, B., 213
Beattie, J., 164
Becoming, 5, 7, 13, 17, 21, 54–55, 130, 296
Behaviorism, 19
Being, 5, 7, 9–10, 14, 16 *ff*., 21, 34, 53, 54–55, 130, 296, 321, 353 *ff*.
Being-for-itself, 353 *ff*.
Being-in-and-for-itself, 356–357
Being-in-itself, 353 *ff*.
Being-in-the-world, 350

Being-toward-death, 349
Belief, 257–258
Bentham's theory of fictions, 214, 216
Berdyaev, N., 343
Bergson, H., 233–235, 338
Berkeley, G., 158–161, 270
Binswanger, L., 327
Blanshard, B., 282
Blondel, M., 316
Boehme, J., 120
Boethius, 38
Bonaventure, 104
Boole, G., 256
Bosanquet, B., 203, 279
Boundless, 2
Bowne, B., 271, 272, 273–274
Bracketing, 330
Bradley, F., 203, 204, 280–282, 308
Brentano, F., 327, 328–329
British Empiricism, 153–164
British Neorealism, 292–298
British Utilitarianism, 215–223
Broad, C., 277
Brown, T., 164
Brunner, H., 343
Bruno, G., 120
Buber, M., 343
Bultmann, R., 343
Bundle of perceptions, 161–162
Butler, J., 37
Buttrick, G., 343

Caird, E., 203, 279
Caird, J., 279
Calkins, M., 203
Calvin, J., 119, 120
Cambridge School of Analysis, 307–313
Campanella, T., 120, 125–126
Camus, A., 342
Care, 351
Carnap, R., 299, 304–306
Carneades, 48
Cartesian philosophy, 133–140
Carus, T., Lucretius, 47
Categorical imperative, 176, 177
Categories, 64
Category mistake, 313
Catharsis, 78–79
Causation, 68–69
Cause-effect, 11
Charlemagne, 93
Chemistry, 13
Chinese Communism, 253–254
Choose thyself, 345
Christian ethics, 126
Christianity, 40, 230
Christian philosophy, 325–326
Chrysippus, 38
Classical Positivism, 241–245

Classless society, 247, 250
Cleanthes, 38, 40
Clitomachus, 48
Cohen, H., 212–213
Coherence, 275
Common sense, 309
Common Sense school, 164
Communism, 123, 246–254
Complex ideas, 154–155
Comte, A., 215, 217, 241–244, 246
Conceptualism, 102, 113
Concern, 349 *ff.*
Concrete, 189
Condillac, E., 166
Congeniality, 323
Connaturality, 323
Conscience, 88–89
Consciousness, 329 *ff.*
Consensus gentium, 50
Contiguity, 161
Continental Rationalists, 132–152
Contradiction, 253–254
Conventionalism, 245
Copernicus, 120
Correspondence theory of truth, 295
Cosmic mind, 6
Cosmological argument, 98, 108
Cosmos, 1 *ff.*, 14
Courage, 39, 92, 110
Creativity, 29
Creighton, J., 203, 282
Criterion of coherence, 275, 295
Criterion of truth, 50, 88–89 133–134, 259–260
Critical Realism, 288, 291–292
Croce, B., 203, 285–287
Crypto-Jews, 140–141
Cunningham, G., 282
Cynicism, 34–38, 43
Cyrenaic Hedonism, 41–43, 45 *ff.*

Darwin, C., 224, 225–226
Darwinism, 3, 41
Darwin's ethical theory, 226
Dasein, 349 *ff.*
Da Vinci, L., 129
Death, 46
DeChardin, T., 316
Deduction, 63
Deity, 6, 70
Democritus, 13, 17–20, 27, 44, 45
DeRouvroy, C., 241
Descartes, R., 18, 50, 120, 133–139
Dewey, J., 204, 263–267
Dialectic, 10
Dialectical materialism, 246–254
Dialectical method, 180–182
Dictatorship of the proletariat, 247, 250
Dignity, 177

Dilthey, W., 203
Diodorus Cronus, 34
Diogenes, 36–37, 43
Dionysodorus, 25, 29
Disclosedness, 351–352
Divine arbitrariness, 160–161
Doubt, 257
Drake, D., 291
Dualism, 357
Dubislav, E., 299
Dynamic Idealism, 270

Eckhart, 104
Eclecticism, 47, 50–51
Ego-centric predicament, 289–290
Élan vital, 233–234
Elean-Eretrian school, 33–34
Eleatic school, 5–13
Emergent evolution, 237–238
Emotion, 42
Emotive theory of ethics, 301–302
Empedocles, 13–14
Empiricism, 132, 146, 151, 153–168
Encyclopaedists, 165–166
Endurance, 39
Engels, F., 202
Enlightenment, 119
Entelechy, 68
Epictetus, 38
Epicurus, 44 *ff.*
Epiphenomenalism, 126, 233
Epistemological Dualism, 274, 275, 288, 291, 295
Epistemological Idealism, 269
Epistemological Monism, 9, 288, 289, 291, 293, 295
Epistemology, 133, 146–147, 156–157, 170 *ff.*, 252–253, 322
Epoché, 48, 330 *ff.*
Erdmann, J., 202
Essence, 65, 67–68, 321, 329 *ff.*
Eternal recurrence, 231
Ethical Intuitionism, 176, 338
Ethical Naturalism, 295–296
Ethical Realism, 294, 295
Ethical salvation, 209–210
Ethical Skepticism, 215
Ethical stage, 345–346
Ethical theory, 55–56, 101–102, 109–111, 145, 157–158, 163, 175–179, 195–199, 215–217, 219–223, 226, 228–229, 231–232, 234, 239–240, 265–266, 280, 282, 285, 294, 295–296, 321, 336–338
Ethics, 19, 72–76, 90–91, 109–111, 145
Eubulides, 34
Euclid, 34
Eudaemonism, 19–20
Eudaemonistic pessimism, 43
Euhemerus, 43

Euthydemus, 25, 29
Evil, 38
Evolutionary ethics, 228–229, 231–232
Evolutionary Naturalism, 224–240
Excellence, 59
Existence, 349
Existential Humanism, 356
Existentialism, 342–357
Existential psychoanalysis, 355
Existential Realism, 290
Experimentalism, 255

Facticity, 350–351
Faith, 347 *ff.*
Fallenness, 351
Feigl, H., 299
Feuerbach, L., 202, 248
Fichte, I., 202
Fichte, J., 180–184
Finalistic Idealism, 270
Finitude, 352
Fire, 7
First intention, 117
First philosophy, 66–72
Fischer, K., 202
Fiske, J., 240
Fixation of belief, 257–258
Flewelling, R., 271 *ff.*
Foolhardiness, 39
Force, 14
Frankl, V., 327
Freedom, 353 *ff.*
Frege, G., 256, 311
French Encyclopaedists, 165–166
French Enlightenment, 165–168
French Sensationalism, 166–167, 169
Freudians, 41

Galileo, 120, 129–130
Gaunilo, 97
General will, 168
Gentile, G., 203, 287
Geometric method, 133, 141–142
German Idealism, 270
German Idealists, 169–214
German Romanticism, 152
Gestalt, 190, 275
Gilson, E., 323–326
God, 2, 14, 37, 40, 46, 54–57, 66, 69–72, 81 *ff.*, 92, 97 *ff.*, 101 *ff.*, 104 *ff.*, 112 *ff.*, 116, 126, 136 *ff.*, 139 *ff.*, 142 *ff.*, 146 *ff.*, 157, 160 *ff.*, 192 *ff.*, 214, 230, 235, 238 *ff.*, 251, 259, 266–267, 278, 280, 296–298, 317 *ff.*, 347 *ff.*, 356–357
Gödel, K., 299
Golden Rule, 177
Gorgias, 27–31
Greek Enlightenment, 23 *ff.*
Green, T., 203, 275, 279–280

Grelling, K., 299
Grotuis, H., 120
Guardians, 59

Hahn, H., 299
Haldane, R., 279
Happiness, 19, 32, 39–40
Hare, R., 307
Harris, W., 203
Hart, H., 307
Hartmann, E., 211–212, 327, 338–339
Heath, P., 313
Hegelian dialectic, 190–192, 247
Hegelian ethics, 195–199
Hegelian left, 202
Hegelian system, 193
Hegeliansism, 187–204
Hegel's logical Idealism, 188–189
Hegel's philosophy of history, 199–200
Hegel's philosophy of religion, 200–201
Hegesias, 43, 44
Heidegger, M., 327, 342, 349–353
Helvétius, C., 166
Heraclitus, 4, 6–10, 19, 22, 24, 25
Herbart, J., 203
Herzberg, A., 299
Hierarchy of values, 336–337
Hindu, 3
Historical materialism, 247, 248
Historicality, 352
History as philosophy, 287
Hobbes, T., 120, 126–128, 167
Holt, E., 288, 290
Human existence, 349
Humanism, 241, 243–244, 266–268, 356
Hume, D., 161–164
Husserl, E., 327, 329–334
Hylopsychism, 2, 6
Hylozoism, 2, 6, 15

Iamblichi, 29
Idea-for-itself, 194
Idea-in-and-for-itself, 194
Idea-in-itself, 193–194
Idealism, 16, 169–214, 269–287
Idealistic Socialism, 213
Ideal language, 310
Ideals of reason, 174–175
Immortality, 71–72, 90–91, 262
Inauthenticity, 350
Indifference, 38
Individualism, 113–114, 230
Induction, 63
Inductive logic, 217–219
Infinite, the, 2
Innate ideas, 136, 153–154
Insight, 30
Instrumentalism, 255, 263–265
Integral Humanism, 322–323

Intellect, 89–90
Intellectual love, 57
Intelligibles, 117
Intention, 116–117
Intentionality, 328 *ff*.
International law, 198–199
Intuitionism, 176, 233–234
Ionian philosophers, 1–4
Ionian physicists, 1–5
Italian Neo-Idealism, 285–287

James, W., 255, 290, 258–263
Jansenists, 140
Jaspers, K., 342
John Duns Scotus, 112–115
Joint method, 219
Judaism, 230
Juhos, B., 299
Justice, 39, 91, 92, 110, 229
Justinian I, 93

Kant, I., 20, 32, 113
Kantian ethics, 175–179
Kantian Idealism, 169–180, 270
Kantian philosophy of religion, 177–179
Kantian political philosophy, 179–180
Kantian social philosophy, 179–180
Kaufmann, F., 299
Kepler, J., 129–131
Kierkegaard, S., 204, 252, 342, 343–349
Kinesis, 11
Kingdom of ends, 177
Knowledge, 31–32
Knowledge by acquaintance, 295
Knowledge by description, 295
Know thyself, 31, 345
Knudson, A., 271, 274–275
Kraft, V., 299
Kraus, F., 299

Labor theory of value, 247, 249–250
Lamarck, J., 224–225, 229
LaMettrie, J., 166–167
Lange, F., 212
Law of continuity, 148
Law of inertia, 130
Learned ignorance, 118
Lebenswelt, 334, 340
Leibniz, G., 145–152
Leibniz-Wolffian school, 151–152
Lenin, N., 251–253
Lesser Socrates, 33 *ff*.
Lessing, E., 152
Leucippus, 13, 16–17
Lewis, C., 255
Liebmann, O., 212
Lipps, T., 327
Locke, J., 18, 119, 153–158
Logic, 217–219, 263–265

Logical atoms, 309–310
Logical Empiricism, 299–306
Logical Idealism, 188–189
Logical Positivism, 299–306
Logos, 8, 87–88, 331
Lotze, R., 273
Love, 92, 110, 179, 337–338
Lovejoy, A., 291
Loyalty, 285
Lully, R., 146
Luther, M., 119, 120
Lyceum, 50
Lycophron, 29

Mach, E., 244–245
Machiavelli, N., 120, 121–123
Maieutic method, 33
Maimonides, 103
Malthus, T., 217, 246
Man as a useless passion, 356–367
Mannheim, K., 327
Marburg school, 212–213
Maritain, J., 319–323
Marvin, W., 288
Marx, K., 202, 203, 246–251
Master morality, 230
Materialism, 17–20
Materialistic interpretation of history, 248
Mathematical deduction, 130
Mathematical logic, 147
Mathematical theory of motion, 129
Matter, 14, 67–69
McTaggart, J., 203, 308, 277–279
Mead, G., 255
Mechanism, 146
Medieval philosophy, 93–118
Megarian school, 33–34
Melanchthon, 120
Meliorism, 229
Memory, 89–90
Menedemus, 34
Menger, K., 299
Merleau-Ponty, M., 327, 339–341
Metalanguage, 306
Metaphysical agnosticism, 156
Metaphysical Dualism, 53, 137–139, 291, 269
Metaphysical Idealism, 269, 282–285
Metaphysical Monism, 5, 9, 16
Metaphysical Pluralism, 5, 10 *ff.*, 13, 16–17, 290–291, 296
Metaphysics, 4, 40–41, 46, 65–72, 205–206, 236–237, 258, 260–262, 274, 280, 282–285, 319–321
Method of agreement, 129, 219
Method of concomitant variations, 129, 219
Method of difference, 129, 219
Method of residues, 219

Methodology, 133, 141–142, 146–147
Method, Socratic, 32–33
Metrodorus, 47
Middle academy, 48, 50
Might makes right, 28–29, 127
Milesian philosophers, 1–5, 12
Miletus, 1, 34
Mill, James, 217
Mill, John, 217–221
Mill's canons 129, 130, 219
Minor Socratics, 33 *ff.*
Molinism, 316
Moments, 189 *ff.*
Monadology, 148–149
Monotheism, 6, 71
Montague, W., 288
Moore, G., 222–223, 293–294, 307, 308–309
Morality, 18, 196
Moral law, 175–176, 186
Moral world order, 231
More, T., 120, 123–124
Motion, 12
Mounier, E., 270
Muirhead, J., 279
Multiplicity, 12, 13
Münsterberg, H., 213
Mysticism, 279, 139–140

Naïve Realism, 289
Natorp, P., 213
Natural selection, 225–226
Natura naturans, 142
Natura naturata, 142
Negative theology, 81, 118
Negativity, 191, 248
Neo-Hegelianism, 201–204
Neo-Kantian Idealism, 270, 279–280
Neo-Kantianism, 212–214
Neo-Platonism, 80 *ff.*, 94 *ff.*
Neopositivism, 299–306
Neorealism, 288–298
Neo-Scholasticism, 316–326
Neo-Thomism, 316–326
Nero, 38
Neurath, O., 299, 303–304
Neutral Monism, 290, 295
Newton, I., 120, 165
Nicolas of Cusa, 117–118
Niebuhr, R., 343
Nietzsche, F., 229–231, 338
Nihilism, 269
Nominalism, 115–116
Non-being, 17
Norms, 275
Nothingness, 354 *ff.*, 356
Noumena, 20, 57, 354
Nous, 16, 55, 84
Novalis, 152
Nowell-Smith, P., 308

Objective Idealism, 270
Objective mind, 194–195
Occam; *see* William of Occam
Occam's razor, 116
Occam's Terminism, 115–116, 117
Oligarchy, 61–77
Ontological, 20
Ontological argument, 97–98, 136–137
Ontology, 5, 53–54
Optimism, 211–212
Ordinary language philosophy, 307–315
Organic theory of reality, 190
Organic theory of truth, 190
Origen, 81, 86–88
Originator, 3
Ortega y Gasset, 270, 343
Oswald, J., 164
Otto, R., 327
Oxford philosophy, 307, 313–315

Paley, W., 215
Panaetius, 38
Panpsychistic Personalism, 272
Pantheism, 6, 118, 143–144
Pantheistic Personalism, 270, 272
Paradox, 11–12
Parmenides, 6, 9–10, 13, 14, 54
Parseval, A., 299
Particulars, 66–67
Pascal, B., 139–140
Patristic philosophy, 85–92
Paul, 112
Peace, 179
Pearson, K., 245
Peirce, C., 255–258
Perfection, 39
Peripatetics, 38
Perry, R., 288, 289
Personalistic value theory, 275–276
Personal Idealism, 270, 276–279
Personalism, 269–279, 270–279
Perspectivism, 336
Pessimism, 206–208, 211–212
Pestalozzi, J., 168
Pfänder, A., 327
Phaedo, 34
Phaedrus, 47
Phenomena, 20, 53, 328 *ff.*, 349
Phenomenalism, 162, 218, 269
Phenomenal world, 53
Phenomenological Ego, 332–333
Phenomenological method, 330–332
Phenomenological Positivism, 339–340
Phenomenological reduction, 330
Phenomenology, 327–341
Philolaus, 20–23
Philosophical analysis, 307–315

Philosophical anthropology, 338
Philosophical experience, 325–326
Philosopher-king, 60–61, 179–180
Philosophers of the garden, 44, 50
Philosophy of "as if," 214
Philosophy of education, 60–61, 267
Philosophy of history, 199–200, 252
Philosophy of law, 213
Philosophy of loyalty, 285
Philosophy of religion, 40–41, 54–55, 80 *ff.*, 107–109, 150–151, 163–164, 177–179, 200–201, 221, 234–235, 238–239, 251, 262–263, 266–267, 278–279, 285, 297–298, 317 *ff.*
Physics, 25
Pico della Mirandola, 120
Picture theory of knowledge, 289
Pitkin, W., 288
Plato, 24, 29, 51, 52–61
Platonic Idealism, 19, 20, 52–55, 270
Platonic love, 57
Platonic virtues, 56, 57, 58–59, 92, 110
Plato's republic, 57–61
Pleasure, 19
Plotinus, 80, 82–85
Poincaré, J., 245
Political philosophy, 57–62, 76–78, 157–158, 195–199, 219–221
Polystratus, 47
Positivism, 162, 241–245
Pragmatic Communism, 253–254
Pragmatic criterion of truth, 259–260
Pragmatic method, 259
Pragmatic theory of truth, 259
Pragmaticism, 256–258
Pragmatism, 49, 255–268
Pratt, J., 291
Preëstablished Harmony, 149–150
Presentative Realism, 289, 293
Primary qualities, 155–156
Primordial, 298
Principle of contingency, 147–148
Principle of contradiction, 64, 147
Principle of excluded middle, 64
Principle of sufficient reason, 147–148
Price, H., 314
Primacy of perception, 340–341
Process philosophy, 296–298
Property, 249
Protagoras, 25–27
Protagorean Relativism, 42
Psychocentric predicament, 289–290
Psychological Hedonism, 44
Publicness, 350
Pure act, 320
Pure form, 70–71
Pyrrho, 17
Pyrrhonian Skepticism, 48
Pythagoras, 20–23, 24

Pythagorean theorem, 21, 33
Pythagoreans, 19, 20–23

Qualitative Hedonism, 219–220
Quantitative Hedonism, 42, 216–217
Quiddity, 106, 113

Ramsey, F., 308
Rashdall, H., 222–223, 276
Rationalism, 100–101, 132–152
Realistic Personalism, 272
Reality, 280–282, 287
Regulative principle, 173–174
Reichenbach, H., 299
Reid, T., 164
Reinach, A., 327
Relativism, 12, 18, 20, 26–27
Religion of humanity, 241, 243–244
Religious Humanism, 266–267
Religious stage, 346–347
Religious wager, 140
Renaissance philosophy, 119–131
Renouvier, B., 270, 271
Representative Realism, 289, 293
Resoluteness, 352
Ressentiment, 337–338
Ricardo, D., 217, 246
Rickert, H., 213
Rogers, A., 291
Romanticism, 152
Rosenkranz, K., 202
Rousseau, J., 167–168
Royal society, 125
Royce, J., 203, 282–285, 334
Russell, B., 290, 294–296
Ryle, G., 307, 313–314

Siant-Simon, C., 241
Salvation, 208–210
Santayana, G., 291–292
Sartre, J., 342, 353–357
Satisfaction theory, 98–99
Scheler, M., 327, 334–338
Schelling, F., 152, 184–186, 255, 268
Schiller, J., 186
Schiller's Humanism, 268
Schlegel, A., 152
Schlegel, F., 152
Schleiermacher, F., 186–187, 271
Schlick, M., 299, 302–303
Scholasticism, 93–118
Schopenhauer, A., 204–212
Schroeder, E., 256
Schurman, J., 282
Schwegler, F., 202
Scientific Empiricism, 299–306
Scientific Positivism, 242–243
Scientific Socialism, 250
Second intention, 117

Secondary qualities, 155–156
Self-control, 38, 39
Self-preservation, 110
Sellars, R., 240, 291
Semantic theory of truth, 306
Seneca, 38
Sensationalistic Skepticism, 48
Sense and sensibilia, 314
Sensibilia, 314
Sentimentalism, 152
Sextians, 51
Sextus Empiricus, 48
Shakespeare, W., 37
Shestov, L., 270, 343
Sidgwick, H., 221–222
Simple ideas, 154–155
Skepticism, 17, 18, 25, 27 *ff.*, 47–50,
    89–90, 140, 162, 163, 215, 269, 294,
    302
Slave morality, 230
Slaves, 29
Smith, A., 246
Social ethics, 75–78, 196–197
Social philosophy, 40, 168, 179–180,
    195–199, 219–221
Socrates, 20, 24, 30–36, 37, 52
Socratic method, 32–33, 48
Solipsism, 159, 288
Sophism, 17
Sophistry, 29, 30
Sophists, 24–30
Sorley, W., 276–277
Soul, 14, 72, 89–90
Spaulding, E., 288
Speculative Idealism, 270
Spencer, H., 224, 227–229
Spinoza, B., 37, 140–145
Stewart, D., 164
Stilpo, 34
Stoa, 50
Stoicism, 34, 37–41, 50
Storm and Stress period, 152
Strauss, D., 202
Strawson, P., 308
Strong, C., 291
Stumpf, C., 327
Suarezianism, 316
Sub specie aeternitatis, 142–143
Subjective Idealism, 182–184
Subjective mind, 194
Subjectivity as truth, 348
Substratum, 160
Suicide, 41
Summum bonum, 91–92
Superman, 231
Surplus value, 249
Survival of the fittest, 225–226
Symbolic logic, 147
Sympathy, 337–338

Synderesis, 110
Synthesis, 130
Synthetic Idealism, 270

Tabula rasa, 154, 274
Tarski, A., 306
Teleological, 16, 108
Teleological argument, 108
Teleology, 55, 146
Temperance, 92, 110
Temporality, 352
Terminism, 115–116
Thales, 1–2
Thatness, 342
Theistic Personalism, 271
Theocentric Humanism, 322–323
Theodorus, 43, 44
Theogonic wish, 202
Theory of fictions, 214, 216
Theory of truth, 259
Therapeutic Positivism, 312
Theses of Thomism, 317–319
Thesis, 22, 174
Thilly, F., 282
Thing-in-itself, 20, 170, 353
Thomas Aquinas, 94, 102, 104–112
Thomistic epistemology, 322
Thomistic ethics, 321
Tillich, P., 343
Time, 352
Timocracy, 61
Timon, 49
Toulmin, S., 307
Tranquility, 19, 46, 49
Transcendent, 330
Transcendental Idealism, 169–180, 184–186
Transcendentalism, 169–180
Transmigration, 3, 20–21, 56
Triad, 191, 332
Troeltsch, E., 213
Truth, 351–352
Truth functions, 310
Tse-tung, M., 247, 253–254
Tyranny, 61, 77

Unamuno, M., 270, 343

Unity of human existence, 351–352
Universals, 66–67
Urmson, J., 308
Utilitarianism, 215–223, 228
Utilitarians, 41, 42, 215

Vaihinger, H., 212–213
Value carriers, 337
Value hierarchy, 336–337
Value-modalities, 337
Value perspectivism, 336
Value preferential sentiment, 336
Value theory, 239–40, 275–276
Verification principle, 300 *ff*., 311–312
Vice, 38–40
Vienna Circle, 299 *ff*.
Virtue, 31–32, 34–35, 38–40, 41, 43, 73, 77, 91–92, 111
Vitalism, 233–234
Voltaire, 165
Voluntarism, 244

Wahl, J., 342
Waismann, F., 299
Wallace, W., 279
Warnock, G., 314
Warriors, 59
Watson, J., 203
Whatness, 335, 342
Whitehead, A., 204, 296–298
Whitman, W., 271
Will, 89–91, 168, 175 *ff*.
Will to power, 229–230
William of Occam, 115–118
Windelband, W., 213
Wisdom, 39, 92, 110
Wisdom, J., 312–313
Wittgenstein, L., 299–300, 310–312
World Reason, 55

Xenophanes, 4–6, 24

Zeno of Citium, 37, 40
Zeno of Sidon, 47
Zeno of Tarsus, 38
Zeus, 38
Zilzel, E., 299